Aesthetics in the Modern World

Aesthetics in the Modern World

EDITED BY

HAROLD OSBORNE

LONDON
THAMES AND HUDSON

© *Thames and Hudson, London, 1968*

Printed in Great Britain by
Cox and Wyman Ltd., Fakenham

CONTENTS

CONTENTS

INTRODUCTION

The Journal of The British Society of Aesthetics has been in existence
only seven years, but it already forms an impressive body of work
and the Editorial Committee are both gratified and grateful for the
opportunity afforded by their publishers, Messrs Thames & Hudson
Limited, to bring a selection of its papers before the public in book
form. The articles carried by the Journal include some of the papers
read at the conferences and monthly meetings of the Society as well
as papers submitted directly to the editor. My task as editor of this
volume has been complicated. As editor of the Journal since its
inception I have been responsible for the publication of the articles in
it, and now as editor of this volume I am responsible for the selection
of some articles at the expense, necessarily, of others. In performing
this task it has been harder to decide which articles not to include
than which to include.

Students of the contemporary social scene may wonder at the
late formation of The British Society of Aesthetics, following tardily
as it did on the growing and lively interest in the arts and their
appreciation which took place in this country during the 1940s and
1950s. The pre-eminence of Great Britain in aesthetic theory during
the seventeenth and eighteenth centuries at first sight makes it even
more surprising that a national society for the promotion of study,
research and discussion of aesthetics came so recently into the field.
But when we recall the peculiar British genius for the informal and
the amateur our surprise will be the less. The theorists of the
eighteenth century were historians, politicians, churchmen, private
gentlemen, critics and belletrists, with professional philosophers in
the minority, and the same pattern has prevailed once again in our
day. On the Continent and elsewhere a society such as this would
have been supported by a university department, its activities would
have been subsidized and its way smoothed and made easy. As it is,
the Society and the Journal have been dependent entirely on

voluntary labour without subsidy or support except for the generous backing of a commercial publisher, without which the publication of the Journal would have been impossible. In these circumstances the Society has steadily flourished and membership now confers a cachet in itself. It enabled Great Britain to be adequately represented at the International Conferences of Aesthetics held at Athens in 1960 and at Amsterdam in 1964 and its own National Conferences were well and enthusiastically attended. Altogether the Society has provided a focal point for a broadly disseminated but hitherto spasmodic and unorganized interest in the understanding of the arts and their appreciation.

The Journal too has provided the main forum in Great Britain and other Commonwealth countries for papers and research in aesthetics and art theory and has reflected in its pages the most significant body of British thinking on these matters. The term 'aesthetics' has been interpreted widely to include experimental, psychological and sociological aesthetics, the principles of criticism and appreciation and basic discussion of the particular arts, but not so widely as to cover essays in practical criticism or art history. In line with the national tradition, papers have been chosen for originality of idea and liveliness of presentation rather than for formal correctness alone. Illuminative flashes of insight, novelty of approach and suggestiveness in idea and conception are the peculiar prerogative of an amateur concern, and have their special value and appeal where interest extends widely beyond the confines of a professional or specialized group.

The most painful part of an editor's task is the necessity to exclude. So much still clamours for attention when the limit has been reached. In this predicament I resolved to clear the ground initially in two ways. First I have given precedence to British writers, even though the pages of the Journal have always been open to contributors of other nationalities and many of the outstanding articles have come from them and particularly from the United States of America. This decision was not taken from any narrowly nationalistic motives and certainly not because American and other non-British contributions were judged to be in any way inferior or less pungent. Rather the

contrary. Many of these writers who have honoured the Journal
with their papers are already of such prominence in their field that
their work in aesthetics has been widely anthologized and is accessible
in books and in previous collections. It therefore seemed reasonable
to suppose that at a time when anthologies of aesthetics are pro-
liferating there might be greater interest, other things being equal,
from a selection of papers by British writers who are for the most
part relatively unknown in this particular field however prominent
they may be in others. My second decision was to exclude articles
on the history of aesthetics. Without in any way belittling the importance of historical studies for contemporary thought in aesthetics,
I nevertheless felt that in a necessarily restricted collection greater
immediacy and impact might be expected from a forward vision.
For the rest I have set before myself two aims in making the selection.
On the one hand I have wished to make the resulting volume as
representative as possible over the whole field which the Journal
has covered. Subject to that I have tried to give preference to articles
which combine novelty or originality of idea with lucidity of
statement and contemporary relevance.

In arrangement I have eschewed the heads of classification which
have come to seem *de rigueur* in recent anthologies of aesthetics: I have
in mind such headings as 'meaning and truth', 'aesthetic experience',
'aesthetic judgement', 'form and content', 'style', and so forth.
Instead I have arranged the articles in four general sections. The first
group consists of papers with a broadly philosophical intention: there
are discussions of the nature and scope of aesthetics and the problems
which are proper to it; truth and reality in the arts; emotional
qualities and the communication of feelings by means of the arts;
and so on. The second set of papers are concerned broadly with
phenomenological analysis of aesthetic concepts and without intending a comparison among individual papers, these as a group form in
my opinion the most astonishing and original contribution which the
collection makes to contemporary aesthetics. The penetrating studies
of such concepts as the perspicuous and the poignant by Professor
Findlay, of the sublime by Miss Meager, of the interesting by Aurel
Kolnai, of vulgarity by John Bayley, unite a keenness of insight with

a firm grip upon actuality which are rarely to be found in aesthetic or even perhaps in philosophical writing and give the lie once for all to the charge of 'dreariness' at any rate in relation to this kind of work in aesthetics. In the third section there follow two articles which are set together because they share a psychological approach. The last division is given over to articles which deal in a deft and vigorous way with aspects or problems of particular arts.

In each of these sections alternative choices were not only possible but would almost certainly have been made by another person. This kind of editorial weighing and balancing without weights and measures inevitably reflects the individual temperament of whoever is responsible.

Having given this account of the genesis and method of the collection, I want to avail myself of the opportunity for a more general defence of a new volume of essays on aesthetics. No apology of course is needed for rescuing seminal and stimulating work from the comparative obscurity which attends anything that remains buried in the back numbers of a periodical. The value and convenience of greater availability to student and general reader are patent. I am concerned rather with the more fundamental demurrer which is sometimes heard, particularly perhaps from some of those engaged in the teaching of the arts, that involvement with the theory of art, any attempt seriously to understand the principles of appreciation and criticism, to analyse and define what the artist is doing, to chart the psychology of artistic creation and plot the vicissitudes of response, may encourage a too analytical and intellectualized attitude in appreciation and may give rise to a sort of self-consciousness which is detrimental to the fervour of untrammelled inspiration wherein lies the chief strength of the artist and art student. Our wooing of the arts, it is alleged, should be from the heart and not from the head. It is no doubt true, we must admit, that those engaged in academic pursuits are sometimes prone to a too analytical rather than a perceptive way of commerce with the arts. So too those in other walks of life may be obtuse in other ways. Undoubtedly also there abounds a kind of philosophical sciolism, an obsession with half digested popularizations of theory, which can be distracting to the art student, though experience has proved again and again—as witness such artists as Kandinsky, Malevitch, Mondrian and the theoretical excesses of the Surrealists—that a mature artist can combine almost any degree of theoretical ineptitude with unimpaired creative vigour. One must accept too that there is a great number of people who are not plagued in any high degree with the urge to understand themselves or what they are about, and it seems likely that among them are many who have a gift for artistic work. Others are impelled to seek understanding and these are either distracted and their energies diffused by the platitudinous and false or are exhilarated to more fruitful effort by clarity of comprehension. And when all is said and done it still seems likely that artists, as other persons, who have a clear mental grasp however slight of what they and their fellow-artists are about will in many cases derive benefit rather than hindrance from it.

Yet the final justification of aesthetics, as of other branches of philosophy, is practical only at the second remove. It is a part, and in our view an essential part, of that attempt through understanding to come to terms with the human condition which has traditionally been considered the central function of philosophy. Put in more technical language, it is concerned with a region of facts without which any general philosophy of mind must turn out truncated and incomplete. Steadily through the present century and more rapidly in the last twenty years there has come to the fore a growing realization that aesthetic experience is a vital and valuable function the suppression of which leads to the impoverishment of human personality. In the past this has usually been taken for granted and implicit in socially approved behaviour. Since the concept of the fine arts emerged to signalize a rift between the aesthetic and the practical purposes of life it has shown itself in a more conscious conviction that the cultivation of the arts and of the capacity to appreciate and enjoy them which is latent in most of us contribute to the enrichment of the individual and the health of society. Neglect of these things on the other hand, a prime hazard of a predominately technological culture, may leave very many persons crippled and unfulfilled. It follows that these facts, if they are facts, must be taken into account in any systematic philosophy of man and equally in the less formal understanding of, and coming to terms with, life in contemporary civilization to which even the philosophically untrained may aspire. This is what aesthetics is ultimately about. Its justification and its necessity derive from the essential contribution it makes to such rounded and four-square understanding. Not all men seek to understand. It is for those who do seek that this volume is primarily intended.

PART I

Aesthetics as a Branch of Philosophy

RUTH SAW AND HAROLD OSBORNE

The word 'aesthetics' (from the Greek *aisthanesthai*, to perceive; *aisthētica*, things perceptible) was introduced into philosophical terminology about the middle of the eighteenth century by Alexander Gottlieb Baumgarten (1714–62), a pupil of the Leibnitzian codifier Christian Wolff (1679–1754), and it is because of the odd use to which he put the word that the branch of philosophy which is concerned with investigation into the nature and principles of beauty now bears this incongruous name. In a dissertation *Meditationes philosophicae de nonnullis ad poema pertinentibus* (1735) which he wrote at the age of twenty-one Baumgarten first put forward the idea that the current system of philosophical discipline was incomplete and needed to be rounded off by the addition of a science of the 'inferior cognition' which is mediated by the senses on the analogy of Logic which, as the science of the 'clear and distinct cognition' mediated by intellect, stood as a general introduction at the beginning of the four departments of Ontology, Cosmology, Ethics and Psychology into which the Woolffian metaphysics was divided. He worked out this youthful notion with typical Germanic thoroughness and the new science was brought laboriously to birth fifteen years later in the voluminously gestated *Aesthetica* (1750–58).[1] But it was Baumgarten's penchant for poetry and the arts rather than his talent or training in philosophy which led him, having conceived the need for an epistemology or psychology of perception, to write a book about the theory of art and beauty. Etymologically he ought to have given the name 'aesthetics' to the study of perception. Instead he gave it to the theory of beauty, even defining aesthetics in his opening paragraph as 'the theory of the liberal arts . . . the science of sensory cognition' (*theoria liberalium artium, gnoseologia inferior, ars pulcre cogitandi, ars analogi rationis, est scientia cognitionis sensitivae*). Baumgarten was able to take this line because he believed that the 'perfection' of sensory awareness is to be found in the perception of beauty. (*Aesthetica 14: Aesthetices nis est perfectio cognitionis sensitivae, qua talis. Haec autem est pulcritudo.*)

Despite a rough passage Baumgarten's neologism established itself. Kant critized Baumgarten for restricting the word to the field of taste and proposed to apply it in its true etymological meaning to sense perception generally. But in the *Critique of Judgement* Kant reverted to Baumgarten's usage. There was stiffer resistance in England. In 1842 Gwilt's *Encyclopaedia of Architecture*—that rich depository of forgotten Victorianisms—referred to the word as a 'silly pedantic term' and one of 'the useless additions to nomenclature in the arts' which has been introduced by the Germans. But by 1859 Sir William Hamilton could say: 'It is nearly a century since ... Baumgarten applied the term Aesthetic to the doctrine which we vaguely and periphrastically denominate the Philosophy of Taste, the theory of the Five Arts, the Science of the Beautiful, etc.—and this term is now in general acceptation, not only in Germany, but throughout the other countries of Europe.'[2] Hamilton himself made no bones about admitting his own preference for the word 'apolaustic' (from the Greek *apolauein*, to enjoy); for by the time he wrote emphasis had switched from the cognitive aspect of appreciation to the emotional and it was already assumed to be a sufficient and the only criterion of beauty if, in the words of the experimental psychologist Gustav Theodor Fechner, a thing had 'the property of arousing pleasure directly and immediately'.[3]

During the second half of the century the word came to be associated with the extravagant affectations and artistic dandyism which were cultivated under the influence of the French 'art for art's sake' doctrines. W. S. Gilbert's famous parody of the posturing of 'long-haired aesthetes' and the exaggerated medievalism and hypersensitivity of the Pre-Raphaelite brotherhood at least had the effect of bringing our word as current coin on every man's lips so that by the end of the century it had ceased to be merely a technical term in philosophy and had been finally adopted into the general language. It has become a common counter, one of those vague but useful semantic signs whose meaning everyone seems to know though no one is able to define. Even in more or less specialized writing the word is now used as if its meaning were more precise than that of the older terms of criticism and appreciation. Thus John Dewey writes: 'To be truly artistic, a work must also be aesthetic.'[4] In a recent glossary of terms *fine art* is said to be 'that art which is principally concerned with the production of works of aesthetic significance as distinct from useful or *applied* art which is utilitarian in intention'.[5] Even the word 'beautiful' has become subordinate to aesthetic' as in such statements as: 'the beautiful is merely one of many aesthetic categories'.[6]

But although the word has come into acceptance, both the subject matter of aesthetics and the sort of investigation which is proper to it remain controversial. It is therefore our principal endeavour in this article to set out the main views which are held about the sort of study which aesthetics undertakes and the kind of conclusions which are to be expected of it.

The *New English Dictionary* defines aesthetics as: 'the philosophy or theory of taste or of the perception of the beautiful in nature and art.' In this sense aesthetics goes back only to the English writers of the eighteenth century, to the 'inner sense' school of dilettante philosophers inaugurated by the third Earl of Shaftesbury, to their successors of the Scottish 'common sense' school, and to the systematization of their theories effected by Immanuel Kant. Certainly Plato and Aristotle discussed the nature of beauty and art, and the place of artists in the community, but aesthetic theory is not explicitly set out in their work. They assumed as having no need of argument that art is to be judged by its usefulness in the community. Collingwood alleges in *The Principles of Art* (1938) that if we go back to the Greek, we find 'that there is no connexion at all between beauty and art'. Lionello Venturi says somewhat more conservatively, and perhaps more accurately, in his *History of Art Criticism* (1936): 'Regarding aesthetic thought, it is necessary to remember that Plato and Aristotle vacillated between the theory of beauty and the theory of art, without letting the two theories coincide.' If we conceive aesthetics as an autonomous philosophy of beauty, we cannot properly speak of a medieval aesthetics. To the medieval mind the visible world was a symbol of the divine and all created things were 'theophanies' or manifestations of the being of God. But their very conception of symbolism was different from ours. To us the symbol is a physical reality which is endowed with a meaning or a significance beyond itself. But to the medieval mind the physical world had no meaning or importance except as a symbol. We suppress the symbolic instinct in the interest of scientific understanding of the world; the medieval mind conceived the symbolic apprehension of the created world as the only reliable guide to such understanding. The work of art, like all created things, was an image or symbol. It achieved its purpose as revelation of the divine Nature not by illusionary representation of the perceptible world but by evidencing in its own construction that concinnity or mathematical consonance of dissimilar parts in which the beauty of the whole universe was thought to reside. Beauty was not conceived as a value independent of other values but rather as the radiance of truth (*splendor veritatis*) shining through the symbol, which was at the same time the splendour of ontological perfection, that quality of things which reflects their origin in God and enables us through them to attain direct cognitive insight into the perfection of the divine Nature. In medieval thought aesthetics was a branch of theology.[7]

Deliberate interest in human taste and in the factual aspects of the appreciation of beauty as a distinct mode of awareness and a subject for philosophical theory first emerged in the eighteenth century in the context of the general revolution in cultural outlook which resulted from the empirical epistemology of John Locke. It is in this sense that Ernest Lee Tuveson, referring to his essays on 'The Pleasures of the Imagination' contributed to *The Spectator* in 1712, declared that Addison 'wrote perhaps the first real treatise on aesthetics'. This is not of course to say that the awareness of beauty had not been there before. But it was at this time that it became an object of scientific interest and it is perhaps not too fanciful to say that it was at this time that the sense of beauty because self-conscious.

Men not only appreciated beauty but now began to examine and speculate about their appreciative commerce with the beautiful. And out of this new interest was born aesthetics as that branch of philosophy which is described for example by Professor Bullough in his lectures on *The Modern Conception of Aesthetics*, delivered at the University of Cambridge in 1907, as the systematic study of the aesthetic conscious-ness manifested both in the creation and in the enjoyment of works of art, of the world of Art in relation to the productive and receptive consciousness and, finally, of aesthetic culture or the aesthetic consciousness applied to life in general. (It will be observed that the word 'acsthetic' is already so firmly grounded in the language that Professor Bullough defines aesthetics as a branch of philosophy or science in terms of it.) More recently, however, there have arisen important schools of thought which have doubted whether there is a separate and distinct mode of awareness which can be particularized as aesthetic or any group of qualities common and exclusive to works of art as such and the possibility therefore emerges that aesthetics as Professor Bullough conceived it may be illusory.

Traditionally, there is a broad distinction between the normative disciplines on the one hand (Ethics, Logic, Aesthetics and, marginally, Epistemology) and Metaphysics on the other hand, as dealing with the nature of the universe. The former were held in the past to be concerned with Truth, Beauty and Goodness, though nowadays the distinction would be expressed in terms of the concepts occurring in discourse about morals, about reasoning in a very broad sense, and about art and the beauties of nature. The transformation of the description of Aesthetics as 'an enquiry into the nature of beauty' into 'the analysis of concepts occurring in aesthetic discourse' does not raise a problem in aesthetics itself. It marks a change in general philosophical climate and need not concern us; we shall be enquiring into the conditions under which we ascribe or refuse to ascribe beauty to an object, the conditions under which we describe or refuse to describe an experience as aesthetic, whether we conceive ourselves to be investigating the nature of beauty and of aesthetic experience, or describe our enterprise in some other way. Whether there are such 'things' as beauty, goodness, truth belongs to another enquiry. There is one qualification to be made, however; we might be making a factual statement when we say that there is no such thing as beauty or *the* aesthetic experience, namely that we can discover no quality belonging to all the things that are beautiful and to no other things, no quality belonging to aesthetic experiences and to no others.

It was Kant's *Critique of Judgement* which first distinguished aesthetic qualities from the categories of the useful, the pleasant and the good. But the full practical implications of these distinctions were hardly realized outside a narrow circle of professional philosophers until they were obtruded violently upon the general notice by the 'aesthetic movement' associated with the names of Gautier and Baudelaire in France, Whistler, Beardsley and Pater in this country.[8] As often happens when enthusiasm takes charge, the new dogmas were carried to extremes. From the plausible position that the aesthetic quality of a work of art is not dependent on its practical usefulness or even its congruence with conventional morality, some of the leaders of the new movement—either from conviction or *pour épater les bourgeois*—committed themselves to the paradox that a work of art must not serve any purpose. 'Il n'y a de vraiment beau,' said Gautier in the famous Preface to *Mademoiselle de Maupin*, 'que ce qui ne peut servir à rien.' Always works of art have been created for this that or the other practical object. And their appraisal as works of art has always been confused with their effectiveness for the purpose for which they were designed. The ancient Greeks, from whom many of our aesthetic and critical principles descend, were interested primarily in the educational and social uses of works of art. European tradition has emphasized the religious, cultural, moralistic, educational, humanistic and entertainment functions. It is only in our own day, since the turbulence and the extravagances of the 'art for art's sake' movement have subsided, that the practical aesthetician is left with the clear necessity to distinguish between judgements about the excellence of a work of art *qua* work of art and judgements about its importance as a vehicle for cultural or other values.

In the present century practical aesthetics has had to absorb its greatest shock in consequence of the retreat from illusionism in the arts of painting and sculpture, the discovery by painters that a picture need not be a picture of something other than itself. The most characteristic feature of the modern school of painting is its rejection of the representational function of art. Whether a picture represents something else or not, and the degree of accuracy with which it represents, are matters of indifference to aesthetic judgement. In the other arts these views would not have caused a stir. Nobody believed that music or architecture must represent something not themselves. But it had been so taken for granted that a picture must be a picture of something that the denial of the representational function was revolutionary. At the same time a sharp recoil of taste from Greco-Renaissance naturalism made it possible for our generation to appreciate as never before the artistic products of widely removed cultures and periods. We enjoy the surviving art objects of all ages although the cultural purposes which they were created to serve are sunk in oblivion. We do not know and shall never know the reasons why the palaeolithic cave-drawings were made. We can no longer appreciate the motives which inspired ancient Egyptian or Meso-potamian art. We cannot recover the ritualistic or other purposes served by Mexican or African art. Not only has painting become international; it has transcended the bounds of race and time. We have suddenly become inheritors of the art of all time and all peoples. But we enjoy and admire this art out of context, as pure aesthetic objects divorced from associated purpose or function. We have created for ourselves what André Malraux calls a 'Museum without Walls' (Musée imaginaire) which 'imposes on the spectator an entirely new relation to the work of art' and where 'l'œuvre d'art n'a plus d'autre fonction que d'être œuvre d'art'.[9]

Earlier Christian art became invisible after Giotto. From the fourteenth century until the Romantic revolt in the middle of the eighteenth the word 'Gothic' was synonymous with the barbarous, ugly and uncouth. It was assumed that medieval sculptors were trying to do what Donatello, Leonardo and Michelangelo did, that they failed because they were primitive and lacking in 'science'. The revival of interest in the Gothic is usually traced back to Goethe's enthusiasm for Strasbourg cathedral when he came under the influence of Herder in the winter of 1770–71, and to his publication of the paper *Deutsche Baukunst* in 1772. That he had been anticipated in this country is evident from Henry Fielding's description of Allworthy's house in *Tom Jones* (written 1746–48) and from Richard Hurd's championship of Gothic art in his *Letters on Chivalry and Romance* (1762). But the vaguely romantic taste for the 'primitive' strength and grandeur of the Gothic as an antidote to Rococo, which was fostered in Germany by the Schlegels, by Chateaubriand and Victor Hugo in France, but which did not discriminate Romanesque from High Gothic, came no nearer to a true apprehension of the highly sophisticated and almost metaphysical art of a Gothic cathedral than did Strawberry Hill with its fashion for faked mossy ruins and 'romantic' gloom. The capacity to see and apprehend the Christian art of the Middle Ages was hardly recovered before the present century. Romanesque returned to visibility still later, owing largely to the pioneer efforts of Henri Focillon and Émile Mâle. It has taken still longer for the Byzantine to return. Hegel and after him Friedrich Theodor Vischer, whose *Aesthetik der Wissenschaft des Schoenen* (1847–57) in six large volumes set the coping stone on German romantic aesthetics, thought that 'mummy-like' was an apt description of the 'ascetic and ossified' forms of Byzantine painting. The works of Robert Byron, David Talbot Rice and Paul Muratoff helped much to cure this blindness. But it was left to a Greek writer, Professor P. A. Michelis, in *An Aesthetic Approach to Byzantine Art* (1955) to attempt an appreciation in terms of the aesthetic principles inherent in it.

It is easy to forget how very limited was the visual knowledge of those critics of the eighteenth and nineteenth centuries whose writings have until recently had most influence on the development of aesthetic theory and critical sensibility. Winckelmann, whose *Geschichte der Kunst des Altertums* (1764) was the first attempt to trace the evolution of style in Greek art, had seen nothing Greek. The English 'Grecians' Joseph Nollekens (1717–1823) and John Flaxman (1755–1826) knew nothing but a few vase paintings not of the best. Shut off from the art of the Middle Ages and blind to everything outside, the Romantic critics of the nineteenth century were confined to post-Renaissance European art and only a small segment of that was open to any one of them. Théophile Gautier (1811–72), who launched the theory of 'art for art's sake' in 1835, visited Spain but did not see Italy until he was thirty-nine and was never in Rome. Charles Baudelaire (1821–67) had been neither to Italy nor to Spain and knew nothing of the works of Michelangelo, Masaccio, El Greco, Titian, Hals or Goya. When reproduction was in its infancy and reproduction in colour unknown, comparison had to depend upon the vagaries of visual memory and the impressions culled in the course of one journey abroad often had to serve for the remainder of a lifetime. The rapid advances in photography and in the technique of colour reproduction during the last thirty years have wrought a change which, in their own sphere, is not less epoch-making than the electric telephone and the internal combustion engine.

It was modern art which brought back the capacity to see. Beginning with Daumier (1808–79) and Manet (1832–83) modern painters systematically denied the values of strict naturalism. It has been the aim of painters of the modern school, whether or not deliberately and consciously pursued, to divest themselves of the trammels of all the subsidiary functions which works of art have served in the past—even where convenient the function of represent-ation—and to seek to realize in their works simply that common quality which renders all art good in whatever period or style and in the absence of which no construct can be a work of art. 'Their aim was to isolate the essential qualities of character and of structure in a picture which makes it a work of art. What is it, independent of the idea a picture communicates, regardless of the story it tells, purely through the balance of its lines and masses, through its shapes abstracted from any meaning; what makes the picture interesting to look at and makes us continue to find it interesting?'[10] Now that Modern Art has created a new academicism of its own, now that we can all put on a blasé air towards the pictures of the pioneers and of their imitators, it is difficult to realize the impression which this new art at first made. Perhaps something of its impact is suggested where Gertrude Stein makes Miss Toklas say: 'It is very difficult now that everybody is accustomed to everything to give an idea of the kind of uneasiness felt when one first looked at all these pictures on these walls . . . Now I was confused and I looked and I looked and I was confused.'[11]

No similar phenomenon has occurred in any of the other arts, except perhaps to a very minor extent the art of dance. But the effect on criticism has been profound, and general aesthetic theory has had to follow, albeit somewhat haltingly, in the wake of the radical revolution in standards of critical judgement. It is no longer even faintly plausible to judge a painting by its choice of subject matter and by the painter's skill in reproducing or idealizing the 'natural' beauties of his subject. We can no longer sensibly accept, what was taken for granted by Burke and Kant, that the beauty of nature is primary and the beauty of works of art derives from their faithful representation of beautiful nature—together, it was conceded, with a certain symmetry of composition and the enhanced titillation of colour. Aesthetics cannot *assume* that the theory of art is a branch—albeit a very interesting branch—of a wider theory of beauty or that the standards by which we ascribe merit to works of art are the same as those by which we judge the beauty of natural things. The artists and critics are emphatic on the matter. Ortega y Gasset has spoken of 'the liberation of the human imagination from nature'. Picasso with deliberate paradox has said: 'Nature and art being two different things cannot be the same thing. Through art we express our idea of what nature is not.' Malraux is the most brilliant and consistent exponent of the belief which lies at the heart of the modernistic movement, that art is the creation of a new world alongside the phenomenal world of sense appearances, not the expression or reproduction of that world. 'Les grands artistes ne sont pas les transcripteurs du monde, ils en sont *les rivaux*.' Aesthetics still speaks with two voices. Its present dubiety has been expressed by that stimulating Spanish thinker Julián Marías. There are certain natural objects, he says, which are generally considered to be immediately and directly beautiful in themselves: such are a flower, a jewel, a landscape, a woman's face. There are on the other hand certain other objects made by man with a definite purpose, among other things, of being beautiful: such are a statue, a picture, a cathedral, a sonata, a sonnet. 'And,' he goes on, 'aesthetics has always been in doubt as to whether its theme is the *beauty* of the first group of objects, or the structure and requirements of the second, or, lastly, the relationship between the two groups in so far as beauty occurs as an ingredient in both.'[12]

The 'naturalistic' school of aestheticians assumes that the beauty of natural things and of works of art is the same in kind (though of course a work of art which is representational must have the additional quality of creating a good illusion). Both arouse in suitable subjects a special kind of reaction which is called 'aesthetic experience'. The beauty of both is simply a function of this reaction. So John Hospers, writing on the meaning of 'beautiful' offers an ostensive definition of 'aesthetic experience' as follows: 'Almost everyone has had experiences in the presence of the ocean or the sunset, the mountains or the forests, symphonies or poems, which would unhesitatingly be labelled "aesthetic".' Where this outlook prevails the beauty of art becomes a special case within the much wider field of natural beauty. So George Santayana wrote in *Apologia pro Mente Sua* (1940): '. . . nor has my love of the beautiful ever found its chief sustenance in the arts. If art *transports*, if it liberates the mind and the heart, I prize it; but nature and reflection do so more often and with greater authority. If ever I have been captivated it has been by beautiful places, beautiful manners, and beautiful institutions.' Where a writer recognizes an essential oneness between the various fields and manifestations of beauty, one would expect that the amount of attention given to the beauties of fine art would be comparatively little, if only because the other fields of accepted beauty are so much wider, so much more generally accessible and, in general, appear to exercise a more universal appeal. The early English aestheticians did in fact devote the greater part of their space to analysing the principles of natural beauty. The modern naturalistic aestheticians, with less consistency, tend despite their assumptions about the nature of beauty to concentrate almost exclusively on the standards of taste and judgement in the arts.

On the other hand it has become increasingly frequent during the last fifty years for writers on aesthetics to confess frankly that elucidation of the principles underlying the appreciation of fine art is their sole concern. Those who believe that the distinguishing feature of excellence in the arts is something not to be found in nature must necessarily take this line. So, for example, R. G. Collingwood declared that: 'aesthetic theory is not the theory of beauty but of art'. For following Croce, he held that the essence of artistic production consists of 'expression' in a sense that natural objects cannot be expressive. Those writers who, like Conrad Fiedler, Ernst Cassirer and Susanne Langer, have held that art is a symbolic language of feeling must, in consistency, segregate the study of the principles of fine art from the study of natural beauty, because the objects of nature cannot except in a Pickwickian sense be a symbolic language. Professor Louis Arnaud Reid is in line with the predominant contemporary tendency when he says in his lecture on *Aesthetics and Education* (given at Bretton Hall in July 1959): 'By aesthetics I mean here the philosophical theory of art and the arts.' And Miss Helen Knight was voicing the new attitude in aesthetics when she said in her paper on 'The Use of "Good" in Aesthetic Judgements': 'On the whole we commend the works of man for their goodness, and the works of nature for their beauty.'[13]

There is another change in the philosophical climate. It has in the past been held that there are certain main concepts in each discipline which it is its peculiar task to elucidate. There are *the* laws of thought, *the* logical form of an argument or of a proposition, and these are the main concern of logicians; moral philosophers are to be concerned with the central concepts of rightness, goodness and their opposites, and aesthetic philosophers with beauty and ugliness. Now, however, philosophers tend to hold that there are many concepts belonging to a 'cluster' in each sphere of discourse and that it is our job to unravel the web of their interconnectedness. We may throw light on our subject by way of an elucidation of minor concepts and our approach will be unhampered by the accumulated mass of beliefs involved in discussion of the traditionally important concepts. Professor Austin once remarked that he wished aestheticians would concern themselves with the dainty and the dumpy, rather than with the beautiful and the ugly.

However that may be, there are certain questions which arise when we examine the writings of critics, the pronouncements of

artists upon their work and the more or less unconsidered statements
of ordinary men about literature and works of art generally, and
upon their enjoyment of natural objects. It is our job as aesthetic
philosophers to draw out the assumptions implicit in such statements,
to elucidate the meanings of the aesthetic words more or less uncritically assumed, and to exhibit their interconnexions. It is possible
to hold conflicting beliefs without being aware of the contradiction
when it is hidden in a mass of words, and it is certainly possible to
hold a belief in practice which one would reject in theory. For
example, the first spate of comment on a newly erected statue is sure
to contain such remarks as: 'That horse would be winded if it ran half
a mile.' Does this mean that the speaker wishes to commit himself to
the view that every representation must be of an object which is
good of its kind? Must there be no statues of broken down horses,
ugly old men, or was this a particular judgement upon this statue in
terms of subject or the intentions of the artist? Are the intentions of
of the artist aesthetically relevant and if so, how do we find out what
they were? When a critic says: 'Good theatre but a bad play,' what is
his distinction, and what does he mean by 'good' and 'bad' in this
context? If you say: 'It was a good play but I didn't enjoy it,' are you
saying that aesthetic value has no connexion with pleasure, or that
through some personal idiosyncracy you were unable to feel the
normal accompaniment to the appreciation of a work of art? When
you commit yourself to a judgement that a given object is beautiful
are you demanding the agreement of the other people (or would you
be willing to add: 'that is what I think but I may be wrong?') Do you
feel that you are saying *more than* 'I enjoyed it'? If so, what more is
involved? In short, do you think that judgements upon works of art
are matters of taste and that *de gustibus non est disputandum*, or that a
considered opinion upon works of art may be supported by argument? If you hold the former view, do you hold the corollary that
any opinion is as good as any other or do you admit experts in
criticism? If so, how would you describe the expert? Is it contradictory to hold that some opinions are worth more than others?
These are some of the traditional questions of aesthetics which arise
from an examination of aesthetic discourse.

The final question raises an important problem for any normative science. Do moral philosophers know, *qua* moral philosophers, what particular actions or kinds of action are right and wrong, or is their concern merely to elucidate the concepts occurring in any given belief about what is right or wrong? Both points of view have been held, and we may describe the latter view of the function of moral philosophers by saying that they do not make first-order moral judgements, that is judgements directly upon conduct, but second-order judgements, that is judgements about judgements about conduct. Similarly, we may say that it is the function of aesthetic philosophers to make second-order judgements and that this is the demand which disqualifies Plato and Aristotle as aesthetic philosophers. They accept unquestioningly the belief natural to their circumstances of time and place that value is to be defined in terms of the best life for men, that is life within a small community such as their own city state. To hold a given belief uncritically about morals or art is to disqualify one as a philosopher of morals or aesthetics, though of course a philosopher may hold beliefs as a private man.

There is one further difficulty here. It is natural to say that a moral theory which had as a consequence that it is right to break promises and to tell lies is absurd, and it is equally natural to say that a theory of aesthetics from which it followed that a peasant song at a village wedding had greater aesthetic value than an opera by Mozart or Wagner is equally absurd. There must be some kind of at any rate provisional acceptance of moral codes and of great works which have passed the test of critical judgement over a long period, though this acceptance must also be examined.

Charles Peirce defined aesthetics as the 'basic normative science' which institutes a comparison among ultimate values—the 'science of ideals or that which is objectively admirable without any ulterior reason'. Few have followed him in giving this very wide meaning to the word. It is not usually considered to be part of the function of aesthetics to consider why we value the appreciation of beauty or what rank we give to it among other valuable human activities. Nevertheless any theory which did not provide some basis for understanding why we value art and beauty would appear nugatory. For

this reason the theory that objective beauty consists of certain mathematical proportions is apt to seem trivial in modern times when it is
dissociated from the religious or metaphysical background which
gave it meaning in medieval and Renaissance times.

Among modern theories that which perhaps comes closest to
explaining why we value art is the theory that art is a language of
symbolism. The modern theory has little affinity with the medieval
theory of symbolism since it is maintained without the religious
postulate that what is symbolized is the nature of Deity. Moreover
while medieval thought regarded all nature including works of art
as symbols of Deity, the moderns distinguish works of art as being
alone symbolic in the aesthetic sense. It is akin to the medieval
philosophy in holding that the appreciation of beauty is a cognitive
act and that it is immediate, intuitive, or non-conceptual awareness
of that which is symbolized. The theory derives from one of the
facets in the thought of German Romanticism and its more particular origin is usually ascribed to the works of Konrad Fiedler and
Ernst Cassirer. It has been recently popularized by Mrs. Susanne
Langer.

It is a theory which requires very careful formulation. It
distinguishes for example between a symbol and a sign. A sign is
something (e.g. a road-sign or a scientific proposition) which expresses
a meaning that could be formulated and communicated by alternative
means. An aesthetic symbol is something which expresses a unique
meaning that cannot be paraphrased and therefore cannot be con-
ceptualized but is apprehended by direct or intuitive acquaintance
with the symbol. This aesthetic theory must be held distinct from
simple recognition of the fact that works of art do often (but need
not) *contain* conventional or 'subconscious' images. The study of
conventional images is known as iconography and the study of unconscious symbolism, whether from the individual or the collective
or archetypal unconscious, is the province of psychology. Neither is
directly germane to aesthetic concepts. Neither the early Christian
art of the Catacombs nor the modern devotional postcard is better
or worse aesthetically because it contains an effective religious symbol of the 'Good Shepherd'. The pictures of the old alchemists or the

pictures drawn by schizophrenic patients do not become 'art' because the psychologist can discover and elucidate subconscious symbolism contained in them. Nor on the other hand do the paintings made by Picasso become any less fine as works of art because similar subconscious symbolism can be found in them by psychologists.

The theory must also be held distinct from the study of general cultural symbols in Cassirer's sense. The historian may use works of art as documents bearing witness to the religious, philosophical, political, social, poetical or emotional tendencies of a period or a country or the individual artist. But for this purpose an unsuccessful and a successful work of art are equally significant and works of art are only one sort of material among a vast variety of others, all of which may serve as evidence of cultural background or trends and many of which contain meanings requiring to be elucidated in the light of such background and trends.

The aesthetic theory of symbolism holds that successful works of art are symbols in a special kind of way in which no other things are symbols. The manner of this symbolism has not yet been adequately formulated and it is therefore difficult to present or assess the theory.

There seem to be three types of statement made within the context of this theory. (i) It is said that a work of art is a symbol but that what it symbolizes is itself. This statement can hardly be intended to be taken literally. A thing which symbolizes nothing else but itself symbolizes nothing and is not a symbol. Perhaps what is intended to be said is that every work of art is a unique individual, that it is an organic whole which cannot be taken to pieces and built up as a set of relations among its parts, that it expresses a meaning which cannot be completely paraphrased either in words or in any other medium. If this is what is meant, the statement says nothing new in aesthetics.

(ii) It is said that art is a 'language of feeling', but works of art do not arouse in the observer particular emotions which were previously experienced by the artist and were his 'inspiration' to make the work of art. They are symbols to (non-conceptual) cognition so that in the act of appreciation the observer by immediate cognitive contact with the work of art becomes aware by direct intuition of that of which it is a symbol. Moreover that which is symbolized is not particular feelings or emotions but a general pattern or rhythm of affective life.

The view that appreciation is primarily a cognitive act rather than an emotional response seems to be true. We do not actually experience all the often conflicting emotions represented simultaneously on the stage or in an anecdotal painting but in some sense we are cognitively aware of them by an immediate non-conceptual act. On the other hand the view that works of art symbolize fundamental patterns of feeling seems far more dubious. It is intrinsically incapable of verification because we have no other means of knowing these fundamental patterns and rhythms; nor have we any possible means of testing our judgements whether particular purported works of art do or do not express a fundamental rhythm of feeling.

(iii) Finally it is sometimes asserted that works of art symbolize a metaphysical reality of which by our appreciative commerce with the work of art we become directly and immediately aware. This is a view which many modern artists have themselves alleged.

In his essay *The Doors of Perception* Aldous Huxley describes how under the influence of mescalin his ordinary perceptions were accompanied by an intense and inescapable feeling of revelation. He develops the theory that artistic vision in general has this revelatory character and that the works of art which artists create communicate to us imperfectly the revelation of ultimate reality which they have enjoyed. 'What the rest of us see only under the influence of mescalin,' he says, 'the artist is congenitally equipped to see all the time ... It is a knowledge of the intrinsic significance of every existent. For the artist as for the mescalin taker, draperies are living hieroglyphs that stand in some peculiarly expressive way for the unfathomable mystery of pure being.'

The statement that in the act of appreciating a beautiful work of art we have immediate intuitive awareness of ultimate or pure being takes us outside the confines of aesthetics proper. As 'emotive' descriptions of the artistic experience such affirmations are significant and must be treated with respect. Their correct philosophical formulation belongs to the sphere of general philosophy or metaphysics.

REFERENCES

[1] There is a translation of the *Meditationes* by Karl Aschenbrenner and William Holther (Berkeley and Los Angeles, 1955).

[2] *Lectures of Metaphysics*, 1, vii, 124. Sir William Hamilton was described in Ueberweg's *History of Philosophy* (1862–66) as 'the most conspicuous figure in the history of English philosophy within the present century'.

[3] *Vorschule der Aesthetik* (1876).

[4] John Dewey, *Art as Experience* (1934), p. 48.

[5] J. O'Dwyer and Raymond Le Mage, *A Glossary of Art Terms* (1950).

[6] P. A. Michelis, *An Aesthetic Approach to Byzantine Art* (1955), p. 8.

[7] Gilbert and Kuhn, *A History of Esthetics* (1956), p. 130.

[8] The story of the 'art for art's sake' movement may be read in William Gaunt's *The Aesthetic Adventure* (1945) and in the more recent study *From Gautier to Eliot* by Enid Starkie.

[9] *Les Voix du Silence* (1951).

[10] Maurice Grosser, *The Painter's Eye* (1951).

[11] Gertrude Stein, *The Autobiography of Alice B. Toklas* (1933).

[12] *Reason and Life* (Eng. Trans. 1956).

[13] In *Aesthetics and Language*, ed. William Elton (1954).

Sense and Nonsense in Aesthetics*

RUTH SAW

The following exchange is reported from a philosophical discussion in Cambridge: 'A: At least you will admit that 2 and 2 make 4. B: No, not until I know what you want to do with it.' That, in effect, is the first point I want to make about nonsense in general. (We must, of course, settle what we mean by 'nonsense' before talking about nonsense in aesthetics.) There is no utterance, however absurd on the face of it, no utterance however sane and sensible it may sound in isolation, which may not be found to be sensible in its context or absurd in its context. But surely, you may object, there are some utterances for which no context could possibly be found which would make them sensible, some utterances, no matter under what circumstances they occurred, which could possibly be anything other than common sense. There is such a thing as sheer nonsense, sheer common sense: there are, for example, on the one hand strings of words, self-contradictions, logical incompatibility, and on the other hand clear statements of matter-of-fact, well-attested scientific theories. All right, let us try a few.

MEANINGLESS STRINGS OF WORDS

'Ink blot black suddenly how frightening devil damn thee black cream Cornwall synthetic.' This is a string of words I produced beginning with 'ink'. How enlightening for a psychologist! How meaningful and pregnant in the right context! I am sure there are some excellent examples in 'stream of consciousness literature' which would have a place in the plot, but I am not able to lay hands on one at the moment.

* This paper was delivered as a lecture to The British Society of Aesthetics on 7 December, 1960.

SELF-CONTRADICTIONS

'Did you enjoy yourself at the party?' 'Well, I did and I didn't.' You will object at this point that this needs expansion into some such statement as: 'I enjoyed the food but not the company.' But that is just the point. Something which has the perfect form of nonsense, 'something is and is not the case,' is shown to be in its context meaningful and as having a perfectly sensible use. Again: 'Into the same river you cannot enter twice: indeed into the same river you both do and do not enter.' This is a paradox leading us into an extremely profound and enlightening discussion of the conditions under which self-identity may be predicated of an object, or indeed whether we may usefully speak of objects at all.

'LOGICAL' NONSENSE

We may have utterances in which there is not exactly a self-contradiction, but in which there is something 'logically odd', e.g. a conflict between tenses and adverbs:

> Pelican, pelican, pelican Jee,
> We think no birds so happy as we.
> Pelican, pelican, pelican, Jill,
> We think so then and we thought so still.

This is nonsense only in inverted commas, in the same sense in which a novel or a fairy story is 'false'. Taken as they were intended, they are neither nonsense nor false. In case you think examples from literature are not fair, take the following: 'There is not when He was not.' In its context this is a subtle statement of a theological position about the existence of Christ in relation to the temporal universe.

'NONSENSE STATEMENTS' OF MATTERS OF FACT

(From *Saki*): Nicholas: 'There is a frog in my porridge!' Nurse: 'Nonsense, there can't be any such thing.'

As a matter of fact there was, since Nicholas had put it there himself. But his triumph was unjustified, since it is absurd to suppose that under normal circumstances a plate of porridge in its passage from kitchen to breakfast table could acquire a frog. 'You said there couldn't be and there was' is an expression of the opposition between what is *as a matter of fact* the case and what might reasonably be supposed to be the case. The truth is often absurd. In fact we often accept a story as true *because* it is absurd. Nobody in his senses, we say, would have invented such an absurd story; he would know that nobody would believe it. His only reason for telling it must be that it is what happened. The consummate example of such an attitude is that of Tertullian, who, speaking of the absolutely absurd supposition that God was a man and suffered martyrdom, said: 'I believe it because it is absurd.'

PERFECTLY CORRECT CALCULATION

'If I set out from home at 9 o'clock and proceed at a rate of a mile in a quarter of an hour, I shall reach a point two miles away at 9.30.' True? Yes. Sensible? Yes, if an answer to a mathematical problem; no, if an answer to the question: 'Why are you so late this morning?' One form of impudence is to produce a true answer which, while relating to the point in a way, is not related in a relevant way. The question and answer do not belong together. There is even a good use for irrelevance other than impudence. The idealistic Clym Yeobright, in *The Return of the Native*, draws the attention of Eustacia to the many attractions of his beloved native heath. She replies: 'I was not even aware that such a druidical stone existed. I am aware that there are boulevards in Paris.'

'ABSURD' USE OF SCIENTIFIC THEORY

I want to build my house on a solid foundation. Sensible and true piece of advice: 'Then you must not build on this piece of ground; it is sand on a clay bed.' True but silly: 'Then you must not build on the earth. It is revolving at a rate of . . . miles a minute.' There are some contexts in which it is sensible to make mathematical calculations, some in which it is not. 'It has taken me an hour to creosote one panel of fencing and there are twenty-four panels.' 'It should take you about twenty-three hours to finish then.' More or less, but about right. 'It has taken me an hour and a half to produce three typewritten pages of my paper, and it should be about 25 pages long.' 'You should be able to finish it in ten and a half hours then.' Absurdly wrong! It may take me a month or a year, or just possibly two or three hours.

The dictionary definition of 'nonsense' is 'a manifestly false statement'. A statement can be *manifestly* false only in relation to a body of accepted facts or theories, though we may have been obliged to take those facts and theories on trust. If there were an intelligent person brought up with absolutely no knowledge of astronomy, he would rightly think it absurd to say that the earth was in motion. A person brought up normally, having learned that the movements of the planets, the prediction of eclipses, the phases of the moon, can all be explained on the hypothesis that the sun is the fixed centre of the universe, will be talking nonsense if he says that the earth is the fixed centre. He has not the knowledge of the planetary system which would enable him to follow the calculations, but the vast mass of theories which all hang together and which justify expectation should be enough to make him accept an hypothesis even though, as Bacon said, it 'commits the rape of reason on the senses'.

I shall do no more than refer to a common use of the word 'nonsense' to characterize a statement which we very much dislike to think might be true. The small child who has been helping to take caterpillars off the cabbage patch says: 'I shall dream about caterpillars tonight.' His parents, knowing the inconvenience of bad dreams, say: 'Nonsense! You will go to bed and sleep soundly all night.' The only inconsistency here is with one's desires, and unfortunately nothing follows about the truth of a statement from the fact that one hopes it is not true.

Our conclusion is that statements in isolation are neither sensible nor non-sensible. Just as to describe a belief as scientific is to say nothing about its content, but only about the manner in which it is held, so an aesthetic theory is not silly or sensible simply on account of the type of concept embodied in it. We are going to withhold the epithet 'nonsense' from a theory until we have examined its grounds. We may have a predisposition towards those which sound like common sense and away from those which sound far-fetched, but we shall keep an open mind as far as possible and examine, for example, the grounds for holding that the work of art is not a physical object but has its existence in the mind of the artist, and equally we shall not accept without question the view that works of art are to be found on the walls of galleries and standing in museums of fine art. We shall reject theories only on the grounds of internal inconsistency or a failure to take account of the facts. Even here, we are not entirely safe: 'fact' is very often condensed theory. That water quenches thirst and that it is composed of hydrogen and oxygen are facts on different levels.

What then are the facts for aestheticians? I propose the following list, not as complete but as embodying those which, at least, must be explained in a satisfactory aesthetic theory.

1. Some people give up time and energy—in fact, their working lives—to the making of objects intended for delighted contemplation.

2. Many people spend time and energy in contemplating such objects.

3. It is possible to be trained to look at or listen to these objects with increased enjoyment.

4. These objects fall into kinds. Some of them are made by the artist himself in the form in which they are presented to the public. Others, musical scores, blue prints, scripts, etc., need a second set of artists who will then make the object or perform it for the public.

5. Even when objects are intended for use, their makers sometimes consider their value for contemplation as well as for use and they are then enjoyed in the same manner as works of art.

6. Most people agree that it is 'a good thing' that people make and enjoy such objects.

7. It is possible to enjoy natural objects in the same way as works of art, and there is some connexion between the beauty of some of the arts and the beauty of nature.

8. There are experts in the arts.

9. 'Beautiful' is a word suitably applied to the objects described above, and 'aesthetic' to the experience of their delighted contemplation.

10. It is better to enjoy worthy objects than inferior ones.

11. There are many common beliefs inconsistent with one or more of the above.

In the attempt to accommodate these facts many theories of art and beauty have been propounded, some of which can include more of the facts than others. In considering them we should have to determine whether an inconvenient fact was not a fact after all but a theory. Even then we should have to explain why it had been thought to be a fact. Expression theories of art, for example, minimize the importance of, or rather change the status of, actual works of art— pictures, statues, performances of plays, etc. They give them the status of stimuli to the production of works of art in the mind of the spectator. The artist is an artist not in virtue of making the physical object, but in virtue of the work of imagination in his mind. He becomes a practical man when he decides to 'externalize' his work. It is very difficult for anyone holding such a theory to give an account of the place of the medium in the work of an artist, the actual manipulation of paint or stone and the place in inspiration of such manipulation.

To talk sense in aesthetics, then, we must accept our facts, decide what questions we want to ask about them, determine what type of answer is appropriate and so determine our procedure. The topic given to me was Sense and Nonsense *in* Aesthetics, but at this point it seems desirable to consider nonsense *about* aesthetics or rather to distinguish between the epithet as applied by ourselves from within our discipline and as applied by critics of our procedure from outside aesthetics. Our discipline is in the uncomfortable situation of having very few facts which are not claimed by some other discipline, which, moreover, claims to treat them in a much more systematic and adequate manner. In fact, they claim to treat them scientifically. Sociologists, it is said, are the right people to investigate the place and function of art in society and its importance. Psychologists cannot understand why we are not satisfied with their descriptions of our evaluations of aesthetic objects, of our experience when confronted with these objects and of creative activity. It is a sheer matter of fact that people think, feel, behave, in certain ways, that they place value on certain objects and experiences and advance reasons for their preferences. When we have noted these facts and stated laws about these types of behaviour, what more is there to do? If we say there is still the question whether these are good reasons and if they are, what makes them good reasons, then what we say falls within the province of criticism. Critics are fitted by training and experience to offer reasons for valuing certain objects, and the question whether they are good reasons does not arise. Of course they are good reasons or experts would not offer them. As Locke said about logic: 'The Almighty was not so niggardly to man as to make him barely two-legged and leave it to Aristotle to make him rational.' Scientists, moralists, lawyers, critics can all carry on their work without help from philosophers. As for the second part of the question: what makes these reasons *good* reasons? this seems to practical people to be no question at all and they think that even if it were a question, it would be unanswerable. If it were true that there were no questions relating to art and beauty which could not be answered factually, then we should indeed be talking nonsense in the strict sense that we were saying nothing.

What then do we claim to be specifically our job? In the course of reflecting upon our 'facts' we notice that some of them are inconsistent. Moreover, in considering common sense and expert critical remarks, we find that people often hold one theory in the abstract while another is implicit in their comments. One and the same man says, for example, that Congo's pictures could not possibly be works of art, since a chimpanzee has no thoughts and feelings to express, but in looking at pictures painted by human beings he praises them for being excellent likenesses. His first comment shows that he thinks that a picture is no good unless it expresses feelings, yet he praises the pictures by human beings for other reasons. It is even possible for one and the same man to hold that there is no disputing about tastes and that there are experts in the evaluation of the arts, i.e. people whose opinion is more worth having than that of others. Sometimes people's conduct is out of keeping with their avowed beliefs. At the first level of sophistication it is usual to say that it is nonsense to say that one *ought* to admire some objects rather than others: it is a mere matter of fact that one does or does not have certain feelings. Yet these very people take pains to get themselves and their children trained to appreciate music, literature and art. If a boy sits enraptured while a cinema organ plays *The Lost Chord*, why not leave him alone? If there is entirely no sense in saying that one ought, or it is better that one should, appreciate Mozart, we are doing the lad a great disservice. There are many more opportunities for him to hear the things he now enjoys. These are the ways in which our questions pose themselves to us. We want to be able to give an exact and precise answer to the questions: Why is it better to enjoy some things rather than others? What are the properties of the things which 'ought' to be enjoyed? If there is some general property of valuable art objects, what is the relation of this property to the characteristics of a particular work given as reasons for its 'goodness' by competent critics?

In sorting out these relationships and in trying to reconcile theory and practice we are led to propound theories and these theories we must test by application to matters of aesthetic fact not included in those we were first considering. How do we find out what I have listed as facts? Some, of course, are facts in the perfectly ordinary sense of the word, such as our careful preserving over the centuries of pictures and statues, our continued production of great plays and musical compositions. (We might even add, at the risk of misunderstanding, the great sums we are willing to pay for pictures, staging of operas, etc.) Our other facts we establish by noticing what people say, and here is the second source of misunderstanding by non-philosophers. Our attention to what people say is interpreted as an interest in words, and it must be admitted that some philosophers are to blame for this misunderstanding. There is no reason why a geographer should not say that what he was learning was how to use the words 'delta', 'confluence', 'equator', etc., correctly. So he is. And, what is more, he is learning it largely out of books. In the same way we find out how to use the words 'beauty', 'art', etc., correctly by studying their use in actual contexts. It is ironical in this connexion that even here we are told that some other discipline is doing our job better and more scientifically. Philologists complain that we have no feeling for the beautiful fluidity of language and for its changing history. We might say for example that nobody would commit himself to the judgement that an object was beautiful without claiming the assent of all men of sensibility and experience, our grounds being that people themselves make the distinction between what they call beautiful and what they like. They say that they do not know whether a certain work is good, but that they enjoyed it. If, however, they commit themselves, they do not say: 'Well, *I* found it beautiful, but you may not.' If there is any doubt, they do not use the word 'beauty'. Once when making this remark I had somebody in my audience say that the word 'beauty' was rarely used now, that people were much more likely to use some such expression as: 'That is absolutely it,' or even just: 'O.K.' I agreed and said I was willing to accept any manner of signalling recognition of highest excellence in art. A philologist took me to task. This, he said, was to show no feeling for context. Anyone who shied at the actual word 'beauty' was thereby shown to be socially inept, immaturely embarrassed at admitting feeling, and anyone who missed these subtleties was simply not giving a correct account of the use of the word 'beauty'. This seems to me to give the answer to people who claim that to draw inferences about aesthetics from the use of the word 'beauty' is to be concerned with words. What we are concerned with are the conditions under which the word is used, that is to say with the logic of the language of criticism.

This kind of nonsense *about* aesthetics leads to nonsense *within* aesthetics, not the kind of nonsense that issues in far-fetched theory but that which results in irrelevance. Some aestheticians are infected with the desire to be 'scientific' and themselves turn to psychology to give explanations of the value of aesthetic experience. I. A. Richards, for example, talks in terms of the satisfaction of impulses or of appetencies in describing aesthetic experience. Some talk in terms of the social function of art. There are two things to be said about such attempts. Either they are factual or not. If they are factual, then they are assuming that some state of affairs, either of the body or of the community, is desirable. This assumption needs justification, and here no factual examination will do. What we need is a reason for and not a cause of aesthetic delight or aesthetic value. If they are not factual, then they are no more 'scientific' than any other theory. Moreover such theories throw no light whatever on the properties which actual works must possess in order to be called beautiful or which an experience must possess in order to be called aesthetic. It is noteworthy that Richards's very good practical criticism bears no relationship to his aesthetic theory. His description of the distinguishing marks of an aesthetic experience is useless since it is impossible to determine whether or not a large number of non-conscious impulses have been called into play and satisfied in the reading of a poem. To do him justice he denies that there is a distinct state called 'aesthetic' and to be distinguished from other states, but he also says that there is a difference in the *number* of impulses brought into play and satisfied in an aesthetic experience. How does he know? And, we might add: What if there are? All he means is that the experiences of reading good poetry, looking at good pictures, are satisfying.

There is one famous case of an aesthetician using his account of the function of art to distinguish good from bad. The result, however, is not encouraging. Tolstoy believed that art had the function of infecting people with brotherly love and goodwill towards one another. Any picture, play or musical composition is good in so far as it does this work, bad in so far as it divides people from one another. On this criterion Tolstoy rightly concluded that the 'great' plays and operas were worth much less than a peasant song sung at his daughter's wedding with spontaneity and depth of feeling. I should want to object that any theory from which it followed that the plays of Shakespeare, the operas of Mozart, were not works of art must be ruled out of court. The fact of the matter is that any theory of art which makes its value lie in the fulfilment of a function is theoretically allowing that art is expendable. If that same function could be performed in some other way, then we do not need art. If it is objected that the function *could* not be performed in some other way, i.e. that there is a point-by-point correspondence between the state we wish to bring about and the elements of the work, then that is to admit that our theory is not a theory of the function of art but of its importance.

There is another pitfall in aesthetics. Some people, feeling very strongly the importance of art, think that it cannot be 'placed' without reference to some other-worldly reality. This may be true: it may be the case that a satisfactory aesthetic theory presupposes a metaphysical view of the world. If so, then we shall have to set out systematically the whole set of theories with the interconnexions. We ought not to lift the parts of metaphysics which please us out of their context and incorporate them unexamined in aesthetic theory. When we do so, we are in danger of misinterpreting these parts, giving them a meaning which they could be seen not to bear on a closer examination.

We may now say in a more general way what is the proper work of aestheticians. I want first to consider whether a distinction is possible in aesthetics corresponding to the distinction between practical ethics and moral philosophy. The most important part of practical ethics is to give the right answer to the question: Why should I choose this course rather than that? To believe that it is possible to give a sensible answer to this question, or indeed to ask the question sensibly, is to presuppose freedom. To believe that it is possible to give the *right* answer is to presuppose that ethics has some such constitutive principle as that it is 'good' to behave rationally. To give an answer we do not have to persuade people that it is better to behave rationally any more than a doctor has to persuade people that health is better than disease before he can treat them. In morals the typical and most important advice-giving and -seeking situation occurs when one has to decide between courses of action in a particular set of circumstances. The similar situation in aesthetics is trivial. Shall I go to this play or that? when no considerations other than aesthetic ones are involved. Shall I buy this picture or that? again when no non-aesthetic considerations are involved. We do not ask whether we shall admire this picture rather than that. This has led people to believe that there are no important advice-giving situations in aesthetics. But it seems to me that there are, though of a different kind. We ask advice seriously when we find that we are lacking in appreciation of work which is admired by people whose judgement we trust. We may not for example be able to appreciate modern music or painting, and it would be sensible to ask advice about how to set about fitting ourselves as far as possible to enjoy them as other people do. We should do no such thing if we had no grounds for believing that the objects which we are unable to enjoy were worth enjoying. It would be nonsensical to ask an expert to help us to enjoy trash. What we are asking presupposes the constitutive principle that it is good to enjoy worthy objects.

There is an interesting contrast between the moral and aesthetic situations. When we ask: Why should I do this rather than that? the answer would be in terms of principles. Do this because in general terms it is right, in particular it is an instance of speaking the truth, keeping a promise. The answer to the seeker of advice in aesthetics will be in terms of particular works and their properties. Read this, listen to that, and notice such and such features. Practise picking out the melody, or look with your eyes half closed or . . . In morals advice is sought about a particular action and the answer is in terms of a principle: in aesthetics the question is about how to fit oneself in general and the answer is in terms of particular works. We ought to perform actions of a certain type because they are exemplifications of a moral principle. We ought to admire certain specific objects—and it is not obvious at first sight whether or not we can add: Because they are of a certain kind. What we know to begin with in morals is that we ought to speak the truth and keep promises: what we know to begin with in aesthetics is that we ought to appreciate. . . . Here would follow a list of masterpieces. We cannot be called good unless we perform right actions most of the time. We cannot be called 'aesthetic' unless we admire a large number of the objects on our list. (I am sorry for the adjective but there doesn't seem to be one corresponding to 'good'. Equally, there are the two words 'ethics' and 'morals', but only the one word 'aesthetics'.)

While practical ethics presupposes freedom and that it is desirable to act rationally, the philosophy of morals is concerned with what it means to describe an act as right, to consider the legitimacy of what has been presupposed in practical ethics and to consider generally the concepts used in moral discourse and the nature of its reasoning. Similarly in aesthetics we have the philosophy of beauty and art, which has to consider the presuppositions of practical aesthetics, the concepts employed in critical discourse and the nature of its reasoning. We have, for example, to show clearly what is involved in the kind of advice given in answer to actual problems in practical aesthetics. The trivial cases—shall I see this rather than that, read this rather than that?—call for answers in terms of properties of the objects and the assumption that it is these properties which constitute the value of the object. The philosophy of beauty has to consider the problem of the relation of these properties to beauty. Is the assumption that anything possessing these properties will be *ipso facto* beautiful? If not, why not? In morals we can universalize a principle and if we cannot, we think that there is something wrong. *Any* case of telling a lie is wrong in so far as it is considered as a case of telling a lie. Apparently, any case of breaking aesthetic principles may or may not result in a failure. Must we then say that there are no principles in aesthetics but only good reasons for valuing each particular work? It seems to me that this is very likely to be the true conclusion. If we wish to add another right action to the list of right actions already performed, we have only to produce one conforming to one or other of our principles. If we want to add another work of beauty to our list, we shall have simply to wait until an artist in words, sounds, colour, makes one. Even then, we shall have to wait until we are sure that our first pleasure in it was not misleading but that it is a source of continual experience of beauty, even of increasing delight. When we list its properties as reasons for our evaluation of it we shall not expect to be able to extend our evaluation to other works *of the same kind*, but only to future experiences of *this same object*. It might even be a ground for not admiring a new work that it possessed the same properties as an established work. There is plagiarism in art but not in morals. It would be ridiculous to say that you are copying me in trying to tell the truth or in not caring whether you tell lies or not. It would not be at all ridiculous to complain that a fellow poet was copying you literally or, in a less exact sense, that a fellow painter was copying your work.

If, then, philosophers of beauty succeed in producing a theory of beauty, they will have to show how it is related to the specific properties offered as reasons for valuing certain works of art highly.

They will have to consider whether it is possible to produce an intermediate principle, which says in effect: this is the way in which specific works will be able to conform to the general principle. This would be a principle for each *kind* of art, which shows how the general principle may be implemented in painting, poetry, music, etc. It may be that the general principle is such that this is impossible. If art is expression, and if moreover expression is complete in the mind of the artist, then the differences between painting and poetry are trivial and connected accidentally with the nature of art. If art is expression, it would be just as silly to ask whether it were in words or colours or music as it would be to ask whether a kind action were performed with cups of tea or flasks of brandy. If at this point one wished to disagree, one would have to examine the meaning of 'expression', what it was that was expressed, and why expressiveness is a ground for valuing a work. If it seemed to be satisfactory, then we should have to look again at our belief that there are *kinds* of art in an important sense.

The more important type of question asked in practical aesthetics —How can I become able to enjoy ...?—also assumes that it is better to enjoy worthy objects. It assumes as well that to appreciate beauty is an achievement, something to be worked at with hopes of success. Anyone can stand in front of a picture or sit in a concert hall and wait to see what happens to him: he could then describe his experience, characterizing it as pleasant or unpleasant, and in accordance with this the work as good or bad. This is one kind of way to behave in the presence of works of art, and for this way psychological laws are entirely adequate. People of a certain kind and background will tend to enjoy this kind of object, though it would be more accurate to say that they tend to enjoy themselves in the presence of this type of object. When we ask how we can come to enjoy the poetry of T. S. Eliot, it would not be an answer to say that you could be hypnotized so that you could enjoy anything. What you are wanting is not to sit happily while the poetry flows over you, but to have the delight *proper to* that kind of activity, i.e. you want to have an experience which is appropriate to, not caused by, the object. What you will find is that the expert is advising you not on how to make a change in yourself but on how you may come to be better and better acquainted with the object you wish to enjoy. The assumption here is that to enjoy an object established as aesthetically worth-while it is enough to become very well acquainted with it. Suppose it does not work and you begin to voice your dissatisfactions to the expert. 'I now know,' you may say, 'all the allusions in the *Waste Land* and I still cannot enjoy it.' It now becomes clear that the hindrance is in yourself. You may think it unsuitable that a poem should require knowledge of such a wide range of literature. What our expert now attempts to do is to justify this requirement, that is to remove your prejudice. And so it could go on. We have here our next assumption, that a normal person who will take the time and trouble to become acquainted with works of art will be able to appreciate their beauty. These assumptions, drawn from the discourse and practice of practical aesthetics, give grounds to the philosopher for defence of the objectivity of beauty. The talk of 'enjoyment', though, will give him cause for thought. Can we be said to *enjoy King Lear*? Perhaps the use of the word 'enjoyment' is simply the sign of successful achievement and so another support for the view that this is the proper way to describe the appreciation of a work of art. The pleasure of success here is no different from the pleasure of success in any other context, so that it is not specifically of interest to aestheticians.

To sum up. The proper work of aestheticians is to take note of psychological facts, of historical facts about art and criticism, of the judgements of critics and people in general, and to become clear about what we want to do with these facts. We have to be clear about what kinds of questions require a factual answer and about the kinds of questions for which a factual answer would be irrelevant. We have to extract the assumptions implicit in the standards used by artists and critics when they talk about their work. This is a point at which it becomes important to take notice of the facts of the history of art and taste. When art changes its function in society the standards by which people judge it change too. Here I am not speaking of theories about the function of art. Art can have a certain place in the life of a community and it will be evaluated in accordance with this place, but it does not follow that we must believe that art has a function *qua* art. Suppose that art has a magical function in a community. The people of that time value it for its efficacy, but the people of later ages may see that the very qualities which made it effective for its own times make it valuable in quite a different way when viewed out of its historical context. It was for some such reason that Hegel regarded 'aesthetic' theories such as Aristotle's theory of tragic excellence as extra material for aestheticians along with the actual tragedies of the time and not as a contribution to aesthetics proper. To value art for its function is to take it as craft-work, and it seems to be humanly impossible to make objects for use without being concerned with their appearance. In fact it sometimes seems that some of our most pleasing objects are those made with loving care for a given end. The artist is so intent on using his material towards that end that beauty emerges almost as a by-product. Some of our most pleasing flower-pictures are the engravings in old gardening and botany books, and some of our most pleasing objects in general are works of architecture, cathedrals, bridges, ships, aeroplanes, even cars. A satisfactory aesthetic, then, would issue in a clear understanding of the interrelationships among the concepts employed in artistic and critical discourse and of the interrelationships among standards and theories so that it can be seen which standard or set of standards rules out which theories. It would set out the conditions under which an object whether natural or man-made is rightly called beautiful, the conditions under which an experience is rightly called aesthetic. Until people have tried to formulate some such system, or tried to follow through the recorded attempts of aestheticians at such a system, we shall not allow them to tell us we are talking nonsense. We are the people to tell them that they are talking nonsense when they stubbornly hang on to incompatible theories or want to discard inconvenient facts.

Aesthetic Appreciation of Nature*

RONALD W. HEPBURN

I

Contemporary writings on aesthetics attend almost exclusively to the arts and very rarely to natural beauty.[1] Aesthetics is even defined by some mid-century writers as 'the philosophy of art', 'the philosophy of criticism'. Two much-quoted anthologies of aesthetics (Elton's in this country, Vivas and Krieger's in America) contain no study of natural beauty.[2] Why is this so?

For part of the answer we have to look not to philosophers' theories but to some general shifts in aesthetic taste itself. Despite appearances to the contrary (the cult of the open air, caravans, camps, excursions in the family car) serious aesthetic concern with nature is today rather an unusual phenomenon. If we regard the Wordsworthian vision as the great peak in the recent history of the subject, then we have to say that the ground declined very sharply indeed from that extraordinary summit, and that today we survey it from far below. The Wordsworthian nature was man's aesthetic and moral educator: whereas the characteristic image of twentieth-century man, as we all know, is that of a 'stranger' encompassed by a nature which is indifferent, unmeaning and 'absurd'.

The work of the sciences too has tended to produce some bewilderment and loss of nerve over the aesthetic interpretation of nature. Microscope and telescope have added vastly to our perceptual data; the forms of the ordinary landscape, ordinarily interpreted, are shown up as only a selection from countless different scales. 'What is nature?' The question can no longer be answered in terms of macroscopic, readily-discriminable, 'labelled' objects.

* A substantially longer version of this study appeared in a volume published in Italian (publisher Lerici) introducing current trends in English-speaking philosophy.

On the theoretical level there are other and distinctive reasons for the neglect of natural beauty in aesthetics itself, especially in an aesthetics that seeks to make itself increasingly rigorous. Certain important features of aesthetic experience are quite unobtainable in nature—a landscape does not minutely control the spectator's response to it as does a successful work of art: it is an unframed ordinary object, in contrast to the framed, 'esoteric', 'illusory' or 'virtual' character of the art object. And so the artefact tends to be taken as the aesthetic object *par excellence*, and the proper focus of study.

Linguistic or conceptual analysts have been understandably tempted to apply their techniques first and foremost to the arguments and manifestoes lying to hand in the writings of art critics. In the case of natural beauty, however, such a critical literature scarcely exists. The philosopher must first work out his own systematic accounts of the aesthetic enjoyment of nature. And this he has so far been slow—or reluctant—to do.

Having drawn attention to a neglected topic, I now want to argue that the neglect is a very bad thing: bad because aesthetics is thereby steered off from examining an important and richly complex set of relevant data; and bad because when a set of experiences is ignored in a theory relevant to them, they tend to be made less readily available as experiences. If we cannot find sensible-sounding language in which to describe them, the experiences are felt, in an embarrassed way, as off-the-map—and since off the map, seldom visited. This is specially unfortunate if for other reasons the experiences are already hard to achieve.

What, then, can contemporary aesthetics do about the topic of natural beauty?

2

If I am right that systematic description is one main lack here, I ought to supply some account of the varieties of aesthetic experience of nature. But their variety is immense, and mere cataloguing would be tedious. I shall select a few samples both interesting in themselves and useful for subsequent arguments.

We have already remarked that art objects have a number of general characteristics not shared by objects in nature. It would be useful if we could show (and I think we can) that the absence of certain of these features is not merely privative in its effect, but can contribute valuably to the aesthetic experience of nature.

A good specimen is the degree to which the spectator can be involved in the natural aesthetic situation itself. *On occasion* he may confront natural objects as a static, disengaged observer; but far more typically the objects envelop him on all sides. In a forest, trees surround him; he is ringed by hills, or he stands in the midst of a plain. If there is movement in the scene, the spectator may himself be in motion and his motion may be an important element in his aesthetic experience. Think, for instance, of a glider-pilot, delighting in a sense of buoyancy, in the balancing of the air-currents that hold him aloft. This sort of involvement is well expressed by Barbara Hepworth: 'What a different shape and "being" one becomes lying on the sand with the sea almost above from when standing against the wind on a sheer high cliff with seabirds circling patterns below one.'[3] We have here not only a mutual involvement of spectator and object, but also a reflexive effect by which the spectator experiences *himself* in an unusual and vivid way: and this difference is not merely noted but dwelt upon aesthetically.

If this study were on a larger scale, we should have to analyse in detail the various senses of 'aesthetic detachment' and 'involvement' that are relevant here. This could prove a more slippery investigation than in the case of art appreciation; but a rewarding one. The spectator is, of course, aesthetically detached in the sense that he is not *using* nature, manipulating it or calculating how to manipulate it. He is both actor and spectator, ingredient in the landscape and lingering upon the sensations of being thus ingredient, playing actively with nature and letting nature as it were play with him and his awareness of himself.

Secondly: though by no means all art objects have frames or pedestals, a great many of them share a common character in being set apart from their environment in a distinctive way. We might use the word 'frame' in an extended sense to cover not only the physical boundaries of pictures but all the various devices employed in different arts to prevent the art object being mistaken for a natural object or for an artefact without aesthetic interest. Such devices are best thought of as aids to the recognition of the formal completeness of of the art objects themselves, their ability to sustain aesthetic interest.

In contrast natural objects are 'frameless'. This is in some ways a disadvantage aesthetically: but there are some compensations. Whatever lies beyond the frame of an art object cannot normally become part of the aesthetic experience relevant to it. A chance train-whistle cannot be integrated into the music of a string quartet; it merely interferes with its appreciation. But where there is no frame, and where nature is our aesthetic object, a sound or a visible intrusion from beyond the original boundaries of our attention can challenge us to integrate it in our overall experience, to modify that experience so as to make room for it. This, of course, *need* not occur: we may shut it out by effort of will if it seems quite unassimilable. At any rate our creativity is set a task: and when things go well with us we experience a sudden expansion of imagination that can be memorable in its own right.

> And, when there came a pause
> Of silence such as baffled his best skill:
> Then sometimes, in that silence, while he hung
> Listening, a gentle shock of mild surprise
> Has carried far into his heart the voice
> Of mountain-torrents . . .

If the absence of 'frame' precludes full determinateness and stability in the natural aesthetic object, it at least offers in return such unpredictable perceptual surprises; and their mere possibility imparts to the contemplation of nature a sense of adventurous openness. In a painting the frame ensures that each element of the work is determined in its perceived qualities (including emotional qualities) by a limited context. Obviously this is one kind of determinateness that cannot be achieved with natural objects. The aesthetic impact made upon us by, say, a tree is part-determined by the context we include in our view of it. A tree growing on a steep hill-slope, bent far over by the winds, may strike us as tenacious, grim, strained. But from a greater distance, when the view includes numerous similar trees on the hillside, the striking thing may be a delightful stippled patterned slope, with quite different emotional quality—quixotic or cheery. Any aesthetic quality in nature is always provisional, correctible by reference to a different, perhaps wider context or to a narrower one realized in greater detail. In positive terms this provisional character of aesthetic qualities in nature creates a restlessness, an alertness, a search for ever new standpoints and more comprehensive unities.

Lastly: we can distinguish between the particular aesthetic impact of an object, whether natural or artefact, and certain general 'background' experiences common to a great many aesthetic situations and of aesthetic value in themselves. With an art object there is the exhilarating activity of coming to grasp its intelligibility as a perceptual whole. We find built-in guides to interpretation and contextual controls for our response. We are aware of these features as having been expressly put there by its creator. Now I think that we can locate a nearly parallel but interestingly different background experience when our object is not an artefact but a natural one. Again it is a kind of exhilaration, a delight in the fact that the forms of the natural world *offer scope* for the exercise of imagination, that leaf pattern chimes with vein pattern, cloud form with mountain form and mountain form with human form. Indeed, when nature is pronounced to be 'beautiful'—not in the narrower sense of that word, which contrasts 'beautiful' with 'picturesque' or 'comic', but in the wide sense equivalent to 'aesthetically interesting' and 'aesthetically excellent'—an important part of our meaning is just this, that nature's forms do provide this scope for imaginative play. For that is surely not analytically true: it might have been otherwise.

I have been arguing that certain important differences between natural objects and art objects furnish grounds for distinctive and valuable types of aesthetic experience of nature. These are types of experience that art cannot provide to the same extent as nature, or cannot provide at all. Supposing that a person's aesthetic education fails to reckon with these differences, supposing it instils in him the attitudes, the tactics of approach, the expectations proper to the appreciation of art works only, such a person will either pay very little aesthetic heed to natural objects or else will heed them in the wrong way. He will look—and of course look in vain—for what can be found and enjoyed only in art. Furthermore, one cannot be at all certain that he will seriously ask himself whether there might be other tactics more proper and more fruitful for the aesthetic appreciation of nature.

3

Accounts of the aesthetic appreciation of nature have sometimes focused upon the contemplating of single natural objects in their individuality and uniqueness. They have centred upon the formal organization of such objects or their colours and textures. Other writers, with greater metaphysical daring, or rashness, have spoken of the aesthetic enjoyment of nature as leading to the disclosure of 'unity' in nature, or as tending towards an ideal of 'oneness with nature'. The formulations vary greatly and substantially among themselves: but the vocabulary of unity, oneness as the key aesthetic principle, is the recurrent theme.[4]

There are strong influences in contemporary British philosophy that prompt one to have the fullest sympathy with a particularist approach to natural beauty—as the contemplating of individual objects with their aesthetically interesting perceptual qualities; and to have very little sympathy for the more grandiose language of 'oneness with' or 'in' nature. None the less, it seems to me that we do not have here one good and one bad aesthetic approach, the first sane and the second absurd. Rather we have two well-separated landmarks between which lies a range of aesthetic possibilities: and in the mapping of this range those landmarks will play a valuable role.

We must begin by frankly denying the universal aesthetic need for unity, unity of form, quality, structure, or of anything else. We can take pleasure in sheer plurality, in the stars of the night sky, in a birdsong without beginning, middle or end. And yet to make 'unity' in some sense one's key concept need not be simply wrong-headed or obscurantist. I want to argue that there are certain incompletenesses in the experience of the isolated particular that produce a *nisus* towards the other pole, the pole of unity. But there is not a single type of unification or union: *several* notions are to be distinguished within the ideal.

We have already noted the nisus towards more and more comprehensive or adequate survey of the context that determines the perceived qualities of a natural object or scene. Our motives are, in part, the desire for a certain integrity or 'truth' in our aesthetic experience of nature: and of this more shortly. We know also that in all aesthetic experience it is contextual complexity that, more than any other single factor, makes possible the minute discrimination of emotional qualities; and such discrimination is accorded high aesthetic value. It is largely the pursuit of such value that moves us to accept what I called 'the challenge to integrate'—to take notice of and to accept as aesthetically relevant some shape or sound that initially lies outside the limit of our attention.

The expansion of context does not have to be a spatial expansion. What else can it be? Supposing I am walking over a wide expanse of sand and mud. The quality of the scene is perhaps that of wild, glad emptiness. But suppose that I bring to bear upon the scene my knowledge that this is a tidal basin, the tide being out. I see myself now as virtually walking on what is for half the day sea-bed. The wild glad emptiness may be tempered by a disturbing weirdness. Thus, in addition to spatial extension (or sometimes instead of it), we may aim at enriching the interpretative element of our experience, taking this not as theoretical 'knowledge-about' the object or scene, but as helping to determine the aesthetic impact it makes upon us. 'Unity' here plays a purely 'regulative' role. Nature is not a 'given whole', nor indeed is knowledge about it. And in any case there are psychological limits to the expansion process; a degree of complexity is reached beyond which there will be no increase in discrimination of perceptual or emotional qualities.

A second movement away from contemplation of uninterpreted particulars is sometimes known as the 'humanizing' or the 'spiritualizing' of nature. I shall merely note its existence and relevance here, for there have been a good many accounts of it in the history of aesthetics. Coleridge said that: 'Art is . . . the power of humanizing nature, of infusing the thoughts and passions of man into every thing which is the object of his contemplation.'⁵ And Hegel, that the aim of art is 'to strip the outer world of its stubborn foreignness'.⁶ What is here said about art is no less true of aesthetic experience of nature itself. Imaginative activity is working for a *rapprochement* between the spectator and his aesthetic object: unity is again a regulative notion, a symbol of the unattainable complete transmutation of brute external nature into a mirror of the mind.

By developing and qualifying the 'humanization' ideal we can come to see yet a third aspect of the nisus towards unity. A person who contemplates natural objects aesthetically may sometimes find their emotional quality is describable in the vocabulary of ordinary human moods and feeling—melancholy, exuberance, placidity. But not always. A particular emotional quality can be roughly *analogous* to a nameable human emotion—let us say, desolation: but the precise quality of desolation revealed in some waste or desert in nature may be quite distinctive in timbre and intensity. Aesthetic experience of nature may be experience of a range of emotion that the human scene by itself, untutored and unsupplemented, could not evoke. In Barabara Hepworth's remark, once more, to be one with nature in her sense was to realize vividly one's place in the landscape, as a form among its forms. And this is not to have nature's 'foreignness' or otherness overcome, but rather to allow that otherness free play in modifying one's everyday sense of one's own being. In this domain, again, we need not confine ourselves to the contemplating of uninterpreted particulars. In a leaf-pattern I may 'see' also bloodvessel patterns, or the patterns of branching, forked lightning: or all of these. In a spiral nebula pattern I may see the pattern of swirling waters or whirling dust. I may be aware of a network of affinities, analogous forms, spanning the inorganic or the organic world or both. My experience has a quality of *multum in parvo*. If, with Mr. Eliot, one sees 'The dance along the artery/The circulation of the lymph' as 'figured in the drift of stars', something of the aesthetic qualities of the latter (as we perceive them) may come to be transferred to the former. This is not necessarily a humanizing of nature; it may be more like a 'naturizing' of the human observer.

A fourth class of approaches to ideals of 'unity' is concerned with what we have called the 'background' quality of emotions and attitudes, common to a great many individual experiences. Here the background is a sense of reconciliation, suspension of conflict, and of being in that sense at one with the aesthetic object. This particular sort of 'at-one-ness' could hardly be present in art-experience, since it requires that the aesthetic object should be at the same time some part of the natural environment. This is the same environment from which we wrest our food, from which we have to protect ourselves in order to live, and which refuses to sustain our individual lives beyond a limited term. To attain, and sustain, the relevant detachment from such an environment in order to savour it aesthetically is in itself a fair achievement, an achievement which suffuses the aesthetic experiences themselves with that sense of reconciliation. The objects of nature may look to us as if their *raison d'être* were precisely that we should celebrate their beauty. As Rilke put it: 'Everything beckons to us to perceive it.'[7] Or the dominant stance may be that of benediction: the Ancient Mariner 'blesses' the water-snakes at his moment of reconciliation.

This fourth type of unity-ideal could arise in the contemplation of what is itself quite *un*-unified in the other senses, the night sky again, or a mass of hills with no detectable pattern to unite them. It is more strictly a concomitant, or a by-product, of an aesthetic experience that we are already enjoying, an experience in which there may have been no synoptic grasping of patterns, relating of forms or any other sort of unifying.

I suspect that someone who tried to construct a comprehensive aesthetic theory with 'unity' as its sole key concept would obtain his comprehensiveness only by equivocating or punning over the meaning of the key expression, only by sliding and slithering from one of its many senses to another. When one sense is not applicable, another may well be. The fourth sense in particular can be relevant to vivid aesthetic experience of any natural objects whatever.

So much the worse, we may conclude, for such a theory *qua* monolithic. But to say that is not to imply that our study has yielded only negative results. This is one of several areas in aesthetics where we have to resist the temptation to work with a single supreme concept and must replace it by a *cluster* of related key concepts. In searching out the relevant key concepts, the displaced pseudo-concept may yet be a useful guide—as it is in the present case. It is not, however, adequate for all explanatory purposes.

We began our study by referring to the contemplation of uninterpreted individual natural objects in their particularity. This was not a mere starting-point to be left behind in our pursuit of the 'unities'. On the contrary, aesthetic experience remains tethered to that concern with the particular even if on a long rope. The rope is there, although the development and vitality of that experience demand that it be stretched to the full. The pull of the rope is felt when the expanding and complicating of our synopses reaches the point beyond which we shall have not more but less fine discrimination of perceptual quality. It is felt again when we risk the blurring and negating of natural forms as we really perceive them in an anxious attempt to limit our experience of nature to the savouring of stereotyped and well-domesticated emotional qualities. It is even relevant to our fourth type of unity-ideal: for the sense of reconciliation is not an independent and autonomous aesthetic experience, but hangs entirely upon the occurrence of particular experiences of particular aesthetically interesting natural objects.

4

Although recent aesthetics has been little concerned with natural beauty as such, yet at crucial points in its analyses of *art* experience it has frequently made comparisons between our aesthetic approach to art objects and to objects in nature. In the light of our reflections so far we may wish to ask at this point whether the comparing has been fairly done. We have room to examine one example only.

An important part of current controversy is the assessment of the Expression Theory. The Expression Theory saw the artefact as the middle link in a communication from artist to spectator. Its critics see the artefact first and foremost as an object with certain properties, properties which are, or should be, aesthetically interesting and which in their totality control the spectator's response. This is an aesthetic approach that reduces the gulf between art object and natural object. Both are to be approached primarily as individual, self-contained entities, exciting to contemplate by virtue of their perceived qualities. But how far can we accept this comparison? Critics of the critics have pointed out some deficiencies. They have insisted upon the irreducible relevance of linguistic and cultural context to the interpretation of a poem. Identical words might constitute *two* poems, not one, if we read them in two different historical contexts.[8]

We could extend this criticism as follows. Suppose we have two perceptually identical objects, one an artefact and the other natural. They might be a 'carved stone' of Arp and a naturally smoothed stone; a carving in wood and a piece of fallen timber. Or they might be identical in pattern, though not in material; for example, a rock face with a particular texture and marking and an abstract expressionist painting with the same texture and the same markings. If we made the most of the *rapprochement*, we should have to say that we had in each of these cases essentially *one* aesthetic object. Yet this would be a misleading conclusion. If we knew them for what they are—as artefact or natural object—we should certainly attend and respond differently to them. As we look at the rock face we may realize imaginatively the geological turmoils that produced its pattern. The realizing of these need not be a piece of extra-aesthetic reflection; it may determine for us how we see and respond to the object itself. If we interpreted and responded to the abstract painting in the same way, our interpretation would this time be merely whimsical. If we arbitrarily restricted aesthetic experience of both nature and art to the contemplating of uninterpreted shapes and patterns, we could, of course, have the *rapprochement*. But we have seen good reason for refusing so to restrict it in the case of nature-experience, whatever be the case with art.

Take another instance. Through the eye-piece of a telescope I see the spiral nebula in Andromeda. I look next at an abstract painting in a circular frame that contains the identical visual pattern. My responses are not alike, even if each is indisputably aesthetic. My awareness that the first shapes are of enormous and remote masses of matter in motion imparts to my response a strangeness and solemnity that are not generated by the pattern alone. The abstract pattern may indeed impress by reminding me of various wheeling and swirling patterns in nature. But there is a difference between taking the pattern as that sort of reminder and on the other hand brooding on this impressive instantiation of it in the nebula.

A more light-hearted but helpful way of bringing out these points is to suppose ourselves confronted by a small object which, for all we know, may be natural or may be an artefact. We are set the task of regarding it aesthetically. I suppose that we might cast upon it an uneasy and embarrassed eye. How shall we approach it? Shall we, for instance, see in its smoothness the slow mindless grinding of centuries of tides, or the swifter and mindful operations of the sculptor's tools? Certainly, we can enjoy something of its purely formal qualities on either reckoning; but even the savouring of these is affected by non-formal factors that diverge according to the judgement we make about its origin. To sum up: the swing, in some recent aesthetics, from 'intention' to 'object' has been healthful on the whole, delivering aesthetics and criticism from a great deal of misdirected labour. But it has countered the paradoxes of expression-ism with paradoxes of its own. Differences between object and object need to be reaffirmed: indiscernibly different poems or carvings become discernibly different when we reckon with their aesthetically different cultural contexts; and the contextual controls that determine how we contemplate an object in nature are different from those that shape our experience of art. In other words, we have here a central current issue in aesthetics that cannot be properly tackled without a full-scale discussion of natural beauty.

5

That, however, is not the only current issue about which the same can be said. It can be said also (and this introduces our final topic) about the analysis of such expressions as 'true', 'false', 'profound', 'shallow', 'superficial', as terms of aesthetic appraisal. These have been studied in their application to art objects but scarcely at all in connexion with nature. It might indeed be contested whether they have *any* meaningful use in the latter connexion.

I think it can be shown that they have. We can best approach the topic by way of some analysis of an expression which we have used already but not explained. It is a sense of the word 'realize'. Here are some examples of the use. 'I had long known that the earth was not flat, but I never before *realized* its curvature till I watched that ship disappear on the horizon.' Here 'realize' involves making, or becoming, vivid to perception or to the imagination. Auxiliary imagings may attend my realizing of the earth's curvature, the image of my arms stretched out, fingers reaching round the sphere; and the realization of loneliness may involve imagining myself shouting but being unheard, needing help but getting none.

In some cases to realize something is simply to know or understand, where 'know' and 'understand' are analysable in dispositional terms. But our present sense of 'realize' has an essential episodic component: it is a coming-to-be-aware. In the aesthetic setting it is an experience accompanying and arising out of perceptions—perceptions upon which we dwell and linger. I am gazing, say, at a cumulus cloud when I realize its height. I do not discard, or pass beyond, the experience, as if I were judging the height of the cloud in flight-navigation (or the loneliness of the moor in planning a murder). This sort of realizing is obviously one of our chief activities in the aesthetic experiencing of nature. It has been central in earlier illustrations, the contemplation of the rock face, the spiral nebula, the ocean-smoothed stone.

But my suggestion that realizing is 'episodic', occurrent, may properly be challenged. Suppose that I am busy realizing the utter loneliness of the moor, when suddenly I discover that behind sundry bits of cover are a great many soldiers taking part in a field-exercise. Could I, without illogic, maintain that I had been realizing what is not in fact the case? Hardly. 'Realize' contains a built-in reference to truth. It has episodic components, but it cannot be exhaustively analysed in that way. I cannot be said to have realized the strength and hardness of a tall tree-trunk if, when I then approach it, it crumbles rotten at a touch. But surely I was doing *something*: my experience did occur; and nothing that subsequently occurs can alter it.

Now this experience was, of course, the aesthetic contemplation of apparent properties. That they turn out not to be also real properties may disturb the spectator, or it may not. For some people aesthetic experience is interested not at all in reality—only in looks, seemings: indifference to truth may be part of their definition of the aesthetic. If the soldiers appear or the tree crumbles, the aesthetic value of the prior experiences is (to those people) not in the least affected. Others take a different view. One could agree that a large range of aesthetic experience is not concerned about truth but yet attach a peculiar importance to the range that is. I am not sure that the gulf between this and the contrasted view is wholly bridgeable by argument: but some reflections can be offered along the following lines.

If we want our aesthetic experiences to be repeatable and to have stability, we shall try to ensure that new information or subsequent experimentation will not reveal the 'seemings' as illusions. If I know that the tree is rotten, I shall not be able again to savour its seeming-strength. I could, no doubt, savour its 'deceptively strong appearance'; but that would be a quite different experience from the first.

Suppose the outline of our cumulus cloud resembles that of a basket of washing, and we amuse ourselves in dwelling upon this resemblance. Suppose that on another occasion we do not dwell on such freakish aspects, but try instead to realize the inner turbulence of the cloud, the winds sweeping up within and around it, determining its structure and visible form. Should we not be ready to say that this latter experience was less superficial than the other, that it was truer to nature, and for that reason more worth having? If there can be a passage, in art, from easy beauty to difficult and more serious beauty, there can also be such passages in aesthetic contemplation of nature.

Were there not a strong nisus in that direction, how could we account for the sense of bewilderment people express over how to bring their aesthetic view of nature into accord with the discoveries of recent science? Because of these discoveries (as Sir Kenneth Clark puts it): 'the snug, sensible nature which we can see with our own eyes has ceased to satisfy our imaginations.'9 If the aesthetic enjoyment of nature were no more than the contemplation of particular shapes and colours and movements, these discoveries could not possibly disturb it. But they do: they set the imagination a task in 'realizing'.

An objector may still insist that reference to truth is aesthetically irrelevant. To him the only relevant factors are the savouring of perceptual qualities and formal organization. But a formalist might at least be reminded that a major element in his own enjoyment is the synoptic grasping of complexities. A particular colour-patch may be seen as part of an object, as modifying the colour of adjacent patches, and as contributing to the total perceived pattern—all simultaneously. One could argue that the striving to 'realize' should be taken as adding to our powers of synopsis and that for the *exclusion* of it no good reason could be given.

But a more searching anxiety might be expressed. Sometimes indeed such realizings may enhance an aesthetic experience, but may they not sometimes destroy it? When I see the full moon rising behind the silhouetted branches of winter trees I may judge that the scene is more beautiful if I think of the moon simply as a silvery flat disc at no great distance from the trees on the skyline. Ought I to be realizing the moon's actual shape, size and distance? Why spoil my enjoyment? There may be cases where I have to choose between an aesthetic experience available only if I inhibit my realizing and on the other hand a different aesthetic experience available if I do some realizing. In our example, the first experience is of beauty (in the narrow sense); and we could not count on the alternative experience being also one of beauty, in the same sense. It might, of course, be still aesthetically exciting: that is, of beauty in the widest sense. But, the objector might press, even that cannot be guaranteed in all cases. And this is exactly the difficulty we feel about the bearing of present-day science on our vision of the natural world. Sometimes our attempts at realizing are aesthetically bleak and unrewarding; or they may fail altogether, as perhaps with some cosmologies and cosmogonies. Compromises, the balancing of one aesthetic requirement against another, may well be inevitable. One may say in a particular case: 'this is the nearest I can come to making imaginatively vivid what I know about the object. My realizing is still not quite adequate to my knowledge; but if I were to go any further in that direction, I should lose touch altogether with the sights, sounds and movements of the visible world seen from the human point of view. And that would impoverish, not enrich, my total aesthetic experience.' What we should be feeling again is the tug of the rope that tethers aesthetic experience to the perception of the particular object and its perceived individuality.

To be able to say anything more confident about this problem one would need to hold a metaphysical and religious view of nature and science which denied that the imaginative assimilating of scientific knowledge could ultimately lead to aesthetic impoverishment. That possibility we can only take note of in this essay without being able to explore it.

We may recall at the same time, and in conclusion, that some important accounts of natural beauty have, historically, been closely allied with various sorts of nature-mysticism. I have argued that there are in fact not one but several unity-ideals; that it is most unlikely that any single aesthetic experience can fully and simultaneously realize them all; and I believe that with certain of them the notion of full attainment makes dubious sense. Yet the idea of their ever more intense and comprehensive attainment is not without value, and the link with nature-mystical experiences need not be severed.[10]

Very tentatively, I suspect that no more materials are required than those with which we are already furnished in order to render available certain limited varieties of mystical experience, and logically to map them. Those materials provide us, not with affirmations about a transcendent being or realm, but with a *focus imaginarius* that can play a regulative and practical role in the aesthetic contemplation of nature. It sees that contemplation as grounded, first and last, in particular perceptions, but as reaching out so as to relate the forms of the objects perceived to the pervasive and basic forms of nature;

relating it also to the observer's own stance and setting, as himself one item in nature—a nature with whose forces he feels in harmony through the very success of this contemplative activity itself.

But even if something of the intensity and momentousness of mystical experience can be reached along such lines, this would be a mysticism without the God of theism. And surely the absence of belief in transcendence would make this quite different from a mysticism that centres upon it. Different, indeed, in the quality of available experience and in expectations aroused both for the here-and-now and the hereafter: but not so radically different as to make 'mysticism' a misnomer. Belief in a transcendent being means that, for the believer, the 'focus' is not imaginary but actual—in God; and it is doubtless psychologically easier to work towards a goal one believes to be fully realizable than towards a focus one suspects to be imaginary. Rather similarly, in ethics a student may experience a check to his practical moral confidence when he discovers that 'oughts' cannot be grounded in 'is's'. Yet it is seldom that he indulges for this reason in a permanent moral sulk. Perhaps, if I am right, it is no more reasonable to indulge in a nature-mystical sulk. But I begin to moralize: a sign that this paper has come to its proper end.

REFERENCES

[1] By 'nature' I shall simply mean all objects that are not human artefacts. I am ignoring the many possible disputes over natural objects that have received a marked, though limited, transformation at man's hands.

[2] W. Elton (ed.), *Aesthetics and Language* (1954): Vivas and Krieger (eds.), *The Problems of Aesthetics* (1953). Compare also H. Osborne's *Theory of Beauty* (1952), which likewise confines its investigation to art-experience. M. C. Beardsley's *Aesthetics* (1958) is subtitled *Problems in the Philosophy of Criticism*.

Mr. Osborne defines beauty as the 'characteristic and peculiar excellence of works of art'. Professor Bearsley's opening sentence reads: 'There would be no problems of aesthetics, in the sense in which I propose to mark out this field of study, if no one ever talked about works of art.'

[3] *Barbara Hepworth: Carvings and Drawings* (1952), chap. 4.

[4] (a) Graham Hough's *Image and Experience* (1960) contains some suggestive reflections stemming from his discussion of Ruskin and Roger Fry. 'By intense contemplation of . . .

experiences of form and space we become conscious of the unity between ourselves and the natural world' (p. 175). 'It is Ruskin's special distinction to show ... how the experience of the senses can lead directly to that unified apprehension of nature, and of ourselves as a part of nature, which can fairly constantly be recognized, under various mytho- logical disguises, not only as that which gives value to aesthetic exper- ience, but also as one of the major consolations of philosphy' (p. 176).

(b) The nature-mystical interpre- tation of unity-with-nature is briefly stated by Evelyn Underhill in her *Mysticism*. In moments of intense love for the natural world 'hints of a marvellous truth, a unity whose note is ineffable peace, shine in created things' (4th ed., 1912, p. 87).

W. T. Stace, listing the common characteristics of 'extrovertive myst- icism' (to which nature-mysticism belongs), includes the following: 'The One is ... perceived through the physical senses, in or through the multiplicity of objects.' 'The One [is apprehended more concretely] as being an inner subjectivity in all things, described variously as life, or consciousness, or a living Presence.' He adds: 'There are underground connexions between the mystical and the aesthetic ... which are at present obscure and unexplained.' (*Mysticism and Philosophy*, 1960, pp. 79, 81.)

(c) Coleridge wrote: 'The ground- work ... of all true philosophy is the full apprehension of the difference between the contemplation of reason, namely that intuition of things which arises when we possess ourselves as one with the whole ... and that which presents itself when ... we think of ourselves as separated beings, and place nature in antithesis to the mind, as object to subject, thing to thought, death to life.' (*The Friend*, Bohn Ed., p. 366.)

These brief quotations, culled in near-random fashion from very diverse historical contexts, may suffice to show at least the existence of some of the tendencies with which we shall be concerned.

5 *Biographia Literaria*, vol. II, 'On Poesy or Art'.

6 *Introduction to Hegel's Philosophy of Fine Art* (trans. Bosanquet, 1886), p. 59.

7 *Later Poems* (ed. Leishman), p. 128.

8 See H. S. Eveling, 'Composition and Criticism', *Proc. Arist. Soc.*, 1958–9.

9 *Landscape into Art* (1949), Pelican Books, 1956, p. 150. Sir Kenneth Clark is writing of art and artists, but his points are no less relevant to a contemplation of nature that never passes into the constructing of art objects.

10 Compare, once again, Graham Hough, *Image and Experience* (1960), pp. 174 f.

Art, Truth and Reality

LOUIS ARNAUD REID

I return to a very old question, the relationships between the arts and
what we commonly call the 'real' world, 'life', and our experience of
it—life which is outside of or at least in some measure independent of
the arts. Do the arts, all or some of them, in any degree mirror life?
Or can art increase our insight into and understanding of life? Is this
an improper question? Is it degrading to the arts, which have their
own laws and their own autonomy, to attempt to measure them by
reference to anything which is not themselves? Another way of
putting the same range of questions is to ask whether it is proper to
call art (or the arts) in any sense 'true' or 'false'. This is perhaps a more
restricted and biased formula for the question; yet the very restriction
may serve to point the problem more sharply.

It may well be said that these questions are being put in an
impossibly general way. An answer which may be valid of one art
seems not to be valid of another. Of much drama, representative
painting and sculpture, it may be said that they are, more or less,
true to life, or that they increase our insight into life. But much contemporary abstract painting and sculpture seem to give the lie to
this: and it is difficult, at any rate at first sight, to argue that pure
music is true to, or increases insight into, real life.

No one who approaches aesthetics from some knowledge of the
several arts (and not *a priori*), and who has long reflected on these
questions, could possibly expect a *simple* general answer to the
question of the relation between art and reality. Yet he might expect a
complex general answer—or at least he might entertain hope that in
time we might move in the direction of finding such an answer, one
sufficiently general to be true of something called 'art', and yet

flexible enough, open enough, to be applied, with suitable changes, to strongly contrasted examples (such as pure music at the one end and representative drama or painting at the other). If he did so hope, he would assume that general statements in aesthetics are not the impossibility which some recent philosophers have thought them to be.

Let us begin by looking at the question from the angle of what is called 'truth'. The word 'truth' has a number of senses, but those which are chiefly relevant when it is said that art should, or should not, be 'true' are (a) the sense in which we claim that a statement (or, if preferred, a proposition) is true in that it conforms to the facts, or (b) that a likeness, say a photograph of a person, is 'true' because it resembles the original.

The first sense, (a), of the truth of propositions, could be directly relevant (if indeed it is relevant) only to those arts which use words as a medium, for example, poetry and drama. And at first sight there would seem to be some relevance here. We are accustomed to think that we do very much value the truth of some of the statements in great drama or poetry, and could quote reams from Shakespeare to illustrate it. On the other side we have a quite violent statement of George Boas: 'the ideas in poetry are usually stale and often false and no one older than sixteen would find it worth his while to read poetry merely for what it says.'[1] This does at any rate compel us to ask whether, even when the truth of the ideas in poetry or drama is more important than Boas suggests, it is not so much the truth to the facts that we are valuing as something else, namely the impact of a total experience which may contain affirmation of truth but is much more, and which is enjoyed only in so far as we are actually entering into the life of the poem as uttered or the drama as acted. The truth of a statement is, on the commonsense account of truth, its quite impersonal relationship to the independent real; what we enjoy in the poem is not the recording of an abstract relationship, but a total participation, felt and understood throughout a single experience, in a fresh insight. A truth, as such, once recorded, can be docketed and assumed; it does not need to be rediscovered unless it has been lost; once is enough. The insights of a poem, on the other hand, are in a sense discovered in a fresh enjoyment each time: once is not enough. Furthermore, whilst a truth of fact can be stated in a number of ways, or in different languages, and it does not matter so long as it is clearly indicated, what the poem or the drama is saying can only be said exactly in the language of that poem or that drama.

I conclude then that though some forms of art contain statements which are true, truth of statements to fact is not in itself of artistic importance when it occurs.

(b) 'Truth' in the sense of likeness again seems at first sight relevant to the representative arts—such as some kinds of painting, sculpture, mimetic dance and, again, drama. But strong reservations, not altogether dissimilar from those already made, have to be entered here too. Likeness there may be; but it is likeness taken up into art, rendered in the medium, transformed there, and intrinsic to it. It is not the likeness in itself, as an isolable factor, which is artistically important. We value representative painting, for instance, not because it reproduces what we know already, but because it helps us to see the world in a fresh way in and through the medium of the painting. Whereas the criterion of truth as likeness sets up a prior model of natural fact to which the picture is supposed to correspond, just the reverse happens when the art is good. The art itself becomes and sets the standard by which the world is seen in a new way. Oscar Wilde was perfectly right in saying that nature (or at any rate our idea of nature) imitates art, not art nature.

If these things are kept in mind, the sharp differences between the representative arts on the one hand, and non-representative arts like music and abstract painting and sculpture on the other hand, may seem not quite so sharp. Music, as we all know, does set a special problem for any theory which claims that art is 'true' or 'reveals reality', since the world of pure music seems to be so different from our world outside it. On the other hand, as we have just seen, the 'reality' revealed by the representative arts is a fresh construction of reality, seen through art, not a repetition of the ordinary patterns of the world of everyday practical experience: and it is 'reality' which is apprehended inseparably from the medium in which it is embodied. In this respect the 'strangeness' of the representative arts is not so different from the 'strangeness' of music.

The naïve or commonsense model of truth was said to be of a statement or picture conforming to an already existing reality, and the 'reality' supposed to be of the commonsense, or, it might be, of the scientific pattern. This 'correspondence' view of truth and reality has many difficulties which I cannot discuss. I think it is wholly inadequate; but it is the common view and it is on that assumption we are proceeding. The only point I want to draw attention to now is that in its naïvest forms (and sometimes in forms not so naïve) it assumes that, somehow or other, we 'can get at' reality 'behind' our knowledge of it, and so check our knowledge, whereas in fact in so far as we can 'get at' reality at all it must be through our knowing of one kind or another. A commonsense statement or judgement, for example 'The book is on the table', is checked by *another* judgement of perception, not by some bare fact or reality behind it. This, I think, will be found to have some bearing on the question of the truth of art.

We have to assume that there is a world which, in part at least, is given to us, and has an independent structure. But this given world we do not know directly, or as in a mirror. We come to know it, in some sense and some degree, we come to terms with it, through our own active symbolic constructions, the constructions of commonsense, science, philosophy, as well as through a number of other ways of knowing. Sense perception is one kind of construction. The senses themselves are highly selective; in a manner they manufacture the qualities which enable us to adjust practically to the external world; and perception is, in ways familiar to philosophers and psychologists, a highly active synthetic constructive affair. Science in its turn, in its attempts to come to terms with certain aspects of the world of nature, is a system of intellectual constructions, tested against observation and experiment, and enabling prediction and control. Philosophy, in the traditional sense at any rate, takes a wider sweep, trying to understand the nature and claims of values as well as facts, and the relations of values to facts, as well as surveying the different types of knowledge and experience. Traditional philosophy attempts some sort of synoptic perspective, making its own constructions and having its own tests of truth. Each form of knowledge has its own symbols and uses them in its own ways, and through them hopes to cope a little better with the mysterious reality which is infinitely greater than any of our necessarily limited and abstract constructions can cover.

These are all attempts to know, and we call them, in a general and not very accurate way, 'knowledge'. Is art knowledge? Does it increase insight into the world? Does art, like other attempts at knowledge, achieve some measure of revelation?

I think that the answer is certainly 'yes', but 'yes' only in a sense which does justice to the uniqueness of art and to its differences from other knowledge. Through the works of the great dramatists we apprehend dimensions of life not apprehended before. In the worlds of poetry, painting and sculpture (not least in their abstract forms), architecture, films, the novel and the ballet ... we are initiated into experiences of the nature of man or of the forms of the external world (including forms and movements of the human body) which are constantly new and, so long as the arts exist, can never cease. With the arts, human growth in stature is unlimited; without them it is greatly impoverished; education in them is far more important than in this age is commonly recognized—though it is conventionally correct to give them lip service. Perhaps the lack of recognition of the arts may be in part a confused belief lingering from the eighteenth century that they are *not* knowledge, but legitimately pleasant diversions for leisure time. In an age of science and technology they are often relegated to the category of 'extras' in education.

But in claiming the arts as a major form of knowledge, we must be careful not to weaken the claim by trying to assimilate them into other models of knowledge. They are not, as we saw (importantly), 'true' in the naïvely commonsense way of conforming to a 'reality' which we know perfectly well in other ways. Drama is not a picture of life as Tom, Dick or Harry can see it any day, but something which may shake up Tom, Dick or Harry to see and feel life as they never saw it before. Coleridge and Blake are not admitted to the house of knowledge because anyone can see that what they are saying is correct, but because they can teach those who will learn to experience the world differently. Again, it would be absurd in assessing art as knowledge to measure it against science with its empirical tests of validity.

What I am saying is that art is discovery, of its own kind and in its own ways, and indeed that the aesthetic, which is of course much wider than the arts, is a basic and irreducible form of knowledge. The aesthetically sensitive mind is more keenly aware than the commonplace one (though anyone can be educated) of the imaginative suggestiveness of the world of the senses—of colour and texture, of natural organic forms, of the qualities of touch and sound and hearing, of the statics and dynamics of bodily poise, of rhythm, of the relations of shapes and spaces, of the symbolism of gesture and demeanour. The aesthetic delight in *objets trouvés* is by no means confined to fossils and sticks and stones; it is a much wider delight in the incarnate life of man. This delight is extended to the inner life of imagination and thought which, drawing in part from the outer life, outdistances it beyond measure. When all this, valuable aesthetically in itself, but also potential material for art, is gathered into the creative processes of art and there transformed, the actual and potential enrichment of human insight into the world is literally without end. In painting and pottery and sculpture every original work is a new vista of the life of the senses and all that can symbolize. In poetry, the ability to use words, the greatest of all single human powers, can open up new perspectives of imagination and conception, new understanding of love, youth, age, mortality, the Greek hero pitted against fate, the Shropshire Lad against the world and his inevitable end. Metaphysical ideas, religious adoration, the problem of pain, the evanescence and the eternity of love—these and the other human themes come into union with the flesh and blood of living words. Of drama all this is true too, to which are added the special opportunities of drama, from Sophocles through Shakespeare to O'Neill, Ionesco, Fry, Pinter and Beckett.

Nevertheless, if words like 'insight', 'knowledge', 'perspective', are perfectly valid here, it has constantly to be kept in mind that these cognitive words express only one aspect of a *total* experience, that it is only through understanding the nature of the total experience that the 'knowledge' which art gives can be understood, and only through entry into the total experience itself that knowledge through art can be actually attained. Its 'knowledge' is not like the knowledge of commonsense, or science, or philosophy, which can be expressed in words or other symbols which are definable, have a general meaning which is understood in relation to other understood symbols, and in the end by reference to common experience, accessible to all. This latter knowledge is expressible in language which is simply a means to the communication of ideas which are, in a wide sense, abstract. Commonsense and scientific statements, for instance, convey judgements about aspects of the world, expressed with relative precision about those aspects and those only; in this sense they refer to abstractions, and they have done their work as statements if they convey their limited meaning. This is their intention, and they aim in the main to do no more. (I am not denying that even the ordinary use of words may have other—e.g. persuasive or aesthetic—intention also.) But art—even that art which uses words—is not stating or representing abstracted truths; it is presenting embodied meaning— meaning which is not abstractly general but concretely individual, belonging to the texture of this whole which is presented, now. And to know this meaning one has to give oneself wholly to it and live in it, perception and imagination and intellect and feeling and will, in a total experience which is, in the widest sense of the word, 'enjoyed' or 'lived through'. In particular, feeling—and feeling in a cognitive sense[2]—is an intrinsic part of it. If then one speaks of 'insight' or 'knowledge', or 'understanding', or 'perspective' through art experience, it is insight which is bound up with all this, nothing less. Being so bound up, the insight can only exist in the experience, and is in no way translatable. There is no substitute for the way of knowing through art, for it is knowing *in* art. Blake's words could be applied to art:

> Never seek to tell thy love
> Love that never told can be;
> For the gentle wind doth move
> Silently, invisibly.

To know love, one must love. To know art, one must be united with art.

I said, a few moments ago, that obviously we must not expect the arts to submit their insights to the same sort of tests, empirical tests, which science applies. What I have just said makes it more obvious still. On the other hand, the use of the words 'insight', 'knowledge', does imply claims to apprehend 'reality' in some sense, so that the question does fairly arise how insights of art are to be distinguished from illusions, the valid from the spurious. I do not profess to have a detailed worked-out answer to this, and even if I had, it would be a large subject. I can only offer a few brief comments.

The arts do not submit their insights to tests of 'reality' outside of themselves, as naïve commonsense might require, or as, at first sight, the sciences may seem to be doing. They are tested, as it were, from within their own integrity. Is this an escape and an evasion? I do not think so, and I believe that a glance at the nature of the testing which science applies will show that even the picture of science as submitting its hypotheses to the test of an empirical 'reality' *outside* it, is a misleading pictorial illusion which may lead on to the present somewhat artificial contrast between science, as having its feet firmly on the ground, and the arts which soar uncontrolled into the upper atmosphere. I want to argue that science as well as the arts is tested from 'within its own integrity'.

I briefly criticized the commonsense view of truth as conformity to reality outside knowledge by saying that the reality with which true statements are supposed to conform can only be known via knowing. Clearly, we cannot get at it in any other way; we cannot know it without knowing it. Now as regards scientific truth, it is artificial to suppose that the hypotheses 'inside' science (or 'inside' the scientific mind) are confirmed (or falsified) by sheer facts which are 'outside' it. I am not, as I said, denying that there is an independent reality which has a structure to be discovered as far as possible, and that wildness of speculation has to be checked by that which is not speculation. But what happens in fact is, very roughly, this: what are compared, in making scientific checks, are deductions from hypothetical constructions (one mode of apprehension), and judgements of perception. Ideas are not compared with, or tested against, bare facts or 'reality', but against *judgements* of perception, which are another mode of apprehension. These judgements of perception—experimenting and observing—have obvious advantages, being fairly simple to carry out by trained people, being direct, repeatable, 'public', etc. But experiment and observation and their results are *within* science itself, and are indivisibly part of its whole attempt at coherent systematic insight. In that sense verification (or, perhaps, very much better, falsification) by 'fact' is within the system of science itself. Science is tested 'from within its own integrity'.

The insights of art are not testable by 'public' sense experience. Since appreciative understanding of art involves the whole person, relatively impersonal tests of anything of a kind remotely resembling experiment and observation are 'out'. Again, judgements of art are value-judgements. In science, both the intellectual processes of theory-making and the relatively simple judgements of sense perception used in observation or experiment are carried out in an attempt to be as objective as possible. I would not deny what Professor Polanyi[3] tells us about the personal involvement of the scientist (imaginative, aesthetic, religious . . .). But in the end factual generalization is the aim, and empirical tests are factual. Feelings and values are at this point irrelevant: the judgement must be based on the direct delivery of the senses which are shared in common between observers, and about which there can be no important dispute. But when judgements of value are crucially involved, as they are in art, there is no such impersonal way of testing. Even if there are many 'observers', as there are, each has to enter into the experience of the work with a proper involvement, as a person, with all his capacities working as a whole. He may, and does, try to be 'objective' in a sense, but if so, his objectivity is of quite a different kind from the (at least relatively) value-free judgement of scientific fact. Further, whilst the scientist is on certain occasions as far as possible trying to isolate one observable from everything else and to cut out much context as irrelevant, the critic of art is all the time aware of the wholeness and individuality of what he is experiencing; his testing is of that and nothing else.

But though judgements of artistic insight cannot possess the same kind of objectivity as the factual and relatively impersonal judgements of science, that is not to say that there are no standards of judgement, nothing to differentiate the genuine and important from the spurious or trifling. This question of 'standards' is immensely difficult: I cannot discuss it. All I can say now is that just as a general philosophical theory of scientific truth must be built upon the critical understanding of the work of science, so a general philosophical theory of the validation of artistic insights must be built upon the findings and reflections of the fully equipped critic of the arts. The critic is, of course, an expert in his own particular art, and is not, as such, a philosopher. But the philosopher of the arts, in so far as he is not himself an expert critic,[4] must wait upon the critic (though with a wary philosophical eye), and learn from his considered judgements. I say advisedly, the 'fully equipped critic'—for judgement of the soundness, the validity, sometimes the depth and greatness of art, requires much more than technical competence; the adequate judging of deep and great art itself requires great capacity, maturity and experience. In the case of representative arts such as literature and drama, it requires experiences of life outside art, in so far as the values and truths of life become assimilated to, and are part and parcel of the embodied content of these arts. In the greatest examples of literature and drama there may almost be said to be a testing of life and these arts against each other: experience of life feeds and illuminates the understanding of the arts, and deep understanding of the arts feeds and illuminates the understanding of life. And all this can be said without weakening one whit the claim that art is tested from within its own integrity; the criteria of 'life' are not applied to art like so many templates; it is the insight into life within the integrity of the art which is being assessed; and the 'life' and the art are different stresses in one single continuous reality.

The main generalization holds good of music too, although possibly not the secondary one about 'life'. It is the fully equipped critic of music who can sift the genuine from the shoddy, the style from the clichés, the superficial from the profound. He gives judgement on its depth, significance, greatness, though it is in part the job of the philosopher to analyse what these mean. The critic of music, however, does not require—at any rate in the same direct and obvious sense—the experienced understanding of life outside music, as the critic of drama and literature does. I would not want to dog-matize about this: how far does depth of experience of life, depth of personality (in so far as that can be distinguished from musical activities) affect the composition, performance and criticism of music? I do not know perhaps a great deal. But at any rate the life references of drama and literature do raise special questions for criticism in these fields which are not in the same way relevant to music.

Finally, there is the 'verdict of time'. I need say nothing about this, except that, admitting the absurdities of changing fashions, there is an objectivity and a public security about it which, although certainly not exactly comparable with the public security of scientific truth, is yet important when we are claiming that art, even music, is a major mode of insight into the real. I shall have a word more to say upon music and 'reality', but I will leave it to my summing up.

I began the paper by posing the question of the relation of art to life in terms of 'truth', in the ordinary naïve common-sense meaning of correspondence with fact, as well as in terms of 'reality' and knowledge and insight. I did so in terms of truth because that is a way in which the question is commonly thought of. I have com-mented on the superficiality of the correspondence-with-fact account of truth, and tried to show that both commonsense and science test their claims to truth against relatively simple public *judgements*, and that the tests of science fall within the system of science itself. I said that grasp of this narrowed the apparent gap between science as validating its judgements and the arts as supposedly having no such obligation, as being fancy-free. The arts do not have to submit to the tests of science but they do have to submit to their own, and these —in this respect (but in this respect only) like science—are made 'from within their own integrity'. Though some of the arts, the representative arts, refer to life, their 'truth' is not measured by their simple correspondence with life but by the validity of insights integral with their embodiment. The 'truth' of a Rembrandt portrait permeates the whole painting; the fact that an original is represented is assimilated into the painterly work.

Ordinary statements are abstract, but they have to be made because we have to say one thing at a time; and they have to 'correspond' in *some* sense if they are to be true. But in fact, these propositional statements are paper-thin, and they have absolutely minimum significance taken by themselves—'The Prime Minister lives in Downing Street'; 'Double the pressure and the volume is halved.' What gives true statements importance is not bare 'correspondence', but their relationship to the system of the rest of knowledge. This is true of science; an isolated statement of fact has minimum significance; it is its exemplification of a generalization, and the relation of that generalization to systematic scientific thinking which contributes towards scientific truth in the more important sense of the word. So in representative art it is not any paper-thin abstracted 'truth to fact' which counts, but insights which are intrinsic to the work of art as a systematic entity. Insight in art is, once again, 'insight within its own integrity.'

The life-reference which (taken up into the body of the work) occurs in the representative arts has no direct place in abstract arts like abstract painting and sculpture, or music. They are not 'true' to the independent world even in the guarded sense that the representative arts are. Or to put it better—since knowledge is an infinitely richer conception than truth—these arts do not, at any rate in any direct way, deepen our knowledge and insight into the real world in the plain ordinary sense as, for example, poetry can do. But though they do not, we must not jump to the conclusion that in no sense do they increase our insight into 'reality', into worlds we had not entered before. Abstract painting and sculpture do not represent the 'things' anyone can see: but they do certainly reveal new aspects of the relationships of space and colour and movement which the ordinary eye does not see (any more than the ordinary eye sees the patterns of things revealed by science). And music certainly reveals a 'reality' of the relationships of sounds in time which is never known at all except through music.

All this compels us to revise our commonplace ideas of 'reality'. Why should we limit 'reality' to what the plain matter of fact man assumes it to be—ready-made and complete, what commonsense and science can show? This assumption underlies the naïve conception of truth—of a world of solid substantial reality, to which the insubstantial fabrications of mind have to conform, to which they must submit. But this is far too shallow. I have suggested that the 'knowledge' which even commonsense, and certainly science, can possess of the real world is a knowledge through constructions of the mind. The physical aspects of the 'real world' of an Einstein are known in a marvellous construction of intellect. Our apprehension of 'reality' grows daily through the work of the masters, and it grows by those very *inner* creative constructions which our plain man, with his feet, as he imagines, on the ground, is so superior about. So it is with the arts, and with music as a shining example. The musician is a creator, if ever there was one, out of natural materials, and what he creates is new 'reality', and a new vision of reality. It is one of the great additions to reality, and it is always going on. Only a prejudice that the 'real' is the natural apart from man, could make this sound strange. The real world for man (contrast it with the imagined 'real world' of an animal) consists of the whole ongoing endless discovery which is his cultural history. It *is* ongoing and endless, and this is why it is not absurd to speak of 'new' reality. William James and I think Bergson spoke of the 'unfinished universe'. Why not? It is certainly unfinished if cultural creations are included. The idea is perhaps less old-fashioned now than when it was new. Whether the physicists' idea of continuous creation, of an expanding universe, is sound or not, I cannot judge. But whatever is true of the physicists' world, it is beyond any doubt that the reality both made and revealed by art is an expanding reality. Music for instance, is certainly not representing the given 'real'. But it is revealing new reality in new creation—continuous creation—and its universe is always expanding. To use religious language for a concluding moment: if the 'world groaneth and travaileth in creation' and man is a 'fellow-worker with God', then music and the other arts are a part of this cosmic enterprise, entering into it in their own unique ways.

REFERENCES

1 George Boas, *Philosphy and Poetry*, p. 9. Quoted in Jessup, 'Truth as Material in Art', *The Journal of Aesthetics and Art Criticism*, Vol. IV, No. 2, December, 1945.

2 See my *Ways of Knowledge and Experience*, p. 79.

3 In *Personal Knowledge*.

4 He must, I should say, be *something* of a critic if he is to know what he is talking about.

Emotions and Emotional Qualities:
some attempts at analysis

RONALD W. HEPBURN

Works of art have, no doubt, something to do with emotion, but it is notoriously hard to determine what, precisely, this something is. Do works of art 'express' emotion, or 'evoke' it, 'represent' it, 'master' it, 'organize' it or 'purge' it? Or can they do several of these things—or all of them? From the constellation of problems here, problems on the border between aesthetics and the philosophy of mind, let us break off some manageable fragments for discussion. The fragments, I think, are important ones: but be it said at the start that many of the topics I shall *not* single out for treatment are every bit as important in aesthetics as those I do. There is no attempt in this article to produce a general or comprehensive theory of 'art and emotion'. That would need a book.

Certain writers make a sharp distinction between the way in which ideas, concepts, meanings, can be *in* works of art and the emotions, feelings, which a work is said to *evoke*, to *cause*, in the reader or spectator. According to this view if we often transfer emotion-epithets to works of art and call them 'jolly', 'joyous' or 'frenzied', we are well aware that we *are* transferring them, that in the last resort it is we who are made jolly or frenzied, and that our epithets are in fact characterizing the poem or piece of music in terms of its effects on us, not in terms of its own qualities. We are entitled to claim that meanings and ideas are 'objectively' in the works concerned: they can, for instance, be adequately and most often unambiguously specified. But since there can be no equally sensitive control of emotional response, we are here in the realm of the subjective.[1]

There are, however, a number of analyses which claim that emotions and feelings can be *in* works of art just as certainly as meanings and ideas can be in them. On this view if I say: 'The music is joyful,' I may not be speaking of my own feelings but of what I hear as a 'phenomenally objective quality of the music itself'. It is not the case, for instance, that listeners tend to report wildly divergent emotional qualities when attending to the same pieces of music: some experimental work has shown that if subjects are asked carefully to concentrate on the music (and not on their own feelings and fantasies), their reports on the music's emotional qualities are convergent. If, however, they are allowed to report on their own emotional states, their reports diverge noticeably. As O. K. Bouwsma put it: 'joy and sweetness, and sadness [can be] in the very words you hear'; or, more characteristically of the author, 'the sadness is to the music rather like the redness to the apple, than it is like the burp to the cider'. 'The mood of a landscape', wrote Otto Baensch, 'appears to us to be objectively given with it as one of its attributes belonging to it just like any other attribute we perceive it to have. . . . The landscape does not express the mood, but *has* it. . . .'[2]

Of these two accounts of emotion and art-objects I think the stronger *prima facie* case can be made out for the second, the account which claims that emotional qualities can be described, with perfect propriety, as *in* works of art. We speak of a musical note as being 'high' or 'low'—the highness or lowness being heard as phenomenally in the note. From this there is a gentle transition to speaking of a phrase as 'incomplete', 'questioning' or 'nimble', again reporting the heard quality of the sound, and on to emotional qualities in the strictest sense like 'melancholy', 'tender', 'plaintive'. Similarly in visual art there is a gentle transition from speaking of a shape as having a 'three-dimensional look' to having an 'awkward, unstable look' to having a 'comic' or a 'melancholy' or 'angry' look. Without any sense of incongruity we can bring together in one description of a shape words from different parts of this scale; for example, the shape is 'comic *and* awkward', 'comically awkward'. At no point is there a shift from talk about the figure to talk about the spectator's response.

Note that the class of 'emotions proper' is not at all sharpboundaried. In one direction we gradually approach it from expressions (like 'awkward', 'graceful', 'elegant') that primarily describe manner-of-acting or -appearing. These tend to carry loose implications about what is *non*-behavioural. If, for instance, we say: 'John rose to his feet awkwardly,' we are normally taken to imply that he lacked inner composure as well as outward grace. But the implication is certainly a loose one. A Bishop might mount the pulpit with great dignity (manner of acting); but the implication that he then experienced an inner sense of reverence and solemnity would be false if such moments had long ago lost their power to move him. Yet the outward dignity might remain.

There are, however, some emotion-words, well within the territory of emotions proper, that make essential reference to the non-behavioural. Sadness, nostalgia, depression, ecstasy—one may experience any of these and manage to inhibit most or all of their behavioural concomitants. The spectrum-scale from manner of acting to emotions with essentially 'inner' aspects is important to our present study; since works of art can display not only the former as emotional qualities but also the latter, which is the more remarkable feat.

Again—to resume the main argument—there are occasions when I may wish to say the following: 'The drawing (or the rondo) was joyful, but *I* was not joyful.' If I say: 'This curve is graceful, and that jagged line intersecting it is tense and menacing,' I do not mean that *I* feel graceful on looking at the curve and then tense and menaced on looking at the jagged line. Instead I may feel vaguely excited, delighted, or be entirely unmoved.

To claim that the emotional quality can be in the work of art is not of course to say that the word 'in' is used in precisely the same sense as when an emotion is said to be 'in' you or 'in' me. People experience emotions: works of art do not. (Cf. Bouwsma, op. cit., p. 78.) But nothing substantial would be gained by restricting the multi-purpose preposition 'in' to the case of emotions being 'in' persons. Had this been a *genetic* study, a study of the mechanisms by which aesthetic effects are produced, then we should have had to work out some theory of emotional 'projection' and explore the analogies, hints and clues that we go on when attributing emotional qualities to such inanimate things as carvings, lines, shapes and configurations of sounds. But our enquiry is phenomenological; we are asking what our experience is like, not how it is stage-managed.

Some elementary examples from music may help to clarify our claims so far. Within the classical idiom we feel that in most contexts a dominant seventh, and more so a thirteenth, 'want' to move to the tonic chord. The music wants, strives, to reach its resolution: the wanting is not mine who hear the chord, but the music's. This is one of *its* vicissitudes. If the music modulates into a 'bright' key, the brightness is not my brightness but again the music's. The music has its own phenomenal career. Suppose my radio is switched off while a thirteenth or leading-note of an ascending scale is being played in a work of the classical period. It can readily be shown that I do not take this chord or note as a mere stimulus of unrest in me— an unrest that would be relieved by any tonic-chord stimulus in the same key, played fortuitously, say, by a boy in the street with a mouth-organ. What needs its resolution is that particular chord on the radio, not the disquiet aroused in me. But what of the gentleman who, hearing from his bed someone playing a seventh on the piano and carelessly leaving it unresolved, left his bed and resolved it himself? This is not really a counter-example to our theory. For, first, it was upon the same instrument that the seventh had to be resolved—not simply by humming or whistling the tonic chord in the warmth of bed. Second: we laugh at the story precisely because we normally objectify the uneasiness and disquiet as being in the music itself, one of its vicissitudes, and do not think of it as being transferred to the hearer so as to become *his* vicissitude instead.

Furthermore, one tends to be relatively detached from emotions in music. A piece of music may be in despair, but I who listen enjoyably need by no means be in despair. Almost callously I can relish and savour the anguish of the music: compounding its despair with my delight. The emotion I feel, if any, is often a radically transformed version of the emotional quality of the music itself and not identical with it. Awareness of this transforming process helps to distance the music and the emotional qualities in it from me and my (hearer's) emotions. I have also an emotional *inertia*: even when the emotion I feel is roughly identifiable with the emotional quality of the music, the music's emotion may be intense but mine sluggish. It may be uninterruptedly gay or wild, while my emotional response may be intermittent and fluctuating. In my ordinary perception of the external world I posit various abiding material objects, my house, my telephone, my watch, although my actual perception of these is intermittent and subject to the variations of perspective and lighting. Not very differently I posit a continuing emotional progress in the music, despite the fact that I do not experience, do not 'have', each successive emotion while the piece plays.

It might be tempting to argue that even if 'This tune is vivacious' does not mean: 'This tune makes me feel vivacious now,' still it must mean: 'This tune *tends* to make me, or most careful listeners, feel vivacious.' But I doubt whether this is so. As a psychological generalization it may be true that quite often vivacious tunes make us feel vivacious; but I may properly judge a tune to be vivacious by simply recognizing in it the presence of vivacity as a characteristic, without myself—or anyone else—ever feeling vivacious on its account.

Try another sort of analysis. 'This musical phrase has emotion E' means: 'The hearer of the phrase would experience emotion E (would come to have emotion E), *if . . .*' *Prima facie* one feels that this conditional sentence must be completable. But what exactly would complete it? Try: '. . . if the phrase were repeated several times, repeated until emotion is experienced.' That would not do; repetitions might cause the phrase to go dead on the hearer, to pall or exasperate or seem banal. Or try: '. . . if the phrase were played in isolation, under non-distracting conditions.' Again, no; since out of its musical context it might well take on a quite different emotional tone. These failures do not prove a conditional-sentence analysis to be impossible, but it is hard to think of any other continuations after the 'if' that are not vulnerable to just as sharp objections.

One might try to make a last ditch defence of the stimulus-response model of emotion in works of art by saying this: 'If works of art do not evoke full-blooded emotions, they at least arouse *images* of emotions.' 'Image of an emotion' is not an expression for which we often have a use—perhaps because having an emotion is not an affair of any single special sense, as seeing and hearing are. But it can easily be given a use. With emotions such as fear, exhilaration, despondency, the emotion-image would be a combination of kinaesthetic, visceral, visual or verbal images. And just as, for example, visual images by themselves are most often schematic—a vague shape standing in for the appearance of a house—so with emotion-images: the kinaesthetic image of clenching fists may stand in for a constellation of occurrences and tendencies that make up 'being angry'. Suppose, then, that this is what we understand by an emotion-image. It needs no fresh argument to show that we often see or recognize what emotion is in a work of art without necessarily imaging any emotions at all. We can recognize anger without incipient clenching of fists, tranquillity without imaged relaxing of muscles.

Lastly, we can recall Coleridge's plain words in the *Dejection Ode*: 'I see, not feel, how beautiful they are.' We might substitute for 'beautiful' a more specific human-emotion word like 'fearsome', 'serene'; and the sentence need not be uttered in Coleridge's mood of dejection.

We have been working so far with an unexamined and far too crude conception of emotion itself. Unless this crudeness is removed, our whole project of critically discriminating between rival accounts of emotion and art works may well be jeopardized. It is not just that we may have to go a certain way with physicalists and behaviourists and admit that emotions have much to do with overt, public behaviour. This does have to be admitted. But some recent philosophical analyses of emotion-concepts[3] have shown that when, for instance, we say 'A feels remorse', 'B is indignant', 'C feels bitter', we do something far more complex than claim A, B and C behave in certain identifiable ways and experience types of inner turmoil. Where is the extra complexity? Roughly speaking, it lies in the way concepts like 'remorse', 'indignation' give interpretations of a situation, interpretations that go beyond the recording of acts and feelings occurring at any particular moment. 'C feels bitter about the way he was treated' carries as part of its meaning 'C believes he *ought not* to have been so treated', 'C believes he was treated *badly*'. That is, being bitter involves making certain evaluations, not simply having feelings or acting in particular ways. It is logically impossible to *hope* for something one does not favourably evaluate; or to *feel contrition*, unless one acknowledges oneself to have done something wrong. Traditional accounts of emotion used to give central place to determinate, recognizable *feelings*—inner and private. Emotion-words were the labels of these feelings. The current opinion refuses to give pride of place to such feelings, and (in the case of some writers) denies even the *existence* of feelings specific to particular emotions. Instead their analyses are given in terms of situation-appraisals plus an undifferentiated general excitation.

In the rest of this article I want to draw on these recent analyses of emotion to the extent that they seem sound and helpful. In other respects, however, we should regard them as being every bit as much *sub judice* as our two accounts of how emotions are communicated.

First of all they can be invoked to support and reinforce the view that emotional qualities can be in works of art. Suppose I read a poem or attend a drama. I say: 'This is jolly,' or: 'this is pitiable'; and my judgement is possible only if I have made a conspectus, an overall survey of the situation presented, and deemed it appropriate to jollity or pity. Clearly, my judgement is an acknowledgment of qualities in the work itself. With a particular play I may say: 'No not pitiable really'; and justify my remark by making value-judgements about the characters and situation concerned. 'He is not to be pitied: he is too much morally at fault.' The finale of an opera may ring false, because it has simply set aside all the pain and conflict that happened on the way to it. These, we judge, need to be reckoned with in the finale—as necessarily modifying, qualifying, its brash or headlong gaiety.

With emotional qualities like 'pitiable' or 'jolly' we are thinking of the presentation in a work of art of imagined human predicaments. These comprise the 'situations to be interpreted'. But a work of art *as a whole* may express a distinctive emotional quality, which is not simply that of the human predicaments it presents. Indeed it may present none: or those it does present may be determined in their precise quality by stylistic factors and the individual handling of the medium. For instance the emotional quality possessed by a human figure in an El Greco painting is determined both by the dramatic situation depicted and by the colouring, design and texture of the painting throughout.

At this point, instead of pressing on with more analysis, a few points can be made of a general evaluative nature. We are, I think, exploring one of the chief sources of aesthetic value—both within art and in aesthetic experience of natural objects and events. First, within art: the complexity of the gestalts, the situation-conspectuses, the fusions of medium and human situation, all contribute to an unusually fine discrimination of emotional quality; and the savouring of this can be counted as one of the basic aesthetic worthwhile-nesses.

On aesthetic experience outside art two points can be offered. We could construct a scale on the following lines. At the one end are occasions when my emotions are based on awareness of only a minute part of my environment, and that sluggishly: or based on a stereotyped, generalized and meagre impression of it. I am sunk in apathy and passivity. I make no complex gestalt of my situation in its particularity. For example, I am aware only of the monotonous drumming of trainwheels as I sit in my compartment. My emotion is a dull, undifferentiated depression. At the other end of the scale my emotions are functions of an alert, active grasping of numerous features of my situation, held together as a single gestalt. In my compartment I make into one unity-of-feeling the trainwheels drumming, the lugubrious view from the window (steam and industrial fog), and the thought of meeting so-and-so, whom I dislike, at the end of my journey. My depression is highly particular-ized. Or again, if one is in love, an encounter with the loved one may acquire a specific, unrepeatable emotional quality—meeting-so-and-so, on that particular day, in that particular park, with that wind and those exhilarating cumulus clouds overhead. Our scale, again, is a scale of increased emotional discrimination.

But, as Kant reminds us, the world is not a given totality: my synopses can be complex but never complete. And it is one of the many distinctive things about works of art that our synopses of them can be complete: they are limited wholes, and in a great many cases wholes constructed so as to facilitate their being grasped synoptically. Disconsolate in the knowledge that synopses of nature are forever partial and ragged, we may turn to art in relief.

Especially important here are the contrasts between apathetic and alert perception, between a sluggish, passive and stereotyped impression and the active enterprise of organizing and unifying a situation. This makes it obvious that however we finally decide to describe the spectators' emotions in aesthetic experience, it will not be simply in terms of emotion-transfusions or emotion-shots. For that is a language of passivity—the spectator as suffering manipulation, as having an emotion conjured up in him.

Further: if we locate one source of aesthetic value in fineness of emotional discrimination, we have a second source in the sense of alert conspectus-grasping itself, in the exhilarating activity of unifying far larger and more variegated 'manifolds' than we are accustomed or able to do in ordinary experience.[4]

Some pages ago I invoked Coleridge to testify that one can 'see, not feel how beautiful' things are, and suggested a reasonable extension to seeing, not feeling emotional qualities of specific kinds. But this use of Coleridge comes dangerously close to being *mis*use. Coleridge *was* dejected: and surely with some reason. Yet why should he have been if aesthetic appreciation on its emotional side is simply the recognition of emotional qualities as in objects? Coleridge compels us to make some qualification to our account so far. One is not always content to say: 'This music has the emotional quality of exuberance, but I am not in any way stirred up by it.' This could very well be a discontented report; and the discontent can be of more than one kind. In some cases I may feel like a forlorn child looking through a window upon a party to which he has not been invited. Tiredness, anxiety, or some other psychological factors impair my responsiveness. Again, I might say: 'I see what it is expressing, but it is too insipid to make a real impact on me.' I cannot feel that music as violent, fearsome or exuberant any more. Perhaps the musical idiom has gone jaded on me or is over-familiar: or it now sounds anaemic because of more powerful effects obtained by more recent musical developments.

It might be asked of this last case: Why not retain the language of recognizing emotional qualities here? If a work is insipid, that could count as a quality of it as it is perceived by us today. But this would not really meet the case. It is a loss of *impact* that we are lamenting: the work fails to rouse us—and this is undeniably causal language, unlike the language we have so far examined. So it looks as if the model with which we have been working will not meet all aesthetic requirements.

Confirming this suspicion is the existence of a small class of emotions about which we seem able to speak *only* in the language of stimulus-response, cause-effect. For instance in talking of that famous Surrealist fur-lined cup, we do not say: 'This painting is sick, nauseated,' but rather: 'It makes me feel sick; it is nauseat*ing*.' We speak similarly about giddiness. Not: 'This is a dizzy picture,' but: 'It makes one feel dizzy—it is a dizzy-making picture.'

The vocabulary of emotion-arousal may play a subordinate part in our talk of art-appreciation, but we seem unable to do without it. The two vocabularies (emotion-arousal and recognition of emotional quality) have interestingly different 'logics'. A conductor may say, while rehearsing an orchestra: 'Now we'll take the vivacious passage once again—two bars after M.' Or: 'Clarinets, you made that lugubrious phrase sound almost skittish.' These and like remarks can be quite intelligible in their context, as they contain a reasonably clear descriptive content. But suppose the conductor says: 'Now back to the thrilling section again,' or: 'You messed up the exciting (or overwhelming) passage.' Members of the orchestra may well disagree over which bars are meant. That is to say, these emotion-words contain far less descriptive content, are in fact not emotional-quality words but response-to-stimulus words. We sense an oddness when someone says in a casual, unmoved voice (but without intending sarcasm): 'Yes, that was a sublime movement, wasn't it?' And we could add to the list of such words 'awesome', frightening', 'dreadful', 'harrowing', 'touching', 'exhilarating', 'hilarious' in most senses: all of which report on the successful arousal of emotion, not merely on the detection of an emotional quality. It is more logically odd to say: 'That was exciting, overwhelming music, but it didn't in the least excite me or make me feel overwhelmed' than to say: 'That was tender or sad music, but I did not myself feel tender or sad.' With ingenuity, no doubt, contexts could sometimes be found that would mitigate the oddness. It is over-simple to speak of two quite distinct vocabularies, for there are shadings, gradations, from one to the other.

To people who wish to deny the occurrence of a great many qualitatively specific inner feelings evoked in the spectator there must be a great attractiveness in the emotional-quality analysis. For that model suggests that the host of nameless spectator-feelings can be replaced by an indefinitely large range of phenomenally different 'looks', patterns of words, shapes or sounds. I want now to argue, however, that we cannot deny the occurrence of highly particular-ized (and aesthetically relevant) feelings: that to have such feelings is not the same thing as to apprehend looks, aspects and situations; nor is it that plus an undifferentiated excitement.

First, let us deal with the complaint that the hosts of nameless feelings are postulated purely *ad hoc* by theorists attempting to patch up bad theories that seem to require them. Perhaps some of the theories are bad. But to make this complaint is not to demonstrate that no such specific feelings exist. Emotions, agitations, feelings of various kinds, get themselves named only when there is some utilitarian point in their having names—particularly if they tend to recur frequently in ordinary human experience. But as we earlier reminded ourselves, art deals very little in the repetitive and stereo-typed. Its slant on the world is often in striking contrast to that of workaday utility. The probability, then, is that its emotions should show the same contrast: their namelessness is no argument for their non-existence.

Are there such qualitatively distinctive, highly particularized feelings? Some people's aesthetic experience, including mine, prompts the answer Yes. It is difficult to say much more than that.

Only introspection can confirm or rebut such a claim. Argument cannot. But if someone hesitates to admit such qualitatively distinctive feelings in art, it may be worth directing his attention for a moment to dream experience. For the same distinctiveness can also sometimes be found there. If we agreed about dreams, we might in the end carry the insight back into art. With the forms in a dream, then, there may go a feeling peculiar to that dream, one that is quite definitely aroused not merely recognized as an emotional quality. On waking I may recall the forms, the dream-events, savouring their character and 'look', and yet lose memory of the precise feeling they evoked, and I may *know* that I have lost it. On other occasions I may be haunted by the feeling, the unnameable particular foreboding or exaltation or whatever it was, and lose altogether the 'look' of the dream-shapes that originally touched it off. *Mutatis mutandis*, the same can be true of the look and the feeling aroused by a peculiarly haunting melody, poem or painting. I recall the notes and the character of a musical phrase, but know very well that it no longer evokes the same poignant and not elsewhere obtainable emotional response that it once did evoke. I can individuate my emotion to the extent of saying: 'I once had it; it is now lost. I am trying to recapture it.' I can attain *half*-descriptions of it—'strange, remote, nostalgic'— but I utter the words aware of their inadequacy and using them only as hook and bait for the return of the unique experience itself. 'Looks' can be imaged, a painting recalled in memory, a tune 'heard in the mind's ear'; general and familiar human emotions can be imaged; but the only way in which these highly specific feelings can be recalled is by actual *revival*, by re-experiencing the feelings themselves, with more or less intensity. These differences should prevent their being assimilated either to the recognition of looks and sound-gestalts or to the arousal of emotions that can be analysed in terms of general excitation plus situation-appraisal.

To sum up and conclude: (*i*) Of the two ways of speaking—the evocation of emotion and the recognition of emotional qualities— the latter is truer to our actual experience in probably a majority of aesthetic contexts.

(*ii*) Yet a significant place needs to be left in aesthetic theory also for the *arousal* of emotion.

(*iii*) This leads us to ask: 'What is it for an emotion to be aroused in one?' Sometimes this may mean that one interprets a situation in a particular way and experiences a general excitement. But this analysis fits not every case. Although excitement may often be undifferentiated, it sometimes is most highly particularized and this differentiation is taken very often to be one source of aesthetic value.

REFERENCES

[1] See for, example, H. Khatchadourian, 'Works of Art and Physical Reality', in *Ratio*, Vol. II, pp. 148 ff.

[2] See Bouwsma, 'The Expression Theory of Art', in *Aesthetics and Language*, edited Elton, pp. 73 ff.; M. C. Beardsley, *Aesthetics: Problems in the Philosophy of Criticism*, pp. 328 f.; O. Baensch, 'Kunst und Gefühl', quoted by S. Langer, *Feeling and Form*, p. 19.

[3] See, particularly, E. Bedford, 'Emotions', *Proc. Arist. Soc.*, 1956–7; J. R. Jones, 'The Two Contexts of Mental Concepts', *Proc. Artist. Soc.*, 1958–9.

[4] On these themes see, particularly, H. Osborne, *Theory of Beauty* (1952).

I have indicated the bearing and relevance of these two observations to this study as a whole. It may be pointed out, however, that in the course of them I have referred both to the recognition of emotional qualities and to the 'having' of emotions *tout court*. I have not, however, forgotten about the distinction between these: it is taken up again in what follows.

The Language of Feelings

HUW MORRIS-JONES

I

A work of art is a product of human skill and ingenuity which in some way is emotionally charged. The effects of this on the observer or reader may be very varied. It can be consoling, puzzling, entertaining, disturbing. It may intrigue, deprave, excite or amuse. Some works of art have provoked riots. Others have apparently left the recipients satisfied, catharized, all passion spent. One effect, however, would be lethal: a work of art must never be boring, though it may have boredom as its motif. Thus Beckett's play *Waiting for Godot* depicts boredom, but it would be dismissed as a failure if it were itself boring.

This connexion between art and feeling has been a worrying theme for philosophers since Plato's day. From Plato to Ryle philosophers have been suspicious of human emotions and of artists who seem to be unduly concerned with expressing or exploiting them. Here lies the source of 'the ancient quarrel between philosophy and poetry', as Plato called it, and his puritanical dismay at the emotional impact of certain forms of dramatic and representative art in his day. The ancient quarrel is repeated in the traditional philistine contempt for art and artists in the English empirical philosophers, for whom David Hume shall be a representative spokesman: 'Poets themselves, though liars by profession, always endeavour to give an air of truth to their fictions, and where that is totally neglected their performances, however ingenious, will never be able to afford much pleasure. . . . This is common both to poetry and madness, that the vivacity they bestow on the ideas is not derived from the particular situations or connexions of the objects of the ideas, but from the present temper and disposition of the person.'

It is because so many philosophers have shared the assumption that there is something discreditable in the creation and enjoyment of poetry or music or of other works of art, though these are the ones most mentioned, that much aesthetic discussion has been so misleading and irrelevant. It appears at its crudest in what I propose to call Primitive Positivism. Though it is not so much in the fashion as it was, it tends to recur from time to time. It is the view that things like poems or songs or paintings are the products of involuntary emotional spasms or a series of such spasms somewhat analogous to crying or laughing. Carnap, in his *Philosophy and Logical Syntax*, puts it like this: 'Many linguistic utterances are analogous to laughing in that they have only an expressive function, no representative function. Examples of this are cries like "Oh, Oh," or, on a higher level, lyrical verses. The aim of a lyrical poem in which occur the words "sunshine" and "clouds" is not to inform us of certain meteorological facts, but to express certain feelings of the poet and to excite similar feelings in us. . . . Metaphysical propositions, like lyrical verses, have only an expressive function, but no representative function. Metaphysical propositions are neither true nor false, because they assert nothing. . . . But they are, like laughing, lyrics and music, expressive. They express not so much temporary feelings as permanent emotional and volitional dispositions.'

What this seems to be saying is that art is expressive in the sense that the artist finds relief either of 'temporary feelings' or of 'permanent emotional dispositions' in the composition or fabrication of a work of art. We naturally wonder why this is so, why 'express' his feelings or disposition in this way rather than any other. What quirk of human psychology induces a man who is sexually aroused to write a love lyric rather than to find relief in a less indirect form of satisfaction? And, more perplexing still, why should anyone else, apart from psychiatrists or those fond of pseudo-psychological speculations, be interested in the product of these 'expressive functions'? It seems clear that those who write like this have little experience of art and no understanding of it.

2

There is a more sophisticated version of the view that works of art are to be conceived of primarily as phases in the autobiography of the artist in Croce's definition of art as 'expression'. It is more sophisticated only in the sense that it involves a more elaborate conceptual apparatus, but this does not enable it to avoid the same objection. Thus Croce's definition is summed up in the phrase 'all art is lyrical'. What this comes to is that art is a spontaneous expression of feeling, though Croce is at pains to explain that this is a misleading way of putting it. Feelings do not, so to speak, pre-exist their expression, they do not lurk in the darkness while we search and find our appropriate form of expression for them. The expression is the feeling. The poem is what the poet feels, the song what the musician feels. We, the readers or listeners, may be unable to recapture that feeling because of some fault in its communication (for expression and communication are distinct processes, communication being the object we are presented with, the written poem, the marble sculpture, the musical composition). Art, as Croce proposed to use the word, refers solely to the feelings of the artist, felt or expressed by him: this, no more, no less, an emotional episode in his life-history.

If so, then those interested in him would presumably be interested in such episodes, his friends or relatives or literary historians with an interest in psychiatric analysis. Apart from these, who else? Most of us are interested not in him but in the works of art, in this novel or poem, this sculpture, this piece of music. Our interest in these may arouse our curiosity about the artist, and knowing about him may assist us in fully appreciating the artistic object which is the focal point of our attention, but such knowledge is not a necessary condition of aesthetic appreciation and is definitely not a substitute for it. Whatever excitement gripped the artist at some moment of time in the past is of concern solely to those whose interests are not primarily aesthetic. To speculate about it is to deflect attention away from the object which is central in the aesthetic situation. To use the object as evidence for what the maker felt like in the past is to make unverifiable inferences which are in any case aesthetically irrelevant. It is not logically necessary that a tragedy can only be written by someone who has himself undergone tragic experiences. Nor is it psychologically necessary in the sense that it is an invariable historical fact that all the world's tragedies have been written by tragic characters. What information is available does not bear this out; it is in any case often too scanty or uncheckable. But we who are concerned solely with the artistic object itself are not concerned with it. We gaze at the Parthenon and our delight has no connexion with what we may or may not know of the feelings of Iktinos, Callicrates, or Phidias and the many craftsmen who built it in the years between 448 and 438 B.C. We look at it now, in the bright light of day, on the Acropolis, or at the sculptures in London or Athens, and it is what we perceive now that determines our present delight.

3

Should we then say that what is aesthetically relevant is the connexion between the work of art and the feelings of those who are exposed to its effects? Thus there were those like Clive Bell and Roger Fry who postulated a unique aesthetic feeling, a thrill which indicated that one was receiving the genuine aesthetic stimulation, due to a kind of built-in device in the emotional equipment of some people who are sufficiently sensitive to pick up these signals in the proper order and intensity. When this registered it apparently guaranteed the authenticity of that which provoked it, for the aesthetic experience was assumed to be unique and self-confirmatory.

Others have agreed in stressing the emotional effect of the arts on the reader or observer, but have tried to avoid the mystery-mongering associated with the idea of a unique aesthetic emotion. Thus to quote I. A. Richard's well-known phrase: 'When we look at a picture, or read a poem, or listen to music, we are not doing something quite unlike what we were doing on our way to the Gallery or when we dressed in the morning.' Richards took a leaf from Aristotle, who countered Plato's condemnation of the poets and dramatists with the concept of catharsis through pity and terror. So Richards may be said to have answered Hume by his distinction between the two types of communication. It is only in respect to the first type of communication that the criterion of truth and falsehood is appropriate, for it purports to give information which can be verified or falsified. In the other type, which includes art and religion, the criterion is irrelevant, for they do not give us information. 'Art and religion tell us nothing.' Therefore to say that poets are liars is absurd; for the poet is not saying anything either about the world or himself which is a contribution to our knowledge, nor is his language to be tested by the methods and techniques we adopt when such information is given. What art does is to have an emotional effect. It produces a heightened sensibility, a greater subtlety of insight, a greater width of sympathy and delicacy of discrimination, which are transferred thereafter from the aesthetic situation which induced them to our responses in non-aesthetic situations, in our dealings with other things and persons. And this, it is assumed, is a morally desirable result. The therapeutic consequences claimed for aesthetic experiences are recommended on moral grounds. What we are therefore presented with is a theory which is a hybrid of psychological theorizing and moral preferences. *Qua* aesthetic theory it is open to exactly the same objections as the expressionist theory. It shifts the focus of attention away from the work of art to its alleged effects. And one basic difficulty is that these effects are not so easily correlated with the nature and structure of the work of art. In describing the emotional consequences of exposure to the effects of art we are describing episodes in the biography of a spectator or reporting on such episodes in our own life-history. One may well be deeply moved by reading a poem or listening to music, but the genesis of such feelings may be affected by purely casual or contingent factors, by highly personal and private associations, by the circumstances of the moment which affect one's mood, or by other factors such as temperament and disposition. Therefore it cannot be assumed that one's emotional reactions are induced and controlled solely by the work of art and that the nature of the conditioned experience can enable one to make statements about the quality or value of such work of art. The aesthetic 'thrill', however it is analysed, is no criterion for the aesthetic nature or value of the object with which in the experience of the observer it is connected. It is as irrelevant to discuss art in terms of the feelings of the observer as to discuss it in terms of the feelings of the artist.

The connexion between a work of art and feeling must be described in such a way that one can locate the feeling in the work of art itself, in such a way that one can legitimately talk of discovering and discriminating the feelings appropriate and relevant to it. So that when we say that a play or music or sculpture is tragic or happy or sombre, we are not describing what the artist felt like nor are we describing how we feel when we look at or listen to them. It is not I who am tragic or happy or sombre, but the play, the poem, the song, the painting or whatever it is. What I do in saying that they are such is to *recognize* the sadness or happiness, and I implicitly claim that others should recognize them too, if they have undergone those perceptual and imaginative experiences which constitute an ex- haustive appreciation of those works of art. It is a claim which is testable. There is a 'control' which will enable the critic to exclude what is casual or contingent and to focus on the distinctive emotional quality of the art object itself.

It is not very helpful, however, to say, as some writers do, that a work of art 'embodies' feelings, unless the metaphorical nature of this concept is conceded and a fuller analysis of its meaning is given. We must be told how a work of art 'embodies' feelings, whose feelings, and how an observer may recognize the feelings which are 'embodied'.

To take the latter point first. Recognition does not mean sharing or any empathic participation by the observer. One recognizes feel- ings without oneself having those feelings, otherwise the contem- plation of tragedy would be intolerable. We can recognize the presentation of grief without being grief-stricken ourselves. Nor is it a necessary condition of recognition that one should have undergone the presented emotion on some other occasion. For the conditions of understanding the presentation of feelings are similar to those for the understanding of statements made in a language one has learnt. One learns to talk not merely by learning the rules of grammar of a language and acquiring a vocabulary, but also by acquiring a sensitive appreciation of its nuances, the subtler changes of meaning following a slight change of emphasis, and the intricate field of suggestion and innuendo depending on the play of inflection and stress. All these are governed by convention and usage which are acquired in a variety of ways. But having learnt them we are thereafter free to make statements in that language which will be intelligible to others as well as to ourselves, though such statements to our knowledge may never have been made in that language before. Similarly in the artistic presentation of feelings we can recognize what we do not necessarily feel ourselves and have not ever felt, because art is a kind of language of feelings whose conventions and usages we have learnt and each work of art bears the same relation to artistic forms and conventions as does speech to language.

4

A work of art is something made or composed in such a way that it becomes emotionally charged. Our critical vocabulary contains terms which refer to both these factors. So we refer to its craftsmanship, its organic unity, its neatness and efficiency as an exemplification of skill. But we also refer to its vitality, its dynamic properties, and the many synonyms for liveliness and life-likeness (not in the sense of being a representation of actuality), which critics use. A work of art can be well made, and show marks of great skill, and yet have no spark of life in it. On the other hand the sheer outburst of emotion can never in itself produce art. Dancing for joy may be greatly satisfying to the participants, but not to the observers. That does not preclude the possibility of improvisation in the performance of an artistic skill, but only if it is based upon acquired skills in a traditional art form. Furthermore, we need to describe the place of emotion in art in a way that will not ignore the essentially aesthetic quality of the excitement it embodies and transmits. It is easy enough simply to affect others emotionally. A liberal use of emotionally loaded words constitutes a crude and direct attack on the feelings. But it is not art.

What is required is a way of connecting art and feeling which would stress the aesthetic nature of the transaction which occurs when we read, listen to or see a work of art. And one way of describing the connexion is to talk of art as a kind of language or symbolic system.*

By a language is meant a system of spoken or written symbols used in accordance with known rules. One has to learn to speak and write a language, although of course the learning need not include formal instruction; it can also be 'picked up' by living with and amongst people who speak and write it. And rules include not only those codified in textbooks of grammar, but also the other conventions which affect linguistic usages, when and where the use of certain words is permissible, and other subtle and intricate factors which regulate speech as a form of social behaviour. A language will contain paradigms of usage which reflect the various determinants controlling them and which function as models to illustrate what is intelligible and communicable in that language. Those determinants include of course many non-linguistic factors, moral, social, historical and so on. But they are all public and intra-personal regulations. Or, to use Wittgenstein's simile, a language is a public game, it requires at least two to play it. Hence there cannot be a private language, for a player who made his own rules could unmake them as and when he wished so it would cease to be a game at all, at least the sort of game language is. A private language is a self-contradiction. Privacy, in the sense of a man talking to himself in a language only intelligible to himself of things only he perceives in a withdrawn fantasy world of his own, is the mark of irrationalism and madness. Strictly such a man is neither talking nor thinking.

Collingwood, in his *Principles of Art*, makes this same point. He argues that language is a social institution, part of a social culture, or as Wittgenstein puts it, of a 'form of life'. Learning a language therefore is part of the process of the socialization of personality. Learning to speak is a part of our learning to live with other persons, to think and feel in ways characteristic of our society. So we learn to talk

---

* No great originality is claimed for this. Cassirer, Collingwood, Langer and Read have all referred to art in terms of language or symbols. Although my use of this concept is in some ways different to theirs.

before we learn to think. We learn to recognize feelings in the behaviour pattern of others before we recognize our own feelings. Strictly one cannot have private feelings any more than one can have private thoughts. The language in which I think is the language in which I describe and make intelligible my feelings. And natural languages embody the thoughts and feelings characteristic of the societies whose languages they are. Different natural languages reflect different ways of life.

In a cognate way different art-forms are also specialized 'languages'; that is, they also reflect culturally determined ways of thinking and feeling limited by the expressive scope of the symbolic media they use. Thus one can say things in music one cannot say in sculpture, and vice versa. Musical feelings are different from sculptural feelings. But what can be said or felt in either will be intelligible and recognizable by those who share common social conventions and cultural traditions and the specific symbol-systems which have developed out of them and have been conditioned by them.

It has been argued against this concept of language that it is highly conservative, and that the stress on the authority of paradigmatic usages is to inhibit change, to circumscribe the range of linguistic expression to what has already been said, to limit one to the clichés and stereotyped verbalisms which are the stock moves in the language game. This extension of language to cover the arts, however, meets this challenge. For it is the artist who is constantly wrestling with his medium to modify and change and amend it, for change in art is always a process of modification. There are no nodal points in the history of art, no clean breaks. New art forms come into being as adaptations of old ones. The novel first appears in the guise of biography, before it generally develops its own conventions and rules. As indeed happens to the wider conventions of social life. New situations arise, new demands and stresses arise in personal relationships, and so there are modifications and adaptations of social as well as linguistic usages. Thus the artist explores and exploits the changing ways of feeling and gives them a habitation and a name.

If therefore it be asked *whose* feelings a work of art expresses or embodies, it can be answered that they are those feelings known by those who speak and feel in a common language, who have learnt the rules, techniques and conventions which are features of the specialized artistic 'languages' of this society. These feelings are not to be conceived of as private episodes in the biographies of certain individuals, of the artist or of the person who contemplates his work. In the same way statements of beliefs in a poem or a novel can be intelligible without asking if the artist held such beliefs or whether the person who reads his work holds them. If one speaks the language in which the belief is expressed, and if that language is correctly used, then one can understand what the statement means without imputing it to any one in particular. Recognizing a feeling is like understanding the meaning of a statement, and the conditions of understanding are the same as those which govern the apprehension of a feeling.

This apprehension or recognition is a necessary factor in that complex and subtle process we call an aesthetic experience. And it is this detachment from the imputation of the feeling to any actual person, artist or observer, which makes it aesthetic. It is this which enables the artist, for example, to treat all manner of themes however tragic or horrible and make them objects of aesthetic contemplation, an experience which has its own rare and peculiar kind of pleasure. It has a kind of excitement which has analogies in the thrill of scientific discovery or in the solution of mathematical problems, or in finding meaning and significance in what was previously baffling and obscure. But a work of art solves an aesthetic problem, not a moral, political or scientific one. Its achievement is the presentation of feelings which are recognizable by those who know the language of those feelings.

I have tried to indicate what 'knowing the language' implies and includes. It includes the social and cultural conventions of which a particular art form is a specialized development. And the artistic achievement is appreciated by those who share these conventions and are aware of the scope and limits set by the symbol-system of the art form, and who can therefore read and interpret the language correctly.

Of course misunderstandings occur; as there are failures to understand the meaning of statements, so we can have failures to recognize feelings which are presented to us in art. The analysis of such errors would throw light on the nature of aesthetic appreciation. For what lures us to art is the fact that we do often succeed in recognizing the successful symbolic articulation of feeling. That is why we use such terms as 'dynamic' or 'vital' or 'alive' as terms of appraisal to indicate the establishment of an illuminating and exciting communication between ourselves and a particular work of art.

The Quality of Feeling in Art

HAROLD OSBORNE

In this paper I propose to discuss the view that qualities of emotion and feeling may be ascribed to works of art without implied metaphor, so that when I call a piece of music cheerful my words may sometimes mean what they seem to mean and will not always need to be reinterpreted by the philosopher as if I were saying for example that I, or others, feel cheerful when listening to the music or that I regard the music as a sign that the composer was cheerful when he invented it. This theory of straightforward emotional realism about works of art has been advocated in two papers which have recently appeared in *The British Journal of Aesthetics*. In an article entitled 'Emotions and Emotional Qualities' Professor R. W. Hepburn argued in favour of the account 'which claims that emotional qualities can be described, with perfect propriety, as *in* works of art'. And in 'The Language of Feelings' Mr. Huw Morris-Jones wrote: 'The connexion between a work of art and feeling must be described in such a way that one can locate the feeling in the work of art itself, in such a way that one can legitimately talk of discovering and discriminating the feelings appropriate and relevant to it. So that when we say that a play or music or sculpture is tragic or happy or sombre, we are not describing what the artist felt like nor are we describing how we feel when we look at or listen to them. It is not I who am tragic or happy or sombre, but the play, the poem, the song, the painting or whatever it is. What I do in saying they are such is to *recognize* the sadness or happiness, and I implicitly claim that others should recognize them too, if they have undergone those perceptual and imaginative experiences which constitute an exhaustive appreciation of those works of art.'[1]

To avoid talking at cross purposes the point should be made at the outset that this theory is not concerned to assert merely that emotions and feelings may be objectively present in works of art in the same sort of way that thoughts and ideas are sometimes present in them, as part of their representational content. It is not in dispute that emotional situations are described or depicted by some works of art just as they are described or depicted in newspaper reportage, amusement novels, comic strips, advertisement posters and musical reviews. What the theory alleges is that a work of art itself, or some part of it, may be apprehended as characterized by emotion or feeling. Emotional epithets are applied in this way to non-figurative art which reflects no images of a reality other than the work itself. Where a work of art is representational it is a common thing for critics to pronounce whether the emotional character of the work itself, or some part or aspect of it, is congruent or at variance with the emotional situations depicted or described in it. The theory to be discussed is a theory about the attribution of emotional qualities to works of art themselves not a theory about the mechanisms by which information can be communicated about emotional situations real or imaginary.[2]

I do not propose to dispute the factual basis upon which the theory rests. It seems to me to be sufficiently attested that our experience of works of art does sometimes carry with it apprehension of apparently objective qualities such as cheerfulness, melancholy, boisterousness, restlessness, severity and so on. Even with very simple stimuli such as uncombined colours and sounds some experimental psychologists, following Bullough, classify subjects who tend to report the emotional effect of the stimulus upon themselves apart from those who ascribe to it an emotional character objectively. In *The Experimental Psychology of Beauty* (1962) Professor C. W. Valentine records that in certain experiments by Bullough and C. S. Myers in order to clarify whether the comment 'cheerful' meant that a colour itself was cheerful or that it made the observer feel cheerful subjects were asked for an explanation 'and generally they were very decided, some emphatically asserting that it was the colour itself that appeared cheerful, not that it made them feel cheerful, while to others it appeared absurd to speak of a colour being itself cheerful' (p. 56). There are indeed many people to whom upon reflection it seems absurd to speak of a work of art or a sense impression as having feelings and who nevertheless find it the aptest description of their experience in contact with aesthetic objects. It is undoubtedly a very odd way of talking unless you assume that sentences attributing emotional qualities to works of art are to be understood in a figurative sense. We have not direct awareness of the feelings of other people but infer them from observed demeanour, and we verify our inferences by their subsequent behaviour and their verbal reports of their own introspective observations. Yet the theory seems to be claiming that we directly apprehend affective states in aesthetic objects which are not sentient beings. Nor would matters be helped by assuming that we are indulging in the ancient practice of animism and employing the language of personification, as when the poet speaks of 'the remorseless stone'.³ For always of a sentient being or an object personified as if it were a sentient being it makes sense to ask whether it is really cheerful or only seems cheerful. Despair may lurk concealed beneath the antics of the clown. But of a piece of music it makes no sense to ask whether it is really sad or only sounds sad; for the music is the sound. The picture is the visual appearance: it makes no sense to ask whether that appearance is really sombre or whether it only appears so.⁴ And in its modern form at any rate this theory of straightforward emotional realism in aesthetics does not invoke personification. Professor Hepburn says explicitly: 'People experience emotions: works of art do not.' Yet on the next page he can say: 'A piece of music may be in despair, but I who listen enjoyably need by no means be in despair.'

I do not wish to repudiate but rather to accept that our experience of works of art brings with it *prima facie* apprehension of 'phenomenally objective' emotional qualities. But I am puzzled to know what import attaches to such statements as 'the music is cheerful' after you have said that the cheerfulness to which the statement refers is not something experienced by the work of art (for works of art do not experience emotions) nor something experienced by the listeners nor something experienced by the composer. There is something there which is apprehended; but in what sense is it 'there' and in what sense is it apprehended? I do not believe that the solution lies in a theory that aesthetic experience involves the cognition by direct acquaintance of non-experienced mental states. Professor Hepburn himself says that: 'To claim that the emotional quality can be in the work of art is not of course to say that the word "in" is used in precisely the same sense as when an emotion is said to be "in" you or "in" me.' I want to carry on from that point and ask in what way this apprehended but unexperienced emotion is 'in' the work of art, if indeed it is in fact there.

Theories of the sort we are discussing, which maintain the objective presence of feeling quality in experienced objects other than sentient beings, are not entirely new. An article by Virgil C. Aldrich which appeared in *The Kenyon Review* in 1939 proffered an account of how feeling 'may become objective and thereby be converted into aesthetic quality', and the author opined that the lack of such an account hitherto had been 'the cardinal weakness of current aesthetics'. His argument, which proceeds by analogy, starts with the premise that visual and aural sensation are modes of feeling by which we put out as it were sensory tentacles and so become cognizant of objective qualities—colours and sounds—located in an external environment. When we attend to colours and sounds for their own sake, neither as qualities of physical things in external space nor as 'subjective qualities in and of the native organism of the subject' (he calls this passing from the practical to the aesthetic attitude), we experience secondary (emotional) feelings towards these primary (sensation) feelings and similarly become cognizant of emotional qualities which objectively characterize the visual or aural complexes on which our attention is directed. Aldrich held that objective emotional qualities belong only to constellations of colours and sounds and not to works of art regarded as physical objects; for, he says, 'no physical object as *physical* is ever an object of aesthetic enjoyment'. But in a much discussed article on 'Art and Feeling', published in 1924, Otto Baensch had maintained a still more radical view.[5] He denied that feelings exist only as internal states of sentient beings and claimed on the contrary that they exist 'quite objectively and apart from us' and are directly cognized as non-sensory qualities of perceived objects. 'The landscape does not express the mood but *has* it.' In opposition to the then popular theory of empathic projection he maintained that direct apprehension of emotional qualities is integral to all our awareness of external reality and their separation from sensory qualities results only from later theoretical abstraction. But affective states, he thought, are little susceptible of conceptual scientific study and are not easy of access by attentive contemplation. It is the special function of art to capture and fix the fleeting feelings so that their content may be presented to non-conceptual awareness and be apprehended with precision. 'According to this view,' he says, 'the function of art is not to give the percipient any kind of pleasure, however noble, but to acquaint him with something which he has not known before.' Baensch also foreshadowed the view later developed by Collingwood, and hinted more recently by Professor J. M. Cameron in his Inaugural Lecture *Poetry and Dialectic*, that by the articulation of feeling in the construction of works of art we have an instrument of emotional cultivation and of self-knowledge. 'The separation, the selective condensation, and the internal grouping of the feeling complex to be shaped can only be accomplished,' he wrote, 'by simultaneously creating and forming the object in which the complex of feelings achieves its existence. In practice, the shaping of the feeling and the shaping of the object into which it will be embedded coincide in one and the same activity.'

Both Aldrich and Baensch assume that the emotional quality apprehended as objectively present in a work of art will be identical with an emotion evoked in the percipient. (Aldrich believed that it is the feeling experienced by the percipient in response to a work of art which reveals the corresponding feeling-quality objectively inhering in the work just as the sensation-feeling of yellow reveals the presence of an objective colour-quality yellow in the object. Baensch states: 'We become aware of objective feelings only when we feel them ourselves.') For this reason, besides the rather wild nature of their attribution of feelings to non-sentient things, their theories were open to many of the objections brought against the doctrine of empathy. This defect is absent from the formulations of Morris-Jones and Hepburn, both of whom allow or indeed insist that the percipient need not always himself experience the feeling which he apprehends objectively in the work of art.

Once we have made up our minds to the initial shockingness of language which speaks of feeling qualities inhering in things which do not feel, it is possible to hold with Aldrich that they belong only to aesthetic objects or one may go the whole hog with Baensch and say that although works of art excel other things as repositories of objective feelings, objective feeling qualities permeate all our experience of reality. A modified form of the latter view has recently gained the ascendant among psychologists of the Gestalt school who under the influence of Wertheimer's criticisms have become dissatisfied with the explanations offered by empathy and in place of empathic projection and association have advanced a theory of tertiary qualities. In the context of this theory tertiary qualities are perceptual 'regional' properties which are 'emergent' and not summative (or in the language of C. D. Broad, 'collective' properties which are not 'reducible'). They are held to permeate and suffuse all perception but are thought to be most prominent in works of art, where their apprehension is a large part of what is understood by 'appreciation'. According to C. C. Pratt writers who have adopted this new outlook 'tend to agree on at least three points: (a) Tertiary qualities can only be described by words which also connote subjective moods, but they themselves are not subjective; (b) they are intrinsic properties of visual and auditory perception, not borrowed from any other modality; and (c) they are probably correlated with higher-order stimulus variables.'[6]

The notion that constellations of visual and auditory perceptions display regional, non-summative properties emergent at various levels is by now well established. What is new, and indeed strange, is the idea that emotional qualities are objective in this way, that there are perceived properties of things which are expressive of emotion without provoking emotion in the percipient or being interpreted as the sign of emotion in some other sentient being. The advocates of this new way of looking at things do not, I believe, intend to cut across commonsense notions to the extent that Baensch is supposed to have done. I shall therefore assume in the discussion which follows that the following propositions will be common ground between us. When I speak of feelings I shall mean states of consciousness such as some of those with which I have acquaintance in myself by introspection. I have no acquaintance with feelings of any being except myself. I have grounds for believing nevertheless that some other sentient beings at any rate have feelings, and I do so believe. I do not believe that anything which is not a sentient being has feelings: and in particular I do not believe that constellations of my own or other people's sense impressions have feelings other than the feelings which I have when attending to my own sense impressions or which I believe other people have when they attend to theirs. On the basis of these assumptions the question before us is still what meaning attaches to the statement that emotional qualities are objective properties of appearances or, to put it the other way round, why we think that tertiary qualities, being objective 'regional' properties, are appropriately describable in words which connote feelings and emotions. How do these qualities 'express feeling' if they are neither stimulus nor sign of actual experienced feelings?

The simplest of the answers given alleges that constellations of visual or auditory impressions are said to express an emotion or to have an emotional quality when their configuration is identical with, or very similar to, the pattern of configuration which we often see in the posture and demeanour of persons whom we believe to be under the sway of that emotion. We do not call the swan proud because it makes us feel proud (proud persons do not make us feel proud either), nor yet because we believe that the swan feels proud. We call it proud because the tense grace of the curving neck and smooth stately sweep of its motion through the water make a pattern identical with a pattern we have observed in the demeanour of proud persons. When Milton calls the nightingale 'most musical, most melancholy', he does not necessarily mean to suggest either that the bird is unhappy or that he is unhappy when he hears its voice. He is rather suggesting an objective pattern of melancholy in the nightingale's song—as, indeed, Christina Georgina Rossetti makes explicit in the lines:

> I shall not hear the nightingale
> Sing on, as if in pain.

According to this explanation experienced feeling is the ultimate term of reference for all talk about emotional expression. I say that I am dejected when I am aware of a feeling of dejection in myself. I call a whole group of visual patterns 'dejected-looking' because they have a certain drooping, listless pattern of appearance which many people (including myself) often display in their posture and gesture when I believe them to be feeling dejected. As Kant and afterwards Herbert Spencer believed, the expressive character of music is according to this theory attributable to structural identities with the patterns of sound in ordinary language when spoken under the influence of emotion.[7]

This explanation breaks down in face of the greater potentialities for the expression of feeling in art and the relative crudeness of our abilities to communicate or diagnose emotion from facial expression and bodily gesture alone unless one is also given a clue from the situation and context.[8] It would, for example, not seem plausible to reduce the expressive power of the dance to our familiarity with the quotidian use of gesture. Rudolf Arnheim expressly rejects the explanation which derives the expressive character of tertiary qualities from any similarity to the actual physical manifestations of emotion in human beings. On the contrary, he holds that 'expression is an inherent characteristic of perceptual patterns' and that 'its manifestations in the human figure are but a special case of a more general phenomenon. The comparison of an object's expression with a human state of mind is a secondary process. . . .'[9] He gets over the difficulty by making feeling irrelevant to the expression of feeling. Music which is sad sounds like a sad man looks. But the look of a man who is sad is not sad because it is the look of a man who feels sad. The appearance of the sad man and the sound of the sad music are intrinsically sad irrespective of any reference to an experience of sadness. And once again we must ask, granted that the sad appearance and the sad music have a similar configurational pattern, what is the significance of calling that pattern 'sad' rather than 'jolly' or 'rude' or any other name at all unless there is an inherent connection between tertiary qualities and experienced feelings? Some Gestalt psychologists and some aestheticians have sought to find a bridge in a doctrine of psychophysical parallelism which postulates structural identity between 'expressive' perceptual configuration qualities and patterns of experienced feeling. According to this view, an observed configurational quality expresses an emotion not because it arouses the emotion in us which we unconsciously project upon it, and not because it is structurally similar to the visual pattern of a human being expressing the emotion by bodily demeanour and gesture: it does so because its structure is identical with the structure of the experienced feeling. As was said by Paul Guillaume: 'If the two aspects (inner and outer) are expressions of one and the same psychophysical dynamism, profound analogies should be encountered between them. . . . The mental or central part of the emotion obeys the same dynamic law as the peripheral part; the same rhythms can be detected in the conscious feeling of a man during emotion as in his muscular reactions; the hidden movements of the psyche and the visible or invisible movements of the body image one another; in the language applied to emotions there is often no difference between the terms applied to the internal feeling and those applied to the external symptom.'[10] The pattern-qualities which we observe in the deportment and gestures of other people and the more refined pattern-qualities which we perceive in works of art are therefore expressive because they are identical with the patterns of our own feelings. The music sounds the way an emotion feels.[11] This, if I have understood her correctly, is the sort of thing which Mrs. Susanne Langer was saying when she has spoken of 'symbolic presentation'.

I am myself profoundly sceptical of the notion that a tonal or a visual structure can be isomorphic with the pattern of an affective state. Besides specific emotions (fury over the loss of a penny) we know in introspection unattached, 'objectless' feelings or moods which while they last colour the whole content of conscious experience like a floating charge on the furniture of the mind. Moods of sadness or joy, elation, depression, serenity, restlessness (Locke's 'uneasiness'), apathy, vivacity, irritability and so on are not directed upon any particular stimulus in awareness or tied up with any impulse to particular action. Their causes are often obscure. The feeling fills the whole mind and tinges our attitude to whatever our experience is. When we are sad even joyful news gladdens us the less and we welcome sorrow almost with sympathy. These vague moods of feeling become qualitatively articulated and more precise when they enter into this or that concrete emotion as its affective element, when they are linked to a specific stimulus involving a tendency to action (as sadness becomes grief when linked to the news of a death) or tied in with some situation appraisal (as despondency becomes contrition when joined with a belief that one has committed a sin). But when we use emotional language about works of art we attribute to them the qualities of moods not the feeling tones of concrete emotions. We say that a tune is merry or gay, lively, languorous, melancholy or serene. We do not hear in the music the emotions of regret, remorse, shame, disappointment, jealousy, fear or amazement. Music may express yearning but not home-sickness, amorousness but not love. But the moods are not highly structured as works of art are structured. So far as I can observe, my feeling of sadness or elation is as nearly structureless as anything I know. While it lasts it is here and everywhere, like an atmosphere or an odour, or a diffused toning of colour, lending a special flavour of melancholy or joy to anything that comes into my mind. It has duration, but it has no internal structure. And the word 'rhythm' seems inappropriate to describe the fluctuations and interplay of the various moods in experience. I can find nothing useful in postulating that the higher-level emergent configuration properties of works of art resemble the patterns or rhythms of feeling. It is a statement hard to refute but incapable of proof. It may seem prematurely plausible but takes us nowhere.

I do not believe that we can solve the problem posed by the phenomenal objectivity of feeling qualities except after examining more closely the ways in which emotion-epithets are applied to aesthetic objects. In order to show one way in which such an ex-amination might proceed I propose in the remainder of this article to distinguish three points at which emotional language breaks in upon descriptive accounts of perceptible objects.

1. Speech is fashioned for practical needs and recognizable per-ceptual qualities exist far in excess of the words available to name them in any language. We draw upon a rich stock of epithets descriptive of visible shape: we describe the things we see as short, long, slender, straight, bent, crooked, bulbous, bloated, pinched, spare, tapering, undulant, crimped, angular, pointed, blunt. ... We use another group of epithets which belong primarily to descriptions of the human body but are applied by metonymy to other things: obese, lank, gaunt, svelte, plump, chubby, snub, squat, dumpy. ... Some few shapes have names such as squares, circles, cubes, tri-angles. ... But even so we soon run out of words. Specialists who habitually attend to the shapes of natural objects or artifacts for other than the practical purposes of living know a multiplicity—indeed perhaps a very great multiplicity—of shapes for which they have no names even in the esoteric languages which they often invent. But shapes do not become subjective when language is no longer pro-ductive of names by which to give them a label. They are apprehended in perception as objective shape-qualities of things perceived. Yet when we need to talk about unnamed shape-qualities we are at a loss and begin to use the language of metaphor, analogy and emotion. Our vocabulary for naming three-dimensional shape-qualities is far more jejune. The epithets available for describing configurations of colours are poorer still. And there are no words for naming the shapes which are used in building up structures of musical sound. In exchanging ideas about music, sculpture and colour the scope for descriptive talking, lying between technical language on the one side and metaphorical-emotional language on the other, is very narrow indeed.

It is further to be observed that apprehension of unnamed per-ceptual qualities is with many people inclined to be charged with feeling and indeed most people sometimes achieve awareness of recondite qualities, recognize and pinpoint them, in the first instance at any rate by means of feeling. At this point in the inquiry it becomes necessary to admit the existence of cognitive feelings.[12] It is the experience of many people who have habitual commerce with the fine arts or who otherwise attend to the perceptual qualities of things beyond the ordinary needs of daily living that the more recondite perceptual qualities, those which transcend the ingenuity of descriptive linguistic devices, obtrude into awareness first as feeling tone; only as they become more familiar, or clearer to cognition, the feeling fades and the quality which was first intimated through feeling is later apprehended without affective tone in a more penetrating and lucid perceptual act. Feeling seems as it were to grope ahead of perception and to put out cognitive tentacles in advance of clear apprehension. At this level of apprehension competent appreciation cognizes perceptually without the misting haze of feeling.

2. In aesthetic cognition perceptual qualities which are common to more than one mode of perception—sometimes called 'intersensory qualities'—come into prominence. They are mostly if not entirely emergent regional properties of more or less high-level configurations. Examples of epithets corresponding to intersensory qualities are: pretty, decorative, delicate, stately, majestic, turgid, bombastic, flamboyant, jejune, simple, austere. . . . These are descriptive terms denoting perceptual qualities which are none the less objective because a certain degree of vagueness or imprecision attaches to the language by which we speak of them. It is by reference to characteristics of this sort that critics describe and demonstrate artistic styles and make stylistic comparisons between the various arts. Groups of intersensory qualities form the basis of those definitions of style upon which many art historians rely. Such general characterizations of style as were proposed, for example, by Wölfflin in his *Principles of Art History* and applied more systematically by Wylie Sypher in *Four Stages of Renaissance Style* over the arts of poetry, painting, architecture, sculpture and theatre are justified only in so far as there are high-level configurational properties common to more than one perceptual mode.

But in this sphere also the intersensory qualities which we discern outstrip the fertility of language to name or discriminate them and where language falls short we communicate perforce by metaphor and analogy. Though 'poignant' is an epithet applicable to emotion, it may well be applied in the reaching for exactness to an intersensory quality of perception. Furthermore although intersensory qualities are objective characteristics of perceptual appearances, our awareness of them is often achieved by means of feelings which are cognitive in character. We *feel* that a work of art is dainty, austere, florid, compact. But the feeling is not awareness of an emotional response in ourselves, deflecting attention inwards; it is an outward directed, cognitive feeling. The extent to which apprehension of complex intersensory qualities depends upon feeling, varies from person to person; but in general as appreciation becomes more competent and sure, reliance on feeling diminishes and perceptive cognition is cleared of feeling tone. In this sphere also feeling seems to probe ahead of perceptual awareness and as our sensitivity expands our reliance upon feeling recedes. The choice is not, as is sometimes represented, between emotional response to an art object and technical or intellectual analysis. People of greatest talent and experience appreciate for the most part by lucid and comprehensive perceptual apprehension of high-level emergent qualities.

3. The recondite sensory qualities merge without any sharp dividing line into the intersensory qualities, and there is no fixed boundary between the latter and emotional qualities.[13] Whether such terms as serene, pompous, majestic, stately, solemn, lugubrious, sprightly, comic, express perceptual or emotional qualities, or a combination of the two, can only be decided—with difficulty—from the context in which they occur. The emotional or 'expressive' characteristics *are* intersensory and *are* configurational or emergent and often impinge directly upon awareness in the act of perception.

Much of the confusion which attends emotional qualities and their attribution to aesthetic objects derives from a failure to segregate two categories of emotional qualities. They are too often all lumped together wrongly as 'physiognomic properties'—a term introduced into psychology by Heinz Werner and adopted generally without sufficiently careful analysis.[14] Physiognomic perception refers primarily to perceiving expressions of anger, joy, fear, sorrow or any other emotion in the object perceived. When a man is described as tall or short, contorted or suffused, we are mentioning his perceptual qualities. When we say that he is angry or merry we are speaking of physiognomic properties. But since we do not believe that feelings are experienced except by sentient beings, we cannot sensibly ascribe physiognomic properties (in this primary meaning of the term) to anything which is not a sentient being or for the time being regarded as such. If we perceive something as joyful, sad, friendly, etc., we assume it to be the appearance of a person who is experiencing (or simulating) these emotions or we more or less deliberately personify what we see. With children and primitives the separation between sentient and insentient is less sharp than with sophisticated adults. But in so far as the distinction is there we do not attribute emotions to insentient things except by analogy or phantasy. Artists, and particularly poets, personify natural objects and speak of 'angry sunsets', 'weeping willows', and the rest. Children, to whom personification comes easily, tend to project their own emotions upon the inanimate, and it would be idle to deny that empathic projection plays an important part in many people's appreciation of literary art. Since we do not personify musical compositions as such —nor indeed pictures or buildings or poems—it is not meaningful to describe them as joyful or sad, merry or morose, any more than we should refer to them as friendly or hostile, angry or afraid, rancorous, hilarious, jealous or contrite. It is a manner of speaking in which the words do not say what they seem to say.

It is necessary on the other hand to recognize that there is a more elementary, less differentiated manner of perceiving, sometimes called 'perceiving emotionally', in which the thing perceived is not held aloof from the percipient but is apprehended in terms of the significance it bears for him. When I become aware of something as awesome, ominous, sinister, menacing, reassuring, stimulating, charming, soothing, interesting, I am *perceiving emotionally*. The qualities apprehended in the object stand in polar relation to the attitude of the percipient and the one is complementary to the other. The anger of the angry man and the repentance of the penitent belong to them whether or not I perceive it or interpret correctly what I perceive.

But when a man perceives emotionally the perceived qualities of the object and his attitude towards it are correlative and complementary. In his genetic study of value judgement W. M. Urban spoke of 'affective-volitional meaning' in this connexion. Heinz Werner used the term 'signal things'—things 'whose characteristics are determined by the condition of the perceiver, not by their physical properties or relationships to other objects'. And it was with this mode of experiencing the world in mind that J.-P. Sartre, in an essay written in 1939 under the influence of Husserl, said: 'L'émotion est une certaine manière d'appréhender le monde.' A recent study by Sylvia Honkavaara explicitly distinguishes this type of perception by the name 'dynamic-affective attitude' from physiognomic perception.[15]

In practical and scientific perception the emotion of the percipient is separated from the perception and attention fastened on those aspects of the appearance which serve as signs of the properties which an object has independently of the relation in which it stands to the subject. In aesthetic perception the attitude of the subject changes and attention fastens upon the appearance itself without ulterior motive but with the sole purpose of apprehension. Or, still within the aesthetic, non-practical attitude, one may attend rather to the emotional qualities of the presentation: one may perceive the object as menacing, louring, exhilarating, comic or sombre.[16] (Some works of art make a point of emphasizing such emotional qualities while blurring or suppressing the objective perceptual qualities of what they depict.) But because in the aesthetic attitude one is not only detached from practical interest and concern but also from normal emotional involvement, the emotional qualities themselves appear as detached in perception and enter into awareness as it were cut off and anchored in the object, as if presented for observation and savouring rather than as the polar obverse of the observer's own emotional response. For in aesthetic perceiving I cut adrift from emotional involvement just as I cut adrift from practical involvement: when I perceive a design as sinister or mysterious I do not respond as if to the implication that I am in danger from it or with curiosity to discover the secret. I savour and enjoy the quality it has of being sinister or mysterious. When spontaneous practical concern is held in abeyance the close fusion of mood and object which is characteristic of emotional perceiving is disrupted and the mood-implications of the object are enjoyed without the vicissitudes of the mood-experience.

Language is very but not quite consistently defective of terms by which to discriminate moods and their complementary mood-qualities at this level of experience. Most but not all mood-words have to do double duty to indicate both the felt mood and the objective counterpart. We do not indeed have an inclination to apply the word 'merry' to the object of merriment: we call it 'comic' or 'funny'. We do not say that a person confronted with a ghost is in a 'sinister' mood: we have in this case no word for the emotion, though 'awe' comes nearest to it. On the other hand we apply the words 'gay' and 'cheerful' to that quality of a landscape or a colour ensemble which is the correlate of a mood of gaiety and it is difficult to find any alternative way of saying what we want to say. But we do not want to say that the landscape is experiencing a cheerful mood. Nor do we intend to imply that we can only perceive cheerfulness or gaiety by being ourselves in a gay or cheerful mood. We condemn gay colours as incongruous to our mood at a funeral. Like most mood-words 'sad' (and still more clearly the French *triste*) has a dual connotation which is readily apparent to those who are at all sensitive to the uses of language. In its primary signification of mood we cannot say that music is sad, for nobody really wishes to imply or pretend that a constellation of sounds can feel the mood we call sadness. We can say the music is sombre, dismal, depressing, lugubrious, mournful, grim. But 'sad' has not only this primary sense. When we call the pudding sad we do not mean that the pudding feels sad. We can say that music or other art objects are sad, cheerful, gay in the secondary senses of these words, when they connote a mood-correlate (as 'funny' is—nearly—the correlate of 'merry') for which there is no separate term.

It is therefore the contention of this paper that a more careful examination of the language in which we describe our emotional experience of works of art would safeguard us from the bizarre theory that unfelt feelings are perceived 'in' aesthetic objects and would release us from the temptation to postulate an implausible isomorphism between the structures of works of art and the un-observed patterns and rhythms of our moods.

REFERENCES

1 *B.J.A.*, Vol. 1, No. 4 and Vol. 2, No. 1.

2 In the language of criticism different categories of emotion statements are habitually mingled in a way which makes them difficult to disentangle. For example on a single page (p. 223) of Erwin Christensen's *The History of Western Art* one may find three short descriptive statements about paintings by Raphael. Of the National Gallery *St. George and the Dragon* he writes: 'The mood is reposeful, hardly what one might expect in a life and death battle.' The *Cowper Madonna*, also in the National Gallery, is 'calm and serene ... Mother and Child are emotionally united, their minds fixed on the future, the Passion. A meditative, serious spirit and a sweet, subdued melancholy underlie the peaceful scene.' And thirdly, in the *Sistine Madonna*, where the Queen of Heaven descends from the clouds as the curtains are drawn back, we are told: 'Though a heavenly vision, she appears simple and unaffected; the unassuming quality is perhaps the secret of her appeal. The Christ Child's serious expression seems to reveal his divinity, as his unchildlike gaze is contrasted with *putti* below. The Virgin, slightly embarrassed at presenting a divine Child, remains floating above the clouds. St. Barbara sinks into the clouds with eyes modestly removed from the Virgin.' The last of these quotations offers the critic's interpretation of the attitudes and demeanour of the depicted figures exactly as though he were describing a scene from real life or a photograph or *tableau vivant*; he says nothing about the emotional qualities of the picture. The second passage combines characterization of the painting, attributing to it serenity and calm, seriousness, sweetness and melancholy, with physiognomic interpretation of the emotions displayed by the depicted figures of the Mother and Child. The first passage attributes an emotional quality to the painting and notes that it is oddly at variance with the theme depicted. In a description of a painting by Domenico Ghirlandaio, Thomas Bodkin has noted that the emotional quality of the picture (which he assumes to be a sign of an emotion felt by the artist when he painted the picture and to be capable of evoking similar emotion in observers) is at variance with the subject depicted. 'The artist has depicted an old man, clad in the scarlet fur-trimmed robe of a Florentine senator and hideously afflicted with elephantiasis, who caresses his grandson. Most of us would be repelled by the appearance of the living man. But the emotion of the artist, reflected through the pictorial harmony he has devised,

recreates in us a mood of unruffled serenity and allows us, as well, to recognize in his presentment the unquenchable nobility of the human spirit shackled in decay.' (*The Approach to Painting*, p. 63.)

When Fra Pietro da Novellara wrote of the lamb in Leonardo's cartoon of the *The Madonna and Child with St. Anne and St. John Baptist* 'that sacrificial animal, which signifies the Passion', he was referring to ideas contained representationally in the picture. So was Vasari when he wrote: 'She (The Virgin) looks down sweetly on a little St. John, who plays with a lamb, while St. Anne looks on smiling and overcome with joy at the sight of her earthly progeny become divine—ideas which were truly worthy of Leonardo's intellect and imagination.' But Peter Murray was referring to the emotional character of the picture itself when he said that it is 'one of the few great masterpieces which stand at the beginning of a formal evolution but have never been equalled in depth of feeling'. (*B.J.A.*, Vol. 2, No. 3.) It is in this sense that Yrjö Hirn writes of 'the melancholy which can be expressed, without any anthropomorphic element, by a mere relation between light and shadow' (*Origins of Art*, p. 138). And it is in this sense that Van Gogh said: 'J'ai voulu représenter par les couleurs les terribles passions humaines.'

3 *Odyssey*, xi, 598. Cited by Aristotle as an example of 'vividness' (*enargeia*) in Homer, along with *Iliad*, xi, 574: 'the spears stood upright in the ground anxious to devour their fill of flesh.'

4 Professor Hepburn has pointed out to me that the distinction between 'seems' and 'is' does have an application in art-works, as when I say 'All modal music may seem melancholy to you at first: but it isn't really.' He adds that this comment does not conflict with the arguments I am here deploying. I believe that I would seek to explain the phenomenon to which he alludes in terms of more and less complete 'actualization' of the music by the hearer. Could his 'but it isn't really' be rewritten: 'but if you successfully apprehend modal music as organic patterns of sound, you will not always hear it as melancholy'?

5 Both this article and that by Aldrich are reprinted in Mrs. Susanne Langer's compilation *Reflections on Art* (1958). In her Introduction she confesses that Baensch's theory strikes her as 'slightly mad'.

6 *Annual Review of Psychology*, Vol. 12, 1961, p. 76.

7 Herbert Spencer believed himself to have shown that 'what we regard as the distinctive traits of song are simply the traits of emotional speech intensified and systematized' and that 'vocal music and by consequence all music, is an idealization of the natural language of passion'. *The Origin and Function of Music* (1857). The theory was the subject of a brilliant attack by Ernest Newman in *Musical Studies* (1905). Kant attributed the charm of music to the following facts: 'Every expression in language has an associated tone suited to its sense. This tone indicates, more or less, a mode in which the speaker is

affected, and in turn evokes it in the hearer also, in whom conversely it also excites the idea which in language is expressed with such a tone.' (Kant's own attitude to music was, however, somewhat ambivalent. He thought that: 'If we estimate the worth of the fine arts by the culture they supply to the mind, and adopt for our standard the expansion of the faculties whose confluence, in judgement, is necessary for cognition, music, since it plays merely with sensations, has the lowest place among the fine arts—just as it has perhaps the highest among those valued at the same time for their agreeableness.' None the less, he opines, 'music has a certain lack of urbanity about it. For owing chiefly to the character of the instruments, it scatters its influence abroad to an uncalled-for extent (through the neighbourhood) and thus, as it were, becomes obtrusive and deprives others, outside the musical circle, of their freedom.') Kant was happy to have lived before the days of public broadcasting.

8 We need not go all the way with psychologists like Carney Landis or Samuel Fernberger who in opposition to Charles Darwin claimed that it is impossible ever to diagnose emotion from facial expression and bodily gesture alone unless one is given also a clue from the situation and context. Darwin himself admitted in *The Expression of the Emotions in Man and the Animals* (1872) that the possibilities of external expression are not adequate to differentiate the varieties of emotion known to popular wisdom and enshrined in the common language.

9 *Art and Visual Perception* (1956), pp. 367–8.

10 *La Psychologie de la Forme* (1935).

11 C. C. Pratt, 'Structural vs. Expressive Form in Music', *The Journal of Psychology* (1938), 5.

12 Whether one speaks of a vague perception strongly charged with feeling or a feeling which is cognitive in that it carries awareness of a presented quality in the way that perception is cognitive, is a matter of convenience. I propose to use the latter way of talking, if only to counter a too sharp distinction between feeling and perception which has been encouraged by the terminology of classical psychology. It is a way of speaking which seems natural to many who have examined this sector of experience carefully but without linguistic preconceptions. Thus, for example, in *Poetry and Experience* Archibald MacLeish says of the word-structure of a poem: 'There is an enhancement of their meanings or perhaps, more precisely, of the significance of their meanings. It is not an enhancement which can be defined by abstract analysis and measurement. But the inability to define in abstract terms does not mean, contrary to notions now in vogue, that an experience is fanciful. It is still possible, even under the new vocabulary, to feel as well as to define. And what is present here is *felt.*' And again: 'Emotion *knows* the difference even though mind is defeated in its busy effort to pinch the difference between the thumb and

finger of reason and so dispose of it. Emotion—and this is perhaps the point precisely—cannot dispose of it. Emotion stands there staring.' And: And the shape of total meaning when it begins to appear is a shape not in the understanding mind but in the recognizing perceptions—those fingers which can *feel*.'

13 Heinz Werner says that we may speak 'in a very real sense not only of the softness of velvet, but also of a colour or a voice'. But it is easy to be led astray by linguistic habits and ingrained metaphor. In this case the opposite of tactile softness is hardness; the opposite of soft sound is loudness; and the opposite of a soft colour is vivid or contrasty colour. The only common feature of these three 'softs' seems to be a low degree of obtrusiveness.

14 *Comparative Psychology of Mental Development* (1948).

15 W. M. Urban, *Valuation. Its Nature and Laws* (1909). J.-P. Sartre, *Esquisse*

d'une théorie des émotions (1939). Sylvia Honkavaara, *The Psychology of Expression* (*The British Journal of Psychology*, Monograph Supplements XXXII, 1961).

16 Aesthetic perceiving has been described as 'living in the immediate present'. In practical life present experience is subordinated to the future and the past. Whenever we are expectant, anxious or apprehensive, when we are hopeful, confident or exultant, these attitudes shape the present experience in the light of its implications for the future. When we are surprised, disappointed, filled with self-congratulation or regret, soothed with the comfortable feeling of familiarity and recognition, we are experiencing the present in the context and colouring of a selected past. All these attitudes are inhibited in aesthetic contemplation: but we may still become aware of 'polar' emotional qualities adhering in the object.

PART II

The Perspicuous and the Poignant: two aesthetic fundamentals*

J. N. FINDLAY

This lecture is the first I have given in the University of London on an aesthetic subject, aesthetics being a topic on which I am not a professed practitioner and in which I make no attempt to keep up with the work of professed practitioners. This does not mean that I think that my lecture will be incompetent or worthless. I even think that the contrary may be the case. For, in my view, contemporary practitioners of aesthetics are so fantastically misguided, so utterly lost in one or other form of unprincipled empiricism, that hardly anything they have to say throws great light on aesthetic questions. They do not believe in their subject, they do not think that there are any peculiar objects or experiences that it deals with, they do not think that the frailest back-bone of governing concepts and principles can be discerned in it, they vaguely drift about noticing trivial minutiae, and what they have to say is in consequence as themeless, as structureless, as unprincipled, as devoid of backbone and as trivial and unmemorable as the material they think it deals with. William James once said that he would rather read a detailed description of the rocks on a New Hampshire farm than certain philosophical character-izations of the emotions: the same is true for me of certain modern treatments of aesthetics. They belong, self-professedly in many cases, to unphilosophy rather than philosophy, they reject the quest for unity and generality in which philosophy consists, and in these circumstances I think it quite right for philosophers to be frankly bored with them.

* A lecture given to The British Society of Aesthetics, 4 May, 1966.

My indifference to the contemporary literature of aesthetics does not, however, mean that I am indifferent to aesthetic issues and to aesthetic experiences. The latter are for me of agonizing importance, and I suffer recurrently from a sort of aesthetic impotence or insensibility which I rate as the most depriving and the most readily fallen into of all forms of impotence. So far am I from holding that there is no such specific thing as an aesthetic experience, that it is just *any* experience in a special context, that I think it a type of experience uniquely marked out, extraordinary in its delight, and often in its difficulty and pain, but above all an experience that is not always nor readily to be had, that it involves the concentration, the mental undistractedness, even the bodily euphoria and lightness that we too often cannot muster at all. I also think that aesthetic issues are of absorbing seriousness and of genuine discussability and decidability whenever anyone has real aesthetic understanding of anything. They take, not the crudely general form of the aesthetic fineness or otherwise of a given work of art or segment of natural being, but the detailed form of the aptness or ineptness, the sense-making or surd character, the living or merely botched readymadeness of each part of the work of art or natural thing in question. Do Cleopatra's last purple speeches really hang together with the whole dramatic pattern which leads up to them? Do they really express an understandable culmination of her whole personal performance, are they really right or irrelevantly gorgeous? All these and similar questions regarding music, mountains, paintings, buildings, etc., are not only questions that have an answer but ones to which we can pursue the answer in perfectly well-defined and formulable ways. Aesthetic discourse is difficult, but its logic only eludes those who believe in no logic other than that of tautological manipulation and who relegate everything else to contingent fact, to blind experience or arbitrary decision.

If I am deeply concerned with aesthetic experiences and aesthetic issues, I am no less deeply concerned with aesthetic theory. My views on aesthetic theory, or in fact on any philosophical theory, demand that it should have a certain devastating simplicity which is infinitely far from the views or the practice of contemporary philosophers. I

believe that philosophy should consist in the steady turning about
and dwelling on, in various lights, of what is almost, but not quite,
trivial and obvious, till it becomes gradually extended into a fabric
of almost infinite extent and diversified colour, in which all the
details of fact and experience can be encompassed and enveloped, in
which by merely laying something down one has insensibly advanced
beyond it, but in which, however far one advances one has, in a sense,
never left one's starting point beyond one. All the numbers in
certain modern mathematical treatments can be educed from O by
a simple process of 'stroking', one has them all in having any of
them, and it is this sort of slow pushing onward of notions, though
freer and less inevitable than the pushing onward of mathematics,
that I want to find in aesthetic theory and in fact in any philosophical
theory. A theory that merely duplicates the irrelevant variety of
undigested experience I do not regard as philosophical at all. I
believe, in short, in a beauty that represents no peculiar feature of
certain objects and that is connected with no special stance, or pose,
of consciousness, but which is in a sense part and parcel of there being
any object before consciousness, or any conscious aliveness to anything whatsoever, though its absolute inescapability and categorical
involvement in all being and experience does not mean that it is not
more intensely and emphatically present in *some* experiences and
objects of experience than others. Modern philosophy hates transcendental universals like being, goodness, beauty, etc., but it is these on
which, in aesthetic theory, I think it absolutely necessary to concentrate. And I think that the subtle categorical something called
'beauty' can be, if not defined, at least fairly effectively pinned down
in a systematic philosophy of mind, which must, however, be of an
a priori and rational character and not merely a contingent and
empirical one. I take my cue, in short, from the classical aesthetic
writings of Kant and Hegel, and in modern times from those of
Brentano, Meinong and Husserl. I should also like to mention my
respect for the entirely forgotten *Ästhetik* of Stefan Witasek. This
line of research into the beautiful and our experience of it can be
developed and deepened, but only in its own manner. The positive
aesthetic observations thrown up by other approaches can, I think,

be without difficulty fitted into it. It is the classical aesthetic to which I think we shall have to return after having erred and strayed from its ways.

The type of approach to aesthetics that I am recommending will be clearest if contrasted with some other approaches that I consider gravely inadequate. I consider gravely inadequate any merely intuitive, enumerative aesthetic which, perhaps holding beauty to be some unique property of objects, or the object of some unique thrill or sensation in ourselves, then goes on to connect it with a large number of further characters in the world—smoothness, symmetry, organized unity, certain specific golden proportions, or what not. I consider that such intuitive approaches to aesthetics can at best provide the field of phenomena, the taking-off ground, from which aesthetic theory must soar up, and in which it must deduce profound unity and simplicity. Such merely intuitive aesthetic approaches merely invite controversion. They may *say* that certain characters have a necessary aesthetic significance or appeal, but this plea can always be controverted by personal and social facts and, if not, by logical possibilities. We can readily imagine, and have in fact actually met, people who do not aesthetically care for Palladian proportions, for maximally pure, saturated colours, for diatonic harmonies, classical profiles, French Alexandrines, etc., etc. Every reason for judging X to be well-formed can, with sufficient mental elasticity or perversity, become a genuine reason for judging X to be very ill-formed, and the whole modern aesthetic appreciation consists in trying to like objects aesthetically because they are *not* naturally likeable. Such intuitive methods are merely the dogmatic preliminaries to a theory which really, by its unity and simplicity, makes us feel that we know *why* we value certain objects aesthetically and why we vary our judgements on different occasions. What is wrong about such intuitive methods is their quasi-empirical character, their air of naïve discovery of what happens to be the case, even though what they discover is much too abstract and general to be, in an ordinary sense, a matter of experience.

If quasi-empirical approaches in aesthetics are inadequate, overtly empirical approaches are much more inadequate. And here I rank all psychological and sociological treatments which base themselves on observation, experiment or history. Such treatments may provide us with invaluable material for aesthetics, but their root inadequacy lies in their total inability to account for the normative, the cogent, the impersonal, the authoritative character of aesthetic values, their claim to rise above mere liking, mere custom, mere arbitrary selection: one is distorting the phenomenology of the situation if one does not recognize that all our deeper aesthetic experiences seem or claim to be of this character. The beauty of Dante's *Paradiso*, for one who fully understands it, does not seem to depend on one's special tastes or interests, religious beliefs, cultural background, etc.: it seems authentic, indefeasible, part of what one is dealing with. A value-free world is, in fact, a non-empirical figment, and among the many values inherent in things and there for our appreciation, are aesthetic values. One may, of course, regard all this phenomenology as *mere* phenomenology; one may think that, though there *seems* to be a difference between the authentically admirable and the merely admired, there really is no other difference than the appearance in question, the claim, the desideratum, the performative institution (or would-be institution) of a norm or standard. Canons of taste are canons laid down by someone for everyone, much as Boileau laid down the rules for all future French versifiers. The turning of a seeming aesthetic discerner into an actual aesthetic arbiter or dictator is, however, too large a transformation to be intelligible: we cannot understand how one should really be the latter while one seems to oneself to be the former.

It is here the place to say something about the modern version of empiricism which assumes a linguistic form. Here concepts and their necessary interrelations are seen as depending on facts of verbal usage: we use an expression B in any circumstances in which we use an expression A, and so what A means entails for us what B means. We never use an expression X in circumstances where we use an expression Y and vice versa, and so X and Y come to be mutually incompatible, contrary notions, and so on. Nowhere is there the slightest suggestion that it is the relations among notions, intelligible contents, which to some extent govern the rules of usage: to think

this would be to commit the error of believing in pre-existent meanings, meanings which antedate linguistic usage, and this would be,
for the view in question, to believe in a language before the existence
of language. The relations of necessitation, incompatibility, com-
patibility, subordination, mutual favourableness and so forth, are all
reflections of the way we *use* our expressions and linguistic forms,
and so all the august structure of the *a priori* has its roots in the factual
and empirical: in the way that certain animal beings happen to talk.
And the only profitable way to study concepts and their relations is
to study them at work in language: phenomenology, or the study
of the necessary forms of being and experience, must be linguistic
phenomenology. It is further held that the forms and workings of
our concepts as shown in language are infinitely more complex and
varied than philosophers, with their passion for simplicity and
generality, like to suppose: this is particularly true in a rather
nebulous field like the aesthetic. There we encounter in men's
ordinary usage no single simple concept of the beautiful but a vast
number of aesthetic concepts, tangled up in the most varied ways.
We have such concepts as that of the ironic, the ethereal, the robust,
the grotesque, the pure, etc., etc. I remember Austin devoting a
whole session to a discussion of the philosophically despised aesthetic
category of the 'dainty', and its contrary the 'dumpy'. Such investigations of aesthetic language are of course immensely valuable: they
show us how the phenomenology of the aesthetic world is vastly
more complex than is readily supposed. But they are philosophically
unsatisfactory because they fail to subordinate the rich material they
have garnered to truly illuminating, directive concepts. It is not
enough for a philosopher, like a battery hen, to scrabble about among
variety, and to pick out from it any and every chunky concept he
happens to find there. Concepts must be found which gather details
into unity, which cover a series of cases graded by genuine and deep
affinities, which hit upon a real mutual belongingness of features
which is *in* our data and not arbitrarily imposed by ourselves, and it
must be the sort of concept which is naturally extensible or stretch-
able, which can be broadened to cover new cases or features, which
shifts while remaining the same in the only sense in which 'being

the same' is of interest for philosophy. Such concepts which really range over important affinities, and which stretch to cover new cases, are in fact the sort of concepts with which Austin himself works, the concept of the 'performative' for instance: Wittgenstein's concept of family relations, which illuminates so many features of ordinary speaking, is likewise not itself a family-relations concept.

As opposed, therefore, to all quasi-empirical or overtly empirical theories of aesthetics, I myself opt for a transcendental theory, one which connects the beautiful and other objects of aesthetic appreciation with conscious experience as such, and so explains the all-pervasive, highest-level character of aesthetic principles and notions, and their elevation above personal and social contingencies. We carry them everywhere with us because they are part and parcel of being conscious of anything whatsoever. A transcendentalism that went further and showed aesthetic principles to be inherent in the structure of being would be still more worth while, and it is a sort of metaphysical transcendentalism that I believe, in fact, to be true. I shall not, however, try to take such very high ground in my present lecture. All that I have been saying will of course arouse violent resistance from those who believe that no metaphysical or transcendental account of the world is possible, and that nothing we can do in thought can either anticipate or reinterpret the facts which confront us in experience. This type of empiricism is to be rejected, however, because it does hardly anything except create insoluble philosophical puzzles and antinomies which it is not my business to go into this evening.

Leaving these generalities, we have first to inquire into the sort of field that aesthetic investigations are concerned with. Brentano divided the attitudes of the conscious mind into three basic species: there was *mere* conception or presentation, having something before one or present to one, without taking up any further conscious stance towards it; there was the theoretical acceptance of something as real, true, existent, believable and its opposing rejection as unreal, false, non-existent, not believable; and there was finally the other, non-theoretical acceptance or rejection which is present in our feelings, our desires, and our practical decisions. In all of these we are for or against something that comes before us and have varying attitudes to its existence or non-existence. There are of course innumerable amended forms of Brentano's masterly ground-plan of mental life, his map of mental geography, and we may well doubt whether pure presentation has that priority in mental life which Brentano gave to it, whether it is not perhaps rightly regarded as a deficient mode of attitudes far more involved and existential. However this may be, the value of the scheme is that it places the aesthetic field very satisfactorily—the aesthetic field is one of suspended conception, of pure having something before one for contemplation: it is a field essentially divorced from the Yes-No of belief and conviction, as it is divorced from the other Yes-No of practical concern with its necessary involvement in reality. When we are aesthetically minded we are interested in what comes before us purely as an instance of character and regardless as to whether there really is, or is not, such a thing or sort of thing; and our interest is, moreover, not concerned, as practical interest always is, to bring what is merely thought of or intended into the field of reality or to push something from the field of reality out into the field of the merely thought of, intended. It is important to note that what I have pinned down as aesthetic interest is in a sense latent in all interest, and is in no sense a peculiar interest that grows up alongside of other interests, directed to a special class of peculiarly pleasing, or in a special sense *sweet*, objects. Whenever one is interested in anything, however much this may involve locating or not locating it in the real world, and putting forth effort to keep it in or remove it from or project it into the real world, one is also interested in noting what the thing is like, explaining it, savouring it, taking it apart and putting it together again, and so forth. What makes interest aesthetic is merely that this exploring, considering, deeply probing attitude is prised loose from its normal complement of conviction and commitment and allowed to develop its own zest, to become an activity pursued for its own sake and not as a mere ancillary to coping with reality. Certain types of object or content may, by their remarkable character or structure or situation, more readily arouse this detached form of interest than others and certain types of relaxed mood, or personal or social situation, may likewise more readily provoke it. But the peculiar zest called the aesthetic is in a sense intrinsic to consciousness of a certain degree of subtlety and development, and ready to spring forth *whatever* the object before us and *whatever* the occasion. At any moment organisms with a sufficient richness of disponible energy must be ready to swing over into a mood which we call 'disinterested' since it lacks the involvement with reality and with practice characteristic of ordinary interest. Do I, you may ask, think that animals sometimes view the world aesthetically? I answer that I do not know, but that it is in principle possible. I believe the nature of mind to be something so profoundly unified, so all-or-none, that none of its possibilities can be realized without all the others, just as all the possibilities of higher geometric pattern are implicit in every fragment of three-dimensional space. There are, I should say, no radically different types of conscious mind, only minds of different degrees of elaboration or development. I think with Pythagoras that earwigs cannot be utterly different from Einsteins, and with Leibniz that the sleeping monads present in pokers are not utterly different from the lucid monads which give lectures on philosophy. This is why I do not believe in bull-fights or factory-farms, and why I do not doubt that cats, cows, birds and other less exuberant animals may at times fall into a zestful, purring meditation which I should not hesitate to call 'aesthetic'. Aesthetic attitudes are not, therefore, the special perquisite of a long-haired class produced in certain relaxed societies; they are latent wherever consciousness is; they are, if you like, consciousness itself, in its purest, least instrumental self-activity and self-enjoyment. What I am saying of course involves persuasive definition, giving concepts a simpler, more marked form than they have in ordinary use. But I should hold that it is not I, but the materials on hand, which themselves persuade us: they offer to our probing regard a simple salient something which genuinely gathers together a whole field of phenomena which belong together and whose most remarkable members we should not hesitate to call 'aesthetically arresting' or 'aesthetically fine'.

In my wild excess of persuasive definition I shall not follow many aesthetic philosophers, e.g. Hegel and Croce, in making the sensuous

an essential feature in the notion of an aesthetic attitude. I think this
a most unsatisfactory limitation, and one that we do not follow in
practice. There is certainly contemplative pleasure in probing
sensory quality or sensory structure, or in probing the fine fit of
sensory quality or structure with certain notional suggestions that
are, as we say, *expressed* by them. But there is undoubtedly contemplative pleasure in exploring and savouring notional structure as
such quite apart from the sensuous vehicles in which it is embodied,
and it is both natural to call such pleasure 'aesthetic' and also natural
to say that it is aesthetic *in exactly the same sense* as sensory structure,
or notionally impregnated sensory structure. The structure of a
Henry James story, the coming together and falling apart of the
characters, the incidentals that precipitate crucial moves in the
history—all these constitute a pattern of absorbing aesthetic interest,
even if we ignore the labyrinthine intricacy of the Jamesian sentences,
the queer, terse, yet wholly suitable names of the characters and the
stilted, arrested diction necessary to their communication. There is
aesthetic delight in a well-constituted joke. It is not in virtue of a
mere metaphor that we are said to take aesthetic pleasure in a
mathematical proof or a scientific theory or a philosophical argument. The dry Moore, as much as the flowery Plato, is a purveyor of
irresistible aesthetic delight, and the appeal of many of the doctrines of
Wittgenstein regarding atomic facts, language-games and what not,
is perhaps more essentially aesthetic than anything else. Philosophers
have in fact been so starved of aesthetic pleasure by many analytic
writings that they are unable to identify an aesthetic assault when it
hits them, and quite often mistake it for the assault of unassailable
truth. I am not saying that the senuous is not very important in the
aesthetic realm, since the fully realized presence of many things to
consciousness is essentially a sensory presence. The beauty of colours
can be enjoyed in poetic imagery or even in imageless thought, but
it is idle to deny that it is more fully enjoyed when the colours are
sensibly before us. In the same way I do not doubt that many logical
patterns can be enjoyed in a poor set of diagrams or symbols, or no
diagrams or symbols at all; but who can doubt that they are more
effectively and fully had when they have an apt diagrammatic or

symbolic expression? To this should of course be added the satis-
factions of communication which are by no means adventitious to
aesthetic experiences. The level at which we are aesthetically affected
is so high, so impersonal, so indifferent to primary impulse that it is
essentially, and not accidentally, one that we desire and seek to share
with others, and in which we are sustained by their agreement.

The aesthetic field is therefore a field involving an ἐποχή, a suspension both of conviction and practical commitment. Does this
vague, negative result lead to anything? It is not possible that anything whatever should become an object of such suspended contemplation, and that the carrying out of such contemplation should
give satisfaction and delight? Is any place left for aesthetic discourse,
which always aims at an ultimate coincidence of attitudes and that
not of the bludgeoning, arbitrary sort one knows from the ex-
positions of Stevenson? It is, I should say, not quite the case that
anything whatever is a suitable object of aesthetic concern: for an
object to come before us aesthetically it must do so *perspicuously* and
poignantly. These are the two aesthetic fundamentals mentioned in my
title: and I have made use of the somewhat flowery expressions
'perspicuous' and 'poignant' because I mean by 'perspicuity' not any
and every sort of clearness or lucidity but a peculiar sort relevant to
aesthetics, and by 'poignancy' not any and every sort of impressiveness and stirringness but a peculiar sort relevant to aesthetics. You
may say, if you like, that I am talking in a circle since you have to
know what 'aesthetic' means in order to identify the sort of lucidity
and impressiveness that I mean, but I do not think that this is the
case. One can quite well pin down perspicuity and poignancy without bringing in a notion so complex as the 'aesthetic'. By the perspicuity relevant to aesthetics I mean a presence to consciousness which
has broken through to success and mastery, whatever impediments
and obstacles there may have been in the way of such success, but
which also involves a certain stationariness or arrest. One's vision
revolves and moves within a relatively restricted orbit and does not
attempt to go beyond it, nor to explore those connexions which
place one's object in the real world. The arrest is, further, a practical
one; one is not concerned to pass on to the next stage, to go on to the

next thing, and so on. And by the poignancy which is relevant to aesthetics I mean not any and every shockingness or impressiveness, but the kind of shockingness and impressiveness that expends itself in vision, that in a sense luxuriates in the latter and that does not pass over any far-flung reorganization of view nor into practical reorganizations. In the aesthetic situation, however feebly induced, one is necessarily rapt, caught up, fascinated, under a spell; and this is the reason why genuine aesthetic appreciation is so difficult for many and why some hardly ever succeed in bringing it off at all. To try to banish ecstasy from art, as from religion, is merely to substitute for it something quite different which operates at a quite different level. Some people intensely dislike the intense gaze or glazed stare of aesthetic enjoyment, and go to any lengths to avoid it or discourage it. But to do so is to substitute connoisseurship, historical information, factual analysis, or the manipulation of value-tickets, for genuine aesthetic appreciation. The perspicuity relevant to aesthetics is one of relatively arrested, masterful vision which luxuriates in its own light; and the poignancy relevant to it is the energy, the intensity of that vision.

The perspicuity I am trying to put before you is one which dwells on character and structure, and is indifferent to context and existence: if it moves over to consider the latter, it does so only in order to see them as embellishments of internal content. Within the limits of its chosen content, it is absolutely unselective: it plays upon what is before it from all regards and angles no matter what otherwise pleasing or unpleasing features may stand revealed; but beyond those limits all is ignored, irrelevant, dismissed, no matter again how attractive or unattractive it may be. All this means that aesthetic perspicuity is in a sense indifferent to content, and this further shows itself in the comparative ease with which it moves from one object of aesthetic contemplation to another, and is in fact naturally led to do so, though the guiding affinity is aesthetic and not factual or practical. In aesthetic contemplation, we may say, it does not really matter what one dwells upon provided it appears with the relevant completeness and clearness: to have favoured objects of contemplation is in a sense to cease to be aesthetic in one's attitude. All this does not mean that, in aesthetic contemplation, one is *self*-absorbed or *self*-concerned, that one is interested in one's own attitude more than one's object: aesthetic concern is ecstatic, *object*-absorbed, *object*-rapt, if any attitude is so. But its raptness has, none the less, something detached about it in that it would shift to another object, and fasten its gaze upon it with more or less equal intensity, and this willingness to shift is in a sense part of the perspicuity concerned and gives to the perspicuity a certain objectivity distinct from that of other traits of objects. When we admire objects aesthetically it is in a sense only the clearness with which they show themselves to us that we admire and delight in.

The perspicuity we are dealing with is a feature so fundamental to consciousness that it is not at all on a level with other detailed psychological facts or poses: it is in fact nothing beyond a loving, lingering prolongation of our orientation to one object (an object being merely whatever is illuminated in *one* such orientation). In aesthetic perspicuity our conscious focus rests upon something, plays over it, so that what it is playing over is brought home to us more notably than in more cursive experience. But though thus funda-mental to conscious experience aesthetic perspicuity has innumerable psychological factors of detail which occasion and determine it and which differ from occasion to occasion and from person to person. The object which is perspicuous is an object intended or given, and this may differ utterly from the object which actually is there. It is an intentional object whose coincidence at certain points with an object in the real world must not lead us to compare it with the latter. It will be high-lighted, attentively stressed, in a manner in which the real object is not and cannot be high-lighted or stressed at all. Certain of its actual features will be determinately given, and others will be lost in an indeterminate haze whether or not they are actually present. And to its actual features will be added others that do not coincide with anything real, which either relate what stands before us to standards and models and objects of comparison in our own mind, or which simply represent illusion or mistake. A distinction between an intentional object and a real object with which it more or less adequately coincides is necessary in all fields: we must always distinguish between an object *as given* to a certain percipient or thinker and an object as it really and completely is. But in practical and scientific attitudes we are not greatly concerned with this distinction, and we scuttle hastily back and forth between the one and the other. In the suspended consciousness of aesthetic perspicuity it is, however, all-important to distinguish the intentional from the actual object, for what is dwelt upon, savoured, explored, made to show itself, is the object as it is for a rather restricted shaft of consciousness, or for a continuous illumination playing over a restricted field, and it would be simply wrong to bring into such an object features that are really there but on which no conscious illumination plays.

There are a few more points connected with aesthetic perspicuity. The first is that the *unity* of what is perspicuously presented is a necessary consequence of its perspicuity. Whatever items are given perspicuously are also given as forming a unitary pattern, are seen in togetherness and mutual relatedness, and not as mutually disparate and disconnected. This does not mean that whatever items are given perspicuously must be given as having objective connexions of an important sort; the lightest and most personal connexions are sufficient, as in many of the almost enumerative passages of T. S. Eliot. But if two items do not come together in a single picture or presentation then, in a sense, neither is fully perspicuous, and the one distracts us from full *approfondissement* in the other. Such distractions of course are one of the basic sources of aesthetic dissatisfaction, and they coincide with defective perspicuity. Neither of the rival distracting objects is freely and clearly held before the mind, but each has its vision cut off and impeded by the vision of the other. Another equally important point must be a firm rejection of the view of emotions as playing an absolutely essential and central role in aesthetic *approfondissement*, as suggested by many forms of the expressive theory. There are of course deep and characteristic emotions excited by aesthetic *approfondissement*, but these are the fulfilment, rather than the essence, of aesthetic activity. And there is further no doubt that emotions are extremely interesting objects of aesthetic appreciation, whether savoured in their misty interiority in ourselves, and whether married to gestures and facial expressions in

sincere persons or actors, or in portraits or other simulacra, or
whether clinging suggestively to poetic combinations or words or to
musical combinations and sequences of tones. But they enter the
aesthetic sphere either as attendant on perspicuity, and so properly
aesthetic, or as characters or features themselves rendered perspicuous,
brought luminously before us and dwelt upon. And in this second
role emotions are in no sense privileged aesthetic contents: a pattern
of tones or colours *not* connected closely with a particular emotion,
but clearly showing us what it is, is as essentially an aesthetic object
as a pattern held together by an emotional significance which pervades it throughout. What is aesthetically important about emotions
like gaiety, dreariness, scheming hatred, jealousy, etc., is not what
they are but that they should be well-displayed; and if this good
display involves our own personal entering into them and reliving
them, this is an incidental rather than an essential feature of the
aesthetic situation. We have to be moved in various ways by poetry
and music and architecture in order fully to appreciate what they are
about, what they mean to set before us; it is, however, as an essential
constituent of the aesthetic *object* that emotions are here aesthetically
relevant. We may say, therefore, if we like, that when emotions
enter the aesthetic sphere they do so in service to the intellect and to a
sort of intellectual activity, and not in their own right. This is part of
what Kant meant by calling aesthetic feelings 'disinterested'. And
we may say, further, that in so far as aesthetic objects take that two-
tiered form called 'expressive', in which a sensuous or other form is
linked with an inner notional meaning—a feature by no means
essential to aesthetic enjoyment, which may be either confined within what is sensuously given, or entirely liberated from it—emotions
are not the essential matters to be expressed. A complex set of
numerical or quantitative relations, a contrast of qualities, a strange
affinity of seeming disparates, the remarkable logic of some ingenious theory, the atmosphere of a historical period, etc., etc., may
be what is well expressed in a piece of poetry or prose or music, and
not any specific emotions connected with the latter.

What I have said has perhaps made clear the sort of retarded,
restricted conscious illumination that I call 'aesthetic perspicuity' or

simply 'perspicuity'. The word 'poignancy' serves, however, to provide some valuable complementary buttressing to the force of 'perspicuity'. For it is plain that the perspicuous may in a sense be *too* perspicuous, it may degenerate into the obvious, the unarresting or commonplace, and there is no aesthetic derogation so ruinous, not even that of ugliness or badness, as that some object makes practically no impression on us at all. There are a vast number of perspicuously, but not poignantly, given objects which are obviously excluded from the courts of beauty. While a series of geometrical figures, squares, octagons, circles, may have a perfectly perspicuous structure, this is generally considered to be too obvious, too regular, too lacking in poignancy to be aesthetically important: only when such simple forms are marshalled in the complexities of Byzantine architecture and adorned with mosaics as gorgeous as they are plain, are they aesthetically poignant, whereas such rich and subtle varieties of curvature as are found in the best Art Nouveau or Baroque or Gothic readily achieve poignancy. Municipal gardening which marshals tulips in monochrome droves, and even arranges them in the pattern of clocks, etc., has a strident obviousness which puts them on the side of the ugly, whereas the ever varied cunning of the Japanese garden is always poignant and unobvious. The more facile forms of Ming porcelain, of Egyptian architecture, of recipe-bound classicism, etc., are perspicuous but not poignant: they show what they have to show perfectly, but we cannot bear to dwell upon it. The same is of course characteristic of all that overripe, florid art which the Germans call *Kitsch*, art in which something is shown to us by so many devices, and all so familiar, that what is shown is infinitely unpoignant. The worst cases of Baroque and Art Nouveau and late Gothic decoration are a case in point, and so are the Romantic German paintings of the late nineteenth century: Islands of the Dead positively reeking with mournfulness, floral Elysia inhabited by human and semi-animal nudes freed from all restraints of decency and taste, Madonnas of consolation administering artificial compassion to still exhibitionist grief, etc., etc. The more purple novels of D. H. Lawrence show that we too are capable of insalubrious work of this unpoignant kind and even of canonizing it.

The lack of poignancy may, like the lack of perspicuity, assume different forms. It may take the form of simple flatness and feebleness and unmemorableness; it may take the form of would-be impressiveness which breaks down through obviousness and repetitiousness, and so is in a sense quasi-impressive; it may take the form of internal discrepancy, in which one presentation robs another of poignancy and perspicuity, or in which there is a discrepancy between sensuous and notional pattern, etc., etc. There are innumerable ways in which an object may be aesthetically unsatisfactory, in which its presentation may fail to achieve the poignancy and perspicuity in which aesthetic goodness consists. There is no better way towards the understanding of aesthetic goodness than to plumb the depths of aesthetic badness in all its myriad varieties. There has, we may note, been something artificial in my distinction between perspicuity and poignancy: they are simply two sides of the suspended consideration from which belief and practice are put at a distance. Perspicuity stresses the relation of such consideration to its object, the impartial truth or fulness with which that object is, in its relevant traits, presented or given. Poignancy, on the other hand, stresses the relation of such consideration to the subject, the intensity with which it sustains itself in our subjective life. Aesthetic satisfaction or pleasure can be said to be a higher-order satisfaction of consciousness in itself *qua* consciousness, in its own luminous fulness, which is none the less essentially camouflaged as an absorbed interest in some object. It is the higher-order character of aesthetic satisfaction which explains its universality and necessity: it is not a satisfaction connected with any special object or any special attitude towards objects but only with the consciousness which we all have and in which we inevitably develop a higher-order zest.

I now wish to develop the implications of my view that the aesthetic consciousness is just consciousness in its purest form, rejoicing in a somewhat squinting, self-deceiving manner in itself, rather than in any object. The first is that no ordinary, first-order character of objects is inherently an aesthetic character of an object or capable of being judged as aesthetically good or bad. Any first-order character of objects enters the ranks of aesthetic objects in so far as it is perspicuously and poignantly presented and while its precise place in those ranks may seem to depend on its character alone, it really can be seen on reflective analysis to depend on the perspicuity and poignancy with which it is presented. There can of course be no doubt that some objects and characters more naturally tend to arouse and sustain that brooding contemplative interest that we are considering, while others readily lose this stimulating power and becoming obvious and unnoticeable. Some objects are by their nature perspicuous and poignant and I should not myself doubt that some of this perspicuity and poignancy is no matter of chance fact, but an entirely *a priori* matter holding for all conscious life whatsoever. The varied play of qualities, the empty immensity of space with which they contrast and which they serve to bring out, the systole and diastole of experienced time, such basic cosmic arrangements as those represented by solid earth, reposeful water, freely circulating air and all-revealing light, the encounter of person with person which alone gives sense to the whole cosmic scene: all these, I should hold, are features inherently arresting and significant for consciousness and need only be shorn of a few irrelevances in order to create perspicuous and poignant experiences. But in the vast majority of cases what is perspicuous and poignant depends on attitudes and approaches which vary almost indefinitely from person to person and which may, moreover, be voluntarily varied by personal or social education. The beautiful is, and may be, sought in infinitely various directions: it will reveal itself wherever the barriers which hinder the emergence of perspicuity and poignancy can be overcome. For us certain collocations of items are too complex and too varied in their suggestions to be perspicuously and poignantly presented, and are accordingly not aesthetically satisfactory: to an angelic taste it would be perhaps precisely such collections which by their freedom from gross obviousness would give supreme aesthetic satisfaction. For us again certain collocations of items seem too gross and obvious in their structure and suggestions to be aesthetically significant, but it is these very frequently that are most poignantly and perspicuously given to a less developed, less sophiscated taste.

Does my view mean that there is no such thing as deformity in the world? (I avoid the unfortunate restrictiveness of the word 'ugly'.) It means nothing of that sort. Deformity exists wherever it is impossible, for one reason or another, to achieve poignancy and perspicuity in presentation: when the elements of what is presented detract from one another, when expression is not felt to harmonize with content, when long habituation has rendered something banal and obvious, and so on. There is no object, however beautiful, which cannot in appropriate circumstances pass over into the class of the jarring and banal or the merely feeble, though in some cases, owing to deep-set necessities of our nature or contingent empirical tendencies, this does not happen at all easily. And the judgement that sees banality or feebleness and jarringness in what previously seemed entirely harmonious and well-expressed may be quite as much a correct judgement as the previous one.

Am I preaching a shameless relativism? Not at all. I consider that there is a class of aesthetic values rooted in the fundamentals I have mentioned that are entirely absolute: in our delight in consciousness as such we necessarily like the unified, the successfully expressive, the poignant and so on. But the objects in which we discover these higher-order properties are not objects as they are in nature or reality but intentional objects, objects for us, and that means objects particularly stressed and seen in particular contexts and in the light of particular comparisons and paradigms, objects interpreted in a particular manner and played over by interests which may be peculiar to a period, an ideology, a region, a personality. Gothic buildings were differently seen by Palladian architects from the architects of the Gothic Revival. They were seen by the former in a heaven filled with idle mythological abstractions and not towering up to an ultimate mystery; they were seen in an atmosphere that loved daylight rather than dim gorgeousness, etc., etc. Considering the intentional objects that the Palladian architects and the Gothic Revivalists had for their judgements, the judgements of both might have been well founded. There is, of course, a general obligation laid upon all of us to have the richest and most varied aesthetic judgement possible, and from that point of view there is something reprehensible, improper, about a merely external, unsympathetic view of an aesthetic object, and a demand that we should understand it as did the people who created it, and who first enjoyed it. From this point of view the Palladian estimate of Gothic architecture was misguided, and the Gothic Revival estimate was better. It is not, however, clear that we are always obliged to give absolute priority to the creator's understanding of a work over and against our own understanding of it. Often indeed this would lead to a much impoverished interpretation. Our enjoyment of the primitiveness and childlike quality of many works of art is an enriching circumstance which must certainly have been absent from such works when they were created, and when sophistication and Daedalian skill must rather have appeared in their workmanship. What emerges from all I am saying is the absoluteness of aesthetic values, but also their higher-order character: they attach to things through features of cognition and the immense variety of such things, and their connexion with personal taste, readily lead to a mistaken doctrine of boundless relativism.

One additional point remains to be considered before I end this lecture. Does my point of view fall in with the bifurcation once again rampant in Oxford between naturalism and non-naturalism? Am I on the side of the lady naturalists or the prescriptive non-naturalism of the new Whyte's Professor? I take no sides in these parochial disputes, these delicate storms in Wedgwood porcelain. I do not think that aesthetic canons are in any sense a matter of personal decision, having nothing beyond the frail correctnesses of English linguistic usage to give them back-bone and body. Aesthetic canons spring from human nature as such, and not merely from contingent human nature but from that absolute human nature which makes us conscious and rational animals. One cannot remove the perspicuous and the poignant from the aims in which we *qua* conscious develop an ever increasing zest. Even if we deliberately cultivate the obscure and the humdrum, it is a poignant, perspicuous vision of the obscure and humdrum as such that we really hanker after. But of course the precise application of the aesthetic heads of value to the concrete stuff of creation and appreciation involves innumerable contingent and arbitrary factors, whose contingency and arbitrariness can, however, be removed by sympathy. Seeing objects as someone else sees them, we can determine whether his judgement of them is approvable or spurious. The whole field is, further, not one that can be studied in a purely intellectual manner: there is an urgent, prescriptive side to aesthetics as to other values, which pushes our creation or our appreciation in certain directions. Everywhere we have 'oughts' which rest on 'ises' and are themselves partially 'ises', and 'ises' which generate 'oughts': what is really proved wrong is the whole diremption of the factual from the valuable of which modern philosophy is so fond. I do not know whether my theory is naturalistic or non-naturalistic, because I believe the distinction to be ultimately unintelligible.

The Sublime and the Obscene

R. MEAGER

To the devotee of ordinary-language metaphysics, if his ordinary language is English, the aesthetic categories present extraordinary difficulties. Such is the established power of the Anglo-Saxon religion of inarticulacy, such are the complex and opaque veils with which the aesthetic language-dance wreathes them about, that rarely, rarely do the big words appear in paradigm-case nudity. 'Beauty' perhaps is not so elusive. Some things there are to which this concept must apply if it is to be a concept of beauty at all. The class of beautiful things must, for example, include among its members the deft late cut between the slips and the sweet smooth cast whereby the fly is brought to float gently on to the dancing surface at the end of the thirty-foot line. But the case of the sublime is hopeless. There is as good as no primary use of this concept at all. The only use a self-respectingly inarticulate Angle or Saxon can allow himself is one safely beyond the serious pale, where his (gentle, Anglo-Saxon) humour leads him to speak of sublime, say, innocence, or ignorance, or impudence, or unselfconsciousness of one sort or another. Yet there *is*, I think, a primary unironic concept brooding away inside the veils of our reluctance to mention it. It is a concept, or perhaps only a vague ideal, which seems to me to animate much of F. R. Leavis's demands of poetry, for example.[1] As such, it manages to make itself felt still as what Longinus took it to be, incomparably the highest excellence in literature; an excellence clearly felt where it occurs though far from clearly understood. As such, since Leavis eschews generalities except of the safely top-level 'life-enhancement' kind, I turn to Longinus for enlightenment.

To be sublime, Longinus says at once, is to have that consummate excellence and distinction in the expression of thought (if this may be accepted as a translation for *logos*) by which the greatest poets and historians clothe their own works, no less than their heroes' deeds, with immortality. But to be immortal one must first be alive. How can a piece of writing be alive? I think Longinus's answer is, and I am sure it ought to be: not through being an utterance of a sublime mind (sublime minds, alas, die like the rest of us); not through being the description of a sublime object (descriptions, alas, rarely measure up to their objects); but through achieving a special kind of expressive effect. The characteristic effect of sublime writing is that it does not convince or persuade or entertain us; it *transports* us into that state of mind in which the words we read convey not merely an isolated belief, request, exhortation, . . . but a total experience. Of course, transportation by literature is not only achieved by the sublime. To a railway enthusiast, we are told, Bradshaw's tables offer transports. But his reader has to contribute an extraordinary degree of spon-taneous special interest and extravagant flights of fancy to fill out the total state of mind needed if Bradshaw is to work so powerfully on him. To us poor average creatures the tables are a mystery indeed but an untransporting one. The sublime, by contrast, forces its interests and state of mind upon us. We are not presented with a description or report of a situation for our consideration and perhaps, if we are convinced, our piecemeal belief. We are not presented with an account of an action or an attitude for our consideration and perhaps, if we are persuaded, our admiration or condemnation. Our whole considering and admiring or condemnatory mind is captured, our imagination taken possession of, by the words we read or hear; they work in our mind as our own; as words we utter with a whole mind behind them, enforcing a shift of conception and value through a wide area of our own mental habits. We are not only with it, we are in what we read as we are in our own sincere utterances.

It must hastily be added, not to make an exaggerated claim, that this effect too is largely dependent on our reading in a generally receptive spirit, and with the general background of experience and acquaintance with his language and perhaps idiom that any writer presupposes in his readers. But the sublime is independent, as

Bradshaw is not, of the reader's having any *special* personal interest in the topics with which it deals. It deals, however, with topics of such universal and central interest in human life that we are all deeply interested in them.

The suppression of critical detachment in the reader or audience which is here ascribed to the sublime can at most be preserved through a single work for the duration of its reading or viewing (it might perhaps be characteristic of great drama, Brecht not excepted, that it creates a sustained total experience in depth of this kind which maintains its identity and separateness from the audience's general experience of the world throughout the duration of the work). In any case the sublime effect as here expounded is plainly a virtue of particular passages or particular works and not an overall quality of style, like adherence to an exalted vocabulary or the deployment of a profusion of exotic imagery. Characteristically the sublime breaks out from the general tenor of whatever style of writing is being used: 'like a thunderbolt it carries all before it and reveals the writer's full power in a flash'. (Ch. 1.)[2] It has indeed the effect of a mental lightning flash—the effect of a momentary but complete illumination capable of indefinite and rewarding recall and reflection, a living treasure of the mind.

This sense of illumination is important. Most of us have the power and many of us the constant disposition to transport ourselves into imaginary situations, or into other people's shoes, which we think would fit us better or worse than our own. But to effect this ourselves, of our own interest, by our own imaginative powers autonomously used, and retaining our sense of personal identity perhaps with the added emphasis given by free scope for self-expression, in the 'If I were Hadrian VII . . .' 'If I were Sir Alec . . .' frame of mind: this is a very different matter from the transportation achieved by the sublime poet. The poet must induce a much greater shift of attitudes, in unknown readers of no special disposition or interests. He must not reinforce but dissolve his reader's sense of personal identity and the habitual interests, modes of expression, conception and valuation which go to make it up, by imposing a new pattern on these in active depth. He must make his reader's autonomous powers of thought and feeling work on new principles so as to give his words their appropriate mental background of beliefs and values; and he has to do this just by presenting the words themselves; or in one famous instance just by outlining with words a silence. Even if this effect is only temporary and is dependent upon his reader's general willingness to read appreciatively, its achievement is surely proof of consummate skill. But, as Longinus insists, it is not a matter of skill only, nor is the transportation effect a sufficient condition, though it is a necessary condition, of sublime writing. Transportation may be effected by a sensuous assault on our general response to rhythm. This is an allied power of music and to a lesser degree of word-music as well known to the ancients of Athens as to the youth of Liverpool (the Beatles are heirs to an immortal tradition). Transportation of this kind is often, perhaps always, a contributory factor in the sublime, but is not in itself sublime. The sublime has to capture us not by its brute impact on our rhythmic senses, nor yet by our independent predilection for the experiences with which it is concerned, but by the grand scale and the vivid sense of the conception it presents. The sublime is essentially a vivid and vigorous expression of some cosmic imaginative conception or of some powerful and intense emotion. The emphasis is on the power of the expression rather than on what is expressed so powerfully. 'Power' here is to be understood in the sense in which a mathematical formula as well as the Mersey Sound may be powerful. It is clear (if anachronistic) that Longinus drew the Croce-Collingwood line between expressing an emotion and merely venting it or stimulating it. The sublime must be attained by working through the understanding, by presenting a new live expression to be understood conceptually. The command of such expressions is a natural gift, not a technical skill that can be learnt, though skill and experience are necessary to control its exercise so that it results in the significant sublime and not in exotic nonsense.

A transporting passage, then, is only sublime if it effects a sense of significance, of sudden illumination; but a grand conception equally is only sublime if it has the capacity to move us, transport us. This moving quality of course need not be of the ordinary emotional kind; i.e. it need not depend on the expression of those familiar universal troublemakers love, rage, scorn, ambition and the like. And the sublime expression of these, as we see from Longinus's analysis of the Sappho ode which he takes as an example of this form of the sublime, depends primarily on the imaginatively powerful, definite conception of the experienced reality of the emotion, of the modulation of awareness of the world that this brings, and only derivatively on the rhythmic, onomatopoeic or generally non-conceptual emotive reinforcements with which this is underlined. Hence though Longinus lists five 'sources' of the sublime, he himself relegates three of these to contributory status, concerned with the rhetorical and stylistic devices with which conceptions derived from the other two sources may be expressed more economically and forcefully; and his two main sources, the power of grand conception and the power of strong emotion, reduce to a single power to produce vivid expressions of new total experiences of the world or of life. What constitutes the special vividness of such expressions? Consider the general concept of suicide, and the particular conception of it expressed in the 'To be or not to be' soliloquy. The soliloquy can hardly be read without a *sense* of wonderfully increased and deepened understanding of the meaning of suicide, and of life as it appears from a suicidal attitude, growing within the reader. This sense of increased mastery through increased understanding enriched by total shifts of perspective in our dealings with life at large is central to Longinus's conception of the sublime itself, and brings his treatment of the notion surprisingly close to Kant's. Although Longinus is not very explicit in his general characterization of conceptions suitable for sublime expression, his many examples can be made to tie in to an extraordinary degree with Kant's treatment of the notion. Even Longinus's two main sources of the sublime can perhaps be seen to foreshadow Kant's division of the sublime into the mathematical sublime dependent on our power to conceive of the infinite as a whole as incomparably greater than any extendable process of measurement could encompass (the power of grand conceptions), and the dynamical sublime dependent on our power to remain spiritually unmoved in resolution by the overwhelming physical forces of nature (the power of intense and not 'lowly' emotion). This degree of community of thought can also be seen in the similarity between what Longinus says about sublime expressions of grand conceptions and what Kant says about the 'aesthetical ideas' which it is the function of the genius in fine arts to create. There is indeed a strong Kantian ring about many of Longinus's remarks—a ring which is notably absent from the crude empiricist Burke's treatment of a notion going under the same name. Consider the following passage from Longinus's Chapter XXXV:

> Nature judged man to be no lowly or ignoble creature when she brought us into this life and into the whole universe as into a great celebration, to be spectators of her whole performance and most ambitious actors. She implanted at once into our souls an invincible love for all that is great and more divine than ourselves. That is why the whole universe gives insufficient scope to man's power of contemplation and reflection, but his thoughts often pass beyond the boundaries of the surrounding world.

Worthy understanding and expression of the wonders of this spectacle may be sublime without necessarily being charged with the ordinary love/hate/rage/ambition sort of emotion, and it is because many cases of sublime writing, notably in Plato, seem to be innocent of such ordinary emotional import and because many of the ordinary emotions, such as pity and fear, however well expressed, cannot be given a mind-enlarging embodiment, that Longinus separates the two 'sources' of the sublime. But even in the case of the emotion-expressing sublime it is clear that Longinus correctly sees its sublime character to depend on its conceptual expressiveness. All the remarks in his traditional rhetorician's treatment of the special devices of figurative or emotive language hammer home the one general rule: grand words, vulgar words, smooth transitions, broken rhythms, stark economy, profusion of subordinate clauses or repetitious detail or vivid metaphor, all may have their place in reinforcing corresponding conceptually determined sense. And the command of such grand or powerful conceptions is the primary source of the sublime.

Parenthetically, I think Longinus should have argued that the special type of nobility of mind implied by and necessary to the utterance of sublime expressions is indeed simply this command of conceptions, which is plainly separable from (and often separated from) the extra practical nobility of spirit which would lead, for example, to an actual death on a Roman cross in the cause of political independence. There is, perhaps, a practical paradox in the idea of a person who combines the power of sublime conceptions with the impotence of *acrasy* or the meanness of petty selfishness or cowardice; but surely it is no more than a practical paradox, and one exemplified everywhere at a less exalted level of thought and action. If it is allowed that Longinus ought to be speaking simply of the power of grand conception when he speaks of a noble mind, there need be no ambiguity in his concept of the sublime as between its being a moral concept of an excellence in people or actions and an aesthetic concept of an excellence in literary achievement. It can be understood clearly as an aesthetic concept applying primarily to expressions, derivatively to the power of producing such expressions, and by 'family resemblance' to people, behaviour, and natural objects providing examples susceptible of description in such expressions. If this is correct, the concept of the sublime can be seen to be an aesthetic concept though examples of the sublime may clearly have great moral importance. So Ajax, in the episode of Odysseus's globe-trotting visit to Hades to check up on the fate of his ex-*Iliad* cronies, in his shade's silence in reply to Odysseus's inadequate attempt to patch things up, no doubt acted nobly because he *was* noble, or was at least cast in the giant heroic mould of the *Iliad*, whose shadow he here draws across the romance of the *Odyssey*. He became sublime, however, only by accident: by the accident which provided his invariable inarticulacy with the one context in which it could become a perfect sublime expression; the adamantine unforgiving silence to vindicate all silences of all strong silent men since time began. Morals made Ajax's silence honourable and righteously implacable (if it was so); aesthetics made it sublime.

To revert to the special character of sublime expressiveness. We have seen that it must effectively transport us, and transport us with a sense of the amplification of our understanding of the world or of life. The other mark which Longinus continuously emphasizes is the suddenness with which this is done. The poet must somehow jump us out of our normal detached reading attitude, the critical objective attitude of 'This fellow says . . .', and out of the personal habits of thought and feeling on which this is based. To do so usually requires some linguistically unconventional shock-tactics such as those discussed by Longinus under 'figures' as a contributory source of the sublime, and these may easily fail to have the required effect. To leave the safe medium of ordinary objective narration or description; to switch from ordinary indirect speech suddenly without warning or introduction to direct speech[3]—

> And Hector to the Trojans called aloud
> To rush the ships, let lie the bloody spoils,
> If I see one of his own will hold back
> I'll see to it that he dies . . .

in Longinus's example, with its sudden disappearance of the separateness of the writer from Hector, and the corresponding jolt to the reader's separateness from both—is a dangerous project and one that will fail if the reader feels unable to accept the invitation to uncritical immersion in the expression. The result may be weird and precarious, or pompous and inflated, or turgid and a bore, or mechanical and frigid, etc. Longinus is full of the corpses of would-be sublime passages dead from such different diseases. Here of course we find the bathetic or ridiculous encamped about the confines of the sublime. But when the jump comes off, then we, the readers, get a unique experience. 'Our soul is naturally uplifted by the truly sublime; we receive it as a joyous offering; we are filled with delight and pride as if we ourselves created what we heard.' (Ch. VII.) Longinus's account here is often taken to be a case of careless rapture; but I think on the contrary it is a case of careful phenomenological observation, and the key to the sublime. It depends on a delicate appreciation of the expression-situation.

There are two extreme views regarding the relation of thought to expression and Longinus avoids both. He holds neither the crude view that expression is a matter of first think your thought and then find an expression, preferably beautiful, for it; nor the profound but obscure view that thought and expression are one, that to each thought there is just one expression and the expression is the thought. Longinus's own view treats thought and expression as a developing process of interplay between the inner springs to expression and the possibilities of expression provided by the public medium of expression, language. This is clear from Chapter XVI, his extended examination of 'Demosthenes's oath'. Since this well-known critical *tour-de-force* also brings out very clearly the mechanics of a sublime passage as he conceived them to be, I shall examine his examination at length.

The oath was one which occurred in the midst of a speech in which Demosthenes sought to turn aside the wrath of the Athenians by a defence of the policy by which he had brought them to their disastrous defeat at Chaeroneia. I quote:

> Demosthenes is trying to vindicate his policies. What would have been the natural way of speaking? 'You were not wrong to take up the fight for the liberty of Greece. You have precedents for this, as they were not wrong who fought at Marathon, at Salamis, or at Plataea.' But when, like a man suddenly inspired and, as it were, god-possessed, he utters that oath by the heroes of Greece: 'It cannot be that you were wrong, by those who faced death at Marathon ...', through the use of that one figure ...

What Demosthenes achieved through the use of that one figure takes Longinus the whole section to run through. First, however, it is worth noticing the implied account of the expression-situation. Longinus is suggesting that at this point language and the situation between them provided Demosthenes, as they always provide all of us, with various alternative ways of phrasing what he wanted to say. Most of us take the obvious, the 'natural' ways—the clichés—both to think our thoughts (express them to ourselves) and to express them to others. Such thoughts and such expressions meet the bare public practical needs of the situation and die with the situation which brought them into being. Genius takes a new all-round look at the situation, uses a new way of expressing it, and with sufficient command of the potentialities of language achieves a uniquely powerful effect. Longinus's analysis of this unconventional oath shows how with it Demosthenes forces upon (or indeed foists upon) the minds of his hearers a sudden wide-ranging shift in their natural understanding of their and his situation, the understanding naturally resulting from their habitual and naturally egocentric thought- and feeling-patterns. He might have offered the new look to their critical appraisal in the overt argument by analogy suggested by Longinus. But he wanted (badly) to jump them out of their natural standpoint and the critical basis this afforded them, and to persuade them to take the wider, *sub specie aeternitatis* standpoint from which the situation would be seen in his way. The oath, in Longinus's view, provides exactly the shock-tactics necessary. To paraphrase his assessment of it: it as it were deifies those ancestors of his hearers who faced death at Marathon, Salamis, etc., and so recalls them to their pride in these glorious dead; it turns a weak defensive argument into a passionate, strange, imagination-firing exhortation; it has the magical incantatory effect of a paean, removing the scene to be scanned from parochial Athens to all history and heaven too, and it should transform shame and grief at a defeat into pride in the battle as the proper successor of those ancient glories of the race; finally, in it Demosthenes carefully avoids any reference which would point up the small defect in his suggested analogy, the difference between victory and defeat, by dwelling on those who faced death rather than those who won the previous victories, and by winding up with the sonorous reflection that to all such glorious dead the city had awarded a public funeral. The grand, cosmic-historic conception is there; the figure of the oath rams it home in depth into the audience's imagination. To effect this Demosthenes carefully doesn't state his analogy plainly, but it, and the congenial sentiments appropriate to its acceptance, are smuggled in as presupposed to an understanding and acceptance of this unexpected powerful oath. Whether his audience were finally taken in by it is, I think, irrelevant. We, for whom the speech has no practical importance at all and who have had its cunning carefully explained to us by Longinus, can, I think, still respond to its sublime expressiveness and feel its emotive power without changing our ordinary beliefs if any about the rights and wrongs of the case. But while we read it we surely see the matter in the light Demosthenes imposes upon us, and feel the force in our own thinking of the emotional reversal attendant on this conception.

I have been using the term 'powerful expression' very vaguely and freely but I think it can be given more precision. I have suggested

that the power of an expression of the sublime kind is at least largely
due to its inducing a sharp shift in, or a crystallization of, the habitual
somewhat empty or vague general concepts and attendant feelings
and impulses with which the reader confronts experience. The power
is heightened by the fact that the sublime expression doesn't spell
out the changes in mental habits that it requires, but packs them in as
a presupposed punch, so that they are manifest in the consciousness
of the victim rather as an unidentified sense or feeling of portentous
implications than as recognized invitations to change his modes of
thought. It is perhaps the distinguishing mark of poetic as against
prose expression that it sets out to control in this instantaneous way
not only the public, dictionary significance of the words it uses, that
which the reader would understand if he read them in their minimal
commonsense, but also such implications, conceptual, evaluative,
emotional, at all levels of awareness and feeling, as will fit the reader
at least temporarily with the total responsive attitude in which the
words will carry the full particular significance in which in this
particular instance the poet wishes them to be read. So in a prose
context an oath sworn 'by' mortal men instead of e.g. by Jove,
would be intelligible no doubt, but as either religious blasphemy or
fantastic nonsense. In the context of Demosthenes's speech, however,
the oath was skilfully placed and poetic enough in its manner and
reference to enforce the appropriate total shift in its hearers' conceptions, with the attendant shift of feelings that e.g. I should perhaps
regard the loss of my husband as something approaching apotheosis,
or at least as a glorious patriotic sacrifice of historic significance, and
what is the prospect of slavery for myself and subjection for the city
compared with the timeless glory we have won for Athens, home
of human freedom ..., etc.? Here we have not merely poetic
expressiveness in depth but the sudden illumination of the sublime,
with the sudden vastly extended viewpoint and its attendant
emotional reversal. In this way we can understand our tendency to
treat poetic utterance, and *a fortiori* sublime utterance, as powerfully
compact with more than explicit meaning, as reaching indeterminate
depths and ranges of significant effect.

Such expressions then come to us alive with the feeling-suggestion

of the wide-ranging mental attitudes appropriate to them, and these
can be felt perhaps fighting with our own mental habits, perhaps
entirely replacing them at least temporarily. It is also these feeling-
suggestions which make up the general sense that this is an utterance
which will repay repetition and reflection. Whether this promising
sense is honoured in the event is another matter. Longinus indeed
maintains that in the true sublime it is, and perhaps there is a very
top-level sublime at which this is so. But in view of his recognition
that there was a certain important weakness in the analogy which
was the main hidden implication in Demosthenes's oath the repay-
ment can't be a matter of extended understanding of truth in any
simple way. Poetry remains poetry and *a fortiori* oratory oratory; it
may even be that a suspicion of a tension between different feeling-
intimations adds to the liveliness of an expression as a stimulus to
the imagination. However that may be, if we list the characteristics
of Demosthenes's oath, we can see why Longinus took it to be a
model of a sublime expression. It is a sudden flashing figure, its
impact independent of and undisturbed by the somewhat monotonous
hammering note which Longinus elsewhere complains of as general
in Demosthenes's style. The new conception of the situation en-
forced by it on its hearers is on the really grand scale, taking in all
history and heaven too and implying a general emotional reversal
from wretchedness to pride; it is effected in a moment by a single
simple figure though one rich with evocations of the supernatural
and the historic; its sensible effect is reinforced by a telling rhythm
and sentence structure, and all this is soberly calculated (by hindsight)
to evoke depth-support of a very determinate kind. No wonder such
an oath came to his hearers as a joyous offering, uplifting them and
filling them with delight and pride as if they themselves had created
what they heard. In effect they had, and we do, create the major
part of the effect of the sublime on us, by being induced to make the
mental shift necessary to take the words seriously as if from a full
mind, as if they were our own. The power to induce us to do this is,
surely, the highest excellence of which literature is capable (oratory
of course brings in inescapable practical ends and moral criteria);
it accounts for the peculiar intimacy and pride of possession with

which we treat such sublime passages, and also for the irresistible tendency to treat the words themselves as alive within us. Hence the immortality of the really sublime expression.

It lives again in every reading of every person who reads it. So in reading the cosmic words of God at the Creation any atheist must for the moment match those startlingly simple words with the startlingly simple yet cosmic act, the imagination and imaginative creation of light. So when we are told of the 'still small voice' in the heart of the rushing wind and the trackless wilderness our own imagination makes a somersault in our values, shrinking the powers and vast-nesses of this world into spiritual impotence and insignificance. This could be taken as the paradigm pattern of the sublimely expressed conception. It commands us to stand back from the endless private succession of egocentric experiences which make up our own particular lives and to comprehend life itself conceptually as a whole, not with the sense of emptying out the baby and bathwater and thinking merely in empty universal words, but on the contrary with the sense of retaining a precise and emotionally live feeling for its infinite complexity and variousness and endlessly particularized reality. My insertion of 'the sense of' and 'the feeling of' is vital here for a realistic appraisal of the sublime, but its power as an ideal depends as much on its pretensions as on its actual achievement. Essentially, as has no doubt been often recognized, it represents the longing, as old as human thought, to combine conceptual compre-hensiveness with intuitive realization, to crystallize out conceptual thought into intuitive particularity, to produce a Creator-God's-eye view and understanding of our universe.

Whether we ever seriously dwell on these passages in order to un-pack the suggestions of meanings which they set reverberating through our feeling-levels, disturbing wide areas of our established patterns of reaction, rather than simply enjoy the reverberations and the generalized sense of power they bring, is a debatable question. Longinus takes the stern line that the truly sublime must in fact be rewarding to serious consideration, so that it can repeatedly be read by men of intelligence and never fail to stir their souls to noble thoughts; so that it will leave impressed on such minds reflections that reach beyond what was said. The truly sublime of this kind satisfies all men at all times: men of different occupations, lives, interests, generations and tongues. An immensely tall bill; the wonder is that it is ever satisfied at all. But some of the works which Longinus had in mind are with us still and still sublime, and we could perhaps even add a few more to the list.

To summarize then: what is it about the sublime that makes it incomparably the highest excellence that literature has to offer?

(1) its presenting a new, comprehensive and apparently comprehension-enlarging way of conceiving life from some important aspect or emotional standpoint—a creative God's-eye view;

(2) in an expression which comes actively alive in our own thinking, valuing and feeling;

(3) thereby transporting us out of our own thought-habits and concerns, compelling us to drop the 'this fellow says...' attitude of detached critical reading and to embrace the words we read and the experience they bring within the fictional-imaginative compass of the bare Kantian 'I think...' which accompanies all our *own* states of mind at the cost of leaving no trace of itself on any, no mark of distinctive self-awareness. Our personality is taken over, temporarily, by the sublime utterance we read.

Clearly any phenomenon which has such a power, even of a temporary kind, is up for severe moral examination, whether or not it presents itself as an instrument of moral education. Clearly also it will be used as such, however its original writers intended it, and this is the basis of Plato's condemnation of poetry. The sublime emerges from Longinus's treatment as the first and finest of the hidden persuaders, for (see Demosthenes) the sublime may work even if it is only *as though* we had been endowed with a larger vision, a more complete empathetic insight, a more vivid realization, when we hadn't.[4]

Unlike the sublime, the concept of the obscene suffers from obscurity through the all too frequent use of the word for its purely evaluative force with little regard for any particular form of condemnation implicit in it other than, perhaps, a morally based abhorrence of what someone else enjoys. In his *Pornography and Obscenity* D. H. Lawrence seems to treat the obscene in this way and to be concerned merely to shift the application of the concept from what shocked other people to what shocked him. If there would seem to be little connexion between such a concept and the sublime, by rather closer examination I hope to reveal one.

Being shocked at something is not a merely passive reaction. I am not shocked *at* but *by* a live wire unwarily clasped. To be shocked *at* you I must be shocked not at you *simpliciter*, but at your duplicity or turpitude or quarrelsomeness, etc., i.e. at you as falling under some concept which I apply on the basis of my evaluational standpoint.

But obscenity is not just shockingness. Many things, such as your duplicity, turpitude, etc., are shocking without being obscene. And here we do return to our discussion of the sublime. For what differentiates the obscene from the shocking in general connects it closely with the sublime. For properly to say of anything that it is obscene implies, as well as an explicit reference to it as shocking, an implicit reference not so much to other people's enjoyment of it as to a peculiar element of enjoyment in one's own perceptual or imaginative experience of it *as* shocking, thus implying a shift in one's sense of self-commitment reminiscent of that demanded by a sublime expression. Oddly enough I think Kant hit this nail on the head in a remark about the portrayal of the disgusting in art (*Critique of Judgement*, ¶.48):

> There is only one kind of ugliness which cannot be represented in accordance with nature without destroying all aesthetic satisfaction, and consequently artificial beauty, viz. that which excites *disgust*. For in this singular sensation, which rests on mere imagination, the object is represented as it were obtruding itself for our enjoyment, while we strive against it with all our might. And the artistic representation of the object is no longer distinct from the nature of the object itself in our sensation, and thus it is impossible that it can be regarded as beautiful.

Here Kant recognizes both that the response of disgust rests on imagination and that the disgusting object as it were enters fighting into the workings of our mind, inviting us to an enjoyment against which we also feel compelled to strive with all our might. If the striving is completely successful, as no doubt with Kant it would be, we have the comparatively simple morally directed response of disgust. In lesser mortals I think the battle may be less completely and effortlessly won and may indeed constitute a self-sustaining imaginative activity focused on the object. We may then have an object presenting itself to us as obscene.

In order to judge an object or situation or a piece of writing or a filthy postcard to be obscene in the primary, i.e. non-derivative, form of this judgement one must be expressing in the judgement a feeling of one's own perceptual or imaginative response of this characteristic self-condemned pleasure. Of course, as in the case of aesthetic judgements of beauty or sublimity, there are derivative, non-expressive judgements made in the same words but based on repeating other people's first-hand expressive judgements, or one's own produced in a more responsive mood, or on applying to an object one's general moral principles and general knowledge of human nature to yield a judgement as to what *will* evoke from *most people* with less well trained susceptibilities than one's own a genuine expressive judgement of obscenity. It is these last judgements that are clearly inter-personal and are at issue in the courts, and they may well for that reason be in practice the most important judgements of obscenity; but they must nevertheless be recognized as logically derivative from the genuine, first-hand expressive judgements enjoyed, according to the gentlemen of the jury, by their maidservants and daughters.

What is it about obscene objects that evokes this special imaginative experience? Like the sublime but in a different way the obscene effects a doubling up of our sense of self-commitment. Implicit in my regarding the tremendous Alps as sublime is a double conception of myself as not only human, and so small in bodily size and power, but also godlike in my indefinitely extending powers of comprehension and self-determination. In the obscene we also adopt or are given a double sense of ourselves, as not only human, and so subject to human demands for the proper treatment of ourselves and other persons as of human dignity and worth, but also as potentially brutish, potentially mere animal digestive and procreative organisms, subject to inescapable physical processes and needs, and to domination by physical *force majeure*. Combining these two conceptions of persons, we are able in an obscene frame of mind to think of ourselves as using, or suffering the use of, physical violence to dominate our own thoughts or other people's reactions and actions; and able to think humiliatingly of ourselves or of other persons through their bodies as inescapably corruptible, diseased and dirty by standards to which we ourselves are committed.

Characteristic of the obscene, then, is its evoking of a special, self-condemned pleasure—the fantasy pleasure of self-condemned liberation of thought and judgement from human standards of propriety in the fantasy-gratification of immediate physical urges or fantasies of domination. Under this double conception of things or persons, persons can be thought of or acted upon *as if* they were non-rational, usable objects or material bodies; or conversely material things or (presumably) mindless animals can be thought of or acted towards *as if* they were persons, while *at the same time* their real character is also vividly recognized, and from this double view we can derive the characteristic pleasure of the obscene, in the use (or imagined use) of bodies to force the compliance of, or bodily satis-factions to counterfeit the satisfactions of, or bodily humiliations to abase, that elusive source of action, reaction and satisfaction, the free spirit of man. Whereas the sublime at least promises to provide an eternity of significant reflection in a moment of illumination, the obscene pretends to liberate from the permanent yoke of rational standards of thought and desire and action, from the built-in demands of foresight and retrospective reflection and consideration for others implicit in our perennial concern for objective truth and for the enduringly based personal relations, to allow the irresponsible manipulation and enjoyment of bodies as stand-ins for persons in providing the desired sensations and fantasies of the moment.

Since the moral and religious assurance of the Puritan-Philistine era has melted away well-intentioned obscenity has become hard to identify and a serious aesthetic danger. If the attitudes and impulses condemned by orthodoxy are seriously held by a moral reformer to be necessary to a full and satisfying human life, the transporting obscene becomes only uneasily distinguishable from the sublime. There is in the sexual act itself a natural paradox that lies in wait for the unwary realistic novelist. For if it is to be whole-heartedly engaged in and not to provide a dangerous opportunity for power-politics, it seems likely that the sexual act must be experienced in mindless abandonment to sensation; yet it is, and must be thought of as, the vital focus of powerful emotional forces with formative influence on the outlook and personality of the participants. An experience requiring such mindless self-abandonment but of such significance in long-term personal relationships is a standing temptation to abuse. For the novelist there is a corresponding hazard. He has to draw a precarious hairline distinction between the sublime portrayal of the sexual act in its integral connexion with the human situation and the obscene portrayal which will disrupt his readers' concern with his characters while they indulge in mental masturbation if the portrayal is powerful enough or reject it as embarrassingly silly if it isn't. This line is one which Lawrence himself often failed to draw, and perhaps it cannot be drawn. But it represents an objective and not merely orthodox barrier beyond which any writing, however pure in intention, must be obscene.

If this account of the obscene is acceptable, then it emerges as an aesthetic disvalue in literature, the effect of the transporting expression (possibly from the purest motives) of what is a sub-rational conception of human beings and life, simultaneously evoking the reader's awareness of its shockingness (possibly strenuously denied to himself) and awareness of the condemned pleasure he takes in it. So, in the twentieth century after he wrote (probably), we can add to Longinus's list of the diseases to which attempts at the sublime succumb, the obscene.

REFERENCES

[1] cf., e.g., his discussion of 'the tragic experience' in 'Tragedy and the Medium', *The Common Pursuit*, Peregrine Books, pp. 130 ff.

[2] This and following translations from Longinus are taken from the *Library of Liberal Arts Press* edition, 1957, translated by G. M. A. Grube.

[3] My attention was drawn to this point by F. N. Lees's paper published in the previous number of this *Journal*.

[4] My understanding of Longinus was mediated, and my appreciation of him stimulated, by the Introduction and Notes to D. A. Russell's edition, which the author was kind enough to let me study in typescript.

On the Concept of the Interesting

AUREL KOLNAI

I. 'INTEREST' AND 'INTERESTING'

When, as they often do, people speak of an *interesting* work of art—an interesting picture, novel, etc.—they obviously do not mean exactly the same thing as when they speak of a *good* or beautiful or significant work of art. Interestingness is supposed to be, to put it crudely, only one among the criteria of aesthetical goodness or value; and one that is probably more widely applicable to the literary than to other artistic domains, as indeed outside the realm of art it seems to be more natural to talk of beautiful objects on the one hand but of interesting events on the other. The question immediately arises here whether 'interesting' can be maintained as an aesthetical category proper, or as a descriptive concept or an objective quality at all; whether it denotes more than the mere psychological fact of somebody's (say the speaker's, or perhaps many people's) *being interested* in some object or kind of object on a given occasion or in some more permanent fashion. A purely subjective view of 'the interesting' might also draw support from the fact that we have no equivalent with a substantive ring like 'good', 'fine' or 'beautiful' (*beau, schön*) for the participial adjective 'interesting'; the rather closely related quality of the 'exciting' (*spannend*) is signified by a word similar in structure which even more emphatically places in view the effect exercised on the subject's mind. If we set 'interesting' in a parallel with 'pleasing', we miss the analogon of the step towards a claim to objectivity which leads from 'pleasing' to such value-words as 'good' or 'beautiful'.

Sometimes, of course, people do speak indiscriminately of an interesting or a fine picture, an interesting or a good book, etc.; again sometimes, probably more often, they would call 'interesting' just what happens to arouse *their* interest, and quite possibly only on that particular occasion in a particular context. But neither the former nor the latter way of speaking, I suggest, corresponds to the proper meaning of the term as used in careful—and very often, in quite ordinary—discourse. Heaving the private sigh: 'Oh, if only I had something interesting to read!' I am no doubt likely to be using the word in an utterly subjective sense; not so, however, in making the statement: 'This is a most interesting book' or its contrary: 'This is a very dull book.' Most of us are perfectly able to distinguish, and again and again do distinguish, between things in which we happen to be specially interested and things that we hold to be highly interesting. I would not, in a state of severe bodily pain which obliterates all the interest I otherwise have in reading, enounce the judgement: '*Hamlet* is a dull play'; nor would I call a book of history 'uninteresting', *meaning* thereby that it discusses the France of Henry IV, in which I take a comparatively moderate interest, instead of the Spain of the Restoration Monarchy or the Austria of Francis Joseph, in which I happen to be exceedingly interested. '*A* is more interesting than *B*, though I am more interested in *B* than in *A*' is a definitely meaningful proposition, and so is the proposition: 'This is a very interesting problem, though few have seemed to realize it so far.'

As regards the distinction between the special quality of interestingness and aesthetical value as such, a few examples may serve to prove it applicable. The point is not that the contrasting appraisals I am going to suggest are demonstrably true, or even tenable with a high degree of evidence, but that they can be suggested meaningfully and entirely within the bounds of reason, that they by no means sound odd or silly, and that they would obviously be subscribed to by a good many persons familiar with the subject. Gogol's *Dead Souls* is a great novel and supremely interesting, but owing to its crude structural imperfections and the clumsiness of some of its techniques it is far from being an unequivocally good novel; Goncharov's *Oblomov*, also a great novel, is a much finer work of art and on the whole a better novel, though comparatively tedious. Nothing Tolstoy ever wrote is even remotely as interesting as most of what Dostoevsky wrote; but very possibly *War and Peace* is a novel superior in artistic grandeur to any novel by Dostoevsky. Turgenev is vastly inferior in quality not only, I think, to Gogol, Dostoevsky and Tolstoy but even to Goncharov, yet I would venture to say that *Virgin Soil* and *Smoke* approach Gogol and Dostoevsky in interestingness. Goya is incomparably more interesting than Raphael or even Titian, but it might not unreasonably be held that Titian or even Raphael is a better artist than Goya. I can hardly imagine that anybody might find the *Venus of Milo* nearly so interesting as the Egyptian *Scribe*, but perhaps a number of experts, even today, would pronounce the *Venus of Milo* to be the finer statue.

Different people are interested, and paramountly interested, in widely different kinds of things. Therefore, *in spite of* the well-established distinction between 'what I am interested in' and 'what I hold to be interesting', there will also inevitably be a good deal of disagreement between people's *judgements* as to what is more and what is less interesting. But a further, and less trivial, difference is conceivable and, I feel certain, instantiated in reality. Different people also *care about* interestingness in markedly different degrees in seeking for objects, topics or presentations which *they* would themselves call 'interesting'. There is not the slightest paradox in saying that one man takes a greater and another a lesser interest in interestingness. It is a question not simply of *value* on the one hand and personal *opinion* (or scale of preference according to *objects*) on the other, but of *style* or taste. Of two Romanesque chapels X may prefer one and very likely also call it 'more interesting' while Y may take the opposite attitude; but Z may prefer a Renaissance palazzo to both while readily granting that it is less interesting than either. And I mean by his 'preferring' it not only his conviction that it is of greater aesthetic worth but his taking a more intense interest in it, yielding a stronger personal response to it, yet in a mode of experience not dominated by the feature of interestingness.

Herein lies an argument against relativism and in favour of the objective meaning of 'the interesting'. By recognizing the latter, while at the same time according preference to some other quality, the appraiser attests that it is not his preference, indeed not his actual 'taking an interest', that defines interestingness. There is an even more clear-cut and obvious disjunction between the interesting and that which we mean when we speak of somebody's 'interest' or 'interests', or of something 'being in his interest'. My attitude to some object may be completely *dis*interested yet at the same time utterly remote from *un*interested (only very illiterate writers tend to confuse these two words); something that has no bearing at all on my interests may greatly interest me. Inversely, my interest may compel me to turn my attention to some (e.g. financial) matter which, far from engaging my interest, plunges me in deadly boredom. ('Interesting' is a much less ambiguous word than 'interest', even though French businessmen may call a proposal worth consideration 'une proposition intéressante'.)*

If, as Kant suggests, the beautiful is that which pleases without appealing to the spectator's or hearer's 'interest', the interesting might be defined as that which evokes interest similarly without appealing to one's interests. That is what establishes the interesting as an *aesthetical* category. Of course 'interest'—in the sense expressed by the terms 'interested' and 'disinterested'—does not necessarily refer to primary urges and desires, welfare or power, etc.; it refers—I am speaking here as a disciple of Meinong and Professor Findlay—to whatever the subject would wish to come to be, to happen, to persist or to be secured: in a word, to whatever possesses an *existential* significance for him. My possible interest in having a certain Rembrandt in the National Gallery protected against thieves or iconoclasts, or even in acquiring a certain work of art for myself, is a true 'existential' interest, not a properly aesthetical interest (though dependent on an aesthetical interest; but it might more emphatically stand, say, for a patriotic or a self-seeking or snobbish interest). The non-existential character of the aesthetical interest is anyhow implied in the fact that the aesthetic appraiser is a pure 'spectator' or 'hearer', a pure sensuo-mental receptor, whereas for example the moral appraiser also harbours within him, be it ideally or virtually but none the less essentially, the roles of a claimant, a rewarder and an agent. And that non-existential character inherent in the aesthetical

---

* Cf. the Spanish proverb, 'Mande Pedro o mande Juan, lo interesante es cobrar': May Peter rule or John, what matters is to make money.

attitude is definitely proper also to the quality of interestingness. Our interest in the description of a cleverly devised crime springs from no interest on our part in the actual presence and prospering of efficient criminals; nor even is our interest in an ingenious piece of detection an expression of our practical interest in civic order and moral retribution. No doubt the latter does in part underlie the interestingness of the theme as a psychological background; but a similar connexion obtains no less in our appreciation of the beautiful. We admire a fine portrait of, say, a tattered beggar without wishing for the prevalence in our world of destitution, though we in fact might prefer the sight, in actual reality, of 'characteristic' faces, marked with some traces of suffering, to an ubiquitous smile of shallow satiety; but the delight we take in a good representation of, say, lovely flowers, vigorous and graceful animals, or winsome maidens, is likely to be reinforced by the desire many of us may feel for the actual occurrence of such objects in our environment.

2. SUBJECTIVITY AND INTELLECTUALITY

'I find it interesting' and 'I find it beautiful' (or 'sublime', or artistically 'good') seem, then, to be judgements on the same axiological footing, embodying the same claim to objectivity however subjectively conditioned both are; and interest in the sense of pleasurable response to the interesting is a state of mind in the subject, but so are other— more 'standard'—modalities of aesthetic enjoyment. And yet there are some considerations that may lend colour to the suggestion that perhaps the experience of the interesting reveals, as it were, a surplus of subjectivity. I find myself more able to imagine a world purged of human minds of which it would still make sense to say that it contained beauty than a similar world to be credited with any interesting features. Far be it from me summarily to identify beauty with something like a 'harmonious structure' or 'the perfect unfolding of a nature'; but it just *might* be that what we currently *mean* by beauty has some such or kindred connotations; whereas if we think of objective traits sometimes implied in the context of interestingness (e. g. eventful, strange, mysterious, many-sided, etc.) while excluding any reference to the interest they are likely to evoke, the 'exciting' impression they are calculated to arouse, it would seem to be as pointless to pin on them the label 'interesting' as it would be vacuous to call certain substances 'diuretics' in a universe in which no organisms with renal functions existed. Whatever problems of theology (or of the critique of theology) such a remark may involve, it would appear to be more natural to suppose that God, to Whom we attribute cognition and evaluation but no psychic *condition*, is pleased with the beauty of a landscape or a human countenance than to suppose that He is thrilled by the exposition of an interesting plot. Granting that values and valuations are necessarily interdependent, value-concepts in general—at any rate the classic, standard and established value categories—direct our glance to the values or goods themselves, as a 'term' and 'place of repose' for the appreciative mind, rather than to the mind with its evaluative acts and emotive resonances; on the contrary, although an interesting object or experience may absorb the mind more completely than the admirable or the lovable as such, the *concept* of the interesting directs our attention to the mind's being interested as well as to the interestingness of the object and the features underlying it.

Perhaps this has to do with the prominence of interesting activities, e.g. games or sometimes work, or more generally of interesting situations, in which the subject is engaged—in spite of the full possibility of a purely contemplative experience of interesting objects. Notwithstanding the sharp cleavage between the practical and the aesthetical (mental, contemplative, and non-existential) meaning of 'interest'—in other words, the disinterested apprehension of interestingness—in the very idea of the interesting there survives a vestigial reference to subjective interest in its undivided sense and a certain contrast with the straightforward object-emphasis of properly appreciative concepts. Undeniably we think of, say, *Hamlet* or of El Greco's fantastic city of Toledo as 'interesting' independently of whether or not we exist to register their interestingness and be thrilled and upset by them; but we still conceive of them, more than of the beauty of any poem or place or animal body, also in terms of subjective response. We might put it as follows. In our appreciative response to beauty, or value or excellence in the distinctive sense of the word, we are in a certain fashion 'subjugated', 'compelled', and thrust into sheer receptivity; whereas our fascination by the interesting might rather be described in some such words as being *entangled*, however non-existentially, in a developing situation or, as it were, in a web of interacting objects of our attention. Accordingly, and in contrast with the case of beauty, narrative literature rather than the fine arts constitutes the standard artistic field of the interesting (I will not risk any conjecture about music), and there is also a close link between the dimension of the interesting and the domain of *history*. The *Oxford English Dictionary* tells us that the word 'interesting' is traceable back to 1711 but appears to have lost its primary meaning ('that concerns, touches, or affects; important') by 1813 and taken on its present meaning ('adapted to excite interest; of interest') about 1768 but more conspicuously ('an interesting conversation') since about 1843: the parallelism with the rise of historical consciousness is striking. In classic aesthetical theory the concept of the interesting has to my knowledge received little or no attention; and I suppose that the theme must have been peculiarly alien to Graeco-Roman antiquity.

Again, to feel interested and respond to something interesting is a more reflective attitude than the enjoyment of beauty and response to value as such; by no means necessarily more conscious but more conscious of self. Therefore it is, in one sense, more intellectual: not more 'rational' or more susceptible of intellectual elaboration, but of necessity more intimately interfused with thinking. Thus while the simple perception of a shade of colour, to a large extent even outside its possible context, may convey an experience of beauty, to find just one shade of colour as such 'interesting' is a marginal, un-paradigmatic experience of interestingness. Inversely, while we may call a mathematical deduction 'beautiful'—more often the word 'elegant' would be used—this implies a somewhat extended meaning of that concept, and we hardly ever speak of a beautiful problem or discussion but all the more often and naturally of an interesting problem, an interesting discussion or an interesting topic. We further speak of a beautiful friendship but of an interesting situation; or, in regard to a book, of a beautiful style but an interesting (basic) idea or an interesting plot (though in most cases of art-appraisal we may apply the general value-word 'good'). It might perhaps be said that response to the interesting more inevitably connotes a 'cerebral' aspect. But it might no less aptly be said to connote a 'motoric' aspect. *Any* value-experience may, of course, invite us to analyse it, start us thinking, confront us with a problem, or set up in us a change of attitude; the difference is only that puzzlement, thinking or mental stirring of some kind, e.g. a sudden recognition, seem to constitute not mere optional accompaniments of our awareness of the interesting but a condition of its coming to be fully constituted. A mental 'movement' of some such kind enters into the the theme of the experience of interestingness and is part of the very stuff of its object.

3. ASPECTS OF THE INTERESTING

If we candidly ask the question: 'What kinds of things, or topics, are interesting?' we at once come across what I have called the surplus of subjectivity on the side of interestingness as contrasted with beauty or similar qualities. On both sides there are, of course, different degrees of sensibility and, again, divergences of taste; but beyond that a man's selective interests also depend decisively, in a way quite unlike any analogous determination of his sense of beauty, on his personal *history*. Any unfamiliar, exotic product of nature or work of art may strike him immediately, at first acquaintance, as superbly beautiful or exquisite—be it, for example, Persian flowers or carpets, Negro earthenware, or apricots from Hungary or Murcia. To be sure, there are many 'acquired tastes' and discernments taught and developed; but from the moment in early adulthood when my eyes were opened to architectural beauty, it has never, be it ever so faintly, occurred me that, say, the nineteenth-century sham-Gothic church *Votivkirche* in Vienna might in any conceivable sense be more beautiful than (or at all commensurable to) *Maria am Gestade*, a recondite Gothic jewel in the old core of that city which I discovered ten years after first 'admiring' the impressively situated *Votivkirche* as a child. Admittedly our history exerts, casually speaking, a good deal of influence on our tastes; many of our appreciations are firmly sustained and indefectible owing to their early establishment and long standing. But the historical conditioning of our *interests* has a status nearer to logical quasi-evidence. To be uninterested in what one is specifically connected with by actually subsisting ties or by familiarity and memories seems unnatural to the point of absurdity. A painting done by a person whom I have more or less intimately known need not for that reason delight me more or appear to me intrinsically better than other paintings of about equal merit by artists who are complete strangers to me; but how could I help taking a greater, or rather a superadditive, interest in it? Not that our interests cannot change, or that a new interest cannot overgrow an old one; not that a distinctive interest cannot spring from the subject's character or constitution rather than from environmental influence, habitual or functional contact, or historical accident. But any given and traditional nexus is invested with a *prima facie* priority of interest over new and adventitious objects, and is unlikely actually to vanish (as our appreciations, tastes and beliefs do sometimes vanish suddenly or fade out in the course of time). Whatever I can *place* in some more or less familiar context is *a priori* certain to interest me more, other things being equal, than whatever I cannot so place or can only fit into my framework of past experience in an utterly vague and hazy fashion.

The question: 'What is interesting?' is not thereby answered, far from it; a presentation or a resurgence of what is already well known is not as such interesting. But the feature of familiarity provides one starting-point, notably for the interpretation of a person's selective interests. I may not, for example, be greatly interested in the politics or the history of my country of origin or of the country to which I now belong; but these are at any rate likely to interest me more than the politics or history of most other countries, and to interest me for ever to some extent; I could not, on the other hand, suddenly take an interest in Chinese matters as I could suddenly fall in love with a Chinese vase (even if I had seen none so far). Again the presentation of an alien subject-matter will gain strikingly in interest by virtue of *references* to a familiar and intelligible setting or system of co-ordinates. Let us recall once more the primary meaning of 'interest': my 'being affected' by something. Anything I find beautiful or well executed *may* indeed affect me powerfully, though (as such) non-existentially; but what is 'interesting *to me*' affects me in a somewhat closer sense of the word, i.e. in a sense more closely related to my existential concerns—my wishes and fears. In the pattern of my distinctive (though, in themselves, non-practical) interests, a focal part is played by what *must* affect me, as it were, in view of the *circumstances* of my life.

This rather trivial point of view is applicable, in a somewhat toned-down way, even to the *general* question as to what kinds of things are interesting. The interest of people as spectators, hearers or readers is, on the whole, aroused by topics relevant to human concerns and passions. Whatever typically and conspicuously moves men and stirs their souls—meaning, not all men at all times, but vast categories of men and permanent potentialities of human nature—is *per se* calculated to catch our imaginative attention and may be found 'objectively interesting'. Thus themes such as love and hatred, antagonisms and reconciliations, uniting and dividing aspirations, dangers and escapes, sore straits and ingenious solutions, institutional pressures and personal reactions, chance and destiny, projects and adventures, turning-points and developing situations, the surging of forces and their containment or equilibrium, etc. Obviously, what I have been trying to do here is to indicate a certain minimum of interest-conditions rather than to penetrate into the core of interestingness. A thematic approach of this kind, again, tells us little or nothing about the features that lend interestingness to a landscape or a city. It will be objected, further, that a literary (or otherwise de-existentialized) theme is not necessarily interesting in proportion as it refers back to urgent vital interests of men which may have figured in the forefront of our own practical attention and might come to be actualized in the course of our own life. How a man threatened by starvation tried to earn a living, or the cure of a severely ill patient, perhaps even the finding of a mate by a lonely person, the establishment of legal order in a place smitten with anarchy, or the moral reform of an evil-doer, may provide no more than moderately interesting themes. Nor are a hundred thousand casualties in a war *per se* more interesting than a mere hundred. Suffice it to say here that there appears to be a special problem of *transferability* to the mental ('spectatorial' or imaginative) plane of urgent and generally shareable concerns.

I now propose to list five standard aspects of the interesting. Such descriptive classifications have always something random and arbitrary about them; the qualities listed have partly been hinted at already; they are partly overlapping; the enumeration is not exhaustive; on the other hand the qualities listed are in some measure relevant to the aesthetics of literature as such, not merely to the problem of interestingness. Again, I am hardly able to say what *further* conditions are required to make an event, a plot, a narrative or a mode of presentation—or perhaps a work of visual art—which possesses all or some of these qualities *really* interesting to a significant number of more or less qualified hearers or appraisers. But at least I feel sure that the features I am recording do not express personal predilections of mine but would fairly commonly be recognized as aspects of the 'objectively interesting'.

(a) The unfamiliar, the surprising, the abnormal, the eccentric including the 'exotic', briefly the *extraordinary*, provides one standard constituent of the interesting. The domain of the weird, ghostly and preternatural may be mentioned as a classic embodiment of the extraordinary, though it equally falls under the heading (b). It is psychologically quasi-evident that the extraordinary, the unfamiliar, etc., should arouse attention, seeing that all perception presupposes contrast and that whatever is striking, strange and unexpected or improbable, yet real or present, commands some kind of re-orientation on the subject's part. It may signalize a danger which has to be parried, and may be said to act in a 'provocative' fashion. Yet is this not in flagrant contradiction with what we said earlier—that a person is primarily interested in what is *familiar*, known, intelligible and somehow linked or near to *him*? I would suggest that by 'extraordinary', as an aspect of the interesting, that kind of remote, unfamiliar or alien object (or feature or pattern) should be understood which *intrudes* into the normal and accustomed order of things. In the case of arousing a personal interest the intrusion is due to the actual course of events, e.g. something highly improbable comes true within my habitual medium or life or the public pattern of the world I live in; in the case of the objectively interesting, e.g. of a ghost story or a novel of adventure, it is the work of an appropriate technique of presentation. The experience of the extraordinary implies a background of order; and the unfamiliar becomes interesting not as an absolute stranger outside our ken but as a stranger who, so to speak, forces an entrance into the family. In other words interestingness attaches to the *tension* arising from the meeting, clash, or confluence between what is habitual, known and established in *some* sense and what 'strikingly' defies or 'mysteriously' alters the familiar setting.

(b) *Mysterious* matters or situations, in the widest sense of the term (embracing the mystical, the elusive, the problematic, the puzzling, etc., down to the so-called mystery novel), furnish a staple instance of the interesting. They ruffle the surface of calm monotony, pierce the routine-like accustomed order of things, arouse an awareness of unexpected vulnerability, and set thinking (an emotively tinged thinking) in motion. But this again supposes a given context of familiarity, knowledge, and some kind of fairly general 'appeal', i.e. a substratum of intrinsic, primary 'interest' taken in the object. The man-in-the-street, chastely unaware of the taunts held in store for some of us by the theory of numbers, is not thrilled by the *Fermat major* still awaiting its general proof, and would not be interested even though the terms of the problem were made intelligible to him; crime 'mysteries' mostly revolve round one or several murders: the skilful theft of a five-pound note would hardly do. For ignorance to pass into puzzle or mystery a horizon of knowledge is necessary; the inexplicable is only interesting in virtue of its emergence within an apparently foolproof pattern of explanation; mysteries only 'baffle' a mind sufficiently attracted by their content or implications to be set on their unravelling. The mere fact that I do not know why somebody is smiling does not account for the quality of an 'enigmatic smile'. Finally mystical events and influences surmised in actual experience or somehow credibly presented by art, as also mystical states of mind or moods induced in whatever way, owe their peculiar quality and inherent interestingness not to their mere irrationality or impenetrability but to a codified or a vague but in any case ingrained human belief[1]—even though reduced, in many individual minds, to the status of a quasi-belief—in the existence of suprasensible realities and in their accessibility, however limited,[2] to men's cognitive powers. Sheer passivity and impotence on the receptor's part would not allow the tension required for the phenomenon of the interesting to be generated. Objectivized types of the 'mysteriously interesting', such as the *sfumato* and *morbidezza* in pictorial art, imply a penumbra in which contours are still discernible; the heaping up of massive obscurities or stark absurdities results in uninterestingness. Darkness is interesting not inasmuch as it forbids but inasmuch as it challenges the lust of exploring, and disorder not as a whirlpool of absolute randomness but as allowing one to guess at the veiled outlines of some elements of a hidden and perhaps 'higher' order.

(c) *Movement* is certainly fundamental to the interesting, although of course it depends on various factors how far the perception of movement is likely to communicate it to the perceiving mind itself, to 'engage' the latter as it were or entice it into participating in its rhythm. Breathless speed, pauseless action and a crowded flux of multiple impressions may easily produce a self-defeating effect. None the less, the presentation of majestic or idyllic stillness, unless used as a foil for the contrasting theme of some intense dynamism, is definitely at variance with any emphasis on the interesting; it may have great aesthetic value and achieve a compelling effect but it is not in terms of interestingness that its appeal would be described. (There are many things we either deeply and devoutly appreciate or intensely enjoy, things fully satisfying in some sense, which we do not experience as typically 'interesting'.) The interesting affects us, not in a characteristically sustaining or 'fulfilling' or pleasing or convincing or persuasive, but in a characteristically stimulating and 'seductive' fashion. What it tends to accomplish is not so much our lover-like spiritual communion with an object or our awareness of a significance (even endowed with a high emotive charge) as our imaginary *displacement* into another *medium*. By an 'imaginary' displacement I do not mean a hypothetical, a Utopian, an ecstatic or a self-reformatory transposition or conversion but an adventurous 'straying into' an unexplored district which thrusts itself upon our attention: we do not shift our position in the sense of a mental experiment or a practical act but allow ourselves to be enchanted away into an imaginary department of our world, which thus itself takes on a somehow modified colouring and flavour. Consciousness of 'straying' is part of the experience, and the 'new medium' must itself be a mobile one to exercise its pull and induce us to eddy our way into its currents. It is also preferably contiguous and communicating with our everyday world so its 'seduction' may reach us well 'at home' and set us on our journey. It is, further, worth noting that the more developed (and philosophic) mind is less responsive than the more immature to blatant newness and strangeness; it is more attracted by recurrences of familiarity in the changed medium itself, expects it to shed a 'new light' on *the* world as a whole, and is aware of every worth-while journey's being in some sense, to speak with Novalis, a 'homeward' journey. Anyhow mobility seen in the perspective of the interesting means the maintenance of a tension rather than the snapping of a cord; not a leap into disconnected alienness but the embodiment of that interplay of familiarity and unfamiliarity which was last discussed. That mobility, beyond the domains of actual history, narration, play-acting and music, is in some form also represented in various objects at rest in the static visual arts (including architecture) needs no stressing.

(d) The place filled in the context of the interesting by *manifoldness* should be obvious in the light of the above considerations: contrast, distinctions, tension, mobility, and the transitions and fluctuations between the old and the new, the intimately known and the unknown lands, crude novelty and the reawakening of dormant memories, etc., are all linked to it. Uniformity or monotony, on the other hand, is known to be the very soul of boredom. Some might even go to the length of criticizing this statement as tautological. I would not wholly agree for, although a suggestion of monotony may be present in every experience of boredom, yet individual objects, persons, utterances or sights may not only irk but bore us without being expressly or conspicuously repetitive. Again, while as a rule it is hilly, broken and chequered (*accidentés*) landscapes that strike us as peculiarly interesting, some kinds of vast monotonous flatlands may not always bore the spectator and many a one might even find them more interesting than a gently undulating, tame countryside. Manifoldness that lacks the aspects of antithesis, sharp contours and significant distinctness is apt to arouse an impression of triviality. Attention is often more interestingly, more 'stirringly' focused on significant differences against a background of scarcity of features, i.e. of a comparative monotony, than in the midst of exuberant variety. With an eye on interestingness, Heraclitus's splendid phrase: 'Better is hidden than manifest harmony' might equally be applied to *dis*harmony. It remains none the less true that the quest for monistic simplification, whether in a religious and metaphysical or in a scientific, technological and utilitarian guise—but the two contrary tints have a tendency to intermix—is utterly antagonistic to interestingness. The same frigid boredom emanates from Spinoza's conceptual pantheism, Parmenides's construction of a single and undivided Reality in the shape of a Perfect Sphere, and similar monsters of philosophers' inanity including Aristotle's 'God', the self-contemplating 'Cause' (likewise 'unmoved') as well as its Scholastic elaborations, modern irreligious materialism in its various dressings, and the Perfection-nightmares of Utopian speculation. One eminent and imaginative Utopian, Fourier, was indeed keenly aware of this and proposed to incapsulate in the construction of his Phalanstery some provisions expressly designed to satisfy the deep-rooted human need for variety and 'flutter'. But analogously to the ascetical rejection of pleasure and the 'Puritanical' distrust of beauty, both ever-recurrent with varying emphases, there also seems to be implanted in human nature an explicit abhorrence of the interesting and preference for boredom—perhaps not wholly useless as a regulative counterpoise in view of the obvious dangers attaching to unbridled *Reizhunger* (craving for excitement).

(e) Features such as *originality*, marked characteristics of an individual object, vividness, concreteness, a 'peculiar flavour', etc., are generally considered to be salient aspects of the interesting. Usually, in the modern age at least, representations obviously allegorical affect us with tedium whereas symbols which signify more than their surface meaning and character yet do so in a unique and somehow untranslatable fashion—possessing 'a life of their own', and bearers of an autonomous reality beyond their semantic function—may greatly add to the interestingness of a work of art. The interestingness of persons similarly depends on the authenticity of their experience, the individual emphasis and zest exhibited by their attitudes (as opposed to presenting a mere instance of conventional and calculable 'group' or 'class' qualities and principles of behaviour) and the sense of irreducible 'thisness' they evoke—to use a key concept of Duns Scotus, the philosophical upholder of an *interesting* kind of world as against the Hellenistic repose in abstractions more or less typified by Aquinas. The linkage of originality and individuality with the previously discussed marks of novelty or transcendence of a customary order, movement and manifoldness is patent enough; it should be noted, however, that a realistic 'three-dimensional' elaboration of the individual may tend to bar the way to every innuendo of transcendence, to strengthen the impression of a self-contained massive reality of earthly and everyday life, and thus to blight the interest-appeal conveyed by vivid picturing as such. It is not the crude and cussèd impermeability of individual things or persons in itself that is interesting; rather it is the changed light in which the world may appear in virtue of their irruption into its texture and of the discovery that our ordinary conceptual apparatuses are not wholly equal to dealing with them. A mere anarchical squirming of figures without intelligibility, unaccountable in terms of rational and conventional categories, is no more interesting than a plot steeped in banality and plausibility and is powerless even to yield the subaltern interest and shallow diversion which the latter may provide. In other words I would submit that nothing is interesting in its isolated selfhood and total lack of interchangeability[3] and that the individual, the original, the eccentric or the irreducible is interesting *as a feature of the world*: in that it presents the world as an interesting place, indissoluble in a ready-made schematism of concepts and categories, and abounding in hidden adits to unfamiliar chambers. Strange singularities are interesting inasmuch as they remind us that we live in a world familiar yet unexhausted, shot through with the transparency and lure of its out-of-the-way modifications towards which its own laws and pressures may convey us: an *ambit* rather than a Parmenidean spherical orbit.

4. IS THERE A CENTRAL PRINCIPLE OF INTERESTINGNESS?

I am raising the question without daring to propose a conclusive answer. It has, I hope, been shown that several things can with some measure of pertinence be said about the interesting and that there is a certain consonance between them; but I feel that no definition of it would have any chance of proving indefeasible. No matter how acceptable a suggested criterion might sound and how expressively it might seem to condense various relevant points of view into a common concept, it would still be possible that by that criterion *A* ought to be a great deal more interesting than *B* but that in fact most of us would find *B* vastly more interesting than *A*. Tentatively, however, I would incline to look for the key concept of interestingness in the experiential mode of *transcendence*. That is to say, transcendence *of a kind*: the qualification is necessary, for 'transcendence' is not meant to point, in this context, to a higher and 'supernatural' level of being as in the religious context, nor to the explanatory 'true' reality behind apparent reality as in the context of metaphysics or of scientific hypotheses of causation, nor again to a mere exploration or imaginative production of other and alien empirical worlds beyond the pale of ours. (That these motifs may indeed carry a charge of interestingness is not, of course, thereby denied.[4]) It is not so much the 'other world'—in any sense—that glimmers with the light of the interesting but rather the passage of our glance to it and back to the ordinary reality which is our solid habitat—the chink in the wall rather than what lies on the other side of the wall. Interestingness attaches to our experiencing the fact that this world is so made as to render it possible for us to look beyond it; to stray, in fantasy, beyond its fragile and tremulous frontiers into outlying twilight zones. In other words interestingness is an aesthetical, non-existential, quality; it is only marginally that it touches on the problems of transcendence in their really serious sense, involving the concepts of belief, rational argument and extension of fact-knowledge. It clings to our vision of objects rather than to introspection or the endeavour to brighten our own mood, yet it does so with an emphasis on our own subjective condition and imaginative movement. Whether *The Wild Duck* is one of the greatest plays ever written I do not presume to judge, but I think it is certainly one of the most interesting. An Austrian critic once observed that the real hero of *The Wild Duck* was not Hjalmar Ekdal, Gregers Werle, or even little Hedvig, but Hjalmar's ghostly father, old 'Lieutenant' Ekdal, if not the lame-winged wild duck itself, and ultimately landed at the shocking conclusion that perhaps the true hero was not even either of these but the hidden lumber-room in the garret, the magic realm of the simple-minded disgraced old man and the wounded wild bird (and in the third place, of Hedvig, also a kind of banished princess). However preposterous as it stands, the remark nevertheless supplies a key to the bewitching magic of *The Wild Duck*. To be sure, unless its life were geared to the classic vital problems and moral conflicts of the foreground figures (Hjalmar and his wife, Gregers and his father, etc.), an untidy garret-room harbouring a downtrodden old nincompoop and another damaged old bird would not even be particularly interesting, much less the 'hero' of a drama; but as an undisplayed background focus of the actual story it confers upon its tragic course (steeped in bitter comic) a supreme glamour of magical interest. The ghostly core, not to say the unreal nerve, of reality is what supplies it with its dimension of absorbing interestingness.

If the 'transport' hinted at and in a way effected by the interesting must not, then, be confused with the full primordial meaning of 'transcendence' but should be seen as belonging, in the main, to the aesthetical level of quasi-transcendence, it should on the other hand also be distinguished from the psychic function and experiential mode of mere entertainment. Undoubtedly, and not without reason, the word 'interesting' is often used as a synonym of 'amusing', just as it is often used to designate what is spiritually, intellectually or morally important—deep-reaching, far-reaching, abounding in implications. But these are improper or, as it would more properly be said nowadays, marginal or non-paradigmatic uses of it. We may take a great interest in the reception of a divine message or the elucidation of a momentous problem; but here is not the central locus of our experience of the interesting. Again entertainment or amusement (the latter word suggests in English, I think, a slightly more vulgar note) seems to captivate us in much the same way as a characteristically 'interesting' object or activity. Yet there is a difference, I contend, not only as regards the height or wealth of the respective contents but as regards the structure of the phenomenon. Pure entertainment definitely leaves the world exactly the same place as it is; that indeed, forms part of its recreative function. It may be said to 'transport' us into an imaginary world of unproblematic repose with the quasi-implication—neatly ordained to our momentary condition *alone*, altogether dissevered from our actual interpretation of things—of a world with which 'all is right', which needs no search, solicitude or decisive response on our part. But in that kind of transport no transcendence in any sense of the word is implied; we retire, as it were, into a cosy and sheltered corner of the world where no kind of tension or dialogue with our current world as a whole intervenes; we are not engaged in a movement of quasi-transcendence. The weight of things is not here subtilized and tentatively juggled with, but discarded (or else, extrinsically, presupposed as it actually is in our everyday medium, or determined by arbitrary stipulation as happens in games). Whereas our contact with the interesting necessarily sets us thinking, though it is not thinking methodically, responsibly or 'to a purpose'. However inseparably tied to our own subjective condition as part of its very theme, the interesting tends to exercise an *oblique impact*, as it were, on our interpretation of the real world—as a backwash of its imaginative extension, supplementation and (partial) overturn. So far as a piece of entertainment involves a system of fanciful illusions, e.g. that the 'Queen' is superior to the 'Knave' and so on, the illusion is tagged on to our experience of the world; whereas the fanciful illusion underlying the effect of the 'interesting' somehow, in a shadow-like way, *penetrates* the tissue of the world we live in by inserting into it a peculiar super-additive off-world in which we also live (according to the mode of an imaginative and emotive quasi-life). In the literary context, let us compare a good conventional detective story, a self-contained plot inventively thought out and skilfully told, with a properly interesting novel in which crime and its discovery or punishment plays a significant part: various works, say, of Dostoevsky, Dickens and Stevenson. (The *Sherlock Holmes* stories, to which as a whole I would ascribe a saga-like poetic value, or the *Maigret* cycle with its unmistakably poetic distinctive atmosphere, may be regarded as border-line cases, if not as exquisite literary creations in a minor key.) On the level of the merely entertaining crime story the functional machinery of the plot is everything; the adjuncts of verisimilitude and characterization are no more than necessary ingredients in the set scene of its display and the devices of style no more than drops of oil to sweeten its creaking. In the genuinely interesting 'creative' story, on the contrary, apart from the serious thought-content the details—characters, situations, moods, landscapes, etc.—possess an autonomous life; mostly attuned but seldom simply subordinated to the plot or its climactic fulfilment, they claim attention on their own merits. They do not merely presuppose the actual world but represent facets of it and constitute a collateral foreshortened world of their own; not just an articulated unit of happening but a para-mundane medium of experience. As contrasted with the exposition and solution of a puzzle, the unrolling of a preconceived plan or the application of a functional stimulus, they manifest a tentative sub-creation of a world heaving with freedom and destiny, of a play of forces triumphant and curbed, briefly of a kind of history.

Both the *fantastic* and the *comic* stand for modes of experience closely akin to interestingness in that each in its way embodies a classic solvent of the massive density of 'the' world as a rigidified structure, and conveys an image or an innuendo of 'transcendence'. But neither the images of unbridled extra-mundane speculation or fantasy nor insulated comic effects and sustained humoristic perspectives are typical carriers of interestingness: for however strong the 'movement' they may induce, they tend to hit, touch, overwhelm or tickle the receiving mind rather than entangle it in the 'mobile medium' of a peculiar quasi-reality. It would seem that the comparatively immature mind—in the different senses of this highly ambiguous concept: the 'primitive', the pre-Christian and the premodern, and again the crude and uneducated but also the polished yet shallow or desiccated type of mind—is more responsive either to the rankly fantastical, the grossly eccentric and the totally unrealistic or to the pointedly and deliberately comic (or both) than the highly civilized mind endowed with a fine aesthetic perception, and more prone to confuse them with the interesting as such, or less keenly yearning for the interesting as a distinct quality. The novel, the principal area of the interesting, is the modern artistic accomplishment *par excellence*, though it descends from medieval and even late Hellenistic ancestors; and Voltaire's anathema on *le genre ennuyeux*— not very faithfully observed by his contemporaries or by himself— would have surprised the Middle Ages and might not have been explainable at all to the classical Greeks. Perhaps it is the nineteenth century and especially its twentieth-century prolongation up to the Great War that marks the acme of men's interest in the interesting (along with their interest in history). Again, today, in the age of technological neo-barbarism as manifested and symbolized, preeminently, by the cinematographic vision of things, narrative art appears to be decaying owing indeed to its being *rejected*; men still look by no means merely for pleasures and entertainment but also for some kinds of thrills, ecstasies and 'uplift', but they have largely lost, I am inclined to think, their former sensitivity to the interesting: that may be the reason why a number of them seem to be able to read Kierkegaard, a task few people would brave in his own time and for generations more. It is true that much in recent philosophy strikes me as more interesting than the doctrines that predominated in the nineteenth century and their lingering survivals; but the impact of Phenomenology (and kindred currents) derives from the later nineteenth and early twentieth century, and the interestingness of late-Wittgensteinian British philosophizing is mainly due to its aspects originating from Moore and Cook Wilson, which points in the same direction.

REFERENCES

[1] Not only does interestingness require a plausible presentation of the imaginary, but even the critical raising of the problem of factual truth—the theme of belief and disbelief—may heighten the interestingness of a situation. Cf. the scene of Thomas the Apostle ('the Doubter') testing the lethal wounds on Jesus's body after His resurrection (John xx. 24–28).

[2] That limitation is intrinsically necessary; but for it, the very concept of the supernatural would lack meaning and all imagery underlain by it would lose its spell. A free and cheap use of it cannot but produce a jejune and uninteresting impression.

[3] Moore's great motto borrowed from Butler, 'Every thing is what it is and not another thing', apart from its value as a noble philosopher's battle-cry against the fallacies of reductionism, expresses a plea for an *interesting* world. It needs, however, some counterpoise. Indeed a thing is what it is, not 'just' a manifestation of another thing or of any conjunction of other things; but neither is it 'just' what it is. Rather, it would not be *it* unless it also had its place in the context of an indefinite number of other things and represented a world of correlations, similitudes and contrasts, conditions, tendencies, etc.

[4] What makes *Dr. Jekyll and Mr. Hyde* supremely interesting is its *moral point*: that fact that Jekyll is not indefinitely free to play Hyde and reconvert himself into Jekyll as he pleases, but has doomed himself to become submerged in Hydeness—illustrating, as Chesterton rightly insisted, the truth that man is *not* 'two' but one, and thus inwardly *torn* between antagonistic principles of good and evil.

Vulgarity*

JOHN BAYLEY

'I wish,' said Lionel Johnson, 'that those who deny the possibility of an eternity of punishment would realize their unspeakable vulgarity.' A perverse comment certainly, whether entertainingly or merely exasperatingly so will depend on our point of view. But it shows the subjective depths into which a once robustly descriptive word has fallen. The vulgar once signified the mass of the population whose behaviour, beliefs and prejudices, unaffected by scepticism and self-consciousness, presented an unambiguous appearance to the gentle observer. But the vulgar of yesterday becomes the polite and pretentious of today. The word loses its confident status: it no longer signifies those people over there, but these persons among us here. It acquires meanings that are provisional, defensive, patronizingly enthusiastic, or resentful. But in one respect its usage remains unchanged. It is a word that can be applied to other people only, not to oneself. We cannot, unless we have the more than Teutonic self-possession of George Eliot's Herr Klesmer, say: 'I am humorous.' 'I am vulgar' is also not a possible pronouncement in the way that 'I am jealous' or 'I am mean' is.

Oscar Wilde noted this when he observed that: 'Vulgar behaviour is the behaviour of other people.' It belongs to that rare class of words which cannot be evaded by the person to whom they are applied, since he cannot by definition realize why they are applied. If he could, he would cease to be vulgar and become something else. The awareness of vulgarity is the achievement of sophistication. John Betjeman is not a vulgar but a sophisticated poet. His poems, and perhaps the stories of Angus Wilson, have deliberately taken our

* Read to The British Society of Aesthetics, 1 April, 1964.

measure; they make a virtue out of the fact that they might be thought vulgar. So do certain advertising techniques. They exhibit themselves to us with a knowing wink, seeming to say: 'I am not so awful as I look,' or rather: 'I know I am awful so it's no good your thinking I am.' But this is a very particular kind of sophistication, a way of escaping being labelled by fixing the label on oneself. Vulgarity in its proper sense is one of the few attributes that one cannot, in any spirit, claim.

We observers who decree who the vulgar are, and why, divide them—though we may not do so consciously—into two categories. The first we can, and do, safely approve of. Music-hall turns, jolly landladies, waltzes by Offenbach, pictures made of shells and hair (the preservation of hair is for some reason always vulgar: compare Byron's vulgar habit of keeping a lock from each of his mistresses), American cars and opulent interiors—the list could be indefinitely extended. We might call all of them deliciously vulgar. In our appreciation is a strong element of patronage, because they are right outside us, have no connexion with us (heaven forbid!) and hence can be enjoyed quite dispassionately and for their own sake. A knowing Englishman can enjoy this kind of vulgarity as a knowing Russian might enjoy *póshlost*, or a German *kitsch*—two terms which correspond pretty exactly to our first category of the vulgar. We do not give away anything by liking it except our broadmindedness, our humanity, our readiness to be pleased—things which no one minds revealing. Much art and would-be art can be appraised in this comfortable way. The point is that though the object doesn't necessarily know its place, *we* do. The characters of Dickens are often so enjoyed—even by one person at least (his mother) who had served him unawares as a model. But we could hardly do this to Rubens or Stravinsky, or D. H. Lawrence. Whatever we feel about their art we could not be quite comfortable about it; it gets inside us to the point where we cannot but wonder what our reception of it will reveal about ourselves. We *might* call it vulgar, but then this comment would disclose something not so much about it as about us.

And this brings us to the second category, the class of things and beings to whom we apply the word 'vulgar' either because they cause a loss of self-confidence in us or because we detect the absence of self-confidence in them. It is a reaction in which comfortable patronage is replaced by cruelty, and perhaps uneasiness (the latter sharpening the former). In its most upright form it is a distressed awareness of things and people being not what they are (i.e. what we think they should be) but trying to be something different, and failing. It is a reaction to anarchy and nullity. We might call it feudal, in the sense that in a feudal system everything and everybody has a place and a character of their own. But now the rich man doesn't know how to behave like one; the parson and the theologian discard the traditional beliefs and behaviour of their status and try to be 'like everyone else'; the artist has no confidence in himself and his own powers but substitutes for them some theory which brings machinery into his studio, which fills his pictures with squares of plain black paint and his novels with four-letter words. All this might be taken to mean: 'Am I anything? Is anything anything?' And that is what it means to the person who surveys all these lacks and hesitations, these substitutions and evasions and mere nothingnesses, and says: 'Really, what unspeakable vulgarity!'

Such a person is indicating, with the handiest term of dislike available, his sense of unease before a kind of nullity, of things pretending to be what they are not, or trying to find something to *be*. The paradox is that the term 'vulgar' is used in two opposite senses: in an uneasy way for things that are not there, and in a happy way for things that are all too much there. 'How vulgar!' can be a cry of panic and resentment, or of triumph and content. Of all possible terms in a vocabulary of aesthetics it is perhaps the most ambiguous.

And yet it would be a pity to abandon it, for its very ambiguity tells us a great deal about the processes of appreciation. The first category of the vulgar goes with the notion of *taste*. Bad taste or good, but still taste, and indeed if a thing is capable of *tasting* to us, and we of tasting it, can it be bad, or we be wrong? A person or thing with 'character', as the house-agents say, may belong to the first category of vulgarity but never to the second. And if the work of art we are appraising has a taste, a *goût*, a *geschmack*, like nothing else, we are inclined to take it seriously even if we do not care for the taste—

perhaps, indeed, we try and get a taste for it. Whatever has a flavour of its own is likely to be good in some sense. 'There is,' says Hazlitt of Lamb's style, 'an inward unction, a marrowy vein both in the thought and the feeling, that carries off any quaintness or awkward-ness.' Taste again—the gastronomical element in the metaphor is significant. Tolstoy often conveys a powerful individuality in terms of smell. 'The whole room, especially near the old man,' he says of Uncle Eroshka in *The Cossacks*, 'was filled with that strong but not unpleasant mixture of smells—wine, vodka, sweat, gunpowder, and congealed blood—that he always carried about with him.' Tolstoy connects this physical aroma with the *thereness* of the old man, his individuality which can only be expressed in terms of itself. The old man says: 'When you die the grass will grow on your grave and that's all'—but when Tolstoy repeats this comment back to him he refuses to recognize it as his own. If he said it, it was as a part of him, and not something which he was capable of detaching from himself and examining or of acknowledging in the mouth of another. Tolstoy conveys this whole and involuntary individuality in terms of its smell, its taste.

Like the central offender of the trio in the Amplex advertisement, an artist who has a taste in this sense can hardly be aware of it, and this unawareness may put him in the first category of the vulgar. That is to say patronage may play a large part in our enjoyment of his individuality. Rubens is sometimes called a vulgar painter and Keats a vulgar poet—they have a powerfully individual smell which we could not, as it were, tell them of and discuss with them. With Cézanne, say, or with Stendhal, we feel that there could be and is a sort of intelligent and informed interplay of mind between us and them: whereas Keats and Rubens are somewhat in the position of Uncle Eroshka—they could not recognize themselves in our aware-ness of them. Hence the critic feels a kind of superiority, though he may not himself be aware of it as such, which finds expression in his calling their characteristic excellence a vulgar one. The line is: Keats and Rubens are a great poet and a great painter, but they are unaware of something about themselves which I am aware of—hence I am here in the classic relation of the enlightened to the common herd.

This feeling of superiority is never becoming to the critic in the presence of whatever sort of artist, and it should put us on our guard. Not that the critic would necessarily admit it if we pressed him to say just why the poet and the painter were vulgar. He would be more likely to draw our attention to a detail like the Joseph in the Prado *Nativity*, who is regarding the scene from behind the Virgin with the comic resentment of the traditional cuckold. Bellini or Piero would have had better taste than to make such a jest? The critic of Keats might merely indicate his descriptions of women and of kissing. They might say: Rubens and Keats are great artists but they are sometimes vulgar; they have spots of commonness and it is a fault in them. But this is to deny the whole and involuntary character of the artists and say they could have done better had they tried. These things are not lapses or blemishes but the stuff out of which the art and poetry are made. We may think we don't find them in *The Ode to a Nightingale* or the King's College *Adoration*, and mark those works up accordingly; but if we deny that they are still there in some sense, still giving their basic taste to the art, then we are denying something crucial in the whole being of that art.

We do not imagine Rubens or Keats saying: I know I have a tendency to be vulgar and in this picture, this poem, I shall do my best to prevent it intruding—indeed, when Keats *does* begin to say something like this there comes over his poetic personality a kind of paralysis and negation. Conversely, no artist can claim vulgarity, in this sense, as a quality of his work. James Joyce's prose, like John Betjeman's poetry, does lay claim to something like vulgarity for particular effects, and achieves what Joyce's brother calls 'studious meanness'. It would be beside the point to criticize the first sentence of *The Dead*—'Lily, the caretaker's daughter, was literally run off her feet'—for its slovenly banality, for this is precisely the effect it intends. On the other hand the story ends with this sentence. 'His soul swooned slowly as he heard the snow faintly falling through the universe and faintly falling, like the descent of their last end, upon all the living and the dead.' What are we supposed to feel here? That the words, like the hero, are a little bit florid, facile, *passé*? Or is Joyce writing simply to move us, and as well as he knows how?

We have no means of knowing, though this uncertainty is not necessarily a defect but perhaps increases the strange impact and authority of the tale.

Whatever may be the case, there is clearly no question here of Joyce submitting an involuntary odour or individuality to us. With immense exertion Joyce re-created for himself a style that resembles the old literary ideal of *decorum*—that is, of each subject requiring its own proper style. Decorum ensured that the feelings were not the artist's; one wrote about a high matter, such as love of a woman or love of one's country, in a suitably elevated style, not because one felt *oneself* that they required it but because the rules laid down that it should be so. The writer who employs *decorum* cannot possess a single odour, an involuntary individuality of his own. Chaucer and Shakespeare have no smell; they do not involuntarily submit us to their physical presence. They write about grand things grandly and coarse things coarsely, and we cannot catch them *being themselves* about, say, mother love or love of country. Nor can we catch Collins when in the eighteenth century he writes a patriotic ode:

> How sleep the brave, how sink to rest
> By all their country's wishes blest—

or Cowper when he writes a poem on his mother's picture. The principle of decorum is still operating. But Kipling we catch, so to speak, head on! He thrusts his bristling moustache into our faces when he writes in *The Brushwood Boy* that the hero and his mother talked for a long hour as mother and son should if there is to be any 'future for our Empire'. We recoil from this obviously because it is familiar—horribly so. It is like being buttonholed by someone who wants to tell us a smoking-room story and who assumes that we are the kind of person who would enjoy listening to it. Moreover Kipling shows an equal lack of consideration for his—albeit imaginary —characters. Their talk was private; they had no idea of the eaves-dropper who is now portentiously assuring us of its public im-portance.

Could this be vulgarity of the first kind? Might it be just the Kipling odour? Possibly, but there is something in the passage and in the story which makes me think that this is a case of the second category. We have here pretention, decay, uncertainty (how can the Empire endure if its spokesman reflects on it in this strangely feminine, fondling and fated way, as if caressing a collapsed peony?) and above all, emptiness. There is no need, in fact, for my solicitude on behalf of the characters for they don't exist: nothing is real, neither country, home nor parents nor girl nor boy. There is only Kipling, bombinating in the void, and—we begin to feel almost with panic—does even *he* really exist, for we have no sense of him other than in the story? He is the most evasive of authors and yet the most overpoweringly present, too self-conscious to have an involuntary presence and yet not confident enough to create one of his own. We have something of the same rather horrible apprehension of Hemingway in his books—particularly in the love passages of *A Farewell to Arms*—and he extends to us the same paralyzing familiarity—*you* drank the whisky, *you* felt good, etc. There is nothing here but an insistent and insinuating manner, a void like the television screen which seems to be trying to embody itself at our expense, an incubus trying to climb into our consciousness. No wonder our reaction is resentment, fear, and an uneasy sense of feeling slip away from us our own achievement of ourselves, our preserved and preservative self-content. Ford's 'History is bunk' is perhaps the most vulgar remark ever made, in its denial that men and their imaginative works have to live by creating and sustaining their own history.

Art, as Aristotle tells us, is imitation, and to the extent they try to impose their own imitation upon our reality all artists are potential vulgarians. But in his capacity of public performer the artist often pleases us with the sense of pitfalls avoided, embarrassments surmounted and outfaced. Sterne and Byron are like actors whom we watch with trepidation for fear they should—as it were—say or do something which will cause us to avoid the eye of our companion in the theatre. We cannot scrutinize their real being, but they avoid the second kind of vulgarity and part of the pleasure of watching them is to see the skill with which they do it. When Byron says:

> I have not loved the world, nor the world me,
> But let us part fair foes

we feel a momentary nervousness in case he should be looking at *us*

claiming us as a party to this ridiculous pronouncement. But we are
soon reassured; his eye is fixed on the theatre at large; he is walking
the tightrope with virtuosity, and his egocentricity is given a kind of
communal being by our communal appreciation of the fact. But
Kipling and Hemingway seem to have sought us out in private and
their lack of being is trying to substitute itself for our individuality,
as faceless corporations swallow small firms.

The dubious O *tempora! O mores!* metaphor should warn me to
stop there. Nothing would be easier than to equate my second category of vulgarity with a loss of *character* in all its forms, the character
of food, of institutions, communities, countries, landscapes, people.
But such a general noise of disapproval would be neither helpful nor
critical—indeed I cannot evade the suspicion that it might be rather
vulgar! The old times are better than the new, for aesthetic purposes,
on the irrefutably logical ground that they exist—as fixed objects of
appraisal—while the new times do not. I suppose that if I reduced my
second category to an *ad absurdum* I should have to find that nothing
in the past could be vulgar and nothing in the present could not be.

None the less I abide by my distinction. In aesthetic matters we
may apply the word 'vulgar' to two sorts of things. It praises the first
because these enlarge us and increase our potential of appreciation:
it dispraises the second because those diminish us and reduce our
power of being ourselves and hence of acknowledging other sorts of
being. And it must be admitted that the media of today, films and
television, are very well adapted to diminish us, to submit us to a
sort of glutinous ingestion. At the end of the evening we feel we
have gained nothing, we have been lost in the machine and have
received no more nourishment than the audience at a television
dinner-party. Dickens has created characters who are superbly
vulgar in the first sense, but in Mr. Merdle of *Little Dorrit* he introduces us to a man who is the ultimate in second-type vulgarity, a
man who is both repellent and void, a perfect neighbour for such a
dinner-party and the sort of man we might meet in hell. If we did,
our only refuge, like that of Ajax and Don Juan, would be in silence.
Dostoevsky, too, in *The Brothers Karamazov*, has made the devil himself such a figure, and even more gruesomely unreal is his Svidrigailov

in *Crime and Punishment*. The latter, it is true, is not without humour (which is in general incompatible with vulgarity) for as he prepares to blow out his brains he tells a bystander to say that he has gone to America. To America—that is to say (in Dostoevsky's view at least) to nowhere, into the ultimate void where we have all become— 'other people'.

Sculptural Thinking—I

L. R. ROGERS

Artists do think

Some people are very reluctant to admit that artists think at all. They consider them to be instruments, playthings of the gods or of their own deep, dark psychic processes. But the fact that art, whatever else it may be, has also something to do with consciousness, and that artists think, and sometimes think very hard, *in their own terms* is now widely accepted. Of course artistic thinking goes on on many levels, is very complex, and shares many characteristics with other kinds of thinking. In many respects it is fit material for a number of branches of psychology. But questions like: How do painters think in terms of painting? Sculptors in terms of sculpture? Musicians in terms of music?—questions which concern the special and peculiar nature of artistic thinking—can only be answered from the inside.

In this essay I shall attempt to describe some of those aspects of sculptural thinking which are the special concern of sculptors. I think this is worth doing because without some insight into sculptural thinking, without some capacity for following the thought that has gone into a work of sculpture as one would 'follow' an argument or a blue-print, all attempts at critical evaluation are likely to be irrelevant and impertinent. They may tell us a great deal about the work as a public object or private fantasy but they will tell us nothing about it as a work of sculpture.

Ordinary thinking in 3D

Although they disagree about what they are and how they are formed, most philosophers and psychologists agree that all normal people acquire a stock of simple abstract spatial concepts—concepts of lines, planes, angles, spheres, cones, cylinders, curvilinearity, rectilinearity, convexity, concavity, etc. 'We are capable of making abstractions not only in terms of objects and classes of objects, but also in terms of pattern or formal relations as such.'[1] These concepts are abstract in this sense that they are not related to any particular object but are of an extremely general nature. Some of them are of relations in two-dimensional space, others of relations in three-dimensional space.

Without these simple spatial concepts ordinary practical day-to-day living would be impossible. Most people, however, do not develop their understanding of space beyond this practical level; they seldom, if ever, adopt a contemplative attitude towards spatial form or show an interest in the form of a thing for its own sake. Usually they notice only those features of an object's form which serve as clues to its identity. 'We were given our eyes to see things, not to look at them. Life takes care that we all learn the lesson thoroughly so that at a very early age we have acquired a very considerable ignorance of visual appearances. We have learned the meaning-for-life of appearances so well that we understand them, as it were, in shorthand. The subtlest differences of appearance that have a utility value still continue to be appreciated, while large and important visual characters, provided they are useless for life, will pass unnoticed.'[2]

Some occupations—surgery, botany, carpentry, etc.—demand a thorough practical understanding of a narrow range or forms, but only in the spatial arts is thinking in terms of three-dimensional form pursued for its own sake. And of these sculpture is the most thorough and least restricted by functional or material considerations. It is, in fact, the special art that caters for spatial perception and understanding.

Advanced thinking in 3D

The high-level spatial thinking of painters, sculptors and architects is a development of ordinary everyday practical spatial thinking. It is based on the same fundamental concepts, but goes much further. Most people have fairly clear and complete concepts of such simple forms as spheres, cones and cylinders, i.e. they know them 'in the round' and can construct them in various ways from memory. But only after special training are they able to conceive complex three-dimensional forms in the same way.

It is often supposed that in order to grasp forms in their 'full spatial completeness'[3] sculptors somehow combine innumerable silhouettes or projective views. They do not. For although it is true that with forms that are at all complex or subtle it is necessary to turn them round in the hands or to look at them from a number of points of view in order to grasp their formal structure, the knowledge achieved is not like a comprehensive set of still photographs and is not the result of fusing a number of projective views. It is, in fact, more like a mechanic's understanding of the way in which a nut and bolt fit together, or a cook's intimate acquaintance with the structure of an orange she is splitting into segments. What causes people to look at sculpture as a set of silhouettes instead of a composition of forms is its complexity. They can appreciate the three-dimensional structure of a cube easily enough and would be able to construct one without thinking of viewpoints or silhouettes (indeed, they may find this hard to do); but when they look at complex forms and lack the training that would enable them to grasp their formal structure, they have to fall back upon other ways of looking. Sculptors, however, learn to conceive complex and subtle forms as completely and clearly as other people conceive cubes, cones and cylinders.

Learning to think in 3D

High-level spatial thinking is developed in two main ways:

(a) By analysing complex forms, particularly natural forms. In this process simple spatial concepts are employed in attempts to master the forms of complicated objects. There is plenty of evidence in artists' sketch-books, in manuals of architecture, sculpture, painting and drawing to show that in trying to grasp complex and subtle forms artists make use of schematic frameworks, i.e. they make these forms intelligible first by reducing them to simpler, more easily conceived forms or assemblies of forms, and then by analysing the developments of these which lead to the more complex ones. We do something rather similar when we try to understand a sonata, a radio circuit, a factory or a system of philosophy. There is no need to dwell on this. All artists know it from experience and non-artists can verify it by consulting the illustrations and directions in almost any technical treatise, from the How-to-draw-cats level to that of the notebooks of Leonardo and Dürer. This process of objective analysis, especially of the human figure, has been the traditional way of teaching sculptors how to think in terms of three-dimensional form. It has also been the means of handing on traditional knowledge, because students learn to see through the eyes of their predecessors; they inherit their schematic frameworks. In some cases, of course, they learn only the formulae and improve upon them without reference to nature. But more of this later.

(b) By manipulating, combining and performing operations upon easily conceived spatial forms in order to develop more complex forms that are not directly derived from objects. The construction of geometrical patterns is a low-level example of this, the creation of original architecture, engineering and non-objective sculpture are high-level ones. This free exploration of spatial relationships, or 'abstract construction' as I shall call it, was used with great success as a pedagogic method by Moholy-Nagy when he taught the rudiments of spatial design at the Bauhaus. It is being further developed at many art colleges in this country. This process, too, has its analogues in other kinds of thinking, particularly in music and mathematics.

The process of abstract construction may appear to be more relevant to the training of architects, engineers and product designers than to that required by sculptors, but this is not so. Sculptural images are becoming less and less directly concerned with natural objects and modern sculptors are demanding a wider field of expression than sculptors in the past. An adequate training for sculptors today develops both methods of exploring spatial form. Its aim is not simply to equip a sculptor with a knowledge of a number of particular natural forms or types of construction, any more than the aim of a musician's training is to teach him a few bird songs or tunes. It is the general principles of the construction of three-dimensional form which he has to learn, what he will often refer to as 'the logic of form'.

The 'logic' of form

In the polemics of art-educationists the methods of objective analysis and abstract construction are sometimes distinguished as 'the imitative act' and 'the creative act'. This is an invidious distinction. At the moment both these terms are heavily loaded and usually imply a value judgement. Besides, as I shall show presently, the matter is not so simple. Perhaps the terms 'inductive' and 'deductive' might be more useful. They might suggest enlightening analogies, and they at least indicate that what we are concerned with are two inter-dependent phases of thinking. In inductive spatial thinking previously acquired spatial concepts are employed in order to investigate the principles of higher-level formal organization *by discovering them in things*. In deductive spatial thinking previously acquired spatial concepts are developed, explored and combined in order to investigate the principles of higher-level formal organization *without reference to things*.

Obviously this presents the kind of chicken-and-egg problem enjoyed by students of psychogenesis. Piaget, who claims that our first spatial concepts are derived, not from direct apprehension of the properties of objects, but from the actions performed upon them during what he calls the sensori-motor phase of our development, writes that it is: 'because it enriches and develops physical reality instead of merely extracting from it a set of ready-made structures, that action is eventually able to transcend physical limitations and create operational schemata which can be formalized and made to function in a purely abstract deductive fashion'.[4]

A knowledge of spatial form does not consist of so many separate, self-contained items of mental furniture; it is organized into a system. The formal logic of this system is geometry. Its working logic operates in the thinking of the spatial designer. Thought of all kinds has its forms which precede logic—people used syllogisms long before Aristotle formulated them—and transcend logic, which cannot encompass the variety of thought. The forms of sculpture may be clearly conceived, perfectly articulated and of a complexity that would baffle all attempt at formulation in mathematical terms. Only comparatively simple, regular forms can be so formulated. For this reason, among others, the intellectual's dream of a mathematically constructed sculpture is a foolish one. Pursuing the wrong kind of clarity, it would restrict the sculptor to those forms which could be conceived in mathematical terms.

'Imitative' versus 'creative' thinking

The process of objective analysis is not as imitative, nor is it as bound to 'reality', as is often supposed. Many writers[5] have shown that it is wrong to think of an objective world with fixed and steady perceptual characteristics which can be simply transcribed into pictures or sculpture. Our knowledge of form is mediated to us through conceptual processes. We employ a conceptual framework or schema as a kind of net to trap and retain it. Thus an artist who attempts to work faithfully 'from nature' is not and cannot become 'just an eye'.[6] He approaches the objective world with preconceptions; he experiments with various conceptual nets to see what he can catch; he abstracts, whether he wants to or not. If he is a weak artist, he will approach nature with perceptual attitudes entirely derived from his predecessors. If he is an original artist, he will give us a version of reality which is new and teach us a new way of seeing. Once he has done this it becomes common property. Thus the attempt to analyse natural forms may be completely imitative of other artists' work, but it can never be so of nature. On the other hand, it may be creative in that it gives humanity a new way of seeing.

And just as objective analysis is not so tied as may appear at first glance, so abstract construction is not so freely creative as is so often supposed. It is true that three-dimensional space is a realm in which an infinite number of operations is possible. Theoretically there is no limit to the spatial designs that could be conceived, but in practice there is. Artists live in definite times and places and what they can conceive or invent depends very largely on the kinds of spatial organization they are familiar with. They are inevitably limited by the habits of spatial thinking of their society and period. Only a few original artists manage to modify the perceptual and constructive habits of society by inventing new ways of organizing spatial forms. The rest are imitators or *pasticheurs*.

Examples of 3D thinking

Objective analysis and abstract construction constitute, as it were, the poles between which sculptural thinking moves. Most of the world's sculpture has been achieved by combining both methods of thinking. Information derived from natural forms has become material for the metamorphosing powers of the mind, for 'the processes whereby the life of forms in the mind propagates a prodigious animism, that taking natural objects as the point of departure, makes them matters of imagination and memory, of sensibility and intellect'.[7]

Take, for example, the forms of the best West African wood-carved figures. They are perfectly articulated, completely three-dimensional, and free from all vagueness. They convey some information which is verifiable by objective processes,[8] e.g. the positional relationships of head, trunk, limbs, nose, eyes, etc., but since they were made by sculptors who had not been influenced by Western scientific ideas there is no attempt to eliminate subjective influences. 'Accuracy', as it is understood in our civilization, was not their aim. Consequently the forms observed in nature are represented for different purposes. The amount of emphasis they are given, for example, is usually determined by their emotional significance. Thus scarification marks, navels, breasts, genital organs and heads are by objective, scientific standards overdone. These sculptures are conceived with the utmost clarity and impeccable formal logic but abstract construction predominates in them and builds a perfect design out of a minimum of information about the forms of the figure. Their method of articulating arms and shoulders, for example, has nothing to do with anatomical structure but as a logical method of construction it is faultless.

Or take a typical fifth-century Greek sculpture of an athlete. Again, the forms are perfectly articulated, fully three-dimensional and free from all vagueness. But measurement and careful objective analysis have provided a great deal of accurate information which has been modified and translated in order to create an ideally proportioned figure according to the Greeks' notions of perfection. 'He who takes for his model such forms as nature produces, and confines himself to an exact imitation of them, will never attain to what is perfectly beautiful. For the works of nature are full of disproportion and fall very short of the true standard of beauty.'⁹ The transparent intelligibility and beautiful proportions of these figures are results of clear and sensitive abstract thinking working upon the data provided by objective analysis.

In order to satisfy a need for icons that would serve as symbols for their gods the sculptors of the southern Indian bronzes created a formula for the human figure which, like that of the Greeks, is not so much an imitation of the figure as a perfectly logically constructed equivalent for it. 'In their canon of absolute, rather than human, beauty, and the almost mathematical purity and clarity of form, these images are the perfect symbols of the Indian ideal. Although cast in human shape, the abstraction of modelling and iconographic explicitness give them the power of a diagram. Like all Indian images, they were emblematic evocations, not descriptions, of a deity that the worshipper had always in his heart and mind.'¹⁰

Finally, to come nearer home, consider the wind-and-sea-worn geological forms of Moore's goddesses. Through observation and analysis Moore has achieved an extensive vocabulary of form derived from widely different sources. Using types of form belonging to different worlds, the human and geological, as elements for the process of abstract construction, he has built what has justly been called a sculptural metaphor—an ambiguous image of tremendous evocative power. Like many modern sculptors Moore seems to be prepared to cover the whole range of sculptural thinking, from the careful analysis in drawing of natural forms to the purely autonomous manipulation of abstract form elements. And he does not seem to mind whether he works from nature towards abstraction or from abstraction back towards nature.

Thinking in terms of mass and space

There are two kinds of spatial form. One is primarily concerned with mass, with solid or opaque volumes that displace or inhabit space. The other is not so easy to define in a satisfactory manner, although those who have experience of it will have no difficulty in understanding what I am referring to. It is mainly concerned with the voids or spatial relations between material elements.

Put this way it sounds elusive and intangible but it is not so in experience. It is real and positive; it is what the sensitive observer of architecture feels inside a spatial structure like St. Paul's or an interior by Le Corbusier. We might say that the first is structure *in* space, the second structure *of* space. Designing with masses has been the traditional concern of sculptors, while designing with space has been left to architects and engineers. But during the last fifty years space has begun to invade sculpture. We owe this extension of the art of sculpture to the Constructivists and perhaps, above all, to the vision and persistence of Naum Gabo.

These two kinds of spatial form differ considerably in their appeal to our sensibilities, so I shall discuss them separately.

We cannot distinguish the traditional forms of sculpture from those of the Constructivists by saying that they are concerned only with the outside envelope and the way it meets surrounding space. This is to misconstrue the whole nature of sculptural form and sculptural thinking. It might, in fact, serve to define one type of bad sculpture. Sculptors think through the mass; the movements on the surface, the surface forms, are the outward manifestation of movements that must be thought of as continuing through the mass. There is an internal structure which has to be sensed in order to appreciate a work as a three-dimensional design. Sculptors who think only of the outer defining planes of their work are not thinking in a fully three-dimensional way. It is the impacting and articulating of volumes which are conceived all round which is the essence of sculpture with masses, and not to pass from what is implied on the surface to the full realization of the internal structure is to miss the main point of this kind of sculpture.

Traditional sculpture at its best—the southern Indian bronzes and

Greek sculptures already mentioned, for example—is not a mere attempt to create an interesting surface but a translation of the figure into clearly articulated, fully three-dimensional volumes. The same is true of non-objective sculpture. Some of it, it is true, consists merely of an aggregate of surfaces, but at its best it is the result of a fully three-dimensional grasp of total volumes. Herbert Read has suggested in his *Art of Sculpture*[11] that sculpture with masses of the kind I have been describing is at bottom an art of touch rather than a visual art. Certainly it appeals to the sense of touch more than sculpture with space.

Fully three-dimensional thinking is not confined to thinking in terms of mass or tactile form. Some of the work of the Constructivists is made up of other kinds of spatial elements, particularly sheet forms, which are fully three-dimensional, i.e. they do not, like paper sculpture, curve only in one plane but exist in full three-dimensional plastic space. Many Constructivist sculptures, however, exist in a world of two-and-a-half dimensions. They consist of essentially two-dimensional elements related or bent in three-dimensional space. I do not wish to suggest that these forms are inferior or that designing them is easy. I wish only to make the point that for the full exercise of his sensibilities a sculptor will usually prefer 'form in its full spatial completeness'.

Gabo has pointed out that the development of Constructivist sculpture has become possible through the development of plastic transparent materials like glass and perspex.[12] These make it possible to construct volumes with visible interiors and to arrange elements so that they do not eclipse each other from any direction. The sculpture is, as it were, opened up and the interpenetrations and internal forms, which in opaque sculpture are implied by the surface forms, are here clearly visible. At its most developed, in the work of Gabo, we can no longer speak of inside and outside the sculpture. The whole work is a fully three-dimensional development in space.

Because the appeal to the sense of touch is sacrificed some people feel that Constructivist sculpture is not really sculptural. This seems an odd and prejudiced way of regarding it. We should be right to regret the loss of weight and tactile qualities if there were no compensatory extensions of the possibilities of sculpture in the work. But in fact the work of Gabo appeals to us in ways that are not possible with sculpture in masses. There need be no question of competition. Gabo in a brilliantly clear essay on *Carving and Construction in Space* writes:

> ... volume still reminds one of the fundamental attributes of sculpture, and we still use it in our sculptures as often as the theme demands an expression of solidarity.
>
> We are not at all intending to dematerialize a sculptural work, making it non-existent; we are realists, bound to earthly matters, and we do not neglect any of those psychological emotions which belong to the basic group of our perceptions of the world. On the contrary, adding Space perception to perception of Masses, emphasizing it and forming it, we enrich the expression of Mass, making it more essential through the contract between them whereby Mass retains its solidarity and Space its extension.

In other words, sculptural thinking has been developed in a new direction. And it is possible, as some artists believe, that these new developments, with their emphasis on space, transparency, structure and inventiveness are more in tune with the modern spirit than the traditional forms.

REFERENCES

[1] M. D. Vernon, *A Further Study in Visual Perception*, p. 80.

[2] R. Fry, *Vision and Design*, p. 45 (Penguin Books, 1961).

[3] H. Moore, *Notes on Sculpture*: 'This is what the sculptor must do. He must strive continually to think of, and use, form in its full spatial completeness. He gets the solid shape, as it were, inside his head—he thinks of it, whatever its size, as if he were holding it completely enclosed in the hollow of his hand. He mentally visualizes a complex form *from all round itself*; he knows while he looks at one side what the other side is like; he identifies himself with its centre of gravity, its mass, its weight; he realizes its volume, as the space that the shape displaces in the air.'

[4] J. Piaget, *The Child's Conception of Space* (1956), p. 449.

[5] M. Friedlander, R. Arnheim, J. J. Gibson, E. H. Gombrich, L. Steinberg.

[6] Cézanne said that Monet was 'Just an eye, but what an eye!'

[7] H. Focillon, *The Life of Forms in Art* (Eng. Trans. 1942).

[8] I am assuming here some acquaintance with Gombrich's *Art and Illusion* (1960).

9 Plato, *Timaeus*.

10 B. Rowland, *The Art and Architecture of India*, p. 187. (Pelican History of Art, 1956.)

11 H. Read, *The Art of Sculpture* (1956), ch. 3.

12 Gabo, *Sculpture: Carving and Construction in Space*.

Sculptural Thinking—II

Rogers on Sculptural Thinking

DONALD BROOK

Everyone likes to be understood (up to a point), but sculptors have on the whole suffered from a shortage of spokesmen of evident intellectual probity who are able to dust off the grime of the studio and make pellucid utterance. Sculptors are silent, or they speak darkly in parable and paradox, or (like all artists) they chatter the last cry, and the cry before that, like budgerigars. Theirs is the high mystery of hand and eye, and their intellectual offerings to that overwhelming majority of the human race which cannot drive a nail in straight are limited to occasional apologiae such as that of L. R. Rogers. It is therefore disappointing that he should have chosen an artificial problem and dealt with it so plausibly that it almost seems real.

For what is Rogers's problem? He says that it is the problem of explaining to laymen the nature of 'sculptural thinking'. 'Sculptors', he says, 'sometimes think very hard, *in their own terms;*' and 'without some insight into sculptural thinking, without some capacity for following the thought that has gone into a work of sculpture as one would "follow" an argument or a blue-print, all attempts at critical evaluation are likely to be irrelevant and impertinent'.

There are snarls worth untangling here, but they are not the layman's. This irrelevant and impertinent fellow usually says that he doesn't have to be a hen to recognize a bad egg. At the same time, of course, his sympathetic insight into the biological limitations of the hen might enhance his respect for an unusually *large* egg—seen as an oviparous feat rather than as an oviform *objet trouvé*. A sculpture student, too, might make a clay egg, and his teacher might judge his performance. He might also judge the object, and it is important to distinguish these situations since they are easily conflated by the single approval-formula 'that's a good egg'. (Congratulations!) But suppose that the student had been trying to model a sphere; what should the teacher say? That the student had made a good sculpture *by accident*? That he was really rather an unpromising sculptor? Suppose that the student often did this: suppose, for example, that he made some obsessive distortion (this actually happens) which was the despair of his teachers, and yet won all the prizes when the judges were strangers. This whole mess of problems associated with the question whether, and how, works of art are to be taken as performances or are to be seen as themselves (whatever that means) is one of the trickiest in aesthetics, and Rogers might have helped us with it. Instead he *assumes* that sculptures must be judged as performances, he *assumes* that they are all the same kind of performance, and he sets out to help us 'from the inside' by explaining just what kind of performance they all are.

This programme is necessarily abortive, for if there is one thing which emerges clearly from any thorough and protracted study of human artefacts it is that sculptures are *all kinds of performances*. The only thing they all have in common is, trivially, their attributes of spatial and temporal extension, which they share with human heads and public clocks. For the rest, they differ in as many ways as may be imagined. They were made to frighten bad spirits, to weigh gold, to decorate the structural members of stone- and wood-work, to imitate and to surpass nature, to delight a patron, enhance a harpoon, to astonish the native and win competitions, to be seen from one side, to be seen from all sides, and even not to be seen at all, like Butler's enigmatic what-is-it-in-the-iron-box. They were made to be hung on trees, hung on necks, to have nails driven into them, to be chopped up at Dada exhibitions, to provide houses for the ghosts of ancestors and 'atmosphere' for the board-rooms of insurance companies. 'Sculptural thinking,' if it is to embrace the activities of *all* sculptors, can only mean: 'whatever it is that goes on in sculptors' heads (hearts? hands?) when they make what they make.' And since they make the most extraordinary variety of things, they must be supposed to harbour the most extraordinarily various thoughts. The entire 'thinking' suggestion is in fact grossly misleading (along with reading blue-prints, following arguments, and so on). The art of sculpture is an art of *making* things, and the difference between what goes on 'in' a man who is making a portrait head and 'in' a man who is making a table is not a difference between 'sculptural thinking' and 'tabular thinking' as if these were, say, different coloured thoughts, or thoughts with distinctive labels attached. Sculptors and carpenters have a different training, and different habits, interests and immediate purposes. They acquire what have been called 'dispositionals', not all of which become 'occurrent' in the act of making each and every thing that they make. Some sculptors may give themselves instructions while they work; others may be quite unable to say, if asked, what they are thinking or (a more intelligible question) what they are doing.

But of course sculptors think, if this is taken to mean that they teach and are taught, that they arrive at opinions and try to act consistently with the opinions that they hold. And this sort of thing—lore and precept, jargon, slogan and trick of the trade—might be called 'sculptural thinking' so long as it is remembered that what is peculiarly *sculptural* about it is merely that it is thinking about sculpture, and that sculpture is not one kind of thing which differs from all other kinds of thing in any one essential way.

Rogers's own 'sculptural thinking' has lead him to the the (mistaken) conviction that sculptors do not 'combine innumerable silhouettes or projective views'. Well, *he* may not, but many others do and did. It was standard carving technique for at least a millennium to cut out the front profile, and then the side, and then to round off the corners; and Cellini (for example) says, in a letter dated 28th January, 1547:

> These views are not only eight, but more than forty because even if the figure be rotated no more than an inch, there will be some muscle showing too much, or not enough, so that each single piece of sculpture presents the greatest variety of aspects imaginable. And thus the artist finds himself compelled to do away with that gracefulness that he had achieved in the first view in order to harmonize it with the others. The difficulty is so great that no figure has ever been known to look right from every direction.

What Rogers is giving us is not (and could not be) what he

promises—an account of 'sculptural thinking'—but an *example* (his own example) of sculptural thinking. This is, in its way, quite valuable; for although it does not go to the heart of any important aesthetic questions (just as Cellini's observation does not), it nevertheless helps us to see that if we are committed to the view that works of art must be judged as *performances*, then we do well to ask their authors what kind of performance they are. We may be able to make inferences from the sculpture itself, or we may not, but in neither case is there reason to disdain a glance inside the horse's mouth when it is obligingly held open for us.

A kind of contemporary sculpture, approved by Rogers, is evidently Neo-Constructivist and has a pseudo-intellectual rationale (derived ultimately from Bauhaus teaching) which provides its students with hearteningly no-nonsense, lets-get-down-to-business phrases such as 'advanced thinking in 3D', 'high-level spatial thinking', and 'the "logic" of form'. Those quotes around 'logic' are disarming: in Rogers's text they give the impression of resulting from a desire to say outright 'the logic of form', restrained by a—wholly understandable—misgiving as to the propriety or sense of such a phrase. ('So-to-speak' quotes are each-way bets on a small field.) The kind of language in which this contemporary sculptural thinking is conducted is clearly illustrated in Rogers's treatment of West African sculpture. He says:

> Take, for example, the forms of the best West African wood-carved figures [*how do we know which are the best?*]. They are perfectly articulated [*just what is that?*], completely three-dimensional [*since Rogers refers elsewhere to sculpture which is 2½-dimensional, there is no point in making protest here*] and free from all vagueness [*what's vague? Medardo Rosso? But in his case that's good!*]. . . . These sculptures are conceived with the utmost clarity [*conceived, or made, or both? What's the difference?*] and impeccable formal logic [*!*] but abstract construction predominates in them [*they are what is usually called 'stylized'?*] and builds a perfect design [*in the best ones, of course!*] out of a minimum of information about the forms of the figure. Their method of articulating arms and shoulders, for example [*ah! so articulating is joining together*], has nothing to do with anatomical structure [*no?*] but as a logical method of construction it is faultless.

The faultlessness of a logic which joins two arms on to the shoulders of a stylized human body is scarcely a matter for such enthusiastic congratulation. A West African wood carver would find it rather patronizing, unless—more likely—he saw it as a huge joke. Of course, it may not be the mere joining which is faultlessly logical, but the *way* of the joining (the shape of the region of junction). This carries us no farther forward, however, since we need above all things a way of distinguishing between logical and not-logical (or illogical?) shapes and junctions. It looks rather suspiciously as though 'logical' means 'approved', and the hint of a basis of approval ('a shape like a correct argument') is a hint at the unsayable.

The message Rogers has for us is, surely, not that the vocabulary of the new advanced thinking in 3D is effective in the interpretation of alien sculpture—for it is only too patently nothing of the kind— but that we have available for art criticism a vocabulary which deliberately aims to be cool, neutral, objective, scientific-sounding, and that this vocabulary must have some relevance to the sort of sculpture Rogers makes and teaches. It will be surprising indeed if, when we come to criticize those perspex constructions which are hinted at in his text, we do not find that they will be best and most sympathetically interpreted in terms not unlike those that Rogers urges.

SUMMARY OF CONCLUSIONS:

(1) Rogers has a pseudo-problem. There is no such thing as 'sculptural thinking' in the sense in which he is trying to explain it to us. There is only the way this sculptor thinks, and the way that sculptor thinks—as well as the things this sculptor makes and the things that sculptor makes.

(2) Although there is no puzzle about 'sculptural thinking', there are often puzzles about how this sculptor or that sculptor thought, and they are bound up with more evidently *aesthetic* problems about works of art seen as performances by artists. If the artist's intention does count in correct criticism, then we may well want to know (as critics) what Cellini thought, and what Rogers thinks.

(3) The kind of sculpture that Rogers seems to favour has developed in parallel with a critical vocabulary, or bag of nostrums,

derived from various respectable intellectual and scientific disciplines. Geometry (pre-Lobachevsky) and Logic (Aristotelian) are exploited rather than, say, Topology or Cybernetics, in spite of the desire to be 'more in tune with the modern spirit'. No doubt there is some need also to appear reliably old-established; but it would be pleasant to meet a few convincingly modern terms like 'bits' or 'isomorphous' in this kind of art-talk. Perhaps that is the *next* cry?

Sculptural Thinking—III

A Reply

L. R. ROGERS

I shall deal with Brook's rather over-confident misunderstandings one by one, as they occur, and in doing so I shall try to bring out the underlying cause of the breakdown of communication between us.

(1) Having completely failed to recognize the problem I was dealing with, Brook has tried to give it a familiar look by recasting it in the mould of one of the Standard Aesthetic Problems—whether works of art should be judged as performances. But I did not say that works of art should be judged as performances. I was not concerned with works of art or with judging them, but with works of sculpture and understanding them. Nevertheless, it is true that without some understanding of what kind of performances they are we cannot even begin to judge them. We should be like the Chinaman at the concert who clapped after the tuning up.

Now although I was not concerned with judging works of sculpture but with understanding them, I did consider them as performances of a certain kind. This, I think, brings us to the heart of the matter. Brook's main points seem to be that general statements about sculpture must deal with trivialities and that general statements about the thinking of sculptors must be nonsense; we can only say worth-while things about particular pieces of sculpture or sensible things about the thinking of individual sculptors. Sculptures, he writes, 'are *all kinds of performances* (Brook's italics), the only thing they all have in common is, trivially (!), their attributes of spatial and temporal extension, which they share with human heads and public clocks'. Exactly! Brook has inadvertently revealed the source of his own confusion. The attribute of spatial extension, whether of human heads, public clocks, African wood carvings or cauliflowers, is just what sculptors get excited about. They call it 'form'; and they call the capacity for grasping the 3D spatial properties of things the 'sense of form'. The ability to apprehend things as form is not highly developed in many people nowadays, particularly in those who have undergone the spiritual leucotomy that passes for education in some university departments. It does not appear to be very highly developed in Brook, since *the mark of somebody who lacks a sense of form is that he cannot see what there is to be excited about*; he thinks it is trivial.

Those who have not learned to perceive sculpture as form usually adopt one of two attitudes: either they stand in front of it pathetically trying to 'intuit' it, to attain a state of 'pure receptivity' which they hope will enable them to soak it up immediately and unthinkingly; or they stand in front of it asking themselves questions about its antecedents, its dates, the mathematical relations between its parts, its significance as a document for psychoanalysis or anthropology, etc., etc. The first is the failure of the simple-minded, who pray that some unimaginable aesthetic rapture will fall upon them in a golden shower or creep up on them like an attack of vertigo. The second is the failure of the scholar, who wanders round and round the railings of the park watching the people inside having fun but cannot find the gate. Works of sculpture cannot be properly appreciated by gaping at them with our intelligences idling or by thinking *about* them. Appreciation demands that we penetrate the work on its own terms. All sculptures, and all things that sculptors are interested in, have form and however efficient we may think they are as harpoons, magic charms or doorstops, we cannot begin to assess them until we have apprehended them as performances in the realm of 3D form. If we are concerned with giving them marks we may have to be sensitive to all sorts of other things *as well*, but these are expressed in or communicated through the forms or are qualities of the forms.

(2) Brook objects to my saying that sculptors *think* in terms of 3D form. He assumes that what I mean by 'thinking' is something that goes on 'in' a sculptor's head while he is working, and he more or less accuses me of trying to bring back into the machinery of

sculptors' heads the ghosts that Gilbert Ryle has exorcized. On the principle of 'heads I win, tails you lose' Brook has inverted Ryle's arguments to demonstrate that sculptors do not think, they make. The whole point of Ryle's chapter on 'Knowing How and Knowing That' seemed to me to be that intelligent practical activities, such as making sculpture, are as much a manifestation of thinking as the production of philosophical or scientific theories. One man produces theories, another produces sculpture; they both think. A piece of sculpture is as much a record, expression or embodiment of a sculptor's thoughts as a philosophical paper is of a philosopher's thoughts. They think in different terms and of different things, but they both think. I was not trying to prove that sculptors are *intellectuals*. Heaven forbid! They think *in terms* of form and think *about* form only when they are reckless enough to try to do what I am doing.

In any case, actually making sculpture is only one way in which a sculptor's spatial concepts are employed; it is only one part of his skill. When I wrote that sculptors *think* in terms of 3D form I meant that they can perceive and conceive form; that they can recognize, remember, imagine, make, talk about and, to a certain extent, describe form; that they can analyse the forms of things and invent forms of their own; and, moreover, that they are more expert at this than anybody else. Whether one accepts a dispositional analysis of these mental capacities is beside the point. I imagine we may still say 'he is thinking' rather than 'his dispositions are becoming occurrent'.

Why Brook has difficulty with my phrase 'sculptural thinking' comes out clearly when he refers to 'the kind of language in which this contemporary sculptural thinking is conducted ... etc.', and confuses the verbal terms in which I inadequately tried to describe pieces of sculpture with the 'terms' in which sculptors conceive and understand them. My whole point was that thinking in terms of 3D form is a kind of thinking that is conducted by means of spatial concepts which are not necessarily verbalized. Non-verbal thinking is presumably inconceivable to Brook and must therefore be made to disappear, like other awkward problems, by linguistic sleight of hand and abracadabra.

(3) Brook's difficulty with my phrase 'the logic of form' is rooted in the same incapacity. Not to know that stylized arms and shoulders may slither sloppily into each other or be clearly, intelligibly or 'logically' articulated or constructed, and not to be able to see through the term 'logical' (which is commonly used in this way by sculptors and others) to what I was trying to say with it are indicative of a lack of sense of form. Words are always opaque if we do not know the experiences they refer to. But if Brook is going to disallow analogy, how can we talk to people about what they have not experienced?

Rodin said: 'When I have a beautiful woman's body as a model, the drawings I make of it also give me pictures of insects, birds and fishes. This seems incredible but I did not know it myself until I found out. . . . A woman, a mountain and a horse are all formed according to the same principles.' As one's knowledge of form grows one becomes aware not simply of a superficial similarity of shape but of an identity of formal principles in the structure of things. This is what Rodin is referring to. One develops what might be called *morphological insight*, a sense of some sort of logic behind the forms of things. I am sorry if my use of the term 'logic' is offensive but I know no other way of conveying what I mean. Some scientific writers, e.g. the plant morphologist Agnes Arber, the psychologist R. Arnheim, C. H. Waddington and the great D'Arcy Wentworth Thompson, have this insight.

(4) Brook's point about the profiles and silhouettes is based on a piece of misquotation by omission. What I wrote was: 'It is often supposed that *in order to grasp forms in their "full spatial completeness"* sculptors somehow combine innumerable silhouettes or projective views. They do not.' And in case the phrase 'full spatial completeness' was mystifying I quoted the passage from Henry Moore in which it occurs.

Of course sculptors look at silhouettes and of course they are relevant to the making of sculpture. I was trying to distinguish a highly developed sense of form from an undeveloped one. The special perceptual and creative skills required for appreciating and producing sculpture may be developed to a high or low degree. We may be skilled or unskilled performers or observers. The most developed sense of form is one which knows forms in their 'full spatial completeness'. Only those who can conceive and perceive form in this way will *know* what I mean. The Greeks started out with quadrature—projecting the profiles of the figure into the sides of a block—and took nearly 200 years to master the forms of the figure so that they could conceive them in their 'full spatial completeness'. A potter throwing a pot on a wheel may appear to be concentrating on the silhouette of his pot, and in a sense he is, but if he is at all advanced in his craft he is using that silhouette as a clue to the subtle concentric volumes it defines. It is the volumes, their weight, mass, proportion and articulation that he is really concerned with and is thinking of. Profiles may be a useful means of checking the accuracy of a form or of starting a carving from a flat-sided block. Again, with certain kinds of sculpture intended to stand in a niche or in the open air profiles may be very important. But profiles are something that forms *have*, rather as they have light and shade on their surfaces, because they must. Sometimes this property calls for special attention, sometimes it does not. But to be sensing or creating profiles or illuminated surfaces is to be doing something very different from sensing or creating 3D forms. Different kinds of sensibilities are involved. However, there is no point in trying to say in a few lines what Moore in his essays and Read in *The Art of Sculpture* have said so much more eloquently and expertly. I will let Gabo have the last word. 'To think about sculpture as a succession of two-dimensional images would mean to think about something else, but not sculpture . . . sculpture is three-dimensional *eo ipso.*'

Finally I should like to make two points of general interest concerning the relations between philosophers of art and artists:

(a) Brook calls my article an apology and appears to subscribe to the common fallacy that all an artist ever writes about art is an apology for his own work. R. H. Wilenski said the same thing more dogmatically in his *The Study of Art* (pp. 153–4). According to him artists are incapable of an objective outlook on aesthetic matters and their writings must therefore be distinguished from those of the philosopher: 'Any piece of writing on aesthetic by an original artist is always inevitably a defence of his own personality and a rationalization of his own limitations.' Anyone who accepts such an argument must be badly in need of comfort. Obviously what applies to the artist applies equally to philosophers, or to philosophically inclined art historians like Wilenski. How could they produce any aesthetic ideas that showed that they were immoral, perverted, or blind, deaf, or otherwise insensitive to man's most valued possessions? They can no more get outside the limitations of their own sensibilities and personalities than the artist can, as we have seen. One might just as well argue that everything a philosopher writes about philosophy is an apology for his own work. Obviously, if somebody produces wrong ideas it may be useful to inquire why he did so; but the important thing is not why a thing is said but whether it is true. Otherwise we might as well all give up any attempt at objectivity and hand everything over to the psychoanalysts. And what they are apologizing for is anybody's guess.

Artists do know something about art, other people's as well as their own. The 'apology' argument is part of the romantic notion of the artist as a brainless practitioner of 'the high mystery of hand and eye', a creature who is all emotions and muscular skills: a divine idiot if he is good, a plain idiot if he is not.

(b) Now I am afraid I shall have to speak darkly or not at all. A growing love of form often leads to a kind of mysticism, a feeling that contact has been established with some deeper level of reality—what used to be called an 'intuition of being'. In the words of an embryologist (A. M. Dalcq), form can 'entice us to the verge of frenzy. Form is never trivial or indifferent; it is the magic of the world'. Sculptors, like other people, sometimes try to express their experiences in words and to seek philosophical understanding of them. That they often talk a great deal of what disenchanted and unexcitable contemporary philosophers regard as highfalutin metaphysical nonsense or seem to chatter like budgerigars is not surprising. They try to match the importance and excitement of their experiences with important and exciting-sounding ideas. The dry sandy wastes of fashionable British philosophy have little to offer them. At least the metaphysicians recognized these experiences; they were not frightened by them or seduced by a passion for clarity into denying them and spending their lives inside a linguistic goldfish-bowl. What they wrote may not in fact have been an explanation, but it did have the virtue of at least seeming like one.

An Exalted Theory of Ornament:
a study in Indian aesthetics*

PHILIP RAWSON

In the circles in which most of us move who are concerned with
living art 'ornament' is a dirty word. In a seminar of architectural
students one has heard it drop with the same effect as Mr. Kenneth
Tynan's more famous word in a million homes. And I hope you
won't think I am forearming myself against criticism by the sub-title
I have given this paper. It might seem to suggest that I mean to talk
about Indian aesthetics and isolate my subject in the comfortable
cocoon of a closed and dead system where it can do no harm and
merely gives us a little innocent fun. We were asked to be polemical,
weren't we? In fact many of you may think that I am bringing out
not one but many dirty words. Because to most people 'Indian
thought' still means Madame Blavatsky, spirit messages, theosophy
and a special kind of cant mysticism. It may also suggest the spiritual
fascism of a certain half–Ceylonese would–be Brahmin who lived
for many years in Boston and declared in one of his articles: 'There
must be a censorship of art.' I must ask you to clear your minds of all
these prejudices that may arise if you are confronted by Indian ideas
and terminology.

In fact I believe that in the field of aesthetics (as in the field of logic)
a great series of thinkers who lived in India and wrote in Sanskrit
between about the fourth century A.D. and the thirteenth have put
up many ideas which *must* be brought into our present-day debate
on art—ideas which we can use on works of art as one uses a can-

*Paper read at the Annual Conference of The British Society of Aesthetics in
September, 1966.

opener on a can, to get at the meat. Their writings could extend our conceptual armoury. But unfortunately they have never yet been properly translated. Even when a few people have written about them they have left the key terms untranslated and have, like prophets, demanded that we conform to their presentation of the ideas rather than helping us to welcome the ideas as naturalized citizens.

The word 'ornament' that I want to rehabilitate, and perhaps begin to naturalize, always makes us think nowadays of applied fruity swags, at their best like those of Grinling Gibbons; of Rococo ormolu; of ribbons on shepherdesses crooks, and Victorian sideboards. Our Puritan aesthetic has banished 'all that rubbish' in favour of something mysterious called 'expression'—Professor Gombrich's *bête noirè*. This can mean *anything*—the purified organization so aggressively demanded (but never supplied) by the young Le Corbusier (unless you live as Le Corbusier demanded you should, his houses and offices are hell) or those Romantic explosions of paint and howls so neatly sterilized by an accommodating society in rectangular frames or concert halls. The submerged current of Japonaiserie that still runs so strongly through our artistic veins makes us think of ornament as something superfluous, inessential, as trimming which adds nothing to the work but only obscures its beauty. Of course we are wrong—we have thrown out the baby with the Victorian bathwater. It is my thesis that the loss of the concept of ornament from our aesthetic code is both a disaster—and an illusion. My contention is that ornament is a functional aspect of art, embedded in it, not a gratuitous extra.

The Sanskrit term, used by generations of Indian writers, which is always translated 'ornament' is *alamkara*. I don't want to go into philology, and I am quite happy to stay with 'ornament' as a translation.

Every Indian aesthetician or writer on poetics worth his salt discussed *alamkara* at length. And so, although at bottom the idea seems a very simple one, once you begin to take it seriously and speculate about it, it takes you an awfully long way. Perhaps I should mention that the Indian writers were thinking mainly of poetry and drama. But music and visual art were always considered and the code was carefully designed to cover them. This, of course, is an important point. For one of the things which is so remarkable about European aesthetic discussion, and especially about recent statistical-psychological aesthetics, is that people who deal seriously with poetry and people who deal seriously with music have virtually no common ground. They are compelled to talk vaguely of 'expression' without any conceptual basis. Indian aesthetics recognizes a common ground and discusses it.

The simple basic idea is this. One states a proposition: 'This is a girl.' Did you feel your responses stir as I said it? Then one can invoke qualities to stir yet other responses. 'She is a pretty girl.' Not enough! 'She is a blonde girl, with freckles.' Even though the idea of the freckles may have given some of us a special kick, these are all relatively low-powered additions. One could say without going too far into semantics that these statements all represent a fairly neutral kind of communication between us—me and you—although it is certainly true that I have roused in you *feelings*, which go with the straight meaning. You may have suppressed them, but you *had* them. Now, according to Indian writers one can really begin to ornament the proposition with similes. If I say that my girl has 'hair like spun gold', you will think it corny. So it is. Because I am sure very few of us have ever seen spun gold or ever had real feelings in its presence which can be recalled when it is mentioned. It might be better if I said it looked like threads of honey—but that suggests sticky as well as sweet. Corn sheaves suggest dry as well as a bit bleached. The two together might cancel out each other's infelicities, especially if you add to the whole thing a suggestion that somehow the sun's light got into both of them, the honey and the corn. But these images, of course, are awfully banal. This is a pity. It probably means that we have most of us got into a state where we haven't any real feeling echoes available about these things.

But to pursue the banal images a bit further. One can pile up propositions plus similes on to the original girl-idea and begin to draw round her a particular halo. One can, for example, accumulate similes for the same girl as a unit. She is like—a gilded icon, the scent of warm pine trees, sunrise over the sea near Fiume. What do all these images make you think and feel? One by one they add their flavours of memory and feeling, their intimations of colour and touch, to the image of the girl entire. They invoke a halo of other experiences at the utterance of a simple sequence of words. And amongst themselves they have a thread of connexion—icon-pines-glitter-Slavonic devotion. One can also go on to divide the girl up into segments and attach similes to her parts. One can say (if one has ever had much contact with jewels) that her eyes are like melted sapphire, her nails like shell, her teeth like pearls, the Woolworth plastic poppers that she wears like the constellation of Draco, the dragon, encircling the pole. (You may think this extravagant, but she isn't *your* girl.) Here we must realize that our aesthetic perceptions have actually taken a leap into a region where dormant echoes of meaning, feeling and relationship can constellate; where memory-traces associated with jewels and the glitter and remote warmth of a tropical night can cease to be unconscious and come to form part of the *conscious* image of the basic girl. The Indians call this *alamkara* as an instrument of *dhvani* and *rasa*. In some ways the imagery must be false to the girl because she is not your possession. But in other ways it must represent an expansion of the truth. For the imagery combines genuine perceptions, genuinely related to each other, for which it so happens we have no real words.

This is all familiar literary criticism. Anyone who has studied Elizabethan poetry and Shakespeare in the light of their background of Italian and Spanish literature will recognize at once the standard pattern of the tenor (the girl) combined with images (analogies) that clothe her in her halo of trans-normal radiance, i.e. make her aesthetic instead of banal. This is *alamkara*, ornament. It is certainly something added to the tenor, giving it an aesthetic significance as more than an everyday significance. At the same time we should realize that the tenor is *there*, but it is our own responses not our belief in propositional truths which actually constitute the life of the ornament.

To follow the Indian ideas further. The metaphor is a more sophisticated ornament than the simile because it offers us the chance

to make propositions which unite the second terms of two metaphorical elements at a remove above the level at which ordinary
sense would link the first terms. Instead of saying that things about
the girl are like other things, we accept that they *are* these other
things (not in any verifiable sense) and then talk about them.
'Beneath the dark waves glint the silver fishes darting here and there,'
wrote an Indian poet. The hair is the dark water. Her glances are like
the silver fish. Or: 'The gilded galleon rode the sunlit waves, driven
by the trade winds of her longing.' Meaning: 'She combs her hair
getting ready for bed.' Instead of saying: 'Rosy-fingered dawn' as
a stock epithet—an ornament which brings into the image all sorts
of memories and feelings, many of them sensual—one says: 'But lo
the dawn in russet mantle clad walks o'er the dew of yon high
eastern hill.' And she has a more dignified mien, having become a
denser image via metaphor. For all the metaphors and images of
which poetic ornament is composed have almost an infinity of
density, ranging from those which may seem to involve true
propositions to those which seem purely fantastic. All can work only
by appealing to echoes of our own experience. By stepping off
beyond the point at which propositions are true, into the region of
metaphor, the metaphors (the ornament) may follow their own
logic. We thus move into the realm of imagery in which the meta-
physicals and symbolists moved. 'Some that have deeper digg'd
love's myre than I/ say where his centrique happiness doth lie.'
(Donne). Or Mallarmé's cigar ash: '... la cendre se sépare/ de son
clair baiser de feu.' And in much symbolist poetry, of course, the
tenor almost—but not quite—vanishes. However far submerged,
however intangible, it still supplies a focus for the poem and con-
solidates its interest.

All this according to Indian conceptions is ornament. Actually, if
we care to look deeply into the matter, it should be ornament in
our own sense too, if only we had not forbidden ourselves the
notion. In our literary criticism imagery of this kind has come to
absorb our entire interest to the exclusion of other questions such as
unity. Indian theory, however, concerns itself with other kinds of
ornament, and in so doing extends that common conceptual ground

out from under literature towards the foundations of the other arts. It is perhaps as yet hard to see how this concept can help to pick out in, let us say, a good piece of modern architecture what is the particular aesthetic radiance the work possesses. But it can.

At bottom this kind of metaphorical imagery—or ornament—has a particular function according to Indian theory. This is to bond together by means of what can be called prismatic diction man and the nature in which he lives. In similes, metaphors and images are combined elements of man's experience of himself inside his clothes and home, his environment. The environment may be personalized to bring it into contact with man, or man may be dissolved into his environment. The threads of association by analogy which justify the similes and metaphors of poetry are held to be no less valid than the most apparently objective facts. The fact that we happen to have developed a conceptual and terminological usage—'red'—to designate a form analogically relating the experience-content of a particular series of perceptions does not make that form any more 'true' than a genuine analogically structured form which has no accepted usage-designation. A form which has no name but can only be indicated by assembling and juxtaposing references to experiences to which it is common is as real as any named form. In fact this theory insists that art is talking about reality, but a reality which is not enclosed in the pigeon-holes of everyday usage with its conventionally defined and limited 'things' and 'qualities', which of course simply reflect Indo-European linguistic structure with its nouns, adjectives and verbs. A whole realm of experience lies unrecognized and atrophied in us unless art evokes it by collecting and juxtaposing sensuous memory-traces which have no usage upon which to constellate. So said the Indians. This being said, we can follow Indian theory further. Amongst the kinds of ornament recognized in Indian poetics is sound. Sanskrit poets were extremely fond of elaborate sonic effects and rhythmic patterns of great complexity. I have written elsewhere at length about metaphorical form in the visual arts. (See *Indian Sculpture*, 1966).

We must admit, of course, that this idea of ornament will have its own dangers and its own special cul-de-sacs. It is these of which we are nowadays most acutely aware. Obviously it will be possible to accumulate metaphorical ornaments which have no intrinsic relationship to each other. There may be repetitive ornaments—though even here rhythmic patterns may be involved which themselves amount to valid ornament. The weary overloading of the sideboard with swags and curlicues, or of the Indian temple with lifeless foliage and mouldings, did take place. But this would have been *bad* ornament, which would have been condemned by everyone as simply bad art. The Indian idea of ornament was that it represented radiance and the wealth of imaginative allusion. It awoke in an unsoundable depth echoes of meaning and intuitions of relationships amongst our perceptions of the real world which no everyday prose could ever elicit. After all the arguments were settled *dhvani was* one of the functions of *alamkara*.

Nearly everything which I have mentioned is usually gathered nowadays under the rubric of 'expression'. This is a word which to me—and to others more distinguished than I am—seems an almost total semantic blank. I am a dedicated admirer of much of the best art which has been called 'Expressionist'. But 'expression' as an aesthetic concept is, I believe, virtually useless unless it is underpinned by a clearer substructure. And this is something which most of the critics who use it never do, even in their own minds. Of course, like everyone else, I have ideas about the reasons why 'expression' became so popular, especially in writing about the visual arts, and about the history of this development. But only one fact is important to my argument now. It is that soon after 1900 artists and art-lovers were suddenly confronted with an enormous mass of works of art from all over the world, the forms of which they could never hope to understand or appreciate. There may have been something about, say, a Baga mask which awoke a few echoes in their minds. For these masks still represented numinous *faces*. That is, there was a tenor of some kind available to carry the image across to them. But there was too much missing. There were no memories or associations in a Western city-dweller's mind related to the shapes of and to the feelings connected with the gourds, shells or horns which the forms were intended to evoke in the minds of the original customers. The forms, therefore, seemed merely 'significant' in a general way and the fact that a face served as a tenor seemed merely irrelevant, because the European had never known it used as the face of a dancing and moving spirit-figure which would both locate it and arouse vivid responses. 'Significant form' was therefore merely stultified form, muffled 'expression', something resembling the sounds heard on a cheesy old radio set badly tuned to unintelligible music from Cairo. 'Expression' is the only thing we can call this. The tenor has been dismissed as irrelevant. The magnificent figurative 'ornament' of meaningful associations is simply not there. And so we Europeans told ourselves there was no 'message' to get. We were just to feel it *here*, in the belly, a sort of muffled thump. Successfully evolved ornament we would call ornament which works for *us*. But I'm afraid I believe that even with our own great masters we miss an awful lot of what was meant. For literature at least some classic works of criticism such as Lowes's *The Road to Xanadu* or Ellmann's *Yeats* have opened up windows into the echo-world of metaphor and image for people who read the poets. But how very very seldom has anything of comparable value been done for visual art! And how many horrible mistakes of interpretation have been made even by distinguished people in the past! There have always been architectural styles—which we still consider beautiful—which bear obvious ornament such as swags and garlands—works by Alberti, Brunelleschi, Asam and a thousand others. But what is nowadays never admitted is that the actual forms of which most great architecture is composed are in fact ornamental in the Indian sense. If you asked any modern engineer-architect to knuckle down under your accountant and build you something to do the job of the Vierzehnheiligenkirche or St. Peter's, it could be done adequately in stone if not in concrete. But it would probably lack the special radiance of form which great architecture achieves not by adhering closely to its mere use, its mere material, its cost ceiling, but by the suggestiveness of its forms, its detail and its synthesis. Even when they were produced it would have been perfectly possible for the old architects of those buildings to have made utility shelters of stone spanning the same areas, perhaps even better adapted to the customers' demands. Look what happened to Michelangelo's plan for the lantern of St. Peter's!

I have referred to the essential 'tenor' which Indian theory accepts as sustaining and focusing ornament. Because ornament can only be defined in relation to tenor, this is a notion which we should examine a bit more closely. It is not the same as the 'subject' or the 'prose-sense', nor is it even remotely like the meaning of the whole. Rather it is a thread giving extension in either time or place or both. It may play the sort of role that Ortega y Gasset admitted the plot of a novel has to play—like the tent-poles in a tent. It is not the whole, but without it there is no whole. Its importance is structural, giving to the novel its intelligible extension in time, just as the tent-poles give the fabric of the tent its extension in space. We find a 'thread', a tenor, in every good poem ever written, even in Mallarmé. It may be hard to find, but it is there. The concept of the tenor is, I suppose, derived from the practice of medieval music, when the known and often insignificant melody was sung by the tenor voices, giving an intelligible basis of unity to the composition, whilst the other voices supplied the emotionally evocative ornament. So the meaning of the composition was the sum of the significance of all its ornamental parts. But without the tenor there would have been no *sum* of parts, only a succession of items. In the same way the ornamental forms of great architecture are supplied with their tenor by the basic building theme—a space, and its uses. If an architect confines himself to stating merely the tenor of his building, he will make a banality. He will, as it were, merely sing over the little tenor tune or show us the tent-poles. A banality is not made radiant by its usefulness but only by the ornamental evocativeness of the actual surfaces of the forms chosen and assembled. Especially in painting today one can often find a confusion between tenor and ornament which seems to sterilize the invention of many unlucky artists who are bogged down in the Malraux Expressionism muddle. Because, of course, such concepts as these were meant by the Indian scholars to help not hinder the artist, to offer weapons for his armoury and aid in the deployment of all his resources. To identify the two functiona poles of one artistic structure, the tenor and the ornament, can make one able to develop the work to a high instead of a low degree. Great artists of all kinds have in fact done precisely this. It is no accident that *Hamlet* is good and has a tenor or that the same applies to the works of Titian or Rembrandt or Cézanne or, as Schönberg has sufficiently proved, those of Brahms.

What sort of role does the tenor play *vis-à-vis* the ornament in Indian theory? At its simplest level it merely provides a 'story-line', plot, and characters taken perhaps from one of the epics. But this is a banality; without the ornament there is no art. Unless Rama and Sita are clothed in their brilliant robes, unless they speak with gestures whose ramified significance turns them all into complex puns and allusions, unless they move with rhythmic patterns that each context fills with emotive suggestion, unless they speak a figurative poetry which draws into the arena of the play a kind of pageant of associated natural phenomena—all ornament—there is no art. But on the other hand without Rama and Sita—who were used times without number as tenor—there is no art either. Without them allusions fail because they have no context and their echoes never return. The same rhythm or gesture which recurs more than once—for after all the repertoire of possible forms is in a sense limited—without them recurs with no different meaning. Only a moving context can give them a changing meaning. In a very important sense the tenor gives to the ornament its only possibility of realization. For despite the canting of misguided mystagogues we know there is no such thing as 'pure space' that visual arts can 'express', nor is there such a thing as 'pure unconditioned time' which other arts can express. Space and time are apprehended by us, and can therefore play a role in art, only as it were obliquely. They are fictitious entities, given some sort of spurious existence through being called by names which are nouns. Our only access to our spatial and temporal intuitions is via functions of bodies and sequences which we ourselves identify and agree upon. But this is a very large issue indeed. The point envisaged by Indian theory which I want to make is that the tenor in art provides the bodies and sequences which make our exploration of the complexities of ornament possible; and, most important of all, make it possible for the creative artist to produce a genuine *wealth* of imagery. Many artists nowadays, if you know them well, will allow their cynical business sense to emerge. 'You've put too much in that one, old boy! You've enough for five or six.' In fact it is impossible to tie up every single metaphorical thread in a poem or picture. If you operate according to the polarity of ornament and tenor, you can from time to time home safely back on to the tenor and carry on with your imagery. This Yeats, for example, well knew. The alternatives, it seems to me, are to blunder around in a fog of disordered intuitions or to revert to an emotive parsimony which dares not venture beyond the simplest ornament of texture and isolated bits of unconsummated rhythms. The rift between construction today and what one can call Romantic expressionism may well be a direct product of the loss of the polar concepts represented in Indian theory by ornament and tenor. The poles should work together in combination rather than in isolation. Both schools are right; but each has only half the resources it should have.

As to the nature of tenor—I cannot possibly make any prescriptions. To do so would be to damn myself out of my own mouth. All one can do is to discover the tenors of other artists at other times. This one can easily do if one knows more or less what one is looking for. Perhaps it is worth pointing out that the tenor of a poem may itself be suggested by an image like those involved in ornament; or that in art it may be a similar given theme, e.g. Picasso's famous goat (the tenor) whose belly-basket is literally made out of a basket or the bull's head from a bicycle saddle and handlebars. I regret that Picasso was so often unable really to *use* this kind of metaphor as the basis for sustained ornamental thought—in my sense. There is one important aspect of Indian theory on the nature of the tenor, however, one which could have important bearing on one particular confusion which often appears in European art criticism. This is a strict differentiation between the purely aesthetic experience of the *traces* of feelings and the everday experiences of feelings themselves. The way it is expressed in Indian theory is as follows—I quote from my book *Indian Sculpture* (p. 128):

It is of the utmost importance that the spectator should *not* respond to the artistic activities as if they were realities. They must remain purely symbolic. The various devices of theatrical presentation—the stage sets, properties, lights, make-up, costume, gestures, dance-steps, music, eye-movements, verse with its rhythms, rhyme and assonance, even the very atmosphere of the occasion—are expressly meant to prevent the spectator reacting as he would in real life either to the actor or to the person portrayed. He must not behave as he would if he met Mr. X the actor, or as he would if he met the hero Rama whom the actor is portraying. He must not respond to the actor's apparent feelings as he would towards a real person who was actually feeling those feelings. He must not, in fact, actually fall into one of the Permanent Emotional Modes. At the same time echoes of actual feeling-responses drawn from the Modes must continually be touched by these very theatrical means. This inhibition of normal reactions combined with the deliberate evocation of a multiplicity of feeling-echoes results in the actor's expression evoking in the spectator's mind a quite unusual state. For if the mind must not be absorbed in the particular emotions, which are not the purpose of the art, it remains free to be aware of the range and sequence of the responses without any one of them taking over the whole attention. What the mind thus becomes conscious of is not a simple object of cognition—the actor—nor a particular feeling, nor a thought, nor a fantasy—for the actor and the stage are indubitably real and not pro-jected from within the spectator. The mind does become conscious of that peculiar and individual psycho-physical state, for which *rasa*, flavour, is the adopted term, and which we may call an image of the Emotional Mode itself.

The point is that if we experience actual horror, actual desire, actual disgust, there is no art. We do not react before Goya's primitive deity devouring his children as we would before an actual person eating his children. If we did, we would only endure everyday, uninstructed, violent emotion. Thus even the realist cinema, in so far as it is art, can never expect to make us experience an *actual* emotion. We must never react to the art-made image as if it were a reality. This means that certain kinds of 'new-objective' art may be to some extent barking up the wrong tree. For Indian theory is quite clear that the tenor, whilst it must seem objective enough to provide a thorough basis for the structure of ornament, must nevertheless be clearly and decisively *not* an object but only a notional object. The implications of this for all our thinking on art are vast.

Now I must admit I have made it seem as if ornament and tenor supply the whole basis of an Indian aesthetic theory. In fact, of course, these notions represent only one aspect of this theory. There are all sorts of important concepts which call for discussion, some familiar, among them *rasa, dhvani, vasana, sthayibhava.* I have hinted at the presence of many in what I have said. Because this theory is *whole.*

Art and Illusion*

RICHARD WOLLHEIM

I

There is a question that few of those who feel a concern with painting and have the habit of looking at pictures cannot have asked
themselves at some moment or other. The moment most likely was
an early one in their experience of art when, on opening some
illustrated history of art or trailing through the long endless galleries
of a museum, they first became aware of the astounding variety of
styles, modes, manners in which at different times different artists
have recorded the one unique unchanging reality. Once asked, however, the question is usually put aside, quite rapidly, probably with
embarrassment, as revealing a naïvety or literal-mindedness quite
unsuitable in a serious and sophisticated lover of the arts.

It is around this question that *Art and Illusion*[1] has been constructed.
And if I may for a moment contravene the self-denying ordinance
that I have for the course of this lecture passed upon myself and
indulge in a brief tribute to the author of the book, I should like to
say that I regard it as typical of the fundamental and radical character
of Professor Gombrich's thinking that he should take as his starting-
point a question that nearly all of us find it natural to raise, but then
instead of, as many do, thinking it superior to ignore it and pass on,
he should prefer to press into the service of answering it a formidable
and dazzling erudition.

The question might be put like this: Why has representative art a
history? Why did Duccio and Rubens, Van Eyck and Monet,
Uccello and Watteau, all of whom, it must be granted, were interested

---

* This paper was read in a slightly shorter form to The British Society of Aesthetics
on 6 June, 1962. An earlier draft of the lecture appeared under the 'Reflections on
"Art and Illusion"' in *Arts Yearbook* (New York) for 1961.

in depicting the visible world, depict it in such different, such bewilderingly different, ways—so different, indeed, that we have no method, even in the mind's eye, of abstracting these differences, but invariably see the manner as part of the picture, take in the subject together with the style? Are these differences, we might ask, essential or merely accidental? Could the Egyptians, for instance, have depicted the human body in the way the Florentines did, and could the Florentines have represented nature as did the Impressionists?

2

The question why art has a history does not itself fall within the domain of art history. The art historian has done his work when he has recorded the changes that together constitute the history of art, and if we go on to ask why these changes occur, or (more accurately) why change at all occurs, we stand in need of some general body of theory to which we can appeal. There are, however, both in the literature of the subject and in ordinary reflective thought, a number of theories which set out to answer our question, and as good a way as any to approach Gombrich's book would be to do so via a consideration of them—not just because Gombrich himself has something to say about each of them but because, in an uncertain terrain, they provide fixed points by which his own theory can be plotted.

The first theory we might consider is what could be called the *perceptual* theory of artistic change.[2] According to this theory each painter paints the world as he sees it, but each painter sees the world for himself, idiosyncratically, and in consequence the range and diversity of representational art can be accounted for in terms of the varieties of human perception. Giotto, Rembrandt, Van Gogh painted things differently because, and to the degree to which, they saw things differently. Secondly, there is what might be called the *technological* theory of artistic change,[3] according to which the course of art follows the history of technical advance in the skill of representation: to specific inventions and discoveries are attributable the capacity of painters to render certain effects of likeness, to achieve certain tricks of verisimilitude, that were quite outside the range of their predecessors. According to this view Egyptian art exemplifies childish methods because Egyptian artists could do no better, whereas in the work of later artists, say of the Quattrocento, or the High Renaissance, or the nineteenth century, we see evidence of an ever-increasing body of skill in the technique of representation. And, thirdly, there is the theory of *seeing and knowing*,[4] regarded by many as the most sophisticated account of the matter obtainable, according to which successive artists are engaged in a collective and continuous struggle to rid themselves of the burden of knowledge in their efforts to portray the world precisely as they see it. Knowing how things really are—for instance, that the human face is symmetrical along the axis of the nose—is an obstacle in the way of depicting things as they appear to be—with, for instance, only half the face visible when seen in profile. To achieve a purely visual art what is required is to see the world directly, without preconceptions, and it is this battle against the corrupting power of knowledge, this determined effort to recapture the vision of the innocent eye, that accounts for the evolution of the visual arts from, say, the fully 'conceptual' art of Egypt to the fully 'perceptual' art of the Impressionists.

3

None of these theories is in Gombrich's eyes without interest or, indeed, without its element of truth; but against each of them as it stands he brings, either implicitly or explicitly, what amounts to a fatal objection.

The perceptual theory is defective because it accounts only for the fact that art displays diversity, and not for the further fact that it possesses a history. For if art were merely the expression of personal vision, we should have no reason to assume, as we do, that pictures produced in proximity would be marked by a certain 'family likeness', nor should we be able to account for the temporal sequence of styles, which is not just an assumption, but a fact, about the course of painting. To remedy this defect in the perceptual theory some writers of a more speculative temper have postulated a history for human

vision or 'seeing' itself,[5] tracing its evolution from the simple
schematic vision of children, to be found at the dawn of history, to
the subtle and sensitive perceptions of modern man—the idea being
that art could then be geared to the history of vision and so, indirectly,
acquire a history of its own. But any such supplementary hypothesis
either straightway takes us out of the empirical world into a realm
of unverifiable entities or else turns out to be narrowly circular: for
when we ask for the evidence in favour of the hypothesis of visual
evolution, either we are entertained with empty metaphysical
speculation or else we are referred back to the changes in artistic style
that the hypothesis was originally invoked to explain.

By contrast the technological theory has the dual virtue both of
accounting for the historical character of art and of admitting into
its framework of explanation only sensible entities. On the debit
side, however, the technological theory might be said to allow art a
history only at the price of denying it value. For if the story of art is
to be interpreted purely as a story of technical advance, of ever
increasing skill in the production of certain admired effects, it is hard
to see why we should esteem the outmoded experiments of the past.
In their day they had value, being the best that could be achieved. In
our day they may have historical interest, like a spinning jenny or a
daguerreotype, or even for some a certain nostalgic charm, like a
vintage car—but certainly no intrinsic value. Furthermore the
technological theory, while giving us an historical account of artistic
production, leads to a curiously unhistorical conception of artistic
psychology. For according to the theory Giotto differs from Michelangelo and Michelangelo from Degas in that Giotto couldn't do
what Michelangelo could do and Michelangelo couldn't do what
Degas could do. But this in turn suggests that it was not alien to
Giotto to want to do what Michelangelo did, perhaps even what
Degas did. And this conception of earlier painters hallucinated by
images which only later painters were able to realize—conceiving
these images in the mind's eye with a clarity and finesse of execution
that far transcended the limitations of their art, but incompetent to
set them down in line or paint because of the technical backwardness
of their age—such a conception betrays a disordered historical

imagination.[6] And yet it seems demanded by the technological theory.

Finally, there is the theory of 'seeing and knowing'. In various ways an advance upon its rivals, able at once to provide an explanation for many of the phenomena of pictorial evolution and also to furnish a terminology in which a great deal of representational art can profitably be discussed, the theory fails because of its attachment to the simple unexamined distinction between perception and inference, between what we really see with our eyes and what we know through the intellect. But it is to be observed that the acceptance of this distinction is not peculiar to the theory of 'seeing and knowing'. For both the technological and the perceptual theories contain in their different ways a reference to a kind of art which is occupied with the direct transcription of what the artist really sees: in the one case as the end, in the other case as the pattern, of all pictorial art. According to the technological theory a completely naturalistic art is that towards which all representation aspires; according to the perceptual theory, it is its inevitable achievement. The question then arises: Is Naturalism possible?

4

'Neutral Naturalism', as Gombrich construes the term, means a form of art that, outside any reference to style or convention, can be regarded as *the* transcription or portrayal of a particular scene or incident, in which every line or stroke made by the hand is uniquely determined by what is given to the eye. And it is Gombrich's contention that such an art is a chimera. 'There is no neutral naturalism,' he writes (p. 75). To establish this point he uses, as far as I can see, three sets of arguments, which have to be collected from across the length of the book.

In the first place Gombrich employs arguments—most of them familiar enough but here restated with fine lucidity—which relate to the limitation of the artist's media. Take, for instance, the essential problem of colour. Nature produces, as we are all aware, a vast range of chromatic effects, and to achieve this she has at her disposal

two variables: local colour, that is the actual colour of the object
and light, the ever-changing light that plays on the object. The
painter, by contrast—and this is a fact of which we sometimes lose
sight—has only one resource: the actual colour of his pigment, which
is always seen in, or at any rate as if it were in, standard conditions.
The light in a gallery or a drawing-room may vary, brighten and
fade, but such fluctuations are something with which the picture has
to contend, not something that the painter can make use of. However, even if *per impossibile* the painter were able to match what he
sees area for area, it still does not follow that there would be an
identity of colour between the picture and the scene it depicts. For
to assume this in the first place ignores the fact that tone varies with
size, so that a small patch painted with one pigment will most likely
not resemble a larger patch painted with the same pigment (pp.
262–3): and it is of course most unlikely that a painting will be life-
size with its subject. Secondly, the 'mosaic theory of representation',
as Gombrich calls it at one point (p. 263), leaves out of account the
further fact that tone is affected by the relations between the areas
(pp. 259–62). In this context Gombrich cites the 'spreading effect' in
the famous von Bezold arabesque (Fig. 251), but this is only a
singularly striking demonstration of the more general truth that if
you alter the relation between two shapes they will look different
even if they are of the same local colour. And it seems inevitable that
the relation between two shapes on a flat canvas will be different
from those which exist between the two elements in reality that they
are supposed to represent.

The second set of arguments that Gombrich employs against
Neutral Naturalism relate to the phrase 'what we really see'. For it
must be evident that the artistic ideal of portraying things as we
really see them, or of setting down what we really see—and it is
around this ideal that Neutral Naturalism is constructed—could not
long survive a demonstration that the phrase 'what we really see' has
no clear reference. It seems to be an aim of Gombrich's to provide
such a demonstration.

I must say now that I do not follow all of Gombrich's arguments
on this point, but I get the impression that much of it does not really

engage the target upon which he wishes to direct it. For whereas what he claims to be attacking is the proposition that in all cases of seeing there is something that we really see, the proposition that much of the time he in fact attacks is a more specific one: namely, that in all cases of seeing there is some *one* thing that we really see. In other words Gombrich flings down his challenge in the direction of the very general thesis that all our vision has a determinate object. But the thesis that he actually fights and (I would say) conclusively defeats is one that accepts this and then goes on to identify this object in a special way with a configuration of flat coloured patches lying in a two-dimensional field. And this is, of course, merely a particular version or interpretation of the more general thesis. One could continue to think that in all cases of vision there *is* something that we really see, without thinking that it is always something of a specific and identical kind and *a fortiori* without thinking that it is of the kind that, traditionally, empiricist philosophers and psychologists have thought it to be. One could agree (and I am sure one should) with Gombrich that: 'We do not observe the appearance of colour patches and then proceed to interpret their meaning' (p. 219), without being forced to maintain that there is nothing that we really observe.

There are passages in *Art and Illusion* where Gombrich certainly shows himself aware of the difference between the avowed and the real object of his criticism. So, for instance, he writes: 'We "really" see distance not changes in size: we "really" see light, not modifications of tone; and most of all we really see a brighter face and not a change in muscular contractions' (p. 282); and championing Constable's naturalism he writes: 'What Constable "really" saw in Wivenhoe Park was surely a house across a lake' (p. 278) as opposed presumably to a 'flat patchwork of colours' which he had denounced above as being a fabrication of false theory. Now in these passages Gombrich explicitly admits that there is something we really see, and if he still insists on placing inverted commas around the word 'really', this is no more than a pious tribute he pays to the more extreme thesis that he advocates elsewhere: namely, that whenever we see, there is nothing at all of which it can properly be said that it is what we really see.

Of this more extreme thesis I shall have more to say later. Here I only want to point out that the particular form in which Gombrich subscribes to it, i.e. that all seeing is interpretation, might seem to be not only not the obvious contrary, but not even a proper contradictory, of the thesis that it is designed to supplant, i.e. that in all cases of seeing there is something that we really see. For it might be held—I would say justifiably—that in the context of perception the expressions 'what we really see' and 'interpretation' secure and maintain their significance from their mutual contrast: so that someone who wanted (like Gombrich) to deny that there was anything we really saw, ought also to deny the existence of interpretation—instead of (as Gombrich in fact does) asserting it universally.

On the question whether the more limited thesis that Gombrich does establish in this connexion is in any way fatal to Neutral Naturalism I find it difficult to arrive at a stable opinion: partly because the theory of Neutral Naturalism is itself somewhat indeterminate. What the thesis certainly does is to weaken the naturalistic ideal considerably, by breaking any connexion that one might have supposed to exist between it and a specific or identifiable style—for instance, Impressionism. For if there is no one kind of thing that we really see whenever we see, then the art that sets out to depict what we really see will not have any consistent look; there is no pictorial manner in which we can say a priori that a Neutral Naturalist should work. And it certainly seems as though in the three theories of artistic change that we have considered the assumption was that there is such a manner.

The third and final line of argument that Gombrich brings against Neutral Naturalism derives from the role of projection in our vision of art. For even if the artist were able to set down on the canvas an image that literally resembled exactly what he had seen, there would be no certainty as to how the spectator would see the image. For the image would be ambiguous: and ambiguous not just in the theoretical sense that it could be seen in different ways, but in the practical sense (though Gombrich is not always careful to keep these two senses apart) that it almost certainly would be seen in different ways. Strictly speaking, this fact need not be seen as an objection to Neutral

Naturalism when this is defined, as it was above, as a form of art in which every stroke was uniquely determined by what was given to the eye. But such a definition, I suggest, seemed satisfactory because it seemed natural to assume that if there was a one-one correspondence between what the eye saw and what the hand did in obedience to it, there would also be a one-one correspondence between what the hand did and what the eye saw of what the hand had done. If what is uniquely transcribed is ambiguously seen, Naturalism loses much of its point.

5

At this stage of the argument, however, when Naturalism appears to be fatally trapped, Gombrich suddenly calls off the chase. For has not the argument gone too far? 'The old insight that it is naïve to demand that a painting should look real is gradually giving way to the conviction that it is naïve to believe any painting can ever look real' (p. 209). And such a conviction, however ingeniously argued for, must ultimately be absurd. For do we not unhesitatingly regard some painters as more realistic than others—Masaccio, say, than Cimabue, or Gainsborough than Perugino? Are there not even certain painters, like Constable or Monet, whom we consider to have achieved about as much in the mastery of appearance as is humanly possible?

The problem, then, is not so much the existence as the definition of Naturalism: for if there is a respectable form of Naturalism, it cannot be the 'Neutral Naturalism' whose discomfiture we have observed. At this juncture Gombrich suggests a redefinition of Naturalism in terms of the information that the picture conveys. To say, for instance, that a drawing of Tivoli is correct or truthful means 'that those who understand the notation will derive no false information from the drawing' (p. 78; cf. p. 252).

This redefinition has two great merits. In the first place it respects the simple logical point that truth and falsehood cannot properly be predicated of objects: strictly speaking, they are properties of statements and if we loosely talk of a picture as correct or truthful, this is an oblique way of talking about a certain set of assertions that can be derived from the picture (p. 59). The question then arises: What assertions are we entitled to derive from a picture?—or, to put it another way: How much of the picture are we justified in interpreting or decoding? And this connects with the second merit of Gombrich's redefinition, namely, that it emphasizes the 'conventional' element in any form of Naturalism. For in order to know how much of the picture is to be decoded we must be acquainted with the convention or—to use a locution which Gombrich at one point (p. 76) insists is 'more than a loose metaphor'—with the 'language' or 'vocabulary' in which the picture is composed. For instance, it would be quite erroneous to infer from the fact that our drawing of Tivoli is correct 'that Tivoli is bounded by wiry lines' (p. 90). To make such an inference would be to misunderstand the contour-convention in a drawing.

From Gombrich's redefinition of Naturalism two consequences important for his general theory are derived. The first is that though certain forms of art are clearly non-naturalistic, there is no unique form of naturalistic art towards which all forms of representational painting approximate to a greater or lesser degree. To posit the existence of such a style would be to make two further assumptions. First, that the conveying of information is a simple cumulative task, so that a picture containing a certain amount of information could always be revised so as to convey some further piece of information. But it may be that some information can be conveyed only at the expense of omitting other information: in constructing a picture we may have to make a choice. Indeed, Gombrich points out not merely that this may be so, but that in fact it is so—and he illustrated his point ingeniously by comparing three representations of a boat, one by Duccio, one by Constable and one by Turner (Figs. 243, 5, 245), and he shows how, as we cast our eye across the paintings in historical sequence, we get progressively more information about the appearance of the boat as at a certain moment and in a certain light, and progressively less information about the structure of the boat. We are told new things at the price of having to take familiar things for granted. And the second assumption that seems to be involved in the idea of a unique naturalistic art is that there is only one way of conveying a given piece of information. But this also is clearly false. 'The world may be approached from a different angle and the information given may yet be the same' (p. 78).

The other consequence of this revised conception of Naturalism is that we can now see that a 'correct' or 'truthful' form of art could not conceivably have been the starting point of artistic evolution. Defined as it is, it could only be 'the end product' (ibid.) of a long process of trial and error.

And here at last we have the stage set for Gombrich's account of the evolution of representational art: the theory of 'making and matching'. In the beginning, the artist makes a diagram of what he wants to depict—a crude model which, for those who understand it, succeeds in conveying a modicum of information about its object: a schema. Gradually, however, as the schema is matched against the object, deficiencies in its informativeness are brought to light. Suggestions are made as to how these deficiencies could be made good, and both the accuracy and the amount of the information it provided be increased; and so we have the schema corrected. The corrected schema, however, also has its deficiencies, and so the process of making and matching, of schema and correction, unfolds itself. At each step the resultant schema can always be said to be more life-like than the schema of which it is a correction. And so it might seem that, as the process enters an advanced stage, we attain to an art of verisimilitude, a fully fledged Naturalism. And so, in an historical sense, we do. But we should not conclude from this that if only we had used our eyes properly in the first place, this kind of Naturalism could have come into being without the long, painful struggle that led up to it. For such a conclusion would not merely be false; it would be absurd.[7]

6

But, we might reasonably ask, absurd in what sense? What kind of impropriety would attach to the supposition that representational art did not evolve in accordance with the principle of schema and correction? In other words, what is the status of Gombrich's hypothesis?

It must be admitted at the outset that on this point Gombrich himself is singularly unenlightening. In various places he talks of the 'psychology' of artistic procedure as though his theory were a contribution to our understanding of how the artist's mind actually works. But I do not think that this could really be his intention, for, if it were, one consequence would be that his hypothesis would be purely empirical. It would rest simply on observed fact, and would be overthrown if it could be shown that some artists worked or had worked in a way other than that of schema and correction. But I do not think that Gombrich really envisages the possibility of a counter-example to his hypothesis, and this suggests that he puts it forward as a *logical*, not as a *psychological*, truth.

Gombrich's contention is, then, I take it, that the idea of representation necessarily involves the idea of trial and error. It is not merely that in the history of art, as we have it, making always does in point of fact precede matching, but that making must precede matching.

But if making must precede matching, what this means is that we cannot have matching without (i.e. without being preceded by) making. But it does not mean that we cannot have making without (i.e. without being succeeded by) matching. Now this asymmetry is of great importance to Gombrich, for it is in virtue of it that the hypothesis of making and matching acquires its secondary role in his system: that of an *historical* as well as a *logical* principle. In Chapters IV and V Gombrich attempts to define certain very general phases in the history of art by reference to the extent to which making was linked with matching.

In Egyptian art making was virtually independent of matching. And this was because of the peculiar function that the Egyptians attached to the image. As far as we can reconstruct the situation their main concern would seem to have been not to secure a representation of an aspect or element of life—which would naturally have led them to correct the image, once they had made it, in the interests of verisimilitude—but simply to make an object. It is only with 'the Greek revolution' that we have the desire for an image that not merely existed but was 'convincing', that not merely stood for itself but also spoke of things outside itself; and it is at this juncture that, for the first time, we come across the restless, dissatisfied reappraisal of the object with the constant aim of bringing it closer and closer to the reality it attempts to mirror.

Again, Gombrich suggests that the connexion between making and matching can be used to bring out the difference between medieval and post-medieval art. For in the Middle Ages the impact of 'the Greek revolution' was comparatively spent. The image was still regarded as primarily representational, but there was no longer that burning discontent with each and every effort to make it convey information about the world. For this we have to wait till the Renaissance. 'To the Middle Ages', Gombrich writes, 'the scheme is the image: to the post-medieval artist, it is the starting point for corrections, adjustments, adaptations, the means to probe reality and to wrestle with the particular' (p. 148). Between the Middle Ages and the world of the contemporary artist there lies a period where not only is there no matching without prior making (as is necessarily the case) but there is no making without subsequent matching. In this period occurred the apogee of European Naturalism.

7

The highly compressed summary that I have been offering of Gombrich's doctrine might suggest an obvious title for his book: *Art and Naturalism*. Yet if we look to the book, what do we find it called? Something quite different: *Art and Illusion*. Nor is this a mere vagary of the title-page. For when we go on to examine the text itself we find that, throughout, the two sets of terms, 'naturalism', 'naturalistic' on the one hand, 'illusion', 'illusionistic' on the other, are used interchangeably. And there corresponds to this linguistic practice a substantive doctrine. It would appear to be Gombrich's considered view that, within certain limitations, Naturalism *is* illusion, and that a painting is to be regarded as more naturalistic the more effective it is in creating its illusion.

Total effectiveness will of course seldom be within its reach: 'that such illusions are rarely complete goes without saying', Gombrich concedes (p. 234). And there are reasons for this, some of which at any rate in no way reflect upon the skill of the artist. In the first place there is the evident or all but invariably evident setting or context in which the work of art is displayed, which is bound to provide a contrast with the work itself. As the eye passes over the picture, across the frame, to the wall on which it is placed, it cannot but become aware, however cunning the painting may be, of a discrepancy or discontinuity which is fatal to the illusion. In this connexion Gombrich refers to the work of Baroque decorators or *quadratisti*, who were as successful as anyone could be in overcoming these difficulties: and he points out how their choice of subject-matter—the sky, a frieze, a cornice, always something which might actually have existed in the very place where it is portrayed—was guided by their determination to reduce or blur as much as possible 'the transition between the solidly built and the flatly painted' (p. 221).

Secondly, there is the fact that a two-dimensional illusion can only ever work for a stationary eye. Not only must the eye not take in the context of the picture, but it must not move either inside the picture or relative to the picture. For as soon as it does, it will require in the interests of consistency modifications in the perspectival profiles of what is depicted, which of course will not occur. 'As soon as we move', Gombrich writes à propos of a Fantin-Latour, 'the illusion must disappear, since the objects in the still life will not shift in relation to each other' (p. 234).

Finally, even if the visual illusion is complete, totally working, that is, for the stationary eye whose field of vision is wholly contained within the picture frame, it is unlikely to be accompanied by all those other 'expectations' which are, according to Gombrich, an integral part of our recognizing or identifying something as an object of a certain kind: expectations of what we would see if we moved, of what we would feel if we touched the object. 'All perceiving relates to expectations' Gombrich writes (p. 254), and he describes how all painters from the Greeks onwards have struggled to supplement the direct pictorial effects that were within their power with induced expectations. Yet these expectations, even when induced, hang by the slightest thread. We may feel that if we craned our neck a little, the dinner plate would look circular, or that if we reached out our hand, we could touch the bloom—but we have only to try to crane our neck or to contemplate reaching out our hand, and the expectations will vanish and with them the completeness of the illusion.

Gombrich allows, then, that very few naturalistic paintings are totally illusionistic. 'Only in extreme cases . . . are the illusions of art illusions about our real environment' (p. 234). But this does not militate against the view, to which he continues to adhere, that Naturalism depends upon illusion. The illusion may invariably break down: but then who says that a painting is ever totally naturalistic? It would seem an accurate formulation of Gombrich's thought to say that for him the more naturalistic a painting is, the more closely it approximates to a successful and sustained illusion—an illusion, that is, as successful and sustained as the medium permits.[8]

Such a conception of Naturalism is, it seems to me, quite untenable. In the first place it is clearly impossible for Gombrich to hold to such a conception, for it is quite inconsistent with the rest of his thought. Not merely is it out of line with his general notion of art as something conventional, which, for instance, offers up its secrets only to those who 'understand the notation' (p. 90), but more specifically it makes total nonsense of the definition he offers elsewhere of Naturalism. For a picture, it will be recalled, is said to be naturalistic in so far as it conveys (or, more precisely, in so far as there can be derived from it) correct information. But how can we be said to gain information about an object from something that we take to be that object? A *trompe l'œil* painting of a duck, for instance, cannot, at least as long as it succeeds in being *trompe l'œil*, tell us anything about a duck: it is no more informative about a duck than the duck itself would be. If we are to talk meaningfully of information, it is ordinarily required that we should be able to discriminate between, on the one hand, the medium of communication and, on the other hand, the referent or what is communicated. 'It is ordinarily required' I say, but then there is no reason to think that Gombrich feels free to dispense with this convention: indeed it would seem that his leading ideas depend for their significance upon it.

But quite apart from issues of consistency within a particular system, which relate especially to Gombrich, there are other and stronger reasons for rejecting the equation of Naturalism with illusion: if, that is to say, we take illusion *literally*, which, I maintain, we are required to do by the theory. In the first place such an equation completely distorts the attitude that we adopt to naturalistic painting.[9] It is surely quite untrue to suggest that, in looking at the masterpieces of Constable or Monet, we have any temptation, even a partial or inhibited temptation, to react towards them in a way similar to that in which we would to the objects they represent: that we in any way wish to stretch out a hand and join in the picnic, or to assume dark glasses against the glare of the sun.

Not only is Gombrich's conception of Naturalism false to our ordinary attitude to paintings of this kind, but—more seriously I should say—it also conceals or distorts the kind of admiration that we feel for them. For surely when we admire the great achievements of naturalistic art we do so because we think of them as very lifelike representations of objects in the real world: but to think of them in this way is clearly quite incompatible with taking them to be or seeing them as (even in the most attenuated sense of either of these two expressions) the objects themselves. Indeed if we took the picture of an object to be that object, it seems unclear that there is anything left for us to admire. Now this is precisely what Gombrich appears to deny: 'It seems that the better the illusion', he asserts, 'the more we see it as a mirror' (p. 237) and a mirror-image he has already characterized, in the same paragraph, as 'a real illusionist image'.

Of course Gombrich does not deny—that is, he does not explicitly deny—what he appears to be denying: namely, that we admire naturalistic pictures as pictures. Yet I maintain that in substance he does—at any rate in the sections about illusion—and that why he is able to suppress this fact or conceal it from himself is because of the particular analysis to which he adheres of what it is to see something as a picture of an object. For Gombrich, to see something as a picture of an object is to see it sometimes as a picture and sometimes as that object. To admire something as a good or naturalistic picture of an object is to say something about the speed or facility with which we can move between these two different ways of seeing it. What excites us, in other words, is something potential, not something actual or visible: it is the capacity of the picture to arouse a capacity in us.

But now, we must ask, why does Gombrich adhere to this particular analysis of what it is to see something as a picture of an object? And to understand his answer here—which is, roughly, that any other suggestion would be absurd or self-contradictory—we must consider a notion that plays an important role at this stage in the argument: and this is what Gombrich calls 'the inherent ambiguity of all images' (p. 211). Now part of the time what Gombrich means by this is quite clear. He introduces the notion at the very beginning of the book by a consideration of the (now) famous duck-rabbit figure (Fig. 2): a drawing which originally appeared in *Die Fliegenden Blätter* and which can, when accurately reproduced, indifferently be seen as a duck (turned to the left) or a rabbit (turned to the right). Later on Gombrich illustrates the notion by reference to the outline drawing of a hand (Fig. 201), of which it is impossible to tell whether it is a right hand seen from the front or a left hand seen from the back. Having, however, introduced the notion of 'ambiguity' by means of these special cases, Gombrich later goes on to point out (pp. 209–17) that in one significant respect all configurations drawn on a flat surface are ambiguous. For if we take any given configuration, there is an infinity of shapes in space of which it is the correct perspectival profile. Of course if the angle and distance from the spectator are known, the shape is determined—just as ordinarily, assuming the shape to be a conventional or familiar one, we can work out the angle and distance. But if the angle and distance are not determined, we must in principle allow the shape to have any one of an infinite number of values. In this sense, then, all configurations are ambiguous.

So far, I think everything is clear. Starting from a few particular cases which he characterizes as being ambiguous, Gombrich soon extends the application of the concept. But in doing so he extends solely its denotation, but its connotation remains constant. To say of the duck-rabbit figure, or of the drawing of a hand, or of all perspectival profiles, that they are ambiguous is to say, in the first place, that they can be seen in two or more ways, and secondly, that they cannot be seen in more than one way at once. This point Gombrich makes at several places by saying that 'ambiguity . . . can never be seen as such' (p. 211: cf. pp. 198, 200, 223).

But from the very beginning of the book Gombrich assimilates to these cases and wishes to subsume under the general heading of ambiguity another feature that is universally possessed by images: namely, that they are both pictures (canvas) and of things (nature). Just as the duck-rabbit figure can be seen sometimes as a duck and sometimes as a rabbit, so a picture can be seen sometimes as canvas and sometimes as nature. And (this is where the assimilation becomes crucial) just as the figure cannot be seen simultaneously as a duck and as a rabbit, so the picture cannot be seen simultaneously as canvas and as nature. It was the achievement of the earliest artists, Gombrich suggests, that 'instead of playing "rabbit or duck" they had to invent the game of "canvas or nature"' (p. 24): as though these two games were identical in structure. And later the same point is more specifically made. 'Is it possible to "see" both the plane surface and the battle horse at the same time? If we have been right so far, the demand is for the impossible. To understand the battle horse is for a moment to disregard the plane surface. We cannot have it both ways' (p. 237).

But by what right does Gombrich assume that we can no more see a picture as canvas and as nature than we can see the duck-rabbit figure as a duck and as a rabbit? Because—it might be said—canvas and nature are different interpretations. But if this is Gombrich's argument, it is clearly invalid. For we cannot see the duck-rabbit figure as duck and as rabbit, not because these are two different interpretations, but because they are two incompatible interpretations. Gombrich states the principle correctly when he writes: 'We can train ourselves to switch more rapidly, indeed to oscillate between readings, but we cannot hold conflicting interpretations' (p. 198). But it does not follow from this that we cannot hold different interpretations. For Gombrich's specific argument about canvas or nature to be effective, he requires a criterion for distinguishing between conflicting and merely different interpretations. In the absence of such a criterion he has no right to insist, against common sense, that seeing something as a picture of an object *must be* sometimes to see it as a picture and sometimes to see it as that object.

Finally I should like to consider two lines of thought in Gombrich's book which go some way to accounting for his equation of Naturalism with illusion: one which might have led him into the belief, the other which might have helped to sustain him in it. The first is to do with Gombrich's use of the notion of 'projection', the second with his use of 'seeing as'. Gombrich emphasizes, quite rightly, the immense importance of projection in the viewing of naturalistic art. But under the general heading of projection he brings together (I want to suggest) phenomena which, though they can be arranged on a scale, need also to be distinguished rather carefully: by assimilating the phenomena that lie on one end of the scale to those which lie on the other, Gombrich finds support for his view that Naturalism is illusion. The different kinds of phenomena he has in mind can be brought out by a consideration of three examples that he gives of projection. First, the case of Shadow Antiqua lettering (Fig. 172), in which letters are indicated only by what would be their shaded side if they were ribbons standing up, but where we tend to see a top to each letter: secondly, there is the case of the Giandomenico Tiepolo etching (Fig. 185) where we read the garments of St. Joseph and the Virgin Mary as coloured (even if indeterminately coloured): and finally there is the case of *all* representative painting (pp. 158, 170, 191), of Frith as well as of Manet (p. 181), of Van Eyck as well as the Impressionists (p. 184), where we project on to the dabs of paint people and objects as they exist in the world. But 'projection' here has no single simple core of meaning, though all the cases may have what it is now fashionable to call a family resemblance. In the case of the Shadow Antiqua lettering we see something that definitely is not there: in the case of Van Eyck, or even Manet, the most that can be said is that we would not see what we do if it were not for something outside, or in addition to, the 'visual situation'. In the first kind of case there is a genuine deception: in that the man who makes the projection will differ in his beliefs from the man who does not. In the third kind of illusion there is no such deception: and correspondingly there is no difference of belief between the man who makes the projection and the man who cannot make head or tail of an Impressionist or even of a Quattrocento painting. By assimilating the latter kind of case to the former, by subsuming all cases of projection under the single pattern, Gombrich is drawn towards the view that to look at naturalistic art is to experience a kind of illusion.

The second line of thinking to which I have attributed some reponsibility for Gombrich's equation of Naturalism with illusion, at any rate by way of sustaining him in a position he might otherwise have found unacceptable, is connected with his use of the phrase 'seeing as'. Here, however, we are already in the environs of a subject to which I shall soon have to turn and address myself directly: Gombrich's general theory of perception. For it is because of this theory that the phrase 'seeing as' has such great importance for Gombrich: since it is a central tenet within the theory that all seeing is seeing as. Here I only want to point out that this equation (i.e. seeing = seeing as) serves to take the sting out of the other equation with which I have hitherto been concerned (i.e. Naturalism = illusion). For if all seeing is seeing as, this suggests that all vision has a faulty or defective or, as philosophers would say, 'non-veridical' or at least *optional* aspect to it—for is not this the implication of talking of 'seeing something *as an x*?[10] Accordingly, if we believe that all seeing is seeing as, then the vision of naturalistic art would no longer appear to have anything peculiar to it: at worst it would only be an extreme case of the sort of deception in which all vision participates.

But I cannot any longer delay turning to the theory upon which this last consideration depends.

8

Gombrich's general theory of perception cannot be passed over even in a consideration of his aesthetic theory, for it stands in a rather peculiar and certainly significant relation to his theory of artistic change: at all times mirroring it, at some moments purporting to provide it with a ground or base. For it is, as we have seen, Gombrich's view that aesthetic change occurs by means of the mechanism of schema and correction. Without some initial schema, which gradually, step by step, we correct and refine, we would never arrive at anything reasonably naturalistic in the arts. But it is also Gombrich's view that perception displays this same pattern. We acquire visual knowledge of the world by first applying schemata to it and then correcting and refining them in accordance with anticipations rewarded or frustrated, until we arrive at an undisturbed or, as we might say, 'naturalistic' vision. 'The very process of perception', Gombrich writes, 'is based on the same rhythm that we found governing the process of representation: the rhythm of schema and correction' (p. 231).

To some it might seem that this more general theory about schema and correction provides some kind of confirmation for the specific theory. For if the phenomenon of schema and correction is very widespread, as widespread as human vision itself, it is not surprising—one might think—that it is to be found also in the more limited domain of art. And it seems that Gombrich himself is sometimes of this view. I want to argue that the opposite is true and that if the general theory about human vision were true, the more specific theory about representational art would be false.

For if it is true that we can move towards Naturalism in art by means of the progressive correction of schematic images, this implies that we have some means of correcting the images by reference not to other images but, directly, to the object that we are trying to depict. For alteration of one schematic image so as to make it conform to another schematic image could scarcely be called correction; and if this were all that lay within our reach, any progression towards verisimilitude in art would be purely accidental.

Now, of course, Gombrich nowhere explicitly states that we can correct one image only by reference to another; on the contrary, he insists that we can correct the crude (and the less crude) schemata of our making by appeal to perception. But if we accept the general thesis that perception itself operates in accordance with the principle of schema and correction—and if 'schemata' and 'correction' are here used *in exactly the same sense* as that in which they are applied to the process of representational art—then the appeal to perception is no better than an appeal to another image. In both cases we try to judge one schema—namely one we have created on paper or on canvas—by reference to another schema; and whether this second schema has been created by someone else on paper or canvas or (as the general theory of perception asserts) by ourselves in the mind, is surely immaterial.

It would seem, therefore, that Gombrich, by his insistence on the thesis that perception also requires schemata or that there is no reality without interpretation, has cut the ground from under his own original thesis: namely, that by means of a progressive correction of schemata we can arrive at a naturalistic art. And, indeed, it is to be observed that when Gombrich is thinking most evidently under the influence of this view of perception, he does, implicitly at least, abandon his redefinition of Naturalism and settle for a very different view of the matter. On such occasions, that is to say, he suggests that naturalistic painting is painting that satisfies one or other of the two following conditions. Either it is such that nature can be seen in terms of it; that is to say, the test of Naturalism is 'the tentative projection of works of art into nature' (p. 273). Or, alternatively, it is such that it can be seen in terms of nature: 'the question is not whether nature "really looks" like these pictorial devices but whether pictures with such features suggest a reading in terms of natural objects' (p. 304). But it does not seem that either of these further definitions is adequate to what we ordinarily understand by Naturalism—so long, that is, as we also adhere to the view that perception involves interpretation. But it is, of course, only so long as we adhere to this view that we have any need for either definition in preference to the original definition in terms of information.

It would, however, be wrong to conclude from this that we have here a powerful argument against Gombrich's theory of artistic change. For I think it can fairly readily be shown that the thesis that perception always involves interpretation or the application of schemata, is untenable. Not that it is false. For though the thesis is popular with a certain school of experimental psychologists, by whom Gombrich has been strongly influenced, it can be faulted not on empirical but on logical grounds. For to say that a certain perception involves interpretation or the application of a schema surely entails that there is something that is perceived and on which the interpretation is imposed or to which the schema is applied. Now unless we are to be caught up in a infinite regress of perceptions, we must allow that *this* perception itself was not a case of interpretation.

Gombrich seems at times to admit this. He admits it *implicitly*, for instance, when he writes: 'Whenever we receive a visual impression, we react by docketing it, filing it, grouping it in one way or another' (p. 251)—for he exposes himself immediately to the question: What is the 'it' that is the object of all these processes which are, I take it, the various species of interpretation? And he admits the same point *explicitly* on the occasions when he puts forward the retinal stimulus as the candidate for being the original uninterpreted raw material upon which we place our various interpretations. 'Without some initial system, without a first guess to which we can stick unless it is disproved,' he writes at one point, 'we could indeed make no "sense" of the milliards of ambiguous stimuli that reach us from our environment' (p. 231). Or again he writes: 'The stimulus pattern on the retina must of necessity allow of an infinite number of interpretations, none of which can be further confirmed or refuted except on grounds of probability' (p. 278). But of course this particular candidate will not do and elsewhere he produces the argument that effectively disposes of it—'We can never see our own retinas' he writes (p. 217)—for it is clear from his whole discussion that, at any rate in his sense of interpretation, a visual interpretation must be of something visual or seen. But none of this alters the fact that *a* candidate for being the object of our interpretation, for being that which is interpreted, is required if the theory is to be coherent.

9

The strength of *Art and Illusion* must, then, rest upon the more restricted thesis: that of the necessary connexion between the progress of representation in art, on the one hand, and the employment of pictorial schemata, on the other.

The efficacy of this thesis for resolving Gombrich's central problem is something that we have already considered: it provides a clue to the question why representational art has a history—although, of course, it makes no attempt to answer the more specific question why art has the particular history that it has. But even within this limited, though by no means narrow, context the thesis still suffers somewhat from a certain ambiguity or imprecision in its formulation. Representational art owes its history, we are told, to the use of pictorial schemata. But what, we might ask, are schemata? Now it is fairly clear what Gombrich does not mean by talking of 'schemata'. And it is fairly clear what, in a very rough way, he does mean by talking of 'schemata'. But to say exactly what he means is not without its difficulties. I am not going to say that Gombrich uses the word 'schema' in different senses. That would be unwarranted. But what I think would be true to say is that at different times he seems to be working under different conceptions of what a typical instance of a schema would be, and these different conceptions lead to an elusiveness in the thesis taken as a whole. Let me explain:

1. The most ordinary and the most evident thing that Gombrich has in mind when he talks of 'a schema' is any form or configuration that an artist uses to represent, depict, portray an object in the world. In this context a schema has no special degree of complexity or sophistication; it can vary from the simple diagrammatic shapes employed by Gombrich's niece in her delightful copy after Wivenhoe Park (Fig. 244) to the minutely detailed (though inaccurate) image of the whale which figures in the two engravings (c. 1600), one Italian, one Dutch (Figs. 57, 58), which Gombrich reproduces. It is in this general, extended usage of 'schemata' that Morellian connoisseurship might be said to be characteristically concerned with the morphology of a particular sub-set of schemata: roughly, those used to portray certain parts of the body (notably, the hand and ear) or certain natural objects.[11]

2. At other times, however, Gombrich in talking of schemata would appear to have in mind forms or configurations that satisfy

a further condition: namely, that they are highly simplified. The divided oval or egg-shape as an abbreviation of the human head—a matter on which Gombrich has some highly illuminating things to say (pp. 144–8)—is a typical example of a schema in this sense; and it is, I think, very significant that in so far as Gombrich writes or thinks under the direction of this conception of the typical schema, he identifies 'schematic' art with what used to be called 'conceptual' art (e.g. pp. 122–3, 247).

3. At yet other times Gombrich appears to work with a very different conception indeed of what a schema is, and this is when he identifies schemata with those very general and elusive elements which conjointly make up what we call a style. So, for instance, in the course of describing Constable's artistic evolution, Gombrich talks of the painter's 'dissatisfaction with ready-made idyllic schemata, his wish to go beyond them and discover visual truth' (p. 325). But what are the 'idyllic schemata' with which Constable grew dissatisfied? It is evident from the context of the discussion that they are not to be narrowly identified with useful pictorial devices for portraying such things as distant mountains or spreading oaks and ilex. They are, rather, to be taken broadly to include things as general and as 'non-formal' as the choice of subject-matter, the atmosphere in which the subject is invested, and the preference for a certain kind of over-all finish, or lack of finish, in the picture.

Of course, Gombrich performs a useful service by employing the word 'schema' so generously, for he brings home to us how different elements in a picture can have a common function. But at a price. At the price, that is, of making the thesis of schema and correction a bit imprecise.

Basically, the hypothesis of schema and correction relates to the first usage of 'schema' as equivalent to any configuration employed to represent an object. But the existence of the other two usages I have specified leads to confusion in the following ways. First of all, by failing to distinguish clearly between schema as *any* inherited or invented configuration and schema as always an abbreviated or simplified configuration, Gombrich slides from the view that representation always begins with some configuration into the rather more specific view that representation always begins with a simplified configuration: in other words, setting out to explain why art has a history at all, he commits himself in an entirely *a priori* way to a specific, though still very general, account of what that history was: namely, that in the beginning there were simple forms. This assumption emerges clearly in Gombrich's discussion of Palaeolithic art, where he treats the complex cave-paintings of Lascaux as constituting a potential threat or providing a *prima facie* counter-example, to the thesis of schema and correction: and he feels that he can get around the difficulty and save his thesis only by postulating 'thousands of years of image-making' which must have preceded these so-called 'primitive' works (p. 91).

Again, the existence in Gombrich's vocabulary of 'schema' as the correct appellation for highly general pictorial elements such as the preference for one kind of subject matter or method of illumination rather than another, makes it very difficult at times to see how much of the phenomenon of art Gombrich thinks his thesis covers. More specifically, does the hypothesis of schema and correction provide an over-all explanation of 'stylistic' change? Whether it does or does not depends, presumably, on the prior question whether a style can be analysed without remainder into a set of schemata. I am sure that, on the whole, Gombrich thinks that it cannot be (e.g. p. 310). But there are, as I have indicated, passages where he suggests that it can. Until such problems are resolved, the scope of Gombrich's hypothesis remains indeterminate. It is an imperative demand of science that for any quantified statement an unrelenting effort should be made to specify the range of phenomena over which it holds good.

10

In this lecture I have singled out certain elements of Gombrich's book for praise, and I have suggested a number of criticisms. 'But why criticism?' I can imagine an impatient listener saying: 'If you have so high an opinion of the book, as you politely say you have, why spend so much time on criticism? For criticism is easy enough.' And that would be a profound and an enlightening mistake.

The great difficulty in any modern book of aesthetics is to find anything to criticize. For by and large what is not unintelligible is truism. The supreme merit of *Art and Illusion* is that it permits criticism. It states a large number of decidable questions, and gives to them answers that are interesting, clear and lucid. In other words, Professor Gombrich has taken hold of a subject that is habitually given over to vacuity and pretentiousness, and he has bestowed upon it some of the precision, the elegance and the excitement of a science. And eccentrically enough he has achieved this by writing a book that is both erudite and witty.

REFERENCES

1 E. H. Gombrich, *Art and Illusion* (London and New York, 1960). All page and figure references are to the second London edition, 1962: the second edition was reset and references will not correspond to the first edition.

2 Gombrich quotes James Barry as expressing a perceptual theory of artistic change in a lecture delivered to the Royal Academy (pp. 12–14): but the major advocates of this theory are Franz Wickhoff (p. 18) and Alois Riegl (pp. 17–20).

3 Gombrich attributes some such theory as this to Pliny and to Vasari (pp. 11–12): though he is careful to observe that Vasari at any rate 'could not disentangle the idea of invention from that of the imitation of nature'.

4 'Seeing and Knowing' is, of course the title of a book by Berenson in which the theory is expounded in its simplest form. Gombrich's major references are, however, to it in the versions held by Ruskin and Roger Fry (pp. 296–9).

5 Gombrich points out that it was Wölfflin who first gave currency to the catchword the 'history of seeing', though 'it was also he who warned against taking this metaphor too seriously' (p. 17).

6 'We catch a glimpse of the reasons why these limitations will never obtrude themselves within the domain of art itself. Art presupposes mastery, and the greater the artist the more surely will he instinctively avoid a task where his mastery would fail to serve him. The layman may wonder whether Giotto could have painted a view of Fiesole in sunshine, but the historian will suspect that lacking the means he would not have wanted to, or rather that he could not have wanted to. We like to assume, somehow, that where there is a will there is also a way, but in matters of art the maxim should read that only where there is a way is there also a will. The individual can enrich the ways and means that his culture offers him; he can hardly

wish for something that he has never known is possible' (p. 75).

7 In the Preface to the second edition, Gombrich writes: 'I am grateful to one of my painter friends, who helped me to formulate my problem afresh by asking me to tell quite simply what would be the opposite of the view I hold. It would be a state of affairs in which every person could always achieve fidelity to nature. The mere desire to preserve the likeness of a beloved person or of a beautiful view would then suffice for the artist to "copy" what he sees' (p. xii). This is not the contradictory of Gombrich's thesis but a contrary; as such it seems to me a highly misleading means of conveying the content of Gombrich's views. It is certainly true that someone who subscribed to Gombrich's views would reject the view that 'every person wielding a brush could always achieve fidelity to nature'. But so would anyone else in his sane mind. The content of the thesis of schema and correction seems to me to consist in two propositions: (1) The notion of 'naturalism' or 'fidelity to nature' is properly speaking a relative notion, so that when we describe a painting as naturalistic we are really saying that it is more naturalistic than certain other paintings. (2) There is no single serial order in which paintings can be placed according to whether they are more or less naturalistic than others, but there are a number of such serial orders corresponding to different conventions or notations. I am convinced that both these propositions are true:

as well as being inconsistent with some things said in *Art and Illusion*, e.g. the equation of Naturalism with illusion. There is a third proposition, which I also believe to be true, and which is possibly, though not certainly, part of Gombrich's thesis: namely, that the notion of 'what we see' is essentially bound up with how we would depict it or the schema we would use to portray it. Gombrich's preoccupation with the constancies—which are, after all, no more than specific instances or exemplifications of this proposition—confirms the supposition that this is part of his general doctrine.

8 It is perhaps significant that Gombrich at this juncture does not consider sculpture where these limitations of illusion—at any rate the first two—do not apply, or apply to a lesser degree. The fact that *trompe l'œil* can be more readily obtained here might have led Gombrich to shy away from it as the limiting case or ideal of naturalistic representation.

9 I mean by this the psychological attitude that we adopt. My argument would not be affected by any demonstration that, in looking at a picture where a river is depicted as being behind a tree, the eye makes the same kind of accommodation movement as if the river were actually farther away than the tree. (This note is stimulated by an observation made by Gombrich in private discussion.)

10 For 'seeing as' see J. L. Austin, *Sense and Sensibilia* (London, 1962), pp. 10–20.

¹¹ e.g. 'Only a close observation of the forms peculiar to a master in his representation of the human figure can lead to any adequate results', Giovanni Morelli, *Italian Masters in German Galleries* (London, 1883), p. 2, or the statement quoted by Layard: 'What I maintain is that the forms, more especially those of the hand and ear, aid us in distinguishing the works of a master from those of his imitators, and control the judgement which subjective impressions might lead us to prounounce.' Giovanni Morelli, *Italian Painters* (London, 1892), p. 32.

The Idea of Literature

G. P. HENDERSON

The word 'literature' is often used in an honorific sense. A course in
English Literature would hardly be expected to contain anything not
'worth-while'. We speak approvingly about 'works of literature';
we often suggest that philosophical or historical works, for example
(Plato's *Phaedo* and Gibbon's *Decline and Fall* come to mind), can be
read as pure literature independently of our final verdict as to their
philosophical or historical merits.[1] Donne's sermons, surely, can
now be nothing but works of literature—but to say this of them is to
say a great deal. 'Literature', 'literary', and allied terms, just because
they have this common approbatory use, can also be employed to
pillory. Hume's *Enquiries* are more literary in character (more in the
nature of literary set-pieces) than the *Treatise*: to say this is to offer
them dispraise. 'I am no man of letters,' one might say, 'no *doctor ...
otiosus in Musaeo sedens* as Descartes put it,[2] but only a straightforward, business-like writer on economics, sociology or problems of
logic, or an undisguised preacher or political tractarian'. Sometimes,
of course, the word 'literature' is intended to confer neither honour
nor dishonour. If one were writing a comprehensive book on the
literature of the nineteenth century (not 'English literature', but
literature 'in English') one might well be expected to survey, for
example, the enormous mass of cautionary moral tales which were
pabulum for children for so long; or the half-instructive, half-
sentimental literature on botany and gardening (like Mrs. Marcet's
Conversations on Botany, Lindley's *Ladies' Botany*, and so on) which
was published in great quantity in the early and middle years of the
century. There is this non-committal use of 'literature' and allied
terms, then, but it is their evaluative use which interests me here. It

interests me because literature is so often said to be an art-form (in a general sense of the term 'art'). When this is said I take it as some indication that the term 'literature' is being used in an evaluative sense. I want to ask what further explanation can be given of such sayings. In particular, what connexion if any can there be between a work of literature's being a work of art and its also being something else—a philosophical dialogue, a speech in a law-court, a sermon, a piece of description, a character-drawing, a lampoon, a broadsheet? Any of these might conceivably reach the status of a work of art.

I want to keep some distinction between 'literature' and 'belles-lettres'. Indeed a distinction between them may turn out to have important bearings on the question just put, about subject-matter and its influence on literary value. The *Oxford English Dictionary* treats the distinction as one of genus and species. It defines 'literature', in an evaluative use, as 'writings esteemed for beauty of form or emotional effect'. Clearly this definition is broad enough to include 'belles-lettres' in its scope. Where there is a distinction between belles-lettres and other literary modes, the dictionary also indicates, this must be sought in the 'elegance' or 'lightness' of a certain kind which belles-lettres affect. And certainly elegance, urbanity, charm and (might I suggest?) some detachment from its subject-matter are qualities which we expect in many an essay, a 'tale', a fable, a 'romance', a love-poem.

This idea of detachment, however—it is my way of construing the dictionary's 'lightness'—may not be well received. 'What?' you may say. 'Some detachment from its subject-matter in a love-poem? Nonsense!' And in what way were Bacon's essays—take the essay 'Of Empire', for example—detached from their subject-matter? To which I reply: As regards the love-poem, it all depends. Some love-poems are as nothing without the loved one. Some loved ones are as nothing without the love-poem. There is a considerable amount of narcissism in, for example, seventeenth-century lyric poetry. It would not be fair to quote the notorious 'I could not love thee (Deare) so much, lov'd I not Honour more' were it not that Anthea, Lucasta, Prew, Juliet and others so often formed a sounding-board for mere dexterity of language and conceit of thought. Then as regards Bacon's essay: although it contains sage enough observations about the power of kings, and prudential maxims on how that power may be preserved or best exercised, the mainspring of the essay is the phrase 'Princes are like to heavenly bodies . . . which have much veneration but no rest'. Bacon, one might say, was intrigued by this piece of imagery and wrote it out. Hobbes, who also discoursed about the power of princes, was writing out the image of the great Leviathan expressed in *Job xli*, 33; but always and only as believing that this is the image which we *must* use, which we disregard at peril of truth and life alike. Towards the theme 'Princes are like heavenly bodies . . . ,' on the other hand, the essayist's attitude tends to be 'let us see what we can make of it, let us see what we can do with it'. There is an experimentalism, a lightness of treatment here that is quite foreign to Hobbes.

The point I want to make is that in belles-lettres it is not, as it were, vital to the subject that *this* particular way of presenting it should be chosen. The 'lightness' which the dictionary discerns is not lightness of subject matter. Elegant essays can be written about empire or superstition or friendship as well as about the smell of roast pork. The lightness is rather a liberation from any concern with what the poem or work is going to do—apart from giving enjoyment. Really, you feel, it will not make any difference to the progress of empire, to the pursuit or avoidance of roast pork when you become hungry, or to Anthea's responsiveness, that you should write about them in those well-turned essays or precious poems. How much more satisfying to your concern about such matters, if you have any, to write a Discourse on Government, an Address to Gourmets or a love-letter! You *may* get something accomplished, something changed, if you do so.

I am indicating what I take to be a salient characteristic of belles-lettres without meaning to suggest that it is always easy to classify a work as being belles-lettres or not. According to the dictionary, I repeat, the very basis on which we esteem a work of literature as such is its 'beauty of form or emotional effect': if this means that nothing but the manner of its composition or its appeal to what Hume called 'the sensitive part of our nature' counts towards a work's being literature, then we are to leave out, for example, what mainly distinguishes *The Leviathan* from being a collection of polite essays, what mainly distinguishes the *History* of Thucydides from a saga, what mainly distinguishes the *Gospel according to St. John* from being a collection of somebody's dictes and sayings. We are to leave out, in other words, all the power which those works exercise upon us from their possible truth or their authority. So the task of saying why we still feel reluctant to classify them as belles-lettres will be rather difficult: surely it is not just a matter of their being, in contrast to belles-lettres, *unselfconsciously* 'beautiful'? Has their beauty *nothing* to do with their concern with the world, their seriousness and their preoccupation with truth? These questions are most unsatisfactorily vague. It is not even certain that the dictionary definition of 'literature' does restrict the comparison between belles-lettres and other literature in the way of which I am complaining. How deep is 'beauty'? And how comprehensive is 'form'? Such further questions have to be asked. They, and the uncertainty of which I am speaking, indicate how limited in its philosophical usefulness the dictionary definition is.

To what extent can we abstract from considerations about truth, or moral or political validity, in trying to say what we mean when we call a history, a Gospel or a political treatise a work of literature, and *a fortiori* one of art? Some think, completely. I happened to read the following passage in a Cypriot educational journal the other day: 'A history or a philosophical work may sometimes be accounted literature—as happens with the history of Herodotus or the dialogues of Plato—but only to the extent that we lose sight of the subject-matter and the facts or ideas presented, in the pure beauty of the expression.'[3] This is an extreme and, it may be, untypical view. It is interesting that Mr. Kingsley Amis, writing, it so happens, about Max Beerbohm, thinks such a degree of refinement in literary appreciation extraordinary: 'the attribution of incomparability to Max is presumably to be connected with the notion, characteristic of Lord David's [i.e. Lord David Cecil's] Oxford and of Bloomsbury, that style is a self-sufficient entity, to be separated at will from qualities of subject-matter and capable of exhibiting a "charm" or "iridescence" of its own. By such means it is possible not to notice that Beerbohm had nothing to say, or nothing that we commonly distinguish as creative.'⁴ And surely it is right that when a historical or philosophical work is ranked as literature we think of it *in toto*, of the work with all that it has to say. We do *not* mean to assimilate it to belles-lettres. How odd if, in becoming a classic, a history or a piece of philosophy lost, rather than gained, in status— as history or philosophy. How much odder if it lost that status altogether.

And yet, one feels, its status *may* change. Plato's *Phaedo* is a case in point. To an important extent that dialogue is about the immortality of the soul; and yet the urgency has gone out of the particular arguments which it uses. Most people read it now for other things; in particular for the daring way in which it works towards a certain congruence—of the conclusion of a man's life with the conclusion of an argument. Here if anywhere is what the dictionary calls beauty of form. Nevertheless the beauty which the dialogue possesses is no mere formal beauty. It does matter that the discussion concerns the immortality of the soul. It matters still more that there should be not the slightest trace of conventional piety in what is said, but only a trust founded upon argument, and *that* founded upon the notion of the clearest possible seeing as a test of truth. The fact that the argument is expressed in archaic terms turns out to be of little consequence: even if you propose to read and judge the work as general literature, you cannot get away from its philosophical content altogether. Something similar may be said, for example, of *The Leviathan*: setting aside the fact that Hobbes's politics still have a formidable appeal, it remains true that you cannot read this work, call it general literature or what you will, without awe at the very idea that the staple reality of politics is fear: 'the laws of nature . . . without the terror of some power, to cause them to be observed, are contrary to our natural passions. . . . And covenants, without the sword, are but words.'⁵ Beauty goes rather deep here: indeed the use of the word 'beauty' at all in one's comments on this kind of artistic monumentality, may be both inadequate and distasteful.

I want to speak now in a less impressionistic way about the problem: 'What is it for a work of literature, which is not belles-lettres, to be a work of art?'—though I shall gradually return to my original way of speaking. I want to consider, more precisely than hitherto, the relationship between artistic and those other features of a work which may appeal to people's interests—its moral, religious, political or other effects, its entertainment value, and so on. First of all I shall outline the considerations that occur to me (there are ten heads involved) and then I shall comment on the more interesting of them at greater length.

(1) We are accustomed to say that a book (or other form of writing) can be regarded from an artistic point of view, from a moral, from a religious, from an entertainment point of view, and so on.

(2) But it does not follow that these points of view are all on a level, i.e. that strictly the same thing as is artistically regarded may be, for example, morally regarded.

(3) To begin the elucidation of (2), consider a distinction between 'moral content' and 'moral result'. It is well known in a way that the portrayal of cruelty, obscenity or other vices does not necessarily result in a cruel, obscene or otherwise vicious book. The moral content of a book is one thing, the moral effect or result another.

(4) A book may have an overall moral effect or result independently of its literary (artistic) quality. Not all who read read for the same thing, or in the same spirit. The same holds good for looking at pictures. For example, a good painting may be merely erotic in its effect on some people.

(5) The question arises whether a book's literary (artistic) quality is independent of its overall moral effect or result. If a book is to be good literature, does it have to be morally good (or at least acceptable)?

(6) I suggest that to think of moral acceptability as a necessary condition of literary acceptability is not true or false but without

sense. Artistic quality is independent of *any* moral effect, not by being more important in some absolute way but by superseding it. (This is a slightly less strong version of the view that whatever moral, religious, erotic or other passional aspects a work may have, these are all transcended in so far as the work can be regarded as one of literature or art.)

(7) It can still be said, consistently with the foregoing, that part at least of the artistic quality of a work of literature is toti-resultant. That is, the work may be judged artistically successful, tolerable or unsuccessful as handling moral, religious, political, social (and so on) themes in the way it does, with the appropriate competence or with incompetence.

(8) The emphasis here is on *how* the thing is done, not on what is done. The fact that people may make a better job of exalting what we call virtue than what we call vice is a feature of human nature but neither here nor there from an artistic point of view.

(9) In sum, a successful work of literature (*qua* work of art) is neither moral nor immoral: it has no moral characteristics: it is meaningless to call it either good or bad (morally), or even morally tolerable.

(10) The moral result of a work is different from the moral content, but a work of art regarded as such has no moral result. In this sense we may say that the artistic and the moral point of view are on different levels.

In general, a book to be judged artistically must be judged taking into account all its moral features if it has any. *How* it condemns abuses, diagnoses ills, urges reform, resists change or praises endeavour, all these features come into the reckoning. But to put the abuses right, to agree that the ills are as stated, and to join in attempts to reform, or to resist change, are no part of the artistic response to the book. The fact that a book fails to move a reader in *this* way, in spite of the fact that it expresses a message, does not imply artistic failure. On the contrary if it moved the reader in this way it would be an artistic failure, at any rate for him. As it is, what we are to admire in any of the classics of morality is the art of word-usage in one of its broadest settings, namely moral persuasion, and not the moral persuasion for being of the particular moral kind that it is.

I should like now to say something more in explanation or exploration of the main considerations which I have just brought forward. There are plenty of difficulties to be met.

We can begin with the conception of the various points of view from which a work may be regarded. Take the artistic and the moral, again. These may not be on the same level, in the sense (which I have indicated) that the artistic may presuppose the moral. But it might seem that there is nothing stable about this relationship. Would it not be just as easy, you may suggest, to think of the moral as pre-supposing the artistic? Consider the use of the phrases 'the art of oratory', 'the art of preaching', 'the art of persuasion' and so on. Demosthenes, for example, undoubtedly did hold the members of Athenian juries in thrall, and his speeches were the more effective forensically for having their artistic qualities well recognized by an audience to whom speech-making was the breath of life. And it is not only connoisseurs who respond to the art of persuasion. Is not a sermon the more effective for being clearly formed, circumspect in length, and having some grace in delivery and taste in illustration? At least, other things such as sincerity and intellectual respectability being equal, is it not so? Of course it is; and really there ought to be a term to pick out that kind of speech-making or writing in which the issue spoken about is still urgent and in which art reinforces the principal purpose of the work. 'Modern classics' will not do, even where the work is modern. We are looking at the matter the other way round as compared to what this phrase suggests. We are not dealing here with any kind of detachment from the issue involved.

My reply to this difficulty is that it really introduces us to a different-level use of the word 'art'. *Of course* we may change our point of view and regard the artistic as the handmaid of the moral. We must remember that there is conscious and that there is un-conscious art, and that not all art is done for its own sake. But when we speak of art, conscious or unconscious, in this context we mean, I think, a certain 'know-how', knowledge how to adapt means to ends, a professional or quasi-professional skill in assembling and arranging one's material, and so forth. Here it is as if there were rules involved, a generic skill in question. The phrase 'the art of fugue' seems to me to indicate this especially. It is another matter altogether to look at a work, in general, as a work of art. If we do this, we may insist on both of two things: first, that we are not separating form from content in the sense that we are ignoring the moral tendency of the work; and second, that we are not responding to its moral persuasion as such. If I want to make someone indignant about the slums of Dundee or Liverpool, I take him to Dundee or Liverpool or show him 'documentary' photographs of them. I should not dream of taking him, e.g. to the Dundee Art Society's latest exhibition, where I recently bought a water-colour of some not very salubrious slums because I happened to like it. From the beginning I have looked at this picture with complete moral indifference.

A similar point can be made if we consider, instead of the moral point of the view, the entertainment point of view. People differ on the question whether Aristophanes's *Lysistrata* is a good work of art (Greeks in my experience tend to dislike it). If it is, one would want to say that this is partly because it succeeds (at least in one's own particular case) as a work of entertainment: contrariwise, if they are not amused, people condemn it—it is considered 'vulgar' and therefore, they imply, bad art. Now suppose we change our point of view and look at *Lysistrata* primarily as a work of entertainment. Some would want to say it will not entertain unless it is good art. (It is not that *all* successful entertainment must be good art, but making allowance for the peculiarities of period and dramatic convention *this* example must be.) Here either the word 'art' or the words 'entertain' and 'entertainment' are being used differently (compared with when we say that *Lysistrata* is good art as being good entertainment). I think that the meaning is either: 'it will not entertain unless it is done superbly well in its kind' (the 'limitations' of that art-form are not seen as limitations), or: 'it will entertain in the sense in which any work of art entertains; it is an object of sustained interest and of admiration to persons who understand what it is all about; cultivated people strive to get to know it, and so on'—the sense of 'entertain' involved here being clearly different from that involved in saying that *Lysistrata* entertains because it makes you laugh.

The problem of the relationship of art and morality has been a hardy metaphysical perennial, and it has to be recognized in some form or other in many settings. Not only in literature may the apparent moral purpose of a work cause aestheticians to be puzzled. Some recent notes by Sir Herbert Read on the art of Alberto Burri[6] suggest to me that one of the main things which I have just been saying about works of literature may apply more widely: namely, the consideration that where some moral attitude is being expressed, i.e. is expressly intended to be conveyed by a work of art, this fact is aesthetically relevant: it is one of the things which it is appropriate and proper for us to comment upon when we are considering the work artistically. I am coming to Read's remarks: but I wish to make it quite clear first that I am not prejudging questions about the nature and importance of representational *vis-à-vis* non-representational painting (to say nothing of, for example, music); and that I am *not* recommending that one should always look for a moral attitude in a work of art.

Burri's art consists in taking 'old sacks, charred plywood, metal scrap, any characteristic debris of our time', making a composition of them, framing them, and presenting them for public contemplation. Now this art discloses what, if it were really 'painting' that we had to do with, would be called painterly qualities, and to such Read draws attention. 'Against a painted background the old and patched sack, stiffened with glue, is arranged with a couturier-like elegance. The different textures of the patches, the faded and stained colours, sometimes enhanced with a touch of scarlet paint, the rough edges and hanging threads, all contribute to a composition which . . . will be found to possess great beauty and vitality.' Of another of Burri's compositions Read says: 'It is an encrustation of paste, paint, paper. . . . Its charm lies in the play of light on a great variety of textures, some smooth, some rough, some crackled, some dull, some brilliant, all constituting a pattern of inexhaustible interest.' One might suppose very naturally that this was all that was required in the way of explanation or commendation of Burri's art—you simply look at it;

it appeals to you or it does not simply for what it, physically, is, or rather for how it, physically, looks. But there is more to be said. Apparently (I am relying on Read for this) Burri is not just creating charm, not *just* rescuing beauty out of his scrap-heap (as Read puts it). He is also protesting. 'Every patch in the sacking, every gaping wound-like hole, the charred edges and ragged cicatrices, reveal the raw sensibility of an artist outraged by the hypocrisy of a society that presumes to speak of beauty, tradition, humanism, justice and other fine virtues, and is at the same time willing to contemplate the mass destruction of the human race.' (Burri was a surgeon, and a prisoner of war.) It is not that Burri forswears beauty, but rather that he puts up one kind of beauty against another or, as I prefer to say, one kind of artistic excellence against what is conventionally thought of as beauty. In all this Burri's preoccupation with wounds, holes in flesh and stitches is not hard to discern, even before it has been pointed out to us. But this preoccupation, we are told, is not just a pointer to Burri's psychological history: it is a reaction, one may say a moral reaction (though the actual word 'moral' is not Read's), to 'our tragic situation'. Having been told all this, we can take our choice now between two positions: (*a*) that the protest and defiance produced the work of art but, having produced it, are no part of it; and (*b*) that they are a genuine part of it. If, in conformity with my previous view about the moral dimension which may exist in literature, I now go on to adopt the second of these alternatives, I do not want to be understood as suggesting that the (or an) appropriate way in which to respond to Burri's productions is to rush out and join the campaign for nuclear disarmament. Nor do I wish to imply that we cannot respond aesthetically, in a more or less satisfactory way, to Burri's productions merely as patterns of sacking, paint, paste and other material. With these explanations, then, let me come to the question whether it is artistically relevant to be told all that Read has told us.

Even if there were no question of drawing any parallel with literature, and of being influenced by literary works having a moral motif, I should reply as follows—We have no such independent knowledge of the meaning of the word 'artistically' as to let us answer this question summarily. What counts as being artistically relevant depends on what artists do and what they offer us. It would be crude to suggest that nothing but the exercise of the senses, pleasantly or unpleasantly, ever conditions artistic appreciation or antipathy. And if a composition is offered by the artist as a protest— if its 'spirit' is to *be* a protest—then it is hard to know what to say in opposition to this, his own profession. It would be impertinent to say: 'I shall look at the pattern and the painterly qualities—or even if you like the saccarian qualities—of what you put before me, but don't ask me to bother my head with what you say it is all about. That has nothing to do with me!' An attitude like this would be at the opposite extreme from the insistence, equally arbitrary, that every painting *must* have a subject, *must* depict, portray or represent. Here there are no rules, only practices, fashions and tendencies. There is really no 'must' about it—except that in our own present state of society at any rate we must take what we are offered. So on this basis I want to say: It simply adds to the interest of the work that I should construe it as a protest. But this is still the interest of the art-gallery and not that of the market-place. If I were left with less guidance than in Burri's case as to the moral motif of the work, then, clearly, the other, sensuous sort of interest would have to be left to take its chance. There might well be no moral motif: but then I have never for a moment pretended that there cannot be artistic appreciation which ends, as it begins, with the sensuous. If the moral motif is so important that the work is produced regardless of art-galleries or any institution in which they may 'show' or 'exhibit' things, but the agent jabs, tears, stitches, glues and paints at his sacking because he wants to raise it up in the market-place and get people to walk under it to the nearest headquarters of the campaign for nuclear disarmament, then the question whether his product is a work of art is, plainly, an open one. Should it find its way to some museum or gallery where we are freer to bring standards of art criticism to bear, then we can perhaps 'enjoy' it after our fashion, not forgetting what it was meant to be but simply not responding to it as full political animals.

There is a strong temptation to see parallels between certain types of painting and belles-lettres, and correspondingly between certain seriously-minded painting and some serious literature. In particular we may allow that some painting has a message, just as some 'classic' writing has a message, and that without the message we may have very little left in either case. What people call 'pure sensuous beauty' seems ludicrously inadequate as a standard for evaluating, for example, religious painting. You cannot avoid thinking of the formidable mosaic *Christ* at Daphni as signifying the *Pantokrator*—impelling you to regard him as Christ the Ruler of the World, whom you cannot look on and escape. The 'message' is not external to the mosaic to anything like the extent even that Burri's 'message' is external to his composition. In the case of Burri you can abstract message from other aspects of the composition relatively easily. Even in the *Book of Job*, where the morality involved is detestable, you cannot do this. It is part of the artistic portrayal of Job's God that men, including Job, should be depicted primarily as mirrors of the divine power; if you cease to be preoccupied with this idea, the book has nothing to say to you.[7] Parallel, then, let there be between literature in this respect and painting in this respect. To *note* the parallel is harmless. By noting it we do not commit the essentialist fallacy of demanding that significantly the same account be aimed at in speaking philosophically of any and every art form. We do not demand *a priori*, for instance, that it shall be possible for music to express a moral message. Instead, we can leave it as an interesting subject of speculation whether, as Plato thought, it can do so in its fashion or whether there is no basis in music for any such judgement.

Bearing all this in mind, I think it is possible to search a little further still for the quality of conspicuously fulfilling some function or purpose in which some literature and some noteworthy painting resemble one another. The obvious direction in which to do so is that of architecture. In this connexion I want to exploit the notion (employed in a recent symposium[8] by J. O. Urmson) of 'looking to have' certain characteristics. (The notion, if not the phrase, is an old one. Both Hume and Kant employ it after their fashion.)[9]

'How a thing looks' is, of course, of basic importance in aesthetic evaluations. We prize a rose for how it looks, as also for how it smells. Have you ever paused to look how food is arranged on a plate when it is served to you? Some cooks quite clearly take, and give, aesthetic pleasure in its arrangement: others have a more farm-yard attitude. 'Looking to have' certain characteristics is a relatively sophisticated way of looking (if I may be allowed the metaphor). We may say, for example, that many a bridge of Wade's now looks as though it is simply native stone heaving itself up to form a natural collar over a stream; and that many of Telford's look more like defiant thrusts. The Model T Ford looked to have the qualities of endurance and plain-living uprightness in such defiance of all the graces as to be in a perverse way delightful. Engineering and archi-tecture, in fact, readily suggest examples of this 'sophisticated' way of looking. There are occasions when we admire a building not because it is picturesque or awe-inspiring for its height or made of some pleasing fabric, but because in some satisfactory way it looks what it is meant to be. A university residence may be made to look, as a habitation, friendly or forbidding; an Athonite monastery looks as if it were holding up its inhabitants as offerings to heaven—which in a sense is what it is meant to do. As Urmson put the matter, in general terms: '. . . if a thing looks to have a characteristic which is a desirable one from another point of view, its looking so is a proper ground of aesthetic appreciation. What makes the appreciation aesthetic is that it is concerned with a thing's looking somehow without concern for whether it really is like that . . .'[10]

One must emphasize the point that functional looking is a proper ground of aesthetic appreciation and not claim that it is either always or exclusively the basis for our aesthetic judgements in regard to engineering, architecture or anything else. For one thing, we must not forget the notion of 'finish', which can apply to many manu-factured articles. A tool of which we do not know the function can still look 'finished' and be admired as looking so. Another point to be emphasized (and here I think I diverge from Urmson) is that although we may not be concerned with whether, for example, a building that looks secure really is secure, the looking must be con-vincing: that is, it is the looking which constitutes lack of concern in a sense. The building could still look secure and be known to be insecure, but then it is questionable whether this is the sort of looking which would remain a basis for aesthetic enjoyment. It is not that the knowledge alters the looking but rather that the looking no longer does justice to what we know. Aesthetically-important looking, of the functional kind which we are considering, is looking-on-its-merits, so to speak; that is, it is the impression which something conveys either in the absence of any knowledge whether the thing is as it appears or when such knowledge as there is reinforces the impression.

I find it tempting to suggest that ranging from literature, through painting, to engineering and architecture, we have remained in sight of a common functional characteristic in virtue of which a work may be pronounced a work of art—or if we prefer to put it less strongly, to be aesthetically satisfying. Urmson's 'looking to possess some quality which is non-aesthetically desirable'[11] might seem to be extendable to literature and painting and to be the characteristic in question. Yet there must be qualifications to thinking in just those particular terms. In painting, looking to possess is possessing. A religious painting which looks to possess (or to 'express') reverence is reverent. Picasso's *Guernica*, which was not painted just for the fun of it, expresses abomination; there is no question of its just looking to express it. I am making the point, not that painting may not be functional, but that 'looking' is of the essence of painting. In literature, too, the distinction between looking to possess and possessing some quality which is non-aesthetically desirable can be elided. I am speaking once more of literature which is not belles-lettres; and the reason for the elision here must be a different one from what obtains in painting. I think it is that the question whether great literature 'looks to possess' some non-aesthetic quality or other—persuasiveness, cogent argument, magnanimity or moral fervour, for example—does not arise; because the great literature I am thinking of, classical literature, leaves you no chance, or the least possible chance, of taking it impressionistically. Someone who said that the *Phaedo* was impressive literature because it appeared to avoid all sentiment and appeared to argue rationally in the shadow of death would be talking like an ass. We could simply say that he hadn't read the work properly. Of course classical literature may *profess* to do something which it does not do. Spinoza in his *Ethics* appears to, but does not really, carry out his promise: 'I shall consider human actions and appetites just as if I were considering lines, planes or bodies'; but the *Ethics* remains great literature because of the daringness of the main conceptions which this very profession indicates. 'Looking to possess' certain characteristics, then, must be thought of in a rather vacuous way when it comes to painting, literature and perhaps other art-forms as well; but the point remains that in these forms 'some quality which is non-aesthetically desirable' may sometimes be relevant to an aesthetical appraisal.

I now want to end this paper with a query. I have maintained that a work of literature regarded as such has no moral characteristics—is not, regarded as such, morally good or morally bad or even morally tolerable. *Does the scholarly and knowledgeable reader or teacher of literature, then, have any special competence to pronounce on moral matters?* Echoes of an interesting debate on this topic can be heard just now from the School of English in Cambridge. The question at issue in that School (so far as I can gather) is what counts as literary study; and for the most part (again so far as I can gather) 'literary study' is interpreted freely to include preoccupations, such as philosophy and sociology, indulged in to an extent which other Schools of English might feel to be embarrassing. The sort of embarrassment that is possible has been brought into the open by one commentator on the debate—though his observations (some of which I quote) do not all refer to Cambridge directly: '... there is now a real danger that we shall ... regard ourselves as a caste of sages at liberty (no, in duty bound—for to this way of thinking presumption masquerades as "responsibility") to lay down the law on all aspects of social and personal life. Sexual experience, for instance: did it not surprise the lawyers, and the public at large, to find some of the defence witnesses in the *Lady Chatterley* trial impelled by an apparently impeccable logic from deciding on "literary merit" to deciding on the proper way for a woman to treat her lover and a husband his wife? The logic is indeed unbreakable; and the teachers of English who gave evidence were only doing what was their professional duty. Yet I regard the spectacle with misgiving. It is not good for any body of people to be required to speak with such assurance on matters so intricate and so momentous.'[12] These observations answer my query in moderate and fairly acceptable terms[13]. It *is* a move from a decision on literary merit to a decision on questions of social and personal morality. But it is not a move in strict logic: a decision on literary merit does not imply any decision on social and personal questions: what it does imply, when favourable, is merely that if social and personal questions are treated in the work being judged, they shall be treated with some insight, some gravity, some responsibility and some taste. The knowledge of the work *may* then serve us well not just as students of literature but as human beings; but knowledge of literature remains only one source of knowledge of life.

REFERENCES

[1] I am simply quoting a view. It is not one of which I approve.

[2] *Dissertatio de methodo*, I.

[3] Pilabake in *Kupriake Ekpaideusis*. Oct. 1960, p. 20. (Translation mine.)

[4] *The Spectator*, 25 Nov., 1960, p. 845.

[5] *The Leviathan*, Pt. II, Ch. 17.

[6] *The Observer*, 30 Oct., 1960. The quotations which follow are from an article in the series 'Painters to Watch'.

[7] *Job* 'is adapted in every respect to the incitement of terror; and . . . is universally animated with the true spirit of sublimity' (Lowth, *Lectures on the Sacred Poetry of the Hebrews*, trans. G. Gregory, 1787, II, 428, 424. Quoted by J. T. Boulton in his edition of Burke, *A Philosophical Enquiry into the Origin of our Ideas of the*

Sublime and Beautiful (1958), p. 66, n. 13).

[8] 'What Makes a Situation Aesthetic?' *Aristotelian Society Supplementary Volume* XXXI (1957). Reprinted in Joseph Margolis (ed.), *Philosophy Looks at the Arts* (1962).

[9] *Vide* Hume, *Treatise*, Bk. II, Pt. I, § 8 and Pt. II, § 5; Kant, *Critique of Judgment*, Pt. I, § 16.

[10] *Op. cit.*, p. 89.

[11] *Ibid.*

[12] Donald Davie, 'Literature into Life', *The Spectator*, 9 Dec., 1960, p. 945.

[13] Interestingly enough, a reply to them, printed by *The Spectator* of 16 Dec., based itself on the dogmatic theme that 'Literature is fiction' (*loc. cit.*, p. 983). The whole trend of my paper has been against this idea.

PART III

Psychology and Aesthetics*

C. A. MACE

I. SOME CONTRIBUTIONS OF PSYCHOLOGY TO AESTHETICS

Aesthetics is both a branch of philosophy and a branch of psychology. As a division of philosophy it will reflect differences between schools of philosophy as indeed is clearly to be seen in the lucid exposition of Ruth Saw and Harold Osborne.[1] So too with psychological aesthetics: its varied contributions reflect differences between schools of psychology. Behaviourism might be expected to contribute little, if anything, to our understanding of aesthetic experience but it can contribute to our understanding of originality and creativeness in behaviour (e.g. to the understanding of ballet, mime or puppetry). Gestalt psychology through its studies of perceptual organization, and especially perhaps through its concept of 'pregnance', may help to elucidate the aesthetic concept of 'significant form'. The so-called 'depth psychologies', the systems of Freud, Jung and their successors, contain much of which the student of aesthetics must take account. In works on 'the philosophy of mind' from Aristotle to our contemporaries there are to be found statements which report scientific observations, statements of observable fact, relevant to the understanding of the creation and the enjoyment of works of art. It is, however, sometimes convenient to study history backwards, to ask: Where are we now? before we ask: How did we come to be where we are?

In psychology today there is what might fairly be called a New

---

* This paper contains a restatement of the reflections embodied in an address to The British Society of Aesthetics on 1 March, 1961, under the title 'Some Contributions of Psychology to Aesthetics'. In the process of revision less stress has been placed on the contributions of psychology to aesthetics and more on the potential contributions of aesthetics to general psychology, and more especially to the theory of human motivation.

Established Order. It was R. S. Woodworth who, in his *Contemporary Schools of Psychology*, introduced the expression 'The Established Order'. He used it to describe an orthodoxy in psychology prevailing at the beginning of the present century, a system which derived from Wilhelm Wundt and his distinguished disciple E. B. Titchener. This well-established order became, however, the object of powerful attacks on many fronts by many schools, and the history of psychology in the first half of this century is largely the story of the tribal warfare of these schools. Even now there is a sharp division between the 'depth', 'clinical' or 'dynamic' psychologies of Freud and the post-Freudians and the 'academic', biological and experimental psychologists who have entrenched themselves in the universities and created a New Established Order, a new orthodoxy, to be taken as seriously by the student of aesthetics as the powerful bands of heretics of Freudian and post-Freudian 'depth' psychology. The Established Order of 'straight' psychologists are mainly concerned to advance their subject as a natural science sharing certain broad assumptions with other natural sciences—directly with the other biological sciences, rather less directly with chemistry, physics and engineering.

There are two main planks in their platform. The first is that man, like any other organism, is a sort of machine. An organism is an assembly of instruments, mainly of two sorts: (i) instruments for picking up signals from the environment (and from within the organism itself), i.e. the sense organs; and (ii) instruments for reacting to these signals in appropriate ways, chiefly by the movements of limbs. Instruments of the first type can be compared with microscopes, telescopes and radar equipment. Those of the second type are comparable with tools such as hammers, pincers, etc. The two sets of instruments are linked by a complex communication system (and by storage mechanisms which enable responses to be made to past as well as present signals), but for many purposes these intervening mechanisms can be ignored and the machine can be treated as a 'black box', and attention be directed to the processes of 'input' and 'output'.

It is natural to ask of anything described as a machine: What is it for? The answer is given in terms of the concept of 'goal-directedness'. What a machine does, when it is not out of order, is to work towards the attainment of a goal, to achieve a desired end. But machines are of two sorts: those that work towards the goals of the operator, like a typewriter; and those which like a computer or a guided missile direct themselves and behave as if they have goals of their own. It is possible to construct a machine which 'steers' itself as does the guided missile to a moving target. It is possible to build a machine which given a number will always extract its square root, or a machine which can be set so that given two numbers it will give their sum or multiply them or divide the first by the second. Man is an extremely versatile guided missile. Sometimes like a conventional guided missile he is obsessional in the pursuit of a single goal, but more often he changes his goals in (at present) unpredictable ways. He has built into him the possibility of various sets and the capacity to acquire new sets, the capacity to learn new goals. If pressed further about these built-in and acquired goal-seeking tendencies, the psychologist may allow himself to generalize a little by saying that all the goals of an organic machine can be defined in terms of the familiar biological concepts of 'self-preservation' and 'perpetuation of the species'.

The second main plank in the platform of contemporary psychology is the acceptance of a thoroughgoing evolutionary view. What man *is* can be explained by reference to what he *was*. Man is admittedly the most complex of the contraptions which Nature has produced, but he has been produced by a series of very slow continuous changes with no abrupt transitions.

Now this might seem a slender basis for an explanation of the fact that some men create and many more enjoy works of art, but the general lines of a 'biological' approach are sufficiently familiar. Natural beauty and works of art contribute to the satisfaction of biological needs. Maybe this is so. It may indeed be true, as Herbert Spencer suggested, that martial music facilitates the circulation of the blood. It may indeed be the case that the peahen's aesthetic response to the peacock's tail is conducive to species perpetuation. But if we are to pass from bright suggestions of this kind to anything like a systematic aesthetic, we have a very long way to go. Perhaps the first step is to look a little more closely at the concept of 'goal directedness'.

Goal Directedness

To specify the goals of goal-directed behaviour is to say what it is in a situation which makes that situation a source of satisfaction, to say what it is in the situation, or in an object, that is the ground of our liking it. In psychological aesthetics it is to say what it is in a work of art or in nature that releases or evokes the aesthetic response. This perhaps is the central question of aesthetics, and if so the central question of aesthetics is an important part of the central question in the theory of motivation.

It has proved surprisingly difficult to reach anything like general agreement on the answers to these questions: Why do we want what we do want? Why do we like the things we do like?

For this failure to reach agreement there are several reasons. One reason is that biologists and psychologists have overlooked an important distinction to which attention has been drawn by some social philosophers, viz. the distinction between what men actually want, or try to get, and what they achieve or bring about as unforeseen and unintended effects. The distinctions have been illustrated by reference to the entertaining thesis of Adam Smith that men in pursuing their private interests promote (by the operation of a hidden hand) the welfare of society. The constitution of man is such, and the constitution of society is such, that men being allowed to follow their selfish impulses are tricked, so to speak, into promoting the good of society as an unforeseen and unintended effect. The principle can be applied to the so-called biological end of species perpetuation. Few men, and probably none of the lower animals, are consciously concerned with 'perpetuating their species'. By giving rein to their sexual impulses they are tricked into perpetuating their species. So, too, with self-preservation. By following his appetites man may be tricked into nourishing his body. More often than might be expected what a man fancies happens to be good for him. Pain avoidance has not as its intended effect the prolongation of life, but the avoidance of pain.

The goals of goal-directed behaviour are goals that yield satisfaction and with experience their attainment comes to be a foreseen and intended effect. Another source of error in the specification of the goals of goal-directed behaviour has been the tendency to over-abstraction and over-generalization. These goals have commonly been described in terms such as 'hunger', 'thirst', 'sex', 'the love of power', etc. They are, however, rarely, if ever, food as such, drink as such, or power as such. Men rarely experience a longing for food which *anything* edible will satisfy. Even when very hungry they will scrutinize a menu card with discrimination. And so with other urges. The 'love of power' generally takes a specific form—the exercise of power through the control of the purse-strings, the exercise of power through oratory, or even the exercise of power through neurotic illness. And so it is, *mutatis mutandis*, for all the 'basic drives'. An interesting new approach to the study of what men (and beasts) want, what they like to get and what they try to avoid, has been developed by the work of the psychologically-minded biologists who are called 'ethologists'.

Ethologists have described with some detail and precision the perceptual content of what they call 'releaser mechanisms' in instinctive behaviour. What releases an instinctive response is a more or less simple or more or less complex 'sign stimulus' such as the red blob on the beak of the parent herring-gull which releases the impulse in the baby herring-gull to open its mouth to receive the morsel of food which its parent has brought it. Sometimes the releasing percept has an innate basis, but through various processes such as 'imprinting' or other forms of canalization all sorts of other percepts can act as 'releasers', e.g. in the impulse to follow. Innately the young chick is predisposed to follow the hen, but it may accept substitute leaders—a human being, or even a clockwork toy.

Corresponding to a releasing percept there would seem to be also a 'goal percept', a more or less simple or more or less complex percept which tells the organism when it has got what it needs or wants—the percept which accompanies or follows the 'consummatory response' which terminates the chain of action or a phase in some longer chain.

The concepts of 'releasing percepts' and 'goal percepts' are related to others which have long been familiar, some of which are important in aesthetics.

As long ago as 1929 K. S. Lashley, in an article on Nervous Mechanisms in Learning,[2] published a figure illustrating 'equivalent stimuli' for a habit of jumping in the rat.

> 'The animals were trained to jump to a platform presenting a black surface and a white edge seen against the background of the room. The appearance of the platform was then changed . . . by substituting a large white screen on which paper figures were pasted. The animals jumped to any horizontal rectangle, whether black or white, but would not jump to a vertical rectangle or a plain figure. . . .'

'Equivalent stimuli' in this context are all those which evoke or release the jumping response. It is difficult to define these features simply. Some rather complicated formula is required, a formula of the form: 'All combinations of black and white lines in which the horizontal dimension predominates over the vertical and in which etc., etc.' It is this kind of formula which is required to describe releaser percepts and the equivalents which through imprinting or canalization evoke instinctive responses. So, too, goal percepts must be defined. These are the ends of goal-directed behaviour in general.

At this point we can begin to see a confluence of the main stream of general psychology and the minor but not unimportant tributary constituted by experimental aesthetics.

Just as learning theorists have specified the configurations which release the learned responses, and ethologists have specified the configurations which release instinctive responses, so a considerable number of studies in experimental aesthetics have revealed a number of configurations which release the aesthetic response—configurations characteristic of objects and situations which yield aesthetic satisfaction. One of the best known of these configurations is that which incorporates the 'golden section', i.e. in which in a whole of two parts the ratio of that whole to the larger part is the same as the ratio of the larger to the lesser part. Earlier studies of these elements in aesthetically acceptable forms admittedly led to oversimplified conclusions. A painting may be a work of art *partly* in virtue of its containing golden sections or other ratios, but only in part. It cannot evoke an aesthetic response *just* because it contains a lot of golden sections or other significant ratios any more than it does so *just* because it contains a lot of highland cattle or a lot of blobs of blue. But golden sections, like representations of highland cattle or non-representational blobs of blue, can contribute to the 'significance' of aesthetically 'significant forms'. Later studies suggest that the formulae which define the releasers of the aesthetic response have this at least in common with the formulae of releasers of instinctive responses and the formulae for the 'equivalent stimuli' which release the jumping response in a rat: they will always turn out to be very complicated—perhaps formulae of the kind: 'This picture is a work of art; it evokes an aesthetic response in part because lines are disposed in ways which fall within a certain range of *deviation* from the golden section, in part because the objects depicted are so represented as to conform to such-and-such three-dimensional patterns, such-and-such deviations from simple symmetry, and the colours in such-and-such ratios of brightness, hue, etc., and so on.' How complex the formula may be is suggested by the attempts of the expert critic to explain why he thinks a painting to be as good (or as bad) as he thinks it is. Some people are tempted to say that every feature in the painting contributes to the aesthetic effect, and the 'formula' can be nothing less than a certain kind of description of the picture. This, however, may be an overstatement. It is at any rate unproven. What is, if not proven, at least more plausible is that an explanation of aesthetic satisfaction is to be looked for in terms of 'goal percepts' —the sensuous and perceptual experiences which tell us when we have got what we want. But a theory of the 'enjoyment' of natural beauty and the 'enjoyment' of works of art is part of a larger theory about the enjoyment of life. To make this thesis plausible requires a re-examination of the second platform of the New Established Order—the Evolutionary Approach. This re-examination will *inter alia* indicate some of the ways in which aesthetics can contribute to biology and psychology.

2. SOME CONTRIBUTIONS OF AESTHETICS TO PSYCHOLOGY

'To cultivate the pleasures of my senses was throughout my life my main preoccupation. I have never had any more important objective.' If this had not been said by that disreputable sensualist, Giovanni Jacobo Casanova de Seingalt, it could have been the expression of a quite reputable philosophy and psychology of aesthetics. The enjoyment of natural beauty and of works of art consists largely in the exercise of *cultivated* senses.

But first to recapitulate:

In Part I of this paper a brief outline was given of the platform of the contemporary psychologist, and the question was raised: What this sort of psychology can contribute to our understanding of the enjoyment of natural beauty and to our understanding of the creation and enjoyment of works of art. Two planks in the platform called for scrutiny: (1) the concept of goal-directedness; and (2) the evolutionary view. Part I was mainly concerned with the first plank. To do justice to the thesis of Casanova a similar scrutiny must be made of the process of evolution and the process of civilization.

The Evolutionary Approach

Living things in their most complex and 'highest' form are what they are and behave as they do by a sequence of gradual, 'chance' variations some of which have survival value. Natural selection, no doubt, is one of the techniques through which the hidden hand has arranged that both beasts and men on the whole, and in the long run, come to like what is good for them and their offspring. But the concepts of 'evolution', of 'biological needs', of 'survival value', require a closer scrutiny and more careful analysis than they have in general received.

It may be questioned whether all variations are strictly 'chance' variations. It well may be that some variations are favoured by pre-established goal-directed dispositions. Any plausible theory of evolution by gradual change must take account of changes which, however slow, are in their outcome as revolutionary and as dramatic as the transformation of a grub into a butterfly.

In the evolution of man as capable of aesthetic responses there are two dramatic sequences to be noted: (1) the passage from the sub-human level to the distinctively human; and (2) the passage at the human level from barbarism to civilization.

Prescientific psychology was no doubt unduly preoccupied with some of the distinctive characteristics of civilized man, with his higher intellectual processes and his love of the true, the beautiful and the good. Descriptions and explanations of these characteristics lacked empirical evidence. In consequence the first descriptions and explanations of the mental processes and behaviour of sub-human species tended to be 'anthropomorphic'. The discovery of an evolutionary approach led to a swing of the pendulum and to a tendency to describe and explain the mental processes and behaviour of man in terms of the more primitive mental processes and behaviour of the sub-human species. It resulted, too, in the writing down of the intellectual, the moral and the aesthetic elements in the mental life of the sub-human species. This philosophy of comparative psychology had as it methodological counterpart principles such as that enshrined in the well-known Canon of Parsimony formulated by Lloyd Morgan—that we should never attempt to explain the mental processes and behaviour of a living thing in terms of more complex or higher functions when explanations can be given in terms of more primitive functions. This near-tautology is unexceptional as an abstract principle, but in its application biologists and psychologists were inclined to stretch over-simple explanations when closer analysis of the facts would suggest that a more complex explanation is the simplest that fits these facts.

Today there would seem to be among biologists and psychologists a cautious and gingerly movement towards a new anthropomorphism. In this the need to maintain the principle of continuity in evolution is met not by giving explanations of human behaviour in terms of primitive functions, biological and physiological needs, but by the recognition of more complex mental mechanisms in the sub-human species. Nevertheless, however far we may legitimately go in attributing higher mental functions and higher forms of motivation to sub-human species, there remain important differences between distinctively sub-human and distinctively human ways of living, and perhaps even more important differences between barbaric and civilized ways of living. The latter transition has been variously described. Political philosophers have described it as one from a state of anarchy to some kind of constitution. The theologically minded have described it as a transition from the 'state of nature' to the 'state of grace'. Recently an economist, Galbraith, has excited interest by presenting the transition in terms of the emergence of *The Affluent Society*. The concept of 'affluence' is of more than economic interest. There is a psychology of affluence, a psychology of motivation in an affluent society, which has a very direct bearing upon aesthetics.

'Penury' and 'affluence' are relative terms. Extreme penury could be defined as a state in which the whole of a man's waking life and his energy must be devoted to activities required to obtain the basic necessities of life. At the other extreme of the continuum is the degree of affluence in which not a moment needs to be spent in such activities. All the necessities have been provided by inherited wealth and status or in some other way.

What happens when a man, or for that matter an animal, has no need to work for a living? On the genetic approach the simplest case is that of the domesticated cat—a paradigm of affluent living more extreme than that of the horse or the cow. All the basic needs of a domesticated cat are provided for almost before they are expressed. It is protected against danger and inclement weather. Its food is there before it is hungry or thirsty. What then does it do? How does it pass its time?

We might expect that having taken its food in a perfunctory way it would curl up on its cushion and sleep until faint internal stimulation gave some information of the need for another perfunctory meal. But no, it does not just sleep. It prowls the garden and the woods killing young birds and mice. It *enjoys* life in its own way. The fact that life can be enjoyed, and is most enjoyed, by many living beings in the state of affluence (as defined) draws attention to the dramatic change that occurs in the working of the organic machinery at a certain stage of the evolutionary process. *This is the reversal of the means-end relation in behaviour.* In the state of nature the cat must kill to live. In the state of affluence it lives to kill. This happens with men. When men have no need to work for a living there are broadly only two things left to them to do. They can 'play' and they can cultivate the arts. These are their two ways of enjoying life. It is true that many men work because they enjoy it, but in this case 'work' has changed its meaning. It has become a form of 'play'. 'Play' is characteristically an activity which is engaged in for its own sake—without concern for utility or any further end. 'Work' is characteristically activity in which effort is directed to the production of some utility in the simplest and easiest way. Hence the importance of ergonomics and work study—the objective of which is to reduce difficulty and save time. In play the activity is often directed to attaining a pointless objective in a difficult way, as when a golfer, using curious instruments, guides a small ball into a not much larger hole from remote distances and in the face of obstructions deliberately designed to make the operation as difficult as may be. This involves the reversal of the means-end relation. The 'end'—getting the ball into the hole—is set up as a *means* to the new end, the real end, the enjoyment of difficult activity for its own sake. Art has this in common with play.

The enjoyment of the arts takes two forms. There is the enjoyment of the creative artist who enjoys for its own sake the activity of creation. There is the enjoyment of those who do not themselves create the objects the perception and contemplation of which they enjoy for their own sake.

The aesthetic element in play and the association between art and play are indicated by the fact that many forms of play are described as arts—fencing, fishing, cricket, for example. The play element in art is indicated by the fact that writing a play and acting a play are recognized as among the finer arts.

There is another way of describing the transition from barbarism to civilization. When men no longer need to work to satisfy their needs, when there is leisure to be enjoyed, the 'organic machine' begins to work in a different way. Configurations which appear in the field of perception cease to be treated as signals, cease to be merely releasers of instinctive or acquired dispositions: they become objects of interest in themselves, like the scent of a rose or the song of a bird. The instruments of response now work not merely to produce good percepts which signify the realization of biological ends: they work to produce new percepts which can be enjoyed for their own sake. They work, that is to say, in the practice of an art. They also work for the enjoyment of the activity itself, i.e. the organism plays. Gardens are laid out to create a field of perception more satisfying than nature designs when left to its own devices. Trees are planted not for their fruit but for their blossom. Houses are built not merely for protection against the elements but as objects of visual experience to be enjoyed as such. Man ceases to build like the mason wasp or the beaver and becomes an architect.

Man's conceptions of the good life—life that is lived for its own sake—are embodied in mythologies and in descriptions of Heaven. To the American Indians heavenly life is essentially happy hunting, to the American Negro (as presented in Connolly's *Green Pastures*) life in Heaven is a glorious fish-fry enlivened by the performance of miracles. To the ancient Greeks life in Heaven was essentially romantic. In Nordic mythology Valhalla was the setting of the further fighting and feasting of those who had been killed in battle. It is of interest to note that the only thing that is specific in the nebulous Christian conception of Heaven is a disembodied enjoyment of music—a fact which may account for its lack of appeal to the tone-deaf whose happiest days were experienced in fox-hunting or salmon-fishing.

Psychologists have made systematic studies of human conceptions of the good life. They have analysed the motifs of fairy-tales and other forms of 'wishful thinking' in literature, and they have collected relevant information from stories and essays written by children which reveal something of the content of children's ideas about the way life can be enjoyed.[3] The information obtained by systematic empirical studies is illuminated by the spontaneous description of the 'high spots' which are to be found in fiction and autobiography.

Hadley Cantril, a psychologist, in his book *The Why and How of*

Man's Experience, quotes a passage from A. A. Milne's *The House at Pooh Corner*, in which Christopher Robin asks Pooh:

> 'What do you like doing best in the world, Pooh?'
> 'Well,' said Pooh, 'what I like best—' and then he had to stop and think. Because although Eating Honey *was* a very good thing to do there was a moment just before you began to eat it which was better than when you were, but he didn't know what it was called. And then he thought that being with Christopher Robin was a very good thing to do, and having Piglet near was a very friendly thing to have; and so when he had thought it all out, he said 'What I like best in the whole world is Me and Piglet going to see You and You saying "What about a little something?" and Me saying "Well, I shouldn't mind a little something, should you, Piglet?" and it being a hummy sort of day outside, and birds singing.'

Cantril quoted this to illustrate his theme that one at least of the essential components of satisfaction in life is social, the enjoyment of good company. No doubt it is, but *it is the enjoyment of other good things* in good company. Not least significant is the aesthetic component. It is the enjoyment of the taste of honey in good company on a *'hummy sort of day and birds singing'*. Again, the principle is that a satisfying experience is to be defined only by a complex formula: *A simple sensuous experience enjoyed in a certain kind of company in a setting of a certain sort*—a complex configuration of elements.

The same facts are to be seen in spontaneous autobiographical records: Sir Lawrence Jones in his *Victorian Boyhood* writes as follows:

> I suppose it would be true to say that I have had more enjoyment, a more vivid sense of the delight of living, with every faculty at full stretch, when pursuing and killing birds and beasts, than in any other activity. For sheer exhilaration, joined with the height of aesthetic satisfaction, I have known nothing to compare with deerstalking. The hard physical grind, the constant exercise of craft and cunning, the breath-taking beauty of the high tops, the subtle and ever-changing colours of Scottish mountains, the solitariness and the silence, combine to exalt the spirit to the summit of happiness. The thrill of fox-hunting is ecstatic, but that has rarely come my way, and the pleasure is more physical than aesthetic. Grouse-shooting ranks high, for the mountains are there again, with the influence sweet as that of the Pleiades; the mountains, too, stand about the lochs, and make memorable many a day's fishing. But there is deep and quiet satisfaction to be had far from any

hills; in waiting among the bracken, touched by the mild December sunshine, for the noiseless flit of a woodcock through a glade of ancient thorns, trailing Old Man's Beard; or in hiding among bulrushes, rustling drily, to ambush a flight of teal, or a wisp of driven snipe. Stalking grey-lag geese at dawn on South Uist, or slowly circling a flock of golden plover, in vain hopes of a shot, between Hecla and the green Atlantic, bring the same suspense, the same alertness of observation, the pitting of wits, the triumph or the failure which are the ingredients of delight; and always and everywhere is the feel of ambient air, of sun or rain or wind, sharp or caressing.

It would seem that there are important features common to the life of a domesticated cat and the life of an English gentleman. Hadley Cantril in his analysis of the enjoyment of life stresses sociality. Sir Lawrence Jones focuses on killing. Cantril would no doubt agree that what matters in the enjoyment of life is the taste of honey in good company. Sir Lawrence would no doubt agree that it is not killing as such that matters (he would not have enjoyed a day in a slaughterhouse slitting the throats of pigs): it is killing in good company and under conditions in which he and this company were exposed to breath-taking beauty. (He enjoyed fishing in the lochs more than he would have enjoyed fishing on the banks of the Grand Union Canal.)

There would seem, indeed, to be three features common to the high spots in the life of a domesticated animal (Tabby Cat or Teddy Bear) and the life of a gentleman of leisure. First, they are definable only in terms of a complex formula. Second, they all contain an aesthetic satisfaction. Third, they all seem to contain something very primitive—a primitive sensuous compound like the taste of honey or of blood, or a primitive impulse such as 'sex' or 'aggression'.

Examples could be multiplied indefinitely of spontaneous descriptions of states of bliss such as the well-known lines from Fitzgerald's *Rubaiyat*: 'A book of verse, a flask of wine and thou Beside me singing in the wilderness, And wilderness were Paradise enow.' This, again, is a situation definable only in a complex formula—a whole philosophy of women, wine and song. Again the simple primitive appetite, again the essential aesthetic component in the formula.

This is true of the satisfactions enjoyed through art. A picture is not aesthetically satisfying just because of its golden sections or other relations between its parts. An analysis of its appeal requires a complex formula. And great works of art give expression to very primitive impulses, and provide sensuous satisfactions. To use Freudian language, they appeal to the 'Id' as well as to the 'Ego'. Hence the great relevance of 'depth psychology' to aesthetics.[4] 'The Prince and the Princess lived happily ever after.' The assumption is implicit in romantic literature that the sense experience of normal sexual relations is experience to be enjoyed for its own sake, part of a good life.[5] Not only normal sexual relations, but also deviant sexual experience may form material for art—the Oedipus Complex, homosexuality, nymphomania. Sex is almost always there. Not only sex, but all of the main primitive impulses of the Id may function as part of the core of a work of art. It is surely significant that much great art is preoccupied with crucifixions and other forms of torture, with cruelty, with basic 'appetites'. This may indeed be true of the aesthetics of a Greek vase. After all, an amphora not only displays interesting mathematical relations in its proportions. It was designed to hold wine, a matter of some interest to the Id. An amphora designed by Henry Moore with gaping apertures could be a work of art, but a kind of work of art essentially different from the art of the Greeks.

In all art, no doubt, the needs of the Id are safeguarded, but the cultivation of the pleasures of the senses entails the transcendence of the Id, the transcendence of biological and physiological needs. Under the conditions of gracious living men do not, except by accident, eat because they are hungry or drink because they are thirsty. It is not the hunger drive which explains their choice of caviar as an hors-d'œuvre, nor thirst that explains their choice of Napoleon brandy to accompany their coffee. The 'sex' life of civilized men and women is full of biological enigmas. Biologists and psychologists often write about sex as though it were a powerful drive in virtue of which any male is attracted to any female of the species. In point of fact civilized men can be as choosey in selecting a mate as a woman selecting a hat and the basis of their choice is again definable only in a complex formula, in which again there is the characteristic aesthetic factor which forms part of the description and explanation of why civilized men like what they like. There would seem indeed no firm evidence that 'beautiful' women are healthier, more fertile or in any way biologically fitter than those who are plain.

In the state of civilization life itself has become an art. As Bergson observed: 'The comic comes into being just when society and the individual freed from the worry of self-preservation begin to regard themselves as works of art.' The statement could be generalized: the comic is only one of the values with which aesthetics is concerned.

To summarize and conclude:

What is it in a work of art or in nature which evokes the aesthetic response? The answer, it has been suggested, is to be found through experimental and other empirical studies of the kind that have revealed in works of art and simpler aesthetically pleasing objects configurations which embody certain ratios and certain geometrical and other relations. It has been further suggested that in such studies experimental aesthetics becomes integrated with some of the major and central lines of research in general psychology. There are features common to studies of configurations which release an aesthetic response, studies of configurations which release instinctive responses, studies of configurations which release acquired responses, and studies of configurations which constitute the source of the ultimate satis-factions in life. In this process of integration psychological aesthetics can contribute to general psychology as much as it receives. It draws on general motivational theory, on the methodology and the tech-niques of experimentation. It contributes to general psychology by reason of its special concern with some of the 'higher' and most distinctive functions and activities of the human mind. It serves to correct the over-preoccupation of 'general' psychologists with the simpler and more primitive functions and activities and with the more primitive 'physiological' and 'biological' needs. Through its special concern with certain modes of experience and activities which are enjoyed for their own sakes psychological aesthetics can contribute to the understanding of other experiences and activities

enjoyed for their own sake, such as play and other pursuits characteristic of leisure and gracious living in civilized society—of life
generally when the working of the organic machine is no longer
geared to 'the basic physiological and biological needs'. Perhaps the
greatest contribution of aesthetics to psychology is that it opens the
way to a distinctively human psychology in which *psychological needs*
are clearly distinguished from the simpler physiological or biological
needs. The life which men seek to preserve and perpetuate is a two-
dimensioned variable. What they try to prolong and enhance is life
of a certain kind—a certain standard and style of living. Men behave
as if they believed that it is better to be a worried philosopher or a
neurotic artist than it is to be a happy and well-adjusted pig. No
limit can be set to the contribution of general psychology to aesthetics
but the extent and the rate of this contribution may well depend on
the extent to which aesthetics contributes to psychology not only
through its facts and hypotheses but also through the student of
aesthetics asking the psychologist the right questions.

REFERENCES

[1] In the first number of this Journal, November 1960. (Paper I in this anthology).

[2] *Foundations of Experimental Psychology*, Ch. 14.

[3] An example of these more systematic studies is to be found in the report in which Miss Thelma Veness of Birkbeck College analyses the data obtained in an investigation of the ambitions and aspirations of young people. In this study among the useful techniques employed was one in which the young people were invited to write an imaginary autobiography from the point of view of the date of their retirement; and another in which a very brief essay was required under the title 'The Best Moment of my Life'.

[4] Notwithstanding its great relevance this aspect has not been considered in this paper since it is one that would require a separate extended discussion.

[5] A thesis persuasively developed by Alex Comfort in *Darwin and the Naked Lady*.

Psychological Processes in the Reading of Fiction*

D. W. HARDING

One of the unsatisfactory features of psychology at the present time is the contrast between an attempt at very exact definition of concepts and terms in some directions and a toleration of extreme vagueness and woolliness in others. The effort after precision is seen mostly in the planning and interpreting of experiments that lead further and further back into the recesses of methodology and abstract theory; the very high toleration of ambiguity occurs in discussing problems of complex behaviour in civilized societies. If we want to say how a rat learns a maze, we know by now that we shall have to come to grips with exactly defined terms and a meticulously scrutinized conceptual framework. If we are invited to consider the psychological processes that occur in reading a novel, we probably expect some rather vague waffle compounded of psycho-analysis, sociology and literary criticism. If I provide that, I shall have failed in my aim. Although real precision may at present be far out of reach, an effort in that direction is incumbent on anyone who believes that psychology as a science can have something useful to say about fiction.

An initial question is whether we should try to discuss fiction within a framework of general aesthetics. I agree with those who maintain that the numerous and extremely dissimilar activities conventionally grouped together as the arts don't form a separate psychological category. Very few literal statements that apply to a novel, a landscape painting, a porcelain dish and a piece of music will be at all illuminating about any one of those things. A novel is so distantly related to many other sorts of art, and so closely related

* Read to The British Society of Aesthetics on 10 October, 1961.

to activities that are not included among the arts, that an approach through aesthetic generalizations would be restricting and misleading. It may seem, perhaps, that the form of a novel and the style of a novelist can be discussed in terms equally applicable to other arts, but I suspect that it can be done only by substituting metaphor and analogy for literal statement.

Much more important aspects of fiction are illuminated if the reader of a novel is compared with the man who hears about other people and their doings in the course of ordinary gossip. And to give an account of gossip we have to go a step or two further back and consider the position of the person who looks on at actual events. As a framework, then, within which to discuss fiction, I want to offer some statement of the psychological position of the onlooker (of which I attempted a fuller discussion in 'The Role of the On-looker', *Scrutiny*, VI, 3 December, 1937), and then to view the reading of a novel as a process of looking on at a representation of imagined events or, rather, of listening to a description of them. This involves examining carefully—and I believe discarding— psychological assumptions about some of the processes, such as identification and vicarious satisfaction, that have been supposed to occur in the reader.

Part of everyone's time is spent in looking on at events not primarily in order to understand them (though that may come in), and not in preparation for doing something about them, but in a non-participant relation which yet includes an active evaluative attitude. We can say two things of the onlooker: first that he attends, whether his attention amounts to a passing glance or fascinated absorption; and second that he evaluates, whether his attitude is one of faint liking or disliking, hardly above indifference, or whether it is strong, perhaps intensely emotional and perhaps differentiated into pity, horror, contempt, respect, amusement, or any other of the shades and kinds of evaluation, most of them unlabelled even in our richly differentiated language. Attentiveness on any particular occasion implies the existence of an interest, if we take that to mean an enduring disposition to respond, in whatever way, to some class of objects or events. The response almost instantaneously becomes (or is from the start) evaluative, welcoming or aversive. And in a complex, experienced organism an evaluative attitude is usually one expression of a sentiment, if we take that to mean an enduring disposition to evaluate some object or class of objects in a particular way; an event or situation is then assessed in the light of its cognized significance for the object of a sentiment.

To take an example. For most of us a human being is interesting, and conflict is interesting, and a struggle between two groups of people is extremely likely to command our attention. When we observe one of the groups to be policemen a system of sentiments will be activated; according to the way we identify the other group, as men or women, drunk or sober, strike pickets, rowdy students, smash-and-grab thieves, political demonstrators, or what not, so other sentiments will be activated; the apparent brutality or good humour of the contestants will stir yet others; and whether we want to boo or cheer or shrug when the Black Maria eventually drives off will be the outcome of a complex interaction among many mutually entangled systems of sentiment.

The idea—still occasionally held—that the spectator's link with the scene consists mainly in his recognition that similar things might have happened to him—'There, but for the grace of God, go I'— depends on far too limited a view of the human mind. Admittedly the man watching a shipwreck from the safety of the shore may realize thankfully that he might have been in it and isn't, or more subtly that it symbolizes something that might happen to him; but to suppose that this is his chief link with the scene would be a crude piece of un-psychological rationalism. By far the likeliest response, and one that almost certainly accompanies any others, is simple horror and distress that this thing is happening to living people, whom he values as fellow-beings and whose sufferings he can imagine. We have a vivid description by William Hickey of what he felt when he was actually in the traditional role of watching a shipwreck from the shore:

> At half-past five nine ships that had parted from their anchors drove on shore between Deal and Sandwich, a distance of only eight miles; others,

having drifted foul of each other, were obliged to cut away rigging and masts to prevent the dire alternative of going to the bottom together; two were seen actually to founder. A more horrid spectacle I never beheld, yet so interested did I feel on account of the unhappy people on board the different vessels that neither wet nor cold nor want of rest could induce me to quit the beach whilst a ray of light remained. . . .

At eight o'clock I followed the advice of the hostess by drinking some excellent hot punch, and going directly afterwards to bed, where, although anxiety for the sufferings of the many poor drowning wretches kept me awake some time, fatigue at last got the better, and I fell into a profound and deep sleep, which continued uninterrupted for full twelve hours.[1]

It was only by chance that Hickey himself was not in one of the ships, and yet it seems clear that any relief he felt on his own account was a small part of his total state of mind compared with his concern for the victims.

Although the disclosure or reminder of environmental possibilities in a merely cognitive mode is a minor matter, it remains true that the experience of looking on at events does extend and modify, besides reflecting, the spectator's systems of interest and sentiment. A girl who watches a mother caring for an infant is not just reminded of one of the possibilities of her own life; she may also be extending her insight into the sort of satisfaction that a mother gets, perhaps correcting sentimental preconceptions or seeing compensations where she would have anticipated only trouble. In the same way we may learn as onlookers from the panic or the calmness of people faced with a threatening situation, or from the courage or the blind hope with which they meet serious illness, or from the sort of pleasure they show on achieving a success. In ways of this kind the events at which we are 'mere onlookers' come to have, cumulatively, a deep and extensive influence on our systems of value. They may in certain ways be even more formative than events in which we take part. Detached and distanced evaluation is sometimes sharper for avoiding the blurrings and buffetings that participant action brings, and the spectator often sees the event in a broader context than the participant can tolerate. To obliterate the effects on a man of the occasions on which he was only an onlooker would be profoundly to change his outlook and values.

Besides looking on at events in progress we can be spectators in memory or imagination of things past and things anticipated; further, we can release our imaginings from practical limitations and consider what might have been and what might be if the restrictions of reality were suspended. Even in looking on at actual happenings the spectator often grossly distorts what occurs, misleading himself by a variety of unconscious mechanisms; in memory and anticipation the unwitting distortion of fact and probability is even greater; and in fantasy even the intention to control thought by the measure of possibility is largely relinquished. In all the forms of fantasy, whether dreams, day-dreams, private musings or make-believe play, we give expression to perfectly real preoccupations, fears and desires, however bizarre or impossible the imagined events embodying them.

The imaginary spectatorship of fantasy and make-believe play has the special feature of allowing us to look on at ourselves, ourselves as participants in the imagined events—the hero in the rescue fantasy, the victim of the assault, the defendant rebutting unjust accusations, the apparent nonentity suddenly called to national responsibility. In spite, however, of seeing himself as a participant in the story, the day-dreamer or the child engaged in make-believe remains an onlooker too; in all his waking fantasy he normally fills the dual role of participant and spectator, and as spectator he can when need be turn away from the fantasy events and attend again to the demands of real life. But although in waking experience we normally never quite lose grip on the role of onlooker, it remains true that every degree of abandonment to the invented occurrences may occur. We may at times give them, as it were, no more than a sceptical glance, perhaps contrasting them immediately with our present situation; we may let them develop very great vividness although we still remain only onlookers, never letting our real situation be far beyond the margins of attention and always being able at the least necessity to switch back to where we really are; or they may reach the extreme vividness, obliterating everything else, that the night dream possesses, and then, whether as day-dreamers or as psychotics, we have abandoned the role of onlooker and given ourselves up to delusional and perhaps hallucinated participation.

The solitary onlooker and the man engaged in private fantasy are, of course, members of a highly social species and their apparent isolation is unreal; what they see and invent, and what they feel, must be strongly influenced by their culture. In an environment which is highly saturated socially our experience as spectators forms an important part of our cultural moulding. Everything we look on is tacitly and unintentionally treated as an object lesson by our fellow-spectators; speech and gesture or the mere intake of breath, smiles, pauses, clucks, tuts and glances are constantly at work to sanction or challenge the feelings we have as spectators. Needless to say, we can at least to some extent resist our fellow-onlookers' influence; and we in our turn, of course, are sanctioning and challenging and suggesting modifications of viewpoint to them.

The influence of our fellow-onlookers draws our attention to one aspect of events rather than another, changing the emphasis or bringing to mind what we might have overlooked. From this it is only a step—but a very important step—to telling us about events we missed seeing, as in a vast amount of gossip and narrative. Instead of literally looking on we now listen to representations of events; and the social influence of our companion is greater than ever because he not only reports selectively but also conveys what he regards as an appropriate attitude to what he saw. The gossip implicitly invites us to agree that what he reports is interesting enough to deserve reporting and that the attitude he adopts, openly or tacitly, is an acceptable evaluation of the events.

From giving an account of what has happened the next step is to suggest things that *might* happen, a process seen at its simplest in the child's 'Suppose ...' technique: 'Suppose that lion got out ...' 'Wouldn't it be fun if we found a secret cave?' 'Suppose that man was a spy ...' Here at one step we pass into the area of make-believe, whether it takes the form of play with companions, of drama, or of fiction. Imaginary spectatorship now occurs in a social setting. The result is a vast extension of the range of possible human experience that can be offered socially for contemplation and assessment. The ends achieved by fiction and drama are not fundamentally different from those of a great deal of gossip and everyday narrative. Between true narrative and fiction there exist, in fact, transitional techniques such as the traveller's tale and the funny anecdote in which the audience's tacit permission is assumed for embellishments and simplifications that enhance the effectiveness of the story. True or fictional, all these forms of narrative invite us to be onlookers joining in the evaluation of some possibility of experience.

Here I must make two digressions. The first is that the possibilities of experience include grief and disaster. Onlookers gather round accidents and funerals, gossips converse about disease, conflict and misery, newspaper readers want to hear of crime and calamity, the day-dream is by no means always an invention of pleasures and children's make-believe includes its quota of illness, injury and punishment. In all these simpler forms of onlooking we are familiar with the fact that the unhappy chances of life are at least as interesting as the happy ones. It is not surprising, therefore, to find the same thing when we come to fiction and drama; the fact that tragic events are of intense human interest should not lead us into formulating pseudo-problems as to how the contemplation of something painful can be pleasurable. If there is a problem here, it is not confined to tragedy. The spectator, whether of actual events or of representations, is interested in any of the possibilities of human experience, not merely its pleasures.

My second digression is that in saying that fiction represents possibilities of human experience we have to notice that it may be doing so through the medium of physical impossibilities. Tales that deal in the impossible are of two kinds. On the one hand there are tales of wonder which claim that the wonders are real possibilities— like the 'very true' account Autolycus was selling of 'how a usurer's wife was brought to bed of twenty money-bags at a burthen'. Some of our contemporary tales of ghosts and the supernatural, whether offered as fiction or as true report, come into this category, as do some forms of science fiction. But on the other hand physical impossibilities may be used, both in fairy-tales and in some sophistic-ated fiction, as vehicles for presenting realities of experience. In many fairy-tales the wonders are of importance chiefly as providing the least laborious, most compressed and vivid means of representing some quite possible human experience. Everyone longs from time to time to have his own way, untrammelled by reality; the three miraculous wishes offer a dramatic compression of that possibility and allow the consequences to be discussed. Any of us might feel downtrodden and hope to have the tables turned by a benign authority who recognized our merit; a fairy godmother is a brief and vivid way of saying how delightful that would be.

In sophisticated fiction it is a question of the author's technique of presentation whether he aims at verisimilitude or at avowed fantasy. When he chooses to depart from real possibilities we might say with Coleridge that the reader is called on for a 'willing suspension of disbelief'. But it makes less of a mystery of the process if we say that he is willing to participate in a recognized mode of communication, an accepted technique for discussing the chances of life. Basically we are engaged in the 'Suppose . . .' technique of children's conversation.

Moreover in this respect—to return to the main theme—fantasy only highlights what is true of all fiction, that it is a convention of communication. The full grasp of fiction as fiction is a sophisticated achievement. Children come to it gradually, and although little seems to be known about the steps by which they reach it, we can plausibly suppose that the phase of 'lying' fantasy that many children go through is one stage of the process. There is good reason to think that the less sophisticated adult often has only a precarious hold on the distinction between fiction and narrative; so some of the reactions to popular series in broadcasting have suggested, though here again full investigation seems to be lacking. It would appear, too, that some primitive peoples, though they enjoy story-telling as a pastime, regard all the stories as true narrative (perhaps of a remote ancestral past) and have little conception of avowed fiction. The Samoans of R. L. Stevenson's time, having read a missionary translation of his story *The Bottle Imp*, assumed that his wealth really came from his command of a magic bottle, and after a convivial evening with him would sometimes feel sufficiently in his confidence to ask if they might see 'the bottle'.[2] Fiction has to be seen, then, as a convention, a convention for enlarging the scope of the discussions we have with each other about what may befall.

The 'discussion' may seem a one-sided affair since the reader is unable to answer back. But he is none the less active in accepting or rejecting what the author asserts. In the first place, the author offers what he claims to be a possibility of experience; the reader may in effect say: 'No: that action of the hero is inconsistent with what he has said or done before; that monster of iniquity isn't humanly possible; that sudden repentance could never have happened. . . .' Secondly, the author conveys what he regards as appropriate attitudes towards events, characters and actions. He is constantly—but of course tacitly—saying: 'Isn't this exciting. . . . He's attractive, isn't he. . . . Wasn't that tragic. . . . Isn't this moving . . .?' Again the reader accepts or rejects the implied assessments. He may not consciously formulate his agreement and disagreement, but these are the underlying processes that show themselves eventually in enthusiasm for an author's work or disappointment with it. The reader discriminates; and this is true even at the low levels of trivial fiction, though there the discriminations may depend on criteria that better educated or more practised readers have discarded.

The view I have been offering of the reader's active part at the receiving end of a conventional mode of communication contrasts with a good deal of pseudo-psychologizing that sees the process of novel-reading as one of identification and vicarious experience. Those ideas, vague and loose as they have always been, have had such currency that they have to be seriously examined.

We may once more begin with the man looking on at actual events. Unless he deliberately adopts the discipline of detached observation for the purposes of science or painting, he soon in some sense 'enters into' the experience of one or more of the participants. The basic process connecting the onlooker with any event, real or fictional, involving living things is that of imagining. The fundamental fact is that we can imagine ourselves in a situation very different from the one we are in, we can create images of the sensations we should have, we can become aware, in part, of the meanings we should see in it, what our intentions, attitudes and emotions would be, what satisfactions and frustrations we should experience. Suppose you are looking out of the window at torrents of rain lashing down in the street: you can imagine yourself out in it, rain beating on your face, your shoes squelching, your legs wet below the mackintosh, rain getting down inside your collar, hands in your pockets, shoulders hunched—and you can imagine the emotions you might experience out there. Suppose a man is in the street: the same process can occur, perhaps facilitated by the sight of him; and because you assume a fundamental likeness between yourself and him you take it that you have imaginative or empathic insight into his experience. Suppose that you watch a film of a man walking through pouring rain, or read of him in a book, or dream of him at night: the same basic process of imagining is at work. To say that this process has long been understood in psychology would be to claim too much, but it has long been recognized; and to what extent more recent ideas of identification and vicarious experience really advance our understanding is a matter for cautious discussion.

The great difficulty about the term 'identification' is to know which one of several different processes it refers to. The reader may see resemblances between himself and a fictional *persona* only to regret them (and perhaps hope to become different): is this recognition of resemblances 'identification'? He may long enviously to be like a fictional character so different from himself that he discounts all possibility of approximating to him: is this admiration 'identification'? He may adopt the character as a model for imitation, more or less close and successful, and it may be this process to which 'identification' refers. Or he may be given up, for the duration of the novel or film, to absorbed empathy with one of the characters. The fact is that we can avoid all this uncertainty and describe each of the processes accurately by speaking explicitly of empathy, imitation, admiration, or recognition of similarities. We sacrifice little more with the term 'identification' than a bogus technicality.

With this pseudo-technicality we discard the idea that there is something pathological about the processes we describe, or something to be better understood by examining pathological exaggerations of them. It may well be true that a continuity can be detected between absorbed empathy with a character and—at the pathological extreme—a psychotic delusion of identity with a great man, Napoleon, St. Peter, the President of the U.S.A. There may also be a continuum between the everyday imitation of some feature of an admired person (the handwriting of a favourite teacher or the hair style of a film star) and the pathological forms of imitation in which, for instance, psychosomatic processes produce symptoms similar to those of the illness from which a close relative has just died (though in this case devotion is often fused with fear and self-reproach). Even latah may claim to be on the same continuum. But we have not illuminated the ordinary processes by showing that they pass by gradual stages into the pathological and by giving to them all, healthy and morbid, the term 'identification'. We are still left with the perfectly usual and healthy processes of having empathic insight into other people (or representations of them) and of imitating features of their behaviour that we admire. To suppose that these processes are explained by being called identification is to be taken in by verbal magic.

The onlooker's observation of other people or of *personae* in fiction and drama may be accompanied by a preference for some, by specially sensitive or full insight into some, by awareness of likenesses between himself and some (not necessarily those he admires), and by a wish that he resembled some. These processes, occurring with all degrees of clear awareness or obscurity, form part of the tissue of ordinary social intercourse as well as entering into the enjoyment of fiction. An adequate account of a reader's attitude to a fictional *persona* may have to include a reference to them all, as well as to the subtler shades and complexities of these broad types of response. No good purpose is served by blanketing them all with a term like 'identification'.

The spectator who gives himself up to absorbed sympathy with some character of a novel or play is sometimes said to experience vicariously whatever the character undergoes. Among those who want a simple but psychological-sounding explanation for the enjoyment of fiction this idea of vicarious experience or vicarious satisfaction has long been popular. But its stands up poorly to serious examination.

Jung expressed the prevailing view when he said: 'The cinema..., like the detective story, makes it possible to experience without danger all the excitement, passion and desirousness which must be repressed in the humanitarian ordering of life.'[3] Notice that he says 'possible to *experience*', not possible to 'contemplate' or 'imagine'. On this formulation depends any exact meaning that the notion of vicarious experience possesses. Other writers, over a wide range of criticism and journalism, have popularized the idea. It was used, for instance, by the Lynds in *Middletown* and by Q. D. Leavis in *Fiction and the Reading Public*, where she took 'Living at the Novelist's Expense' as one of her leading themes and interpreted much novel-reading as the indulgence of wish-fulfilment fantasies. A contributor to *The Adelphi* (March, 1934), wrote: 'With the lovely heroine, the laundry worker dons silk underwear . . . an evening cloak with soft furry collar. During the day she has stood with damp feet in badly-fitting high-heeled shoes which took two weeks' savings. But now her well-shaped leg is enclosed in stockings of finest silk, and shod by shoes from the Rue de la Paix. For an hour !' And Rebecca West wrote in *Nash's Pall Mall Magazine* (February, 1934): 'George was glad to earn two pounds a week by tedious toil, and for relaxation . . . indulge in remote concupiscence with unknowing film-stars.' (The quotations date from a period when the cultivated could pity wage-earners.)

What can be meant literally by these views? The desires are not in fact satisfied, of course. The implied suggestion is apparently that viewing a film or reading a novel approximates to having a wish-fulfilment dream—as hungry explorers are reported to dream of good meals—and that the spectator temporarily gets a delusive satisfaction through what amounts to hallucination while he reads or watches. That something approaching this may possibly happen to a few rather unusual people would be difficult to prove or disprove. But that it can be at all a usual mechanism is unbelievable. We may in moments of bitterness speak of the cinema or television as a dope, but we don't seriously believe that the spectators are sitting there in the same psychological condition as opium smokers in a dream, supposing themselves actually to be in some world of their fantasy. (They can pass each other sandwiches or stand up to let somebody else get to a seat, all in the real world, though they watch the screen.) It seems to be a case where a vivid metaphor has been taken literally without realization of the extent of pathological disorientation that the supposed psychological process would imply.

We get nearer the truth by starting from the fact that the 'wish-fulfilment' dream is also a *statement* of a pressing need or desire, defining the desire at the same time as it offers hallucinated satisfaction. In expressing interests and affirming desires for which ordinary life provides small scope fiction and drama may indeed have something a little in common with dreams. They may, for instance, give expression to interests and attitudes that are partially checked (perhaps even repressed) in ordinary social intercourse, such as sexuality, cruelty, arrogance and violence. But it is very doubtful whether plays or novels that do this can rightly be said to give *substitute* satisfaction to the spectators' desires. They give perfectly real, direct satisfaction, but to a muted and incomplete version of the desires. The parallel is with the person who exclaims of someone annoying: 'I'd like to knock his block off,' or: 'He deserves to be horse-whipped.' Exclamations like this offer no vicarious satisfaction for impulses to homicide or assault, but they constitute a real social attack and give direct satisfaction to a permissible degree of hostility (and may thereby give very incomplete but still direct satisfaction to a more immoderate degree of hidden rage). They may, if the anger grows or the countervailing impulses weaken, lead on towards actual physical attack; but more commonly they serve in themselves as a safety-valve. So with novels, plays and films, the represented expression of interests and desires usually held in check may in some spectators precipitate overt action to satisfy the desire (for instance, sexual activity or some form of violence), but in other cases the fiction itself will be a sufficient and a direct satisfaction of the slight degree of interest and desire that it elicits or releases.

Interests and attitudes that are repressed or condemned, however, form only a small part of the material of fiction and drama. Entirely acceptable values, too, receive definition and affirmation. The desire for affection (prominent among the desires represented in the films analysed for the Payne Fund Studies of the cinema), the desire for adventure, for achievement, for the courage of one's convictions, for prestige, for cheerful companionship and for endless other things may all be stimulated, defined more concretely and vividly, revived after waning or confirmed after doubt. Although these desires, perhaps thwarted in real life, will not be satisfied in drama or fiction (or through contemplating real people more happily circumstanced), there may still be a highly important gain in having joined with the novelist or dramatist in the psychological act of giving them statement in a social setting. What, after all, is the alternative to defining and expressing our unattained and perhaps unattainable desires? It is to acquiesce in the deprivation and submit to the belief that with our personality or in our circumstances we ought not even to desire such things; and to forfeit the right to the desire is even worse than to be denied the satisfaction.

What is sometimes called wish-fulfilment in novels and plays can, therefore, more plausibly be described as wish-formulation or the definition of desires. The cultural levels at which it works may vary widely; the process is the same. It is the social act of affirming with the author a set of values. They may centre round marble bathrooms, mink coats and big cars, or they may be embodied in the social milieu and *personae* of novels by Jane Austen or Henry James; Cadillacs and their occupants at Las Vegas or carriages and theirs at Pemberley and Poynton. We may lament the values implied in some popular forms of fiction and drama, but we cannot condemn them on the ground of the psychological processes they employ. The finer kinds of literature require the same psychological processes, though putting them to the service of other values.

It seems nearer the truth, therefore, to say that fictions contribute to defining the reader's or spectator's values, and perhaps stimulating his desires, rather than to suppose that they gratify desire by some mechanism of vicarious experience. In this respect they follow the pattern, not of the dream with its hallucinated experiencing, but of waking supposition and imagination—'Wouldn't it be wonderful if . . .' 'Wouldn't it be sad if. . . .'

Empathic insight allows the spectator to view ways of life beyond his own range. Contemplating exceptional people, he can achieve an imaginary development of human potentialities that have remained rudimentary in himself or been truncated after brief growth. He can believe that he enters into some part of the experience of the inter-planetary explorer, the ballerina, the great scientist, the musician or the master-spy; and again this applies at every level from popular entertainment to serious literature. The spectator enters imaginatively, with more or less accuracy and fullness, into some of the multifarious possibilities of life that he has not himself been able to achieve. One of the bonds between ourselves and others, one among our reasons for interest in them, is that they have done things that we have not. A great deal of gossip, newspaper reports, memoirs, fiction and drama, serves to remind us of the human potentialities that for one reason or another we have left to others, but the knowledge of which, in a diversified group with highly developed modes of communication, forms one of our social possessions.

A related source of satisfaction in entering imaginatively into activities far beyond our own range lies in the fact that we can see in very diverse ways of life certain broad types of experience that we know in our own: we view familiar experiences of struggle, dis-appointment, excitement, moral challenge, companionship, in the heightening context (biographical or fictional) of a more remarkable way of life, and the ordinary possibilities of our own lives may gain an enhanced significance as a result—whether the Saturday night dance takes on a Ruritanian glamour, or the determination of a Pasteur or Cézanne redeems our everyday persistence in face of the usual setbacks, or the commonplace failure of courage reveals the Lord Jim in our own personality.

In all these ways the process of looking on at and entering into other people's activity, or representations of it, does enlarge the range, not of the onlooker's experience but of his quasi-experience and partial understanding. For it has to be remembered that the subtlest and most intense empathic insight into the experience of another person is something far different from having the experience oneself.

I have suggested that the processes that are sometimes labelled 'identification' and 'vicarious experience' need to be described more carefully and in more detail for psychological purposes. But we have to go further. For even when these processes have been accurately defined they are totally insufficient as an account of the reader's response to fiction. An account based on them alone neglects the fact that the onlooker not only enters into the experience of the participants but also contemplates them as fellow-beings. It is an elementary form of onlooking merely to imagine what the situation must seem like and to react *with* the participant. The more complex observer imagines something of what the participant is experiencing and then reacts *to* him, for instance with pity or joy on his account. The spectators who watch Othello as he kills his wife are not feeling simply what they imagine him to be feeling; they are also feeling, as onlookers, pity *for* him.

Nor is this part of the onlooker's role confined to the upper levels of fiction and drama. It figures prominently in the response of the most naïve spectator watching, say, one of the old films of the hero tearing along a dangerous road in a car, to the rescue of the heroine on whom disaster is closing in. Do the spectators experience imaginatively only what the hero is supposed to be experiencing— his determination, his anxiety and hope, his concentration on the road, his exasperation at the fallen tree, his conflict before taking a hair's-breath chance on the edge of the precipice? Some part of this comes across but the spectators are in addition responding to the situation as a whole: they are hoping *for* the hero as well as with him, they assess his chances in the light of what they see of the heroine's position, they have ups and downs of hope and anxiety as the situation alters (often in ways that the hero knows nothing about); they may think more of the heroine and her danger than of the hero's supposed feelings, and their taking sides with both of them against the villains introduces another social element that forms no part of the supposed experience of any of the participants.

The onlooker's response to the events as a whole goes much beyond identification with any one of the characters, a point so obvious that one would apologize for making it were it not regularly ignored by those who psychologize about fiction and drama. A clear example of response to the situation as a whole is given by K. O. Newman,[4] who describes '. . . the climax of the last act [of the war play that he saw repeatedly], when a stage-character, believed missing or dead, reappears bodily, hale and hearty, though somewhat tired and bedraggled. The delight of the audience at this auspicious dispensation knew no bounds, night after night, matinée after matinée. His appearance, behind the back of the hero and heroine, engaged in conversation, invariably evoked an excited mutter in the audience, which, at some performances, went as far as an outburst of rapturous applause from the more naïve and impressionable playgoers.' The impulse to applaud was clearly not the outcome of feeling what any one of the characters on the stage was feeling. In viewing a situation like this, commonplace enough, the spectator is contemplating the whole social situation, perhaps anticipating what the characters will soon be feeling, but primarily adopting an attitude *towards* them. His attitude is that of a well-wisher who is not merely anticipating the joy that they will feel but who enjoys the fact that they will be feeling joy. He feels pleased *for* them as well as *with* them. For the reader to know more about the events than the characters are shown as knowing is a normal and frequent feature of novels and plays. Dramatic irony is entirely dependent on it. And, of course, re-reading or re-witnessing a novel or play extends and emphasizes the audience's superior knowledge of events and outcomes. Whenever the reader or spectator is in this position it becomes still more evidently a mistake to describe his response as 'identification' and 'vicarious experiencing'.

Let me recapitulate my main points. The mode of response made by the reader of a novel can be regarded as an extension of the mode of response made by an onlooker at actual events. One process on which the response depends—apart from the elementary perception and comprehension of the scene—is that of imaginative or empathic insight into other living things, mainly other people. But this would give only imaginative *sharing* of the participants' experience. At least equally important is the onlooker's, on the reader's, evaluation of the participants and what they do and suffer, an evaluation that I would relate in further analysis to his structure of interests and sentiments. But there is a third aspect of the process: the reader knows that the characters of the novel are not real people but only *personae* created by the author for the purpose of communication. Many readers, even educated readers, fail to hold this fact clearly in mind and they retain traces of the naïve view of the *personae* as real people, wanting to speculate for instance about the influences that made them what they are when the story opens or what will become of them after it ends. The more sophisticated reader knows that he is in social communication of a special sort with the author, and he bears in mind that the represented participants are only part of a convention by which the author discusses, and proposes an evaluation of, possible human experience.

REFERENCES

[1] *Memoirs of William Hickey*, ed. Alfred Spencer, 9th edition (1948), Vol. II, pp. 5–6.

[2] See J. C. Furnas, *Journey to Windward* (1952).

[3] C. G. Jung, *Modern Man in Search of a Soul* (1945).

[4] *Two Hundred and Fifty Times I Saw a Play* (Pelagos Press, Oxford, 1944).

PART IV

Art as Communication*

ERIC NEWTON

The title of this paper is, I am fully aware, unforgivably ambitious and almost unforgivably old-fashioned. Let me limit your expectations at once—first by attempting to define the ground I propose to cover, and secondly by promising that even that ground will be covered very thinly by the simple method of illustrating what I have to say by examining a single painting.

What I have to say is roughly this. A work of art does not exist until it has reached a state in which it can make its impact on the sensory perceptions of others—people we can call spectators or audience. And yet long before that state has been reached it must have existed (if that is the right word) in the creative mind of the artist. And by that I emphatically do not mean that this private, invisible, inaudible embryo of an unborn work of art bears much resemblance to what will one day be seen by a spectator or listened to by an audience. But it must bear *some* resemblance—roughly the same resemblance as the embryo bears to the adult it will one day become.

It would be fascinating, if it were possible, to trace every stage in the growth between the *moment* of conception—perhaps the interview between Michelangelo and Pope Julius II when the Sistine Chapel ceiling was first discussed, or the moment when Shakespeare, glancing through a copy of North's translation into English of Amyot's translation into French of Plutarch's Life of Coriolanus, paused in his reading and said to himself: 'Something could be made of this'—between those moments (they are always moments) and the day when the ceiling was finished or the first appearance of The

* This paper was delivered as a lecture to The British Society of Aesthetics on 2 November, 1960.

Tragedy of Coriolanus in the Folio of 1623, all kinds of processes had happened which I shall not even attempt to describe, but which I should like to call, generically, *attempts to find a language to fit an idea*—and therefore (even though the idea of communication may not have been uppermost in the artist's mind) attempts to communicate.

Now before communication becomes possible a kind of unwritten agreement must exist between artist and spectator. There must be a certain fund of experience common to both. It is usually an extremely elementary affair, but until the spectator has *seen* a woman he cannot understand the meaning of Leonardo's *Mona Lisa*. And until he can consult his own memory of a naked woman he cannot understand Botticelli's *Birth of Venus*. He refers Botticelli's image to his own remembered image, and finds to his surprise that the two are related but are not identical. Botticelli has added something, and the sum total of that addition is what Botticelli has communicated. He has, as it were, reinforced the dictionary meaning of the word 'woman'.

My object, then, in this paper, is to examine the nature of the artist's inventory of formal arrangements—*visible* formal arrangements. Their purpose is to reinforce and expand the unwritten agreement between artist and spectator. And the task imposed on the spectator is that of *reading* a language with which he is not yet familiar with the aid of a context with which he is familiar.

That brings me face to face with the age-old problem of the relationship between form and content. And it will be convenient to select for consideration a work of art that is intense and urgent in content and courageous and inventive in form. Such a work is Picasso's *Guernica*. Consider by what means Picasso has invented a visible form that will fit an invisible content that must have existed for him, however vaguely, before he began to paint the picture. Its form, we may say, is that aspect of it which is perceived by the eye of the beholder. As such it has recognizable harmony, rhythm, pattern and colour. But as soon as that form is communicated to the mind of the beholder it begins to convey a set of meanings, and those meanings can be conveniently called content. Seen as form *Guernica* consists of a series of curves and angles and of areas of low-toned

colour. If we can imagine a man blind from birth suddenly granted
the gift of sight and presented, as the first object offered to his
inexperienced eye, with Picasso's picture, its form would be all that
he could see. No passage in the picture would 'mean' bull, fallen
warrior, or agonized horse since he had never seen a man or an
animal. But for the normal man the picture would quickly resolve
itself into an organization of meaningful images, and with that
resolution content would begin to emerge out of form. 'In *Guernica*,'
we must then say, 'we are presented with images of a bull, a horse, a
fallen warrior, an arm holding a lamp, a woman holding a child.'
Or to use the language of everyday speech: '*Guernica* is "about"
these phenomena.'

As we contemplate the picture, however, we begin to realize
that we are *not* primarily being offered information about the
appearance of the objects and personages, but that in some strange
way that must be accounted for the imagery is charged with emotion. The horse is agonized, the bull noble but angry, the warrior
defeated, the lamp encouraging. And this happens partly because we
can refer back to our previous knowledge of agonized horses and
stricken warriors. We recognize that the artist has selected and
isolated whatever, in the shape of a horse, will 'mean' *agonized*
horse. Yet all that *could* have been done by a photographer who
took the trouble to inflict pain on a horse or slay a warrior and then
take a photograph of the result. The photograph would, of course,
still convey descriptive visual information, but this time it would be
descriptive information of a more precise kind. And it is evident
from a comparison between *The Massacre at Chios* and *Guernica* that
Delacroix has given us more precise information than Picasso about
the *appearance* of suffering persons or persons inflicting suffering on
others. Delacroix, to put it in its simplest terms, has been more
photographic and his success in conveying emotion has been more
dependent on *what* was depicted (content) than on the *manner* of
depiction (form).

None the less the words 'more' and 'less' are indicative of degree
and not of kind. We feel quite sure that had Ingres tackled the same
kind of subject, he would have been less successful than Delacroix,

and that the reason for his failure would not have been his inability and his unwillingness to describe in paint the appearances of suffering or of cruel persons but his failure to discover the appropriate form. One begins, therefore, to suspect that there must be a hidden correspondence between form and content, and that within the limitations of the stylistic traditions or conventions of the period in which the artists lived certain families of form will refuse to express certain kinds of content: that the smooth, untroubled surfaces of Ingres cannot convey the savagery implied in say Goya's painting *Saturn devouring his Children*: and that however completely Ingres could have *imagined* the man-eating monster, his painting would have failed to convey the innate ferocity of the idea—the 'literary' idea, to employ a useful but inexact word—behind it. The very fact that in describing Ingres's form one cannot avoid using such words as 'untroubled' makes it plain that a correspondence exists between form and the emotion it attempts to convey. A line or a surface cannot in itself be troubled or untroubled, though it can be rough or smooth. To describe a surface as 'smooth and untroubled' is to pass from a fact to a metaphor. And we feel instinctively that an untroubled surface will not express—will not 'mean'—a troubled content.

But we also know that the limitations of the stylistic traditions or conventions of the period in which the artist lived exert an unavoidable steady pressure on his form and therefore, in view of the correspondence noted in the previous paragraph, that same pressure must affect his content. Ingres and Delacroix, by virtue of their inevitable adherence to a 'descriptive' style of painting, are closer to each other then either is to Picasso, despite the difference between their temperaments.

I said just now that form resolves itself into content in the spectator's mind partly because it can refer back to a previous knowledge of warriors and horses; and even though Picasso's form refers less descriptively than that of Delacroix to such knowledge, *Guernica* is still quite easily read as imagery. But the word 'partly' implies that my description of the form-content relationship is still incomplete. In what sense could it be said—if it can be said at all—

that form can resolve itself into content without any help from such references to previous visual knowledge?

Non-figurative or abstract art has attempted for half a century to abandon such references, but no non-figurative artist would admit that in doing so he had abandoned content even though he would probably maintain that he was pursuing a different *kind* of content. Picasso's semi-heraldic image of a bull refers us back to our knowledge of a seen bull. But does Ben Nicholson's painting of a rectangle refer us back to our knowledge of seen rectangles? And if it does, what is its 'content'? If we regard it as a *description* of two rectangles, it adds nothing to our existing knowledge of rectangles. The artist has selected or intensified nothing out of our experience of rectangularity. He would probably maintain that what he had presented us with in his work of art 'is' two rectangles and not a representation of them.

This really does mean that the content of non-figurative art is different in kind from that of figurative art—or rather that it is of only one kind whereas that of figurative art has a double appeal. It refers back, as already stated, to forms already seen and remembered; but I have suggested that it could also be regarded as a formal organization and might convey a certain satisfaction from 'the underlying mathematics' of the design. That same underlying mathematics is, of course, available to us all in every work of visual art and if the work of art contains no representational elements—as in a building, a piece of furniture or a non-figurative painting—it is the *only* ingredient in it that is available. The 'satisfaction' I have postulated that comes from the contemplation of that mathematical ingredient is undeniable. Would it be true, then, to say that 'content' is of two kinds, one operating through the enjoyment of purely mathematical (or harmonious) relationships, the other arousing emotion by virtue of its appeal to our visual experience?

Plato, in an oft quoted passage in which he says that beauty is to be found in geometrical figures, certainly recognizes the satisfaction provided by mathematical relationships. Yet would Plato have denied that beauty is also discoverable in a well proportioned human body? And therefore, presumably, in a marble or bronze replica of that body? But what now concerns me is the problem whether these two kinds of beauty are related. Is it, for example, partly by virtue of their innate mathematics that the shapes that compose the *Guernica* panel succeed in communicating an emotion of suffering and grief? If, as has already been suggested, an 'untroubled' line or surface is inappropriate for communicating trouble, one would suspect that there *is* such a correspondence and that therefore the critic, attempting to estimate the success or otherwise with which Delacroix had communicated suffering in *The Massacre at Chios*, would be better advised to say 'note the acute angle of the shoulder' than 'note the teardrop in the eye'. Even so, the critic must be on his guard to distinguish, if such a distinction can be reasonably made, between the acute angle that invariably indicates pain in real life and the acute angle that the artist has invented as the visual, mathematical *equivalent* of pain.

'If such a distinction can be reasonably made' is certainly a necessary saving clause in attempting to solve such a problem. For there seems good reason to suppose that the connexion between mathematics and human emotion has its ultimate roots in human experience. Vertical lines suggest not only stability but also energy: they repeat the natural line of the tree trunk that seeks the most direct way towards the light. A tower, we say, 'rises', knowing well enough that it does not rise but that we, by the process known as empathy, lift our eyes and our heads upwards as we follow the line from its base to its summit. It would not occur to us to read the tower from the top downwards and say it falls. Horizontal lines suggest even greater stability, for we demand for our comfort a level surface to walk on: but they suggest less energy, for the horizontal is the line ultimately achieved by whatever, from the fallen warrior to the line of the sea's horizon, has given up the struggle or has no need to raise itself upwards and no longer resists the law of gravity. A glossary of such correspondences could easily be compiled. The most imperturbable of all geometrical forms, because the most difficult to overbalance, would be the pyramid, whose weight decreases as it ascends: the most unstable the inverted pyramid for the opposite reason. Diagonals—the line of the tree or the warrior *during* their fall—must involve and therefore suggest movement.

And we know that nothing but an opposing diagonal will arrest their movement and that once the opposing diagonal has arrived the movement will be arrested, since an immovable pyramid will have come into being.

Curvature of various kinds can be added to our glossary until we are at last furnished with a vocabulary that will serve well enough for the most elementary human requirements. We can use it to say 'serene', 'active', 'unstable', 'voluptuous'; but not until we have added recognizable imagery to it can we say 'fear', and still less can we say *Guernica*. But once we have produced the woman, the warrior, the horse and the bull that will enable us to say *Guernica*, we can then return to our glossary and by using all the extracts from it that will serve our purpose we can immeasurably increase the impact of our statement about *Guernica*.

What has just been said about a mathematical basis which could be analysed into a glossary has, of course, always been true of all the arts. The problem of discovering a form that will give content its maximum force was a problem for Giotto just as it was for Picasso. But it was not a problem that was tackled self-consciously or intellectually by earlier artists. The glossary of correspondences was never envisaged until the twentieth century. It would have been unthinkable for Giotto to say that an untroubled line could never depict a troubled mood or situation. And even had he or any other pre-twentieth century artist had the courage to make such a statement, he would never have been logical enough to face its consequences and abandon his own descriptive style (however personal it might have been) in favour of a series of *formal devices* invented for the occasion.

Once the decision to do this has been made—and the sacrifice involved in doing so must always be considerable—the descriptive method of painting at once loses its importance: form becomes its own master—or rather it becomes the aggressively dictatorial servant of content and the 'descriptive' method slinks away unmourned and becomes unnecessary. This may be an old situation; but since about 1907 it has been heightened until it is now almost unrecognizable. One could say that today the observant eye has almost ceased to play a part in the creation of form.

The changeover, as is well known, happened suddenly. Up to the year 1906 Picasso had followed the normal course of isolating and intensifying the emotive object or personage. During the blue period he had been obsessed by pathos and expressed it in paintings of emaciated creatures, deliberately elongated and made cadaverous. The method was still that of Delacroix—the method of selecting a model and of emphasizing or exaggerating whatever in the model would increase the emotional impact he had already decided upon. In 1907, with *Les Demoiselles d'Avignon*, so often hailed by critics as the 'begining of modern art' (though it seems to me, despite its courageous experimentation, a far from satisfactory work of art), the descriptive method is largely abandoned. The new glossary of mathematical form makes its arrival, though it is still rudimentary, operating for the first time as a weapon for the expression of content. It would of course have been more than any human being, however inventive or audacious, could have achieved to produce a completely organized new language of formal equivalents at such short notice. In 1906 Picasso follows tradition. Then, suddenly, a year later tradition loses its importance.

It is surprising that in a major work, and without a longish period of trial and error to prepare for it, the new formal language should have been as coherent as it is. No language, whether verbal or visual, can ever be invented *ab initio*. However unfamiliar it may seem at its first appearance, it must have been developed out of something already seen and already digested. It is tempting to think of the formal rhythms that appear for the first time in *Les Demoiselles d'Avignon* as being based on African sculpture. But apart from the heads of the two women on the right, which stylistically contradict the rest of the painting, it is impossible to discover African idioms anywhere. The schematic treatment of the blue and brown curtains behind the women reminds one of one of El Greco's skies—themselves among the most remarkable examples of stylistic invention in the art of the past. The incisive angular forms of the five nude women probably trace their origin to Iberian sculpture. But the refusal to model by shadow, the attempt to suggest volume by lines superimposed on the flat areas of flesh-colour and the almost total negation of space could come from any school of pre-Renaissance painting—in Picasso's case it would probably be Catalan. What is most remarkable is the rhythmic unity of the picture. The angular pattern of the figures overflows across the whole canvas and holds together the 'negative' shapes left by the gaps between them. In the gaps the treatment of the folds of the curtains, their linear character and the density of the pattern made by them, binds the picture together into a formal, compact unity. It is this replacement of descriptive painting by rhythmic invention that is the startling innovation. The new type of form that Picasso has invented can be used equally well for a woman, a folded curtain or a bunch of flowers. It is in this respect that the traditions of the past, which had operated without a break from the thirteenth century up to 1907, were jettisoned and that a new conception of form—form unfettered by any obligation to be faithful to appearance—took their place.

The effect even on Picasso's most sympathetic and intelligent friends—certainly on Braque, Matisse and Apollinaire—was shattering. It was inevitable that it should be so, for a work of art in a language so unfamiliar and strange does not carry its glossary with it. Only by constant repetition of new forms in varying contexts can we begin to guess at new meanings. It is by the same kind of repetition that the child learns its own language, and if Braque and Matisse could not fathom the meanings of the new *Demoiselles d'Avignon* language, it is not likely—indeed it would have been impossible—that less sensitive or less accomplished visual linguists could do so.

But exactly thirty years later, when *Guernica* came to be painted, Picasso had not only perfected his own gift of linguistic formal invention, but he had established the fact that his paintings could not be read until we had accepted him as a language-inventor. During that period of thirty years he had offered us so many different kinds of syntax and vocabulary that we had accustomed ourselves to the new method of reading. For example, the sensuous curvature expressed in fierce but flowing black line and the clear primary colouring of 1932 were sufficiently reminiscent of the flowing lead lines and the vivid colouring of Gothic stained glass to give us a starting point in the task of deciphering a new kind of content. It turned out to be a new way of emphasizing the indolent sensuousness of the female body. As content that aspect of human experience is familiar, but apart from certain erotic carvings on Indian temples no previous artist had succeeded in discovering a formal language that could isolate and intensify it with such unmistakable impact.

Presumably, in the year 1932 Picasso's own experience of 'volupté' demanded the invention of a new set of formal and chromatic rhythms. But it is quite certain that in 1937 when he came to design *Guernica* those same rhythms would have been quite useless to express the *Guernica* content. They would, in fact, have destroyed its very essence. The genesis of the *Guernica* panel (11 feet high by 25 feet wide) is worth a brief note. During the two years that preceded it Picasso's emotional preoccupations had been largely centred on the Spanish Civil War. Consequently his stylistic invention had developed in the direction of indignation at cruelty and injustice. During those years and especially in the latter months of that period he had been experimenting with shapes of unusual angularity and ferocity—or, to be strictly precise, angularity which became in his hands the equivalent of ferocity. But this stylistic development was often almost independent of the descriptive or narrative content. Portraits of Dora Maar and Madame Éluard painted in 1937 show the same set of angular conventions but contain no implications of anger. It is as though the formal vocabulary he had been evolving to fit a dominant mood had overflowed into paintings that had no connexion with the mood. But parallel with these ferocious paintings and interspersed with them was another series of works left over, as it were, from the voluptuous 'gothic' series of 1932 though far more poetic in their imagery. They vary in mood between suave pathos and tenderness, and in content they are among his most memorable essays in a private mythology dominated by the minotaur. This extraordinary creature, sometimes a symbol of brute strength, sometimes of Caliban-like bewilderment, sometimes triumphant, sometimes subdued and even slain by beauty, is developed in a series of drawings and etchings that culminated in one of the most pregnant and memorable of all his works, the *Minotauromachie* of 1935. This series of mythologies contains the germ of a great deal that was to reappear in a simpler, savager form in *Guernica*. The bull, the frightened horse, the vulnerable woman, the child holding a symbol of hope in an outstretched hand, are all echoes of previous innovations. A familiar melody has been reorchestrated. From a richly elaborated andante it has become a stark allegro furioso. *Guernica* combines the symbolic imagery with the fierce angularity of the years that preceded its appearance.

But also—as was inevitable in the case of so large a picture—its planning is purely classic. If proof were needed that romantic content need not be contradicted by a classically deliberate basic plan, *Guernica* supplies it. Mathematically speaking, the picture is based on a firm central pyramid strengthened on either side by groups whose dominant rhythms are vertical. And the verticals are carried across by further references to verticals within the pyramid itself. The basic architecture of the panel is that of a Greek pediment flanked by columns and despite the almost hysterically expressive separate ingredients it contains, nothing could be structurally firmer than this overall plan. The pyramid rises in two shallow curves, like the silhouette of Mount Etna, to a strongly marked centre line. Within its framework is packed most of the violence and suffering. On the left, the figures of the bull and the woman mourning over her dead child make a compact group tapering *upwards*; on the right the woman with arms outstretched, falling downwards through a burning house, balances the bull in a shape that tapers *downwards*. Nearer to the centre line are two more supporting shapes: on the left the horse-image and the sun-image; on the right the head and the arm that thrusts itself across the point of the pyramid and holds a lamp that adds another vertical.

This is the kind of basic architecture that a Raphael or a Poussin could easily have invented. That Picasso should have used it as a steadying framework is no sign of genius. Any good artist with a feeling for the laws of composition could have arrived at a similar solution to the problem of planning so large a surface. It is not until we begin to *read* the picture in terms of the invented glossary of form and the not very obscure language of accepted symbolism, that it begins to count as a masterpiece. And it seems clear that Picasso in designing it was determined that it should be read entirely in terms of its linear constructions and the alternating masses of light and dark areas, since he ultimately decided to eliminate colour and make his final statement in grisaille, even though he was quite capable of fusing form-content with colour-content in order to double the emotional impact of the final product. He did, in fact, paint in the same year a head of a weeping woman, clearly connected with the mood and imagery of *Guernica*, in which the colour, acid and brilliant, is both appropriate and insistent.

The picture contains a good deal of symbolism; and here again is a painter's device that makes no demands on genius, for symbolism is fundamentally imagery that is valid for the spectator only by virtue of having an accepted meaning. It is, in fact, visually no more than a short cut—a device that overflows into the domain of literature but happens to use a formal instead of a verbal medium. To represent hope by an anchor and justice by a blindfolded woman requires neither talent nor ingenuity. Its presence in a work of visual art is no indication of an urge to increase the impact of emotional content. *Guernica* could conceivably have dispensed with the bull, the horse, the lamp and the formalized sun with rays radiating outwards from an electric light bulb. Even the broken sword in the hand of the fallen warrior is merely an easy way of indicating that he has been engaged in some form of combat with an anonymous adversary. Once the literary content of the symbol has been accepted as adding something, however little, to the message, its function has been fulfilled. Beyond that it can only add a note of obscurity. And this Picasso has succeeded in doing, for his symbols have a life of their own which lifts them out of the category of 'accepted' imagery and gives them a range of meaning that is normally beyond the range of the familiar stereotypes of literary symbols. The bull is another reincarnation of the mysterious minotaur, with all its patience, its pathos and its nobility; the horse is the most arresting item of imagery in the picture's surface, partly because of its central position, partly because it has become the crowning statement of anguish. Packed with 'meaning' though they are, the meaning conveyed by these two creatures is not simple or precise. Equally dubious

is the almond shaped form with the electric light bulb in its centre
that seems to mean the sun—but is it, in its turn, a symbol of hope?
Or does it contain a hint of claustrophobia—the only source of light
in a crowded, violated underground shelter?

But the secret of *Guernica's* romantic impact is found neither in
its classic, architectural symmetry, nor in its symbolism, but in the
innate character of the forms themselves. And this is my central
theme. If one regards them as wilful departures from descriptive
realism, they are distorted with the kind of intelligent recklessness of
which only Picasso knew the secret and which even he could use to
its fullest effect only at certain moments when passionate emotion
and formal inventiveness were working in perfect harmony with
each other. The eye is riveted immediately on certain details in
which the formal invention is working at white heat. The outstretched empty hand of the warrior on the left—its fingers clumsily
grasping the air, its palm crossed by a cat's cradle of brutal lines—is
balanced by the foot and ankle of the woman who rushes in from the
right. These two fragments—architecturally important because they
mark the limits of the pyramid's base—are emotionally arresting
because they establish the kind of linear tension that pervades the
picture. It would be possible, though it would be tedious, to analyse
these formal tensions in detail. Some of them have a childlike
obviousness, others sink in slowly and convey their meaning
gradually to the mind behind the eye. Some are mere rudimentary
simplifications of something that had to be included for clarity's sake
but added nothing to the content; others, which occur at the most
vital points of intersection, are evidently the result of a long process of trial and error, where the lines gather themselves together
into knotted complexities. In particular the horse's head, more
ruthlessly 'distorted' than any other piece of imagery, has been
arrived at after a longish sequence of experimental drawings—
attempts, as it were, to see the inside of the open mouth, to isolate the
teeth, to turn the thrust-out tongue into a dagger, to reduce the eyes
to tiny circles as though they were sightless in death.

The whole process by which the imagery of *Guernica* came into
being tends to disturb those of us who have absorbed in our

childhood the theory that illusionism, though not the whole of art, is a major part of it. We call it for convenience a process of *distortion*, implying that the artist, if he wished, could pin his faith on a close rendering of appearances but finding that this failed to deliver the message he had in mind, he deliberately *distorted* those appearances in order to make them expressive. If that is how we account for examples as extreme as *Guernica* (as well as for less extreme examples that recur by the thousand throughout the art of the world), we cannot help being disturbed, for we are continually comparing in our mind's eye the appearance of a bull or a man with Picasso's description of a bull or a man and trying to account for the difference between the two. According to the theory of distortion an artist continually departs from what he sees in order to express more clearly what he feels. I do not believe that we can ever come to grips with the meaning of any work of art if we think of the artist as a man tethered to the world of appearances but continually straining to lengthen the tether in order to extend his range of expressiveness. To speak of *distortions*, whether they occur in *Guernica* or in the *Pietà* of Avignon, is surely to misunderstand the creative process and to think of the artist as somehow taking his stand at a certain distance (a distance always chosen by himself) from the world of phenomena, and doing his best at that fixed distance to express himself: Velasquez, if that is the image in our mind, has adopted an unusually short tether, the unknown painter of the Avignon *Pietà* a longer one, and Picasso a longer one still. In his *Metamorphosis of the Gods* Malraux speaks of a Truth that exists 'beyond and above experience' and suggests that the great artist subordinates 'what is seen to that which *is*' even though in doing so he may (not *must*, otherwise non-figurative art could never have come into being) make recognizable references to what is seen. This is not an easy notion to grasp, but I believe it must be accepted for all art though it is only in the case of extremists like the Picasso of 1937 that the difficulty becomes acute.

Once the difference between lengthening the tether to 'what is seen' and shortening the tether to 'that which is' has been grasped, the pictorial language of a *Guernica* becomes comparatively easy to read. We are concerned not with departing from what is *seen*, but with approaching more closely to that which *is* and then translating it into some kind of visual equivalent. The invented images of grief, cruelty or hope are no longer pictorial imitations of the gestures and facial expressions of grieving or cruel or optimistic persons. They are translations into line and colour of grief itself made 'readable' by minimal references to women or warriors. In such references the artist need no longer pay even lip-service to human anatomy, or to space and light. The arm holding a lamp need make no reference to bone and muscle, but it must make clear *the act of thrusting*; the head behind the thrusting arm need not possess a body, but it must suggest urgency and perhaps an open mouth to suggest a warning cry. The lamp, on the other hand, must be a recognizable lamp with a recognizable flame, otherwise it will 'mean' nothing but a set of curves with a vertical axis. The vertical axis would have been explicit enough to 'mean' steadiness: but steadiness is not enough. 'Lampness' must be added, and all the artist can do is to glance back at the seen world and hastily borrow a real lamp from it.

When we look at *Guernica*, therefore, we are not looking at a wilful though expressive set of distortions but at a direct translation of 'that which is' into visible terms, and we must judge its success by the excellence of the translation and not by the persuasiveness of the distortion. Clearly the demands on the creative imagination are more severe in the latter case, and not many artists have managed to meet them with so few backward glances at the seen world and so few borrowings. And among those few not many have felt the need so often and so imperatively to found a new formal vocabulary to meet the needs of a new set of emotional impulses. It is in that respect that Picasso differs from his great predecessors.

A Giovanni Bellini or a Turner may spend a lifetime slowly developing the means to an end which had always been in view. Between Bellini's *Agony in the Garden*, which borrows its formal vocabulary from Mantegna, and his *Feast of the Gods*, which uses a vocabulary invented by himself, is a long and steady progress during which he slowly moved towards a style which we can only describe as more suited to his temperament. But Picasso's temperament has none of that steadiness. He can alternate with alarming rapidity between tenderness and anger, between an obsession with the natural and a grasping for the supernatural, and with each alternation he has to lay aside the old pattern of form and invent a new one. That each one of these patterns has had its origin in something already seen—perhaps a drawing or a Greek vase, perhaps an Iberian or a Nigerian sculpture—is only natural. What is unusual is his willingness to find a new stimulant whenever he found himself in the grip of a new mood. The consequence, as far as his 'style' is concerned, is that he is quite incapable of development. For him there is no 'end that has always been in view'. From the paintings of *volupté* of 1932 it would have been impossible to predict the passion of 1937. His life as an artist has not been a steady advance in a known direction but a series of lightning raids in unforeseen directions and on unforeseen objectives, so that his power is never cumulative. He is, of course, capable of building on past successes and returning unexpectedly to old battlegrounds, as though he had left something behind in an earlier raid that had to be retrieved. But such returns are not typical. They occur frequently but only, one feels, in order to give his creative imagination a holiday from the strain to which it had been subjected. It is useless and also insensitive to ask where in this sequence of violent changes and experiments we are to find 'the true Picasso'. Behind each one of them is an easily detectable flavour, not quite the equivalent of a personal hand-writing but certainly the result of a set of personal gifts or preferences. He is, for example, a brilliant draughtsman but not more than an adequate painter. One cannot praise him for his *matière* as one can praise Bonnard or Manet. It is the organization and tension of his line that bears the main burden of each of his major statements. *Guernica*, like so many of his most forceful paintings, is in essence a drawing. And it is well known that a personality can express itself more forcefully and unmistakably in line than in any other medium, whether it be a hurried scribble or a painstaking statement and whether its author is Mantegna, Tiepolo or Ingres. For all the urgency of his content, in which, as with all Romantics, 'beauty' was invariably sacrificed to 'meaning', Picasso is in essence a classical draughtsman. The design underlying the

Romantic detail is always as solidly constructed as in a Raphael, a Poussin or an Ingres.

The illusionist theory must regard the pity and terror conveyed by *The Massacre at Chios* as being dependent in the end on the skill and accuracy with which the artist has described the appearance of persons inflicting cruelty or suffering pain. And since Delacroix has manifestly succeeded in doing this and Picasso has not even attempted to do it, no amount of persuasive argument about the difference between what is *seen* and what *is* will convince those to whom illusionism is a normal procedure that it can be dispensed with. To dispense with it to such an extent—to substitute an equivalent for a description —is a twentieth-century experiment. It is not a necessary one though it can produce results denied to the illusionist painter. Naturally, even the devotees of illusionism are not so blind or so foolish as to equate illusionism with photographic accuracy. They recognize that between Titian and Rubens there is a fundamental difference of approach to life itself and that what Titian has to say about the meaning, *to him*, of the human body is not the same as what Rubens has to say. They are well aware that what makes both artists precious to us is precisely that difference. What unites them is the fact that both of them observe, and observe with enthusiasm, the same object—the trunk of a tree or the naked body of Venus. What gives them their value is that in describing those objects their enthusiasms have been stimulated by different aspects of them and their statements in pigment have therefore a different set of emphases. To be blind to such emphases is exceptional and whoever attempts to describe them has a comparatively easy task, for what he is really doing is to compare two descriptions, both of them heightened by strong personal emotion, with an imagined reality—an actual tree or an actual human body. They prefer the description to the reality, for it carries with it a highly charged comment, which the object described does not. This sensitivity to the comment is what all of us in various degrees possess. It makes our approach to the Titian version or the Rubens version of a tree or a woman comparatively easy. But when we are faced with the languages Picasso has invented the problem is different. The Picasso tree or the Picasso woman is not a comment on an observed object but the creation of a new object. It may be that we have to call it, for clarity's sake, 'tree' or 'woman'. But it is different in kind from the Titian-Rubens tree or woman. Only in the remotest sense is it based on what is seen. It is a separate creation—a metaphor in visual terms. Perhaps after all to call it a symbol would be the least misleading way of describing it.

Perhaps the cleavage I have tried to describe between the commentator and the creator could best be expressed by saying that that age-old intermediary between the artist and what he produces—the artist's model, whether it be a tree or a woman—has disappeared. We look at Titian's Uffizi *Venus* or at Rubens's *Judgement of Paris* and we know that the goddesses with which those masterpieces are concerned could not have made their way on to canvas without the co-operation of real women. Titian and Rubens had devoted their lives to the close study of models and to the technical procedures that would enable them to produce an illusionist account of their appearances, just as Picasso had done before 1906. It was not that either Titian or Rubens thought that the art of painting consisted in the production of such illusionist accounts, but that they took it for granted that without a model there could be no question of isolating and intensifying that aspect of the human body that passionately interested them. For to isolate and intensify implies a concrete object as a starting point for the journey, however long and tortuous the journey may be and however radically the resultant work of art may differ from the model.

That the model herself had been invented in Periclean Athens is unimportant, though both Titian and Rubens must have been unconsciously influenced by Greek sculpture when they contemplated their posed models. But that was not necessary. Gauguin had taken what he thought was a revolutionary step when he left Europe behind and journeyed to Tahiti. The step was *not* revolutionary. Gauguin had merely changed one model for another. The Tahitian girls in his paintings were still the starting points for a journey. But that Picasso's human images are not evolved from models hardly needs saying. What does need saying is that the method of using a model as a starting point always involves the artist in a reference, however disguised, to a seen object: and that a seen object exists not only in space but in time and must therefore carry with it the sense not only of a specific but also a *momentary* appearance, and in doing so the figures in the painting can never be timeless symbols. They can, in fact, never be goddesses.

By Picasso's method the timelessness of the symbol is assured. There never were any models for the *Guernica* panel. 'This happened to those people at that moment' is an inconceivable thought in the presence of such a work. The images are formal embodiments of an abstract emotion: and for that reason they are not descriptions of a specific incident, nor are they anchored to a moment in time.

Rhythm and Imagery in English Poetry*

WILLIAM EMPSON

When I was honoured by being asked to speak here I was doubtful what I could say that would be useful or suitable: I will keep mostly to the subject announced, but I want to begin with some scattered remarks. The field is very large and confused. It is not even clear that you want a theory, because its findings must always be subject to the judgement of taste; I still believe in the Benthamite theory of Ogden and Richards, from *The Foundation of Aesthetics* (1925), but I am not sure what it entails. This is the first century which has tried to appreciate all the art works that ever were, anywhere; and combining this with the first effects of universal education, let alone a variety of revaluations of opinion, was bound to produce a kind of traffic jam. The artist was free to an extent which he often found baffling, and so was the critic. Four major thinkers, Darwin, Marx, Fraser and Freud, gave grounds for the belief that the artist often does not know what he is doing. Darwin, for one reason, because the artist will be exemplifying a stage in an evolutionary trend (one could extract others here), Marx because he will be expressing his society's means of production, Fraser because his mind will be hag-ridden by a group memory of human sacrifice, and Freud because he will be expressing his own unconscious desires; clearly, he had better do what he feels like, and the critic had better say what he likes, he also, in his turn. An interpreter of the art work cannot set out to bring all this to consciousness, where it does not naturally belong; his main function must be to mediate between the unconsciousness of the artist and the unconsciousness of the public he works for. When I was young I did not mind this, but I find now I have become one of the old buffers

* Delivered as a lecture to The British Society of Aesthetics on 3 May, 1961.

who were always made fretful by it. I think that modern art has gone too far, and that aesthetics ought to curb and prune it; and that aesthetics ought to be curbed and pruned too.

Literary critics feel about art-writers much as Christians do about Hindus; they have never had an ideological purge, so they are practically Ancient Night in person. We literary critics may talk a lot of nonsense, but we have been scolded out of talking like they do long ago. The catalogue of a picture exhibition is often very intimidating; a steady iron-hard jet of absolutely total nonsense, as if under great pressure from a hose and recalling among human utterances only the speech of Lucky in *Waiting for Godot*, is what they play upon the spectator to make sure of keeping him cowed. And I suspect they would often have something to tell us if this stern convention did not forbid them; I felt it about Mr. Roland Penrose, always an intelligent and well-intentioned man, in the catalogues of the great Picasso exhibition. In some paintings, I thought, for example one about romps at the seaside where a striped balloon appeared to be in flight, the artist was clearly being jovial about the oddity of the human form; much like the comic postcards which would be found on display not far from the bathing beach he was depicting. At other times it is known that he used his distortions of the human form to express horror at the cruelty of some political event. Art criticism is naturally vaguer than literary criticism, because the whole field of mental activity concerned lies much farther away from the discursive reason; but still it should be possible to say which of these Picasso meant. There was one picture which I thought plainly jovial, as some men had drunk themselves under a table; but the catalogue quoted Picasso here as saying that a painting is not for the drawing-room, it is a political act. Here, you see, Penrose had artfully got round the convention that he is only allowed to talk guff, but this made me feel, ungratefully, that he could have said more.

The effects of the revolt against reason are, I think, also striking in architecture; all the more because there you really do have trade union rules of no criticism in public. I think many English architects accept designs for workers' flats and such-like, believing them to be artistic as well as convenient and quite without realizing that they are grindingly horrible. Horrible because they are meant to be; when they were invented in Germany they were part of the great Surrealist movement of protest against the machine age and the gathering storm. The Dutch, who have always been able to get a cosy feeling into domestic architecture, can still manage to get it into a huge block of workers' flats; but many English architects don't feel that this is clean-lined or in-the-movement enough for them. They cannot learn better because they would think it Philistine to talk about the matter in real terms, just as it would be Philistine to discuss whether Picasso was feeling larky or sickened; so they put up, feeling that the work is just pure and functional and advanced, buildings of a screaming-lunatic horror and terror. At least I met a man at a party who had been putting up such things and this was the best picture of his motives I could extract from him.

I thought I had best begin by expressing some old-buffer prejudices in general but now I will turn to English Literature, which it is my business to know about, and try to examine the fundamentals, the basic tools; as must be the proper thing for a Society of Aesthetics. I am in favour of rhyme and metre for English poetry, but I realize that there is something queerly accidental about the way they arrived and settled into the traditions of Europe; the founders of the Free Verse movement, a generation or two ago, expected a great gain in energy from introducing radical changes there, and it seems time to ask why that didn't happen.

I must be brief about rhyme because I haven't the information which must be available somewhere; it is hard even to find which peoples rhyme and which don't. We Europeans ought to feel curious about the subject; no other major civilization had such a total Dark Age, and we emerged no longer quantitative in metre but clutching the divine gift of rhyme, which Greece and Rome had despised and thought suited to Hercules when drunk. If Homer taught the language of the gods to men, who taught us what by this radical change of ear? Professor Robert Graves has stepped gallantly into the very large breach left here by more official pundits, but I cannot understand why hammering on an anvil rhymes in any sense in which marching or rowing doesn't rhyme, and that seems funda-mental to his argument. The Chinese have always rhymed, but the Slavs as well as the Greeks have only taken to it recently; there was a block of non-rhymers in the middle of the land mass. Rhyme is first used by Europeans for Latin hymns, but they were written in North Africa not Europe, as early as the third century A.D.; and surely a missionary would want to give the congregation what they liked already rather than start a revolution in poetic technique. I have failed to learn whether the Berbers rhymed, but the Semitic language of the Carthaginians was still not stamped out and Semites rhyme; I understand that the Koran is partly in rhymed prose. Robert Graves thinks we got rhyme from the Irish, not from Carthage, but he seems only to quote repetitions or rough assonances in ancient Irish, and the Irish had in any case an early mastery of Christian techniques. Very little can be understood from all this; it is agreed that most poetry since the Dark Age is the better for rhyme, and that classical poetry would be spoiled by it, but explanations of this seem no longer even to be attempted.

I have just learned, however, one interesting fact about the classical quantitative metres, and am eager to pass it on, though perhaps it is well known. Going back to first principles, a syllable may be louder or softer than the one before, used in a stress metre; also longer or shorter, used in a quantitative metre; and then also the note may be higher or lower on the musical scale. There are thus three dimensions, and even when the rules of scansion use one of them the other two may be needed before the result can be beautiful. Chinese poetry scans by ups and downs, but these movements come within one syllable; the rising and falling-and-rising tones of Mandarin are put in one group of syllables, the level and falling tones in the other group, and patterns are arranged with these two. The poetry is intoned, a process like singing which is a recognized skill. We tend to laugh at Chinese poetry for being meaningless except on paper, but we ourselves don't much expect to be able to follow the words of a song. English itself of course is strongly tonal; only the rise for a question is recognized as part of the meaning, but I believe the Chinese now simply learn English as a tonal language, finding that convenient. Well, then, the accents written on ancient Greek marked a rise and fall of tone, so definite as to make the line like singing. This would tend to reduce interest in the loud-soft contrasts, which we too do not feel to be an inherent part of a melody, whereas long-short contrasts do feel part of it. Loudness does, however, become part of the melody for what was called in Purcell's time his Scotch Snap, where the stressed half of an English disyllabic word is given the shorter note

> And *pity mankind* that will *perish* for gold;

but this charming device does not seem widespread. An emphasis for the meaning, as when hymns put *pp* and *ff* for the same parts of consecutive verses, is evidently not felt as part of the melody. Maybe in Greek there was no prosy way to speak the line, which a man would use if he didn't know it was poetry, as there so definitely is in English; although one might think that only the Garden of Eden could have such an inherently musical language.*

Nobody supposes that the Romans had this bird-like tonal quality in their language, and pushing Latin into quantitative metres must have been very artificial. But one should not underrate bulldog grit; they did make some poetry; and I think the method still works in English, often without being noticed; indeed, it usually takes effect as a source of mysterious romantic beauty. Almost all the English poets of the past had been taught Latin poetry, and the English language makes a quantitative metre always possible, so they are not unlikely to have echoed it. In prose, for that matter, the classical system of rhythm, the *cursus* and so on, was part of the practical training for writing formal English, without anybody bothering about the change to stress-accent.

May I then, to set the pattern, remind you of Tennyson's imitation of Alcaics:

> O mighty-mouthed inventor of harmonies,
> O skilled to sing of time or eternity
>   God-gifted organ voice of England,
>   Milton, a name to resound for ages;

* A gramophone record of Professor W. H. D. Rouse reading Homer and Pindar was played at the end of the lecture.

His third verse, I think, is the only other good one:

> Me rather all that bowery loneliness
> The brooks of Eden mazily murmuring
> And bloom profuse and cedar arches
> Charm, as a wanderer out in ocean. . . .

In the following verses A. E. Housman, a Professor of Latin of course, is using the third line of this metre as the last line but one of each verse; and to some extent in all the odd lines of the poem.

> Tell me not here, it needs not saying
> What tune the enchantress plays
> In aftermaths of soft September
> And under branching mays;
> For she and I were long acquainted
> And I knew all her ways. . . .

> Possess, as I possessed a season,
> The countries I resign,
> Where over elmy plains the highway
> Would mount the hills and shine,
> And full of shade the pillared forest
> Would murmur and be mine.

It is plainly a matter of long-short and not of stress, because 'and' in Tennyson and 'the' in Housman are erected into long syllables, with aching tenderness, merely by pausing on them. The other verses have for this penultimate line 'And beeches strip in storms for winter', 'And Traveller's Joy beguiles in autumn'. I find that I can't say the lines so as to bring out this rhythm unless I treat them 'lyrically', that is, let my voice go up and down; and I should think quantitative metre always needs this. Homer smote his blooming lyre.

I think the poem is wonderfully beautiful. But a secret gimmick may well be needed in it to overcome our resistances, because the thought must be about the silliest or most self-centred that has ever been expressed about Nature. Housman is offended with the scenery, when he pays a visit to his native place, because it does not remember the great man; this is very rude of it. But he has described it as a lover, so in a way the poem is only consistent to become jealous at the end. Perhaps the sentiment has more truth than one might think (it is natural to reflect, in addressing this Society); many English painters really are in love with the scenery of England, and nothing else, so they had much better give up their theoretical tiff with Nature and get back to painting it. The last verse of the poem, driving home the moral, is no longer tenderly hesitant and therefore has given up the Alcaic metre.

> For nature, heartless witless nature,
> Will neither care nor know
> What stranger's feet may find the meadows
> And trespass there and go,
> Nor ask amid the dews of morning
> If they are mine or no.

Granting then that we can use stress and quantity at once, I think we have also a way of using stress which the metrists have refused to recognize. Coleridge remarked in the Preface to *Christabel* that all the lines were meant to have four stresses, though the number of syllables varied. He was liable to talk rashly, but he seems cool here and I think we should believe him; and yet it is sometimes a strain to keep the stresses on one syllable each:

> ... Thou heardst a low moaning
> And foundst a bright lady, surpassingly fair,
> And didst bring her home with thee in love and in charity
> To shield her and shelter her from the night air. (275)

It is a cantering cart-horse, and I think it plainly rolls several syllables together to make one stress. This process was recognized in 1929 by Robert Graves, when he said in *The Future of Poetry*:

> In the earlier native prosody the metre was determined by the stress centres of the line and the time-intervals between them. The earlier prosody has never been abandoned by popular poets and is frequently used by poets of culture. Its most familiar use is in nursery rhyme and country ballads:

> > Misty, moisty was the morn,
> > Chilly was the weather;
> > There I met an old man,
> > Dressed all in leather,
> > Dressed all in leather
> > Against the wind and rain.

It was, how do you do? and how do you do?
And how do you do? again (etc.)

Though the syllables number most irregularly, nobody can deny that the pieces scan. I write of stress-centres rather than of stresses, because often the stress is not on one syllable but, as in 'how do you do? and how do you do?' spread over two or three.

Graves was recommending flexibility in general as native to English rhythms, but I think this particular device needs the dignity of being formalized. I am inclined to call it 'jammed stress'; and once you realize that it is frequent, you feel that a great deal is wrong with our standard account of metre. (Maybe Hopkins has named it already, but I can't make his system, or systems, out.)

Not long ago (August 1960) there was a controversy about metre in *The Times Literary Supplement*, and a metrist asserted as a scientific discovery that there are four degrees of stress in English poetry.* I did not understand what had proved that there were no more than four but I readily believe that this fits the facts much better than the crude Dumdi Dumdi we were taught at school, so that a machine programmed to talk verse on four degrees of stress would sound almost as if it understood it. But this would be a case where the machine isn't interesting because it doesn't use the same method as the mind. In most poetry (not perhaps all good English poetry) there is a tension between the pronunciation demanded by the form and that demanded by the feeling, which may for example be colloquial and down to earth or dramatic and exalted. Two rival ways of scanning the line are both being used at once, and the less formal, the more colloquial or dramatic, will commonly use a jammed stress. That is why these quarter-stresses are used, if they are really different from a continuous range; the hearer is able to pick up from them what the two rival scansions are and how they balance. I don't understand the thing, but some unconsciously obeyed rule needs to be postulated. It struck me teaching in Japan and China that recognition of a poetic rhythm is a sudden process, though it sometimes only comes after a good deal of patient reading of the author; and I have known

* Page 94 of *The Function of Criticism*, by Yvor Winters (1957), proves that at least four are needed; the chapter is also good on 'spondees' in sixteenth-century English.

students write convincingly that they had discovered one of these beauties of sound, although their own mouths were hardly able to make the noises at all. I had expected to meet a major obstacle there, and was regularly astonished by the confidence and success with which they pronounced about beauty of sound. The human ear, or inner ear, is somehow cleverer than we understand about this matter; we need a theory about what we already do without a theory. It may be said: Why then not accept the fact that we use quarter-stresses? Because as they stand they are too unconscious, and the next question is what we use them for. We *think* we are giving five whole stresses to one ten-syllable line, and the unconscious activity needs to grow out of the obvious one. These rhythm-handling centres of the mind are largely autonomous but not at all secret. We know that they are clever at counting ten syllables in a jumble, because the poetry of the French and of Miss Marianne Moore depends on that. They cheerfully accept our rule that there are five stresses in a decasyllable; the only point where they go beyond our expectations is in finding two lots of five stresses. Considering what goes on in music, especially in syncopation, we need not be surprised.

The alternative is often there, I think, in very plain and singing lines:

> That time of year thou mayst in me behold
> When yellow leaves, or none, or few do hang
> Upon those boughs that shake against the cold;
> Bare ruined choirs, where late the sweet birds sang.

The rhythm is steady and sober, but the last line is packed enough to put strain on it. All the syllables could be stressed except '-ed' and 'the'; and oddly enough, if you try stressing 'sweet' but not 'birds', and then 'birds' but not 'sweet', both readings have implications in bad taste. 'Only the sweeter birds are sweet enough to be like me' with the stress on *sweet*; 'I am so innocent that I think all birds sweet' with the stress on *birds*. You need equal stress on both, because of the peculiar way our stress-system handles the basic logical constants; only equal stress allows of the logic that these birds are emblematic or typically sweet, so that 'sweet-birds' is practically their name, like 'black-birds'. These spondees of course are frequent in English words, and any system of scanning by Dumdies has to reckon with them somehow. The official scansion, with only one of the words stressed, would turn out here to be a tear-jerking or emotive one. The beginning of the line illustrates the more usual case, where the jammed stress is the more emotive of the two alternatives. *Bare* can hardly be said without any stress, but that could be regarded as thrown in at the start, hardly affecting the rhythm of the line: when separated like this it feels earnest but prosy. If we make it emotive, that is if we make Shakespeare at the age of thirty squealingly indignant with the stealing clutches of time: 'Why, but I can't be friends with an exciting young lord like you; I'm a shambling old man, with no *teeth*'—then, whether it began as a joke or not, the two syllables become practically one noise:

BEARRU ined-choirs where-late the sweet-birds sang.

To call the one noise a spondee makes it a foot in quantitative metre, and we find that reassuring somehow; after all, when all the syllables are stressed in English the language becomes in effect unstressed. But I don't think that describes what usually happens. If you record on a graph the sound of reading a line, two syllables will often make one jagged peak of noise together. We only fail to realize this because of a secret belief that consonants do not make a noise, only vowels; whereas the consonant R at least can be used for a loud and sustained noise, as by dogs. One should of course allow for the feed-back of theory upon both poets and readers; any beliefs they hold must be expected to affect the scansion, and as I say I think they are often affected by knowing classical metres. The jammed stress is unconscious for the theoretical part of the mind, but the practice imposes itself and is then not hard to explain away or explain as something else.

This at any rate clears up how to scan the first line of *Paradise Lost*. We must be allowed to stress *Of*, the first syllable, for the meaning: O *Muse, sing of man's disobedience* does not get said for six lines, so the grammar demanding it becomes lost unless *Of* is emphasized. This means that four stresses together have to start the poem; but we are now ready to explain that they are only two jammed stresses:

Of man's first disobedience, / and the fruit

Even so, you need not suppose a 'weak stress' at the caesura; the five stresses can be allotted in many ways.

If then the rhythms of English are loose, rich and confused, as one can hardly deny, how far is poetry in English likely to gain from strict metres? And is the language really so very heavily stressed, panting and thudding with emphases inherited from our rough northern forbears? The question has only to be asked to suggest a qualification; the English often feel that some Americans quack on with a terrible monotony and no pause for the opposite number to get in a word. For that matter I have known American literature students who believed that regular metres if used by literate authors were always meant as a parody of the unsophisticated—the well known mock-pastoral. The Free Verse movement began in America, and this might simply be because their language is no longer stressed. Greek lost its tones during some Dark Age, and a similar thing may be happening to English. But it is clearly not true that all American accents are unstressed; perhaps only the Boston accent is. I should guess that Miss Marianne Moore really talks without stress, and only could be scanned by counting syllables, so that she was quite right to make her innovation. It is rather surprising, come to think of it, that American poets have not revived classical metres, as they feel themselves forbidden the standard singing line. Forbidden does seem the word; the *vers libre* movement has meant, for many young poets, a struggle to renounce a pleasure which they feel perfectly capable of. Opinion about William Carlos Williams makes the position clear, I think; English critics don't feel he is a poet at all, but the most un-expected American critics will be found speaking of him with tender reverence; they feel he is a kind of saint. He has renounced all the pleasures of the English language, so that he is completely American; and he only says the dullest things, so he has won the terrible fight to become completely democratic as well. I think that if they are such gluttons for punishment as all that, they are past help. But then again I am not sure that we English aren't the ones who are losing the singing line as apart from renouncing it. Serious poetry written to be set to music would be a striking change in the literary scene and may be, though we don't know it, already an impossible one.

(After the lecture a young English questioner rebuked me for disrespect to William Carlos Williams, so this attempt to differentiate the two cultures was a failure like so many. He also felt it was rather queer and disagreeable to talk about poetry in this cookery-book way, because unlike the other arts poetry was just a matter of expressing oneself sincerely. This dogma would convince any real poet that he was not a poet, just as Menuhin would have become certain after a few trials that he was not a violinist if he had been brought up to believe that such a man could play well without having to learn. And yet one cannot leave the sincerity dogma there; poets who had acquired high skill have renounced it for the sincerity of free verse. Perhaps this need not always be called renunciation; the delicious social hints and evasive claims-by-mumble of spoken English are a positive intoxicant though externally drab. One may agree that a poet should be enough in contact with the spoken English of his time, and also believe he has always needed to be free enough from it to sing. Taking for granted that mumbling is the only honest mode of speech is I suppose a fog which has thickened steadily for the last fifty years. Still, I don't deny that some English poetry without rhyme or metre has the distinctive feeling they can give that the words are magically right through satisfying a number of independent conditions—for example, the first version of Auden's *Spain*.)

Turning now to the subject of Imagery, the second half of my title, I have to say that it is a great delusion. The great word 'Imagination' is from the same root, and there must be some good uses for such words, but it is a misfortune that aestheticians refuse to outgrow a stage of thought which can be recognized as inevitable for primitive man. Or, to make the complaint as small as possible, the people who give 'Images' a high specialized meaning need to be more aware of the delusions caused by the ordinary meaning.

The primitive mind, when asked how the ear does its work, tends to say: 'There's a little man in your ear; he listens, and he tells you.' Thus the striking thing about the primitive explanation is that it does not explain anything; the mind feels very rightly that there is room for an explanation here, so then it has to be quieted with a bogus one, as a hungry baby is given a soother. In the same way, when the philosophers asked themselves: 'How do we think?' they thought: 'Oh well, we must have copies of everything inside our heads; God and the triangle and tapeworms and everything are laid up in Heaven to start with, but then also laid up inside each man's head.' These are the man's Images. Now this explanation too, you see, has the distinguishing primitive feature of not explaining anything. When you have got all these things inside your head they have still no connexions with one another; you are no nearer to starting thinking about them than you were when they were outside your head. The point is made very clear by the modern calculating machines, which really are like brains in the sense that all previous machines have been like other parts of the human body. One of them, out of date now I believe, had a huge column of mercury and worked by the times when a wave in the mercury arrived back; you could feed millions of these rhythms into the one column and it would keep them all going till you wanted to take one out, so the column was the memory of the machine. You could say if you liked that that was where it stored its Images, but if you did you would have got a long way away from what you had meant by Images to start with; what you began by meaning was a sort of picture in your head. People do, of course, get these pictures, some people more than others; but they have so little to do with thinking that it is actually hard to say what they are used for, what function they were evolved to fulfil.

In literary criticism, where people are always talking about images, they have to be assumed to mean visual images; whereas the scientific use of the term includes muscular images. To imagine a movement might well be a preparation for making it; and we know that dogs dream of chasing rabbits because we see them twitch as they lie by the fire. You can imagine riding a bicycle, indeed dream of it, and you need not then be seeing any picture of your own legs. I think it often makes a difference in reading poetry whether you get the muscular image, whereas it seems to be hardly ever important to get a visual image. No doubt 'eyes like almonds' doesn't mean what it should unless you 'see' that the eye is *shaped* like an almond, but there the meaning itself is visual. Keats says in the *Ode to Autumn*:

> And sometimes like a gleaner thou dost keep
> Steady thy laden head across a brook.

This is a very strong piece of muscular imagery, though easily not noticed because of a negative kind. The plank over the drain will be green and slimy in autumn, so that you are liable to fall in even without a weight on your head, and the goddess has to take care not to lose her dignity. At any moment a catastrophe will come; one storm will strip the leaves and turn all this scene to winter—that is the point of the last line 'And gathering swallows twitter in the skies'. Necessarily the poet compares this to his disease; he feels 'it is all so glutted with calm that it feels eternal, and yet really I am racing towards death at the speed of an express train'. The effort of balancing in the calm goddess, the muscular image, is the centre of the poem. I am glad to have one example of an Image being beautiful, but even so it isn't what critics usually mean by the term.

It has been known for at least a century that many people don't have visual images, and think without them, but the literary critics have stubbornly refused to pay any attention. Non-visualizers are often intellectuals, and I am sure it does intellectuals good to have their noses rubbed in their sensual corruption; I agree that it's disgusting not to have images; but all the same even people who do have images don't use them for thinking. This was pointed out by a novelist who was working hard at telling the truth about life with the insights of the most recent philosophy, and nobody I think has yet noticed that he refuted the philosopher he was admiring. Sterne, in *Tristram Shandy*, used Hume on the human mind rather than safe old Locke as he chose to pretend; after the book had made him famous he became friends with Hume, but neither of them ever realized that it had refuted Hume. The death of the son of Mr.

Shandy is announced in the novel, and treated with the rather grim coolness of this sentimental author; one of the servant girls, while the death is being talked about, reflects that she will be expected to wear mourning but she can't be expected to buy a black dress; she will have to be given an old green gown of Mrs. Shandy which she had long waited for, and she will dye it black. She goes on talking and thinking about all this perfectly sensibly, indeed rather artfully; but all the time, Sterne keeps on telling us, she imagines seeing the gown as it is now, green, not black as she is thinking of making it. The simple fact that this is possible is enough to prove that Hume is wrong when he takes for granted that we can only think by images. The human mind is an enormously elaborate machine, vastly bigger than any artificial one, and it has extra gadgets in careless profusion; we can sometimes learn from diseases, when a bit of the machine goes wrong, what extremely elaborate things have to go on so that we can do what we regard as elementary. Thus there is a disease where a man can't read, though he can see, but with large letters on a blackboard, where he can trace his finger round the letters, he can switch over to the tactile or muscular centres which sum up a whole shape and in that way he can make out the letter, A or B. One could not have more direct proof that visual images are not enough for thinking.

It was worth evolving visual images, you can suppose, to try out a movement in your head and imagine its results without having to learn by experience; this would clearly have survival value when the experience itself would kill you. But I don't think there is any kind of thinking which can only be done by visual images. I was once discussing these matters in a splendid hall in Leeds, and after trying to imagine what use imagining could be, by way of showing generosity to the opponent there, I said that images must be the only way to play nineteen simultaneous games of chess blindfold, clearly that can only be done by pictures, probably a photographic memory as it's called; and a man spoke up from the back of the hall and said he had played twelve games of chess at once blindfold and had never had any images at all. I gazed at him as if he was a bug-eyed monster. This was the usual case of falling back upon chatter about images

when we don't know how a mind has worked. Certainly what can
go on in his mind is a black mystery to me, but then I couldn't play
these games of chess with the pictures either. (After the lecture this
account was endorsed by scientists in the audience.)

The trouble about Imagism and all its connexions, which are
still crawling about underfoot in the contemporary jungle and
tripping up the innocent reader of poetry, is that it is determinedly
anti-intellectual, and tells us that we ought to try to be very stupid. I
was having a small controversy some while ago about *The Garden* by
Andrew Marvell, and the opponent said it was inept of me to have
said that the word *straight* could mean 'tightly together' as well as 'at
once'; because, he said, the poet was writing about the sea, which is
big, so the image of being crowded into a small space would be inept.

> Meanwhile the mind, from pleasure less,
> Withdraws into its happiness.
> The mind, that ocean where each kind
> Does straight its own resemblance find;
> Yet it creates, transcending these,
> Far other worlds, and other seas,
> Annihilating all that's made
> To a green thought in a green shade.

The poet is comparing his own mind to the sea, and though the sea
is big his head is small. Such would be the position for any poet, but a
mystic might feel himself entitled to large claims. Marvell does echo
the claims of mystics, but he knows very well that he is being
impudent and can only rely upon the humour of a logical analogy.
If one of my sons said he needn't hold down a pay packet because he
could get as much experience by sitting in Appleton House garden
as by learning any skill, I would think it a bit much. Literary critics
nowadays I think lose the impact of the poem because they refuse
to look at it in this real way. Actually the war had finished in England and gone to Scotland when Marvell was at Appleton House,
but he still felt the great estate as an enchanted peace. He had been
directed into a very quiet staff job with frightfully useful contacts;
and it wasn't his fault, though he knew he ought to be fighting the
King. You understand, I am puzzling about what was at the back
of his mind when he wrote these few extremely magical poems.

There is something about the tone of them, as many critics have felt, which though so deliciously relaxed feels like a challenge. But an Imagist reader is not allowed to understand anything. If the poet says the mind is like the sea, then the Imagist reader must have a picture of the sea, in his head, and he must make a unique kind of muscular effort so as never to think of what is being talked about, the other half of the comparison, at all. The belief that poetry positively ought not to mean anything is still very strong, though mainly held by foreigners I think. I have to meet people in the course of my profession who actually hold these delusions; and are prepared to show me that my poetry too, like all other poetry, is merely a collage of logically unrelated images. I think just the opposite; arguing in verse has always seemed to me a wonderfully poetical thing to do, so I cannot understand the idea that it is prosy to speak up for the human reason. If the modern movement is the revolt against reason I have never been in it at all, so I have not left it merely because I am an old buffer.

Literary critics often talk about Images, or the Imagery of a Shakespeare play, meaning the metaphors in it; and this would only be an unnecessary extra word if they meant nothing else. But probably most people would call 'Hover through the fog and filthy air,' at the beginning of *Macbeth*, part of the imagery of the play. They are right, because the feeling that all the characters are doubtful which side will win and who to trust, so that they are all in a fog, is the atmosphere of the play. It struck me during the Civil War in China how extremely right Shakespeare had been to pick on that. So I kept on writing the lines down in the albums which people would kindly bring me to sign:

> But cruel are the times, when we are traitors
> And do not know, ourselves; when we hold rumour
> From what we fear, yet know not what we fear,
> But float upon a wild and violent sea,
> Each way, and move.

The witches only mean there is a fog, giving flying conditions which they find agreeable; but Shakespeare behind them means, as Dickens did at the start of *Bleak House*, that the characters are in a mental fog too. So that makes the fog part of the Imagery. But even in this atmospheric kind of case you do better if you arrive at seeing the point with both halves of the comparison vivid in your mind; both the Vehicle and the Tenor, as I. A. Richards named them in his *Philosophy of Rhetoric*, the thing which is really meant as well as the thing it is compared to. In fact, when Imagery is known to work well, it works by leading an appeal to experience forward till the rational mind feels it can safely deduce something (usually a very plain fact of life, but not always) from the variety of life and the decisiveness of the immediate judgements upon it which have already been shown in the artwork, taking for granted the experienced sympathy of the reader. I can well believe, on the other hand, that Ezra Pound himself is a very bad judge of Imagery; because he is such a clever man, and has such natural good feelings, that he actually hasn't had to do any conscious thinking for fifty years or so. The way his mind decides for him is rather too much above his own head; he is inspired, and hardly to blame when he is mistaken. What his feelings consider good are homely and practical things, and this has to be recognized as more important for a judgement on him than his views.

It is hard to guess what people who talk about Images mean, but I think most of them expect to mean that they are allowed to think about both halves of the comparison; that is, if young Andrew Marvell says the mind is like the sea, they are allowed to think about a unique mind at a selected date and need not only switch on their standard Image of the eternal sea. But the effect of the word 'Imagery' is that they are very strongly encouraged to attend to the Vehicle and not the Tenor, attend to the decorations only; and a massive line of talk preaches to them that they are more high class and artistic if they do so. The first thing to get clear, I think, is that this Imagist account of the human mind (which often sounds to be making it angelic) makes it totally subhuman, subcanine for that matter, the mind of a blackbeetle. T. E. Hulme, who had a very lively mind and no doubt would have learned better if he had not been killed in the First World War, said that thought is prior to language and consists in the simultaneous presentment to the mind of two images. This is not so. A dog could not find its way home across a field if it had nothing more in its head, at a moment of choice, than the simultaneous occurrence of two images. It is fair to suppose that the two images here are the cosy inglenook and the raw plain, one of them desired and the other presented by fact; but the dog would need a great deal more in its head than that. There is a sharply horrible answer to this nonsense talked by Hulme; the condition he describes actually occurs among men lost in the desert, and they know themselves that they must break out of it or perish.

What motive then can be found for the theorists who say that this is all the mind can do? The motive is often both generous and politically well-calculated; deserving to win through the confusion of life, and likely enough to do so. The aesthetician wants to recommend some under-privileged group whose art works are being taken up; such as the ballads of the working classes, or the *Beowulf* of our shaggy ancestors, or the carvings of a primitive tribe. Plainly, any city slicker who wants to snub these worthy people deserves to be snubbed in his turn; and a convenient way to do this is to say that the intellect is a wicked thing: 'Of course these people are blackbeetles. Aren't we all? That's why they're so nice.' The trouble about this line of talk is that it greatly underrates the primitive artworks, which are almost always found to have strict rules carried out with great care, even if rather loony ones; and it regularly happens, when the tribespeople discover what these sponsors have been saying in their favour, that they become as it is called very ungrateful; and they are quite right of course. However, I must not present this as the only impulse behind the anti-intellectualist movement, a very complicated thing, with some of its motives more respectable than this and some of them less.

Surely, it will be said, the Imagist movement has had some valuable effects, for example in the study of the 'reiterative imagery' of Shakespeare. I agree that this has increased our understanding of the plays, but I think the pure theory is wrong even there. This became specially clear in the sheep-shearing scene of *The Winter's Tale*, where modern critics of the Symbolist school have told us that Perdita was not mature, a grave fault in their system somehow, or more definitely that she was afraid of sexual love, or quite definitely that she is self-pitying (and D. H. Lawrence laid down a rule that any little bird would die with its head under its wing in a frost without ever saying a self-pitying sentence):

> O Prosperina,
> For the flowers now that, frighted, thou letst fall
> From Dis's waggon: Daffodils
> That come before the swallow dares, and take
> The winds of March with beauty; violets dim,
> But sweeter than the lids of Juno's eyes
> And Cytherea's breath; pale primroses
> That die unmarried, ere they can behold
> Bright Phoebus in his strength—a malady
> Most incident to maids. . . . O, these I lack
> To make you garlands of, and my sweet friend
> To strew him o'er and o'er.

I think that this critical belief comes solely from being too proud to attend to the story. Perdita is behaving with heroic courage, and far more virtue than would be expected in real life. Despairingly in love with Prince Florizel, the supposed peasant girl announces to a casual visitor that she disapproves of princes marrying peasants (she takes for granted that she wouldn't 'breed by him' without his marrying her); and this affects the audience much more than any imagery, because without her farm-bred innocence *breed* would be a shameless word for her to use. She says she will die if her lover abandons her; and in these poetical speeches, while other persons on the stage are supposed to think she is merely acting up to her grand clothes as Queen of the Festival, she is trying to needle her young man into marrying her. Surely it is too ludicrous to have Imagist critics arguing that she is too immature to accept passion, when the meaning of her words, if you attend to the story, is that she will die if she is separated from her lover. Of course her imagery sounds dying; she is using her imagery to fight for the triumph which she achieves not to betray her own feelings, which many reasons make her want to hide. I think this the greatest nonsense ever talked about dramatic imagery; but of course even here I would agree that recognizing the character of the imagery adds to the effect.

Our President, Sir Herbert Read, has long been one of the

foremost theorists of the Image, and I want to remark that *The True Voice of Feeling* seems to me much the best exposition of the Romantic doctrine; in fact I always recommend it to students who are thinking about that. And I agree with him that the Romantic doctrine is true, or mostly true. But I don't think its truth depends on the part about the Image. During the last hundred years, the Image has been much mixed up with the Revolt against Reason, a game, I feel, which we can no longer afford to play. There is a belief that Imagery was developed earlier or lies deeper than the rational mind, and helps to protect us from that mind, which is always on the edge of some sordid wickedness. I agree that what is meant here contains important truths, but the expression of it (in D. H. Lawrence, for example) has always depended on very tricky, very intellectual and up-to-the-minute uses of language, by which a highly selected part of the mind is called conscious and wicked and diseased and in short mental, but some other part of the mind, which remains shrouded, is called good. But a great deal of our unconscious thinking, in the pre-conscious I think it is called, is quite unromantic and straightforward; the staff go loyally on with their routine whether the inspector is passing or not. One is bound to reflect, after one of these tirades: 'Well, the poor old mind may not be worth much, but it's all you've got, anyway.' One may love a fellow creature for all kinds of reasons, such as that it smells nice; the point where the experience becomes serious is when it loves you back, and then the poor old mind has to come into play, one way or another. Exactly which bits of the mind count as mental was, I think, simply a thing D. H. Lawrence habitually cheated about, on the great superlogical and intuitive principle 'Heads I win, tails you lose'. He was often on the right side, in the various quarrels for which he used this trick about the mind; but it is a misfortune that the whole literary tradition of Symbolism has grown up so completely divorced from the tradition of fair public debate. Chatterley, for example, has always been spiritually impotent and you are supposed to know this from a Symbol, that he happened to become wounded in battle. Surely one knows quite well that this is an infantile type of arguing in the author, tirelessly petulant and spiteful, and not unmental in the slightest degree—as artful as a monkey, in fact. Of course Lawrence did not invent it; I am not sure that the first establishing uses of Symbolism weren't the political propaganda of Dickens, though as usual we can't be sure we didn't catch it from the French.

I don't deny that the revolt against reason was often used with success, as was believed at the time, to liberate artists from pedants who tied them down by false arguments to conventional forms. Most of these liberations went on between the two wars, a wonderful time to be alive, when as Wyndham Lewis said the cultural scene was like a great circus with thrills at every turn. 'Oh, it's a wild life in the Near West,' he said, 'between one revelation and another.' The present age is much duller and quieter, in fact it feels to me simply groggy, as if the Atom Bombs have given it a rabbiter on the back of the neck. All the great movements of liberation are still ticking over and emitting their slogans, but the attacks on the rational mind have nearly all been fielded and directed into simple obscurantism. 'You can't avoid being a Communist unless you're a Christian, and you know you're frightened of Communism, so have a good fright about Hell too. Obviously you can't be a rationalist any more, because the freethinkers have been telling you that for years.' So the residual legatee of all the anti-intellectual movements has been simple old fundamentalism, with a strong flavour of political conformity.

This curious development was described before it had really got started in the horrible book *1984* by George Orwell. If you remember, the story happens in London, and one can't make out whether London is post-Communist or post-Christian; the rulers say it is permanently at war with another state in eastern Europe, and daily hate is drummed up on the telly, but the novel gradually lets it emerge that there isn't a pin to choose between them. On the whole I find the book tiresomely incredible, which is a comfort as what it prophesies is so very ghastly; but I keep feeling that a bit of the prophecy has already come true. This puts me against all forms of the revolt against reason; I think our only remaining hope lies in getting the poor old mind to do its work just well enough.

Content and Form in Poetry

RICHARD KELL

I

Although it has been seriously challenged, the idea that a poem can be divided into content and form is still quite common. Many of us would probably claim that we have sometimes adopted it merely as a convenient generalization, and we might point out that we have often shown our true allegiance by asserting that content and form are inseparable. This assertion, however, is hardly an adequate safeguard. The functional inseparability of two things does not preclude a separate discussion of each and any such discussion must be misleading unless the terms used are clearly defined—as 'content' and 'form' seldom are even when handled by experienced critics. I believe that the 'convenient generalization', far from being useful or even harmless, can be a positive nuisance: for example, there seems to be a fairly widespread assumption that critics who judge a work on aesthetic grounds are interested only in its 'form'. It is for this reason that I am attempting a clarification.

2

How is content to be defined? In popular usage it often seems to be synonymous with subject-matter, 'ideas', 'what the poem is about'. Granted this definition, in discussing the content we are not discussing anything belonging uniquely to the poem: we are concerned with something which could be given, say, in note form or conversation, and which might also be used for a novel, a short story, an essay, a painting, a film, or even a piece of programme music. It is notorious that this use of the word can result in approval or condemnation of a poem for reasons unconnected with poetry.

A less objectionable usage equates content with meaning—though often, one suspects, simply because meaning has been confused with subject-matter or paraphrase or summary (or with all three, since these are apt to be confused as well). Although the possibility of such confusion makes it insecure this equation is an improvement, since the meaning of a poem—precisely what all of it says, down to the implication of the lowliest comma when it is printed—is an intrinsic part of it.

But the meaning of a poem is only one third of its content—of what it 'contains'. The meaning cannot exist without the other two components of language: sound (whether imagined or actually voiced), and rhythm. It is no more logical to say that the meaning is contained by the sound and rhythm than to say that the sound and rhythm are contained by the meaning: all three are functionally equal and interdependent, and all are 'contained' by the poem. So we may say of a poem that it has semantic content, phonic content, and rhythmic content.

Edith Sitwell was rightly taken to task for going to absurd lengths in her evaluation of phonic content, but the extreme reaction that her efforts provoked has been unfortunate. In recent years critics have tended not only to ignore whatever expressive qualities vowels and consonants do possess, but also to assume that a poem has no content except the semantic, and consequently their judgements have often been obtuse and misleading.

Up to now I have kept the term 'content' to show how it might be more precisely defined. If my argument has been valid, however, it is clear that the term can be used only metaphorically: I have defined content as meaning, sound, rhythm, but the poem *is* the meaning, the sound and the rhythm, and it is strictly nonsensical to say that something contains what it is. So the term 'content' is dispensable—and although there is no logical objection to keeping it purely as a metaphor there may be a practical objection, for the very idea of containment is likely to condition our thinking and revive old mistakes.

3

When the term 'content' is used as a synonym for meaning, and when a poem is said to consist of content and form, form must be intended to denote either (1) the sound and rhythm taken together, or (2) the rhythm abstracted from the rest—though we are not then told what becomes of the sound! (It cannot mean the sound alone, for sound without rhythm would be nothing but isolated letters and syllables, and these could not be the sound of a poem.) I have argued, however, that as long as the term 'content' is retained it must be allowed to comprehend sound and rhythm as well as meaning, and if this is true the first use of the term 'form' becomes redundant.

It is doubtful whether this usage (1) had any logical justification in the first place. If the term 'content' cannot logically be applied only to one or more components abstracted from the complex of meaning, sound, rhythm, surely the same is true of the term 'form'. Why should the semantic relations be excluded from form any more than the phonic and rhythmic ones? That we can apprehend sound and rhythm without conceptual meaning (in music or an unfamiliar verbal language), but not conceptual meaning without sound and rhythm, might seem to justify as well as to account for the usage I am challenging; but to grant the justification would be to miss the point that when we *do* know the language—and it is important to remember that without this knowledge we are experiencing something less than the poem—the sound and rhythm can no longer function apart from the meaning.

Clearly, then, if the term 'form' (as so far considered) is taken to denote anything except an abstracted rhythmic pattern (usage 2), 'content' and 'form' become interchangeable terms to denote a complex of meaning, sound, rhythm. Therefore poem = content = form, and the last two terms are dispensable.

4

Although the meaning of a poem is impossible without sound and rhythm, and the sound impossible without rhythm and meaning, the rhythm can be represented in isolation—diagramatically, for example, or by tapping, or with a musical instrument—and perhaps exactly duplicated by an electronic machine. This does not contradict the earlier assertion that in the poem the three components function inseparably. Abstracted, the rhythmic pattern ceases at once to belong uniquely to the poem in question: for instance, a new pattern of vowels and consonants might be fitted to it.

We can now find a legitimate use for the term 'form': it will mean (so far) a representation or idea, detailed or otherwise, of the rhythm of the poem. This representation will be related to the poem much as an X-ray photograph of a man's body is related to the man. If we say that the photograph shows the man's form we cannot possibly mean that the picture-skeleton and the real skeleton are one and the same; of the real skeleton as part of a living body we can know nothing without the flesh that it shapes. To do justice to the term 'form', however, it is not sufficient to equate it only with the abstracted rhythm of a poem. No one will cavil, for example, at the use of the phrase 'sonnet form', yet this is related to rhyme and meaning as well as to rhythm. What we are really concerned with when we use the term 'form' is proportion and distribution, whether these relate to rhythm, sound, or meaning.

Consider a Petrarchan sonnet. Of its linear rhythm (for present purposes synonymous with metre, since only the norm is being considered) we can say—or demonstrate by means of prosodic signs—that its weak and strong beats are equal in number (5/5) and alternating in their distribution; and of its multilinear rhythm that it comprises fourteen iambic pentameters occurring in the ratio 8/6. Of its rhyme scheme (connected with sound) that it produces five rhymes in fourteen lines, with the proportions 4a/ 4b/ 2c/ 2d/ 2e and the distribution abba, abba, cde, cde. Of its meaning that it is broadly divided into two parts with a logical or imaginative link of a certain kind, occupying eight and six lines respectively. Thus, to analyse the form of a sonnet is to indicate the ways in which its rhythm, rhymes and meaning are proportioned and distributed—nothing more. We might be analysing either sonnet form in general or the form of a given sonnet (whether or not it departed from the norm in any respect), but in neither instance would we be discussing the actual stuff of a poem.

On the other hand, if we said 'In the octet Wordsworth expresses a sense of wonder at the holy tranquillity of the evening. . . In the sestet he addresses a child . . . [summary of meaning, not be confused with meaning itself]; his rhymes are *free, nun, sun, -y* . . .; in the line *It is a beauteous evening, calm and free,* the first two words depart from the iambic norm . . .'—then we would be talking about the semantic, phonic and rhythmic aspects of that verbal whole which is an actual poem. Here 'form' and 'content' would be redundant terms as well as misleading ones.

5

Recapitulation: (1) When we are discussing *a poem* the terms 'content' and 'form' are interchangeable and both can be discarded in favour of the terms 'meaning', 'sound', 'rhythm'. Meaning can of course be paraphrased or summarized, but what the paraphrase or the summary says is strictly no more than a rough approximation to what the poem says. (2) Used independently the term 'form' refers not to any poem *per se,* but only to an abstract from a poem or a group of poems; not to the functionally indivisible whole of meaning, sound, rhythm, but only to the proportioning and distribution of these elements. Thus it is possible to discuss the form of a particular sonnet, for example, without quoting a single word of the poem itself.

Architecture and the Human Condition

W. SINCLAIR GAULDIE

In our time, and in this country especially, architecture as an art-form is consistently undervalued, not least by architects themselves. My argument is that this is a dangerous tendency which must be reversed. I rest this argument upon three propositions:

> 1. The urban population in almost every country is increasing both absolutely and in relation to the rural population. If present trends continue over the next hundred years, about 90 per cent of the world population will be living in urban settlements, one-third of them in cities of over a million inhabitants.
>
> 2. This change will be accompanied by an unprecedented alteration in the scale and appearance of the man-made environment, and the rapidity of the change will create grave problems of psychological adjustment for those who are already urbanized as well as for those who migrate into the cities.
>
> 3. Maladjustment between the urban dweller and his environment is already pronounced in the sense that a substantial proportion of the urban population is consciously or unconsciously in conflict with its immediate physical surroundings.

The prognosis, therefore, is not good. Our culture is approaching a crisis with which we are only half equipped to deal. We are already equipped technically to meet the problem of adapting the physical environment to the new situation, but not to meet the problem of helping man towards a sane and healthy adaptation to new and increasingly unfamiliar surroundings. I refer specifically to a *sane* adaptation because there are neurotic escape-routes, such as scotomization and fantasy-building, by which the individual may buy temporary survival at the price of leading a mutilated and blinkered existence: but this is not a level of existence at which the affairs of the twenty-first century can safely be conducted.

There is a real danger that the difficulty of the human problem is being masked by the very existence of these escape-mechanisms and the placebos associated with them, and even that the problem will be overshadowed altogether, until it is too late, by the scale and urgency of the technical and economic challenge. Hence it becomes a matter of necessity to draw attention to the social function of architecture, not simply as a means of fulfilling certain physical needs but as a line of communication with the subconscious through whose agency the process of adaptation may be assisted.

Let us then consider, in broad outline, the nature of the adaptive process. Our species has survived for a long time, successfully adjusting to many different and hostile kinds of environment, through its ability to organize the random evidence of the senses and to extrapolate from it: that is, by using observation, memory, reason and imagination. Associated with this is the ability to rationalize changes in one's state of mind precipitated by or associated with sensory data—or, to put it colloquially, to live with one's emotions. When this mechanism of cognition and imagination is atrophied or weakened, survival is endangered. Simple failure of cognition can obviously kill quickly, equally at the traffic-lights and in the jungle: but more important from our point of view is the psychological confusion, the inability to sort out one's impressions and emotions, which clouds the judgement and erodes the will to adapt until the sufferer becomes in some degree a social liability. This 'corruption of consciousness', to borrow Collingwood's expression, already affects a dangerously high proportion of our population. It is reckoned that one in five of us will receive psychiatric treatment at some time in his life. Considering the known reluctance to seek such treatment, the proportion of bad survival-risks must be very much higher and higher still the proportion whose maladjustment, though not acute, is lowering the general adaptive capacity of society.

If one accepts—and I think one can—the view that the function of art is to help man master these inner confusions by enriching his cognitive-imaginative experience, then it is evident that architecture, as the most public and indeed inescapable of the arts, can have a high therapeutic potential—subject to certain conditions. The first condition is that the building must bear the distinctive stamp of a work of art as opposed to a work of craft: which means that it must be irradiated with an excitement unique and specific to the work and arising from the act of creation which is, at the same time, an act of discovery. The second condition is that the excitement or emotion must be expressed: that is, brought up in the first place to the conscious level of the artist's own mind, clarified, and communicated to the spectator in the aesthetic language proper to the art, so that he also is sent on a voyage of discovery.

It has always been difficult for architecture, as contrasted with painting or poetry, to meet these criteria of high art. The period of gestation is long, the designer's ingenuity often bent to a distracting profusion of functional and technical problems, and only a very powerful imagination can sustain, throughout this long and complicated operation, a high level of coherent emotional expression. It will become still more difficult with the increase in the extent and complexity of the technical matters with which the designer has to deal, demanding as they do that the design-process should become more and more a matter for a team rather than an individual. The difficulty is compounded in our time by the absence of a well-developed language of architectural form, understood both by artist and spectator and capable of reconciling the high technical demands of the building programme with human emotion, human scale and human dignity.

Such a language can hardly be said to exist. It might have evolved naturally, in step with the technical developments of the last hundred years, but this possibility was excluded by the nineteenth-century excursion into historicism and the subsequent rejection of historical stereotypes has left a void which has hardly begun to fill. One of the dangers of this time is that, under pressure of the quantitative need for more building, the void will be filled not by a language in the full sense, constantly developing and adaptable to fine shades of personal expression, but by a code, a limited and explicit sign-system which deliberately restricts the possibilities of personal vagary. By its nature such a sign-system is ill-adapted to the task of enlarging experience by communicating a fresh and personal vision and thus of discharging the therapeutic function of art. Moreover acceptance of such a limited sign-system as a substitute for language tends to stultify the growth of language proper.

Fortunately a high proportion of architects still enter the profession not simply for reasons of status or salary but because it offers the prospect of a lifetime spent in the process of creation. In some of these the creative effort will, from time to time, reach an intensity and clarity of expression which raises it from a craft operation to an operation of art. Therefore, since this is the process by which art creates its language, there is a possibility that an architectural vocabulary and syntax of the necessary flexibility and maturity will in fact emerge before it is too late. I put it no higher than a possibility, since the process itself is liable to frustration by:

(a) The increasing intellectualization and depersonalization of the design-operation, which I have already noted as a necessary condition of meeting functional demands.

(b) The increasing complexity and rigidity of the legislative and economic framework within which the architect has to operate: it is not possible to build high art out of the hopes and fears of the sanitary inspector, the fire-prevention officer and the chartered accountant.

(c) The speed with which mass-communication promotes the decay of idiom into cliché, depreciating the currency of language while it is still fresh from the mint.

I am aware that these arguments appear to be leading to a discouraging and unwelcome conclusion. If man is about to experience a profoundly disturbing metamorphosis: and if survival in the crudest literal sense is to depend on his ability to adapt to it: and if that ability depends on the liveliness of his cognitive and imaginative faculties: and if it is the function of the arts to keep these faculties alive and at full stretch: and if we cannot count on the most public and accessible of the arts to carry out this function—then the outlook is very grave.

It is indeed very grave, but not yet hopeless. The will to create is very strong and not readily broken by technical difficulties, by legal obstacles or by economic pressures. Nevertheless these difficulties are real and are multiplying, and they will proliferate in a society which consistently puts too low a value on the aesthetics of its environment. Architecture is essentially a social art: the architect can ameliorate the human condition only with the support of a society which not merely allows him but clearly asks him to enrich its aesthetic experience.

INDEX

Index of Names